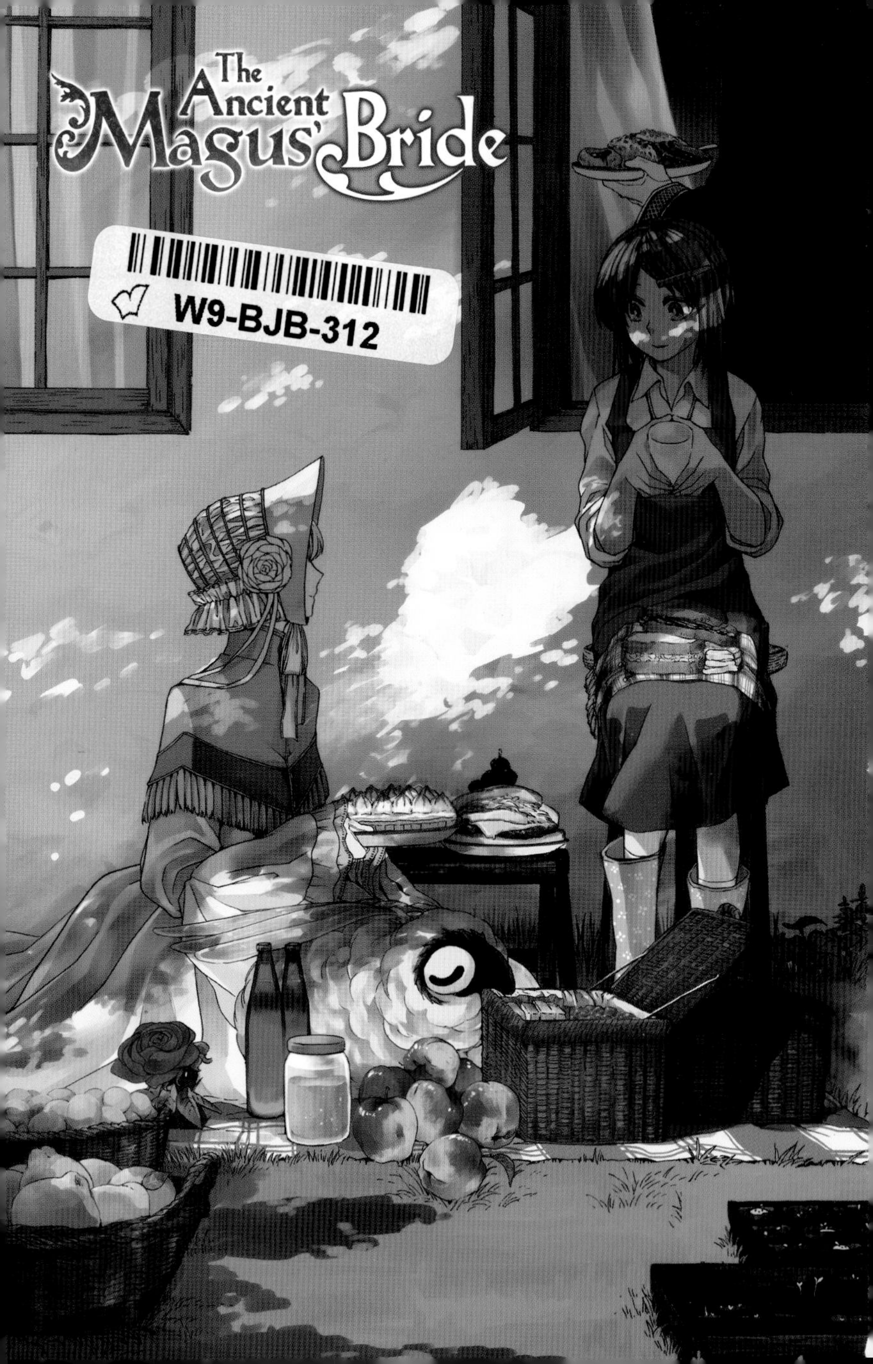
The Ancient Magus' Bride

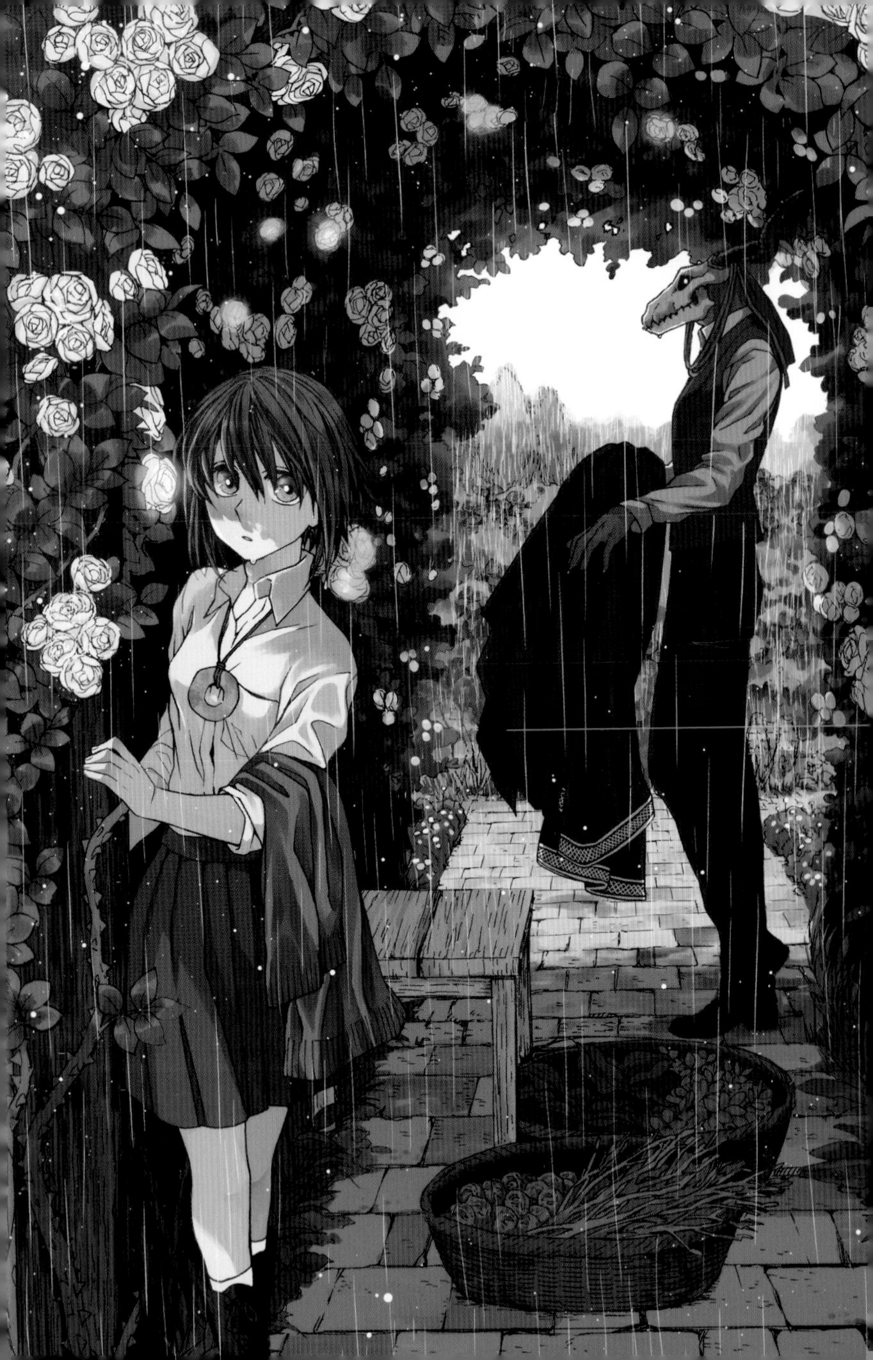

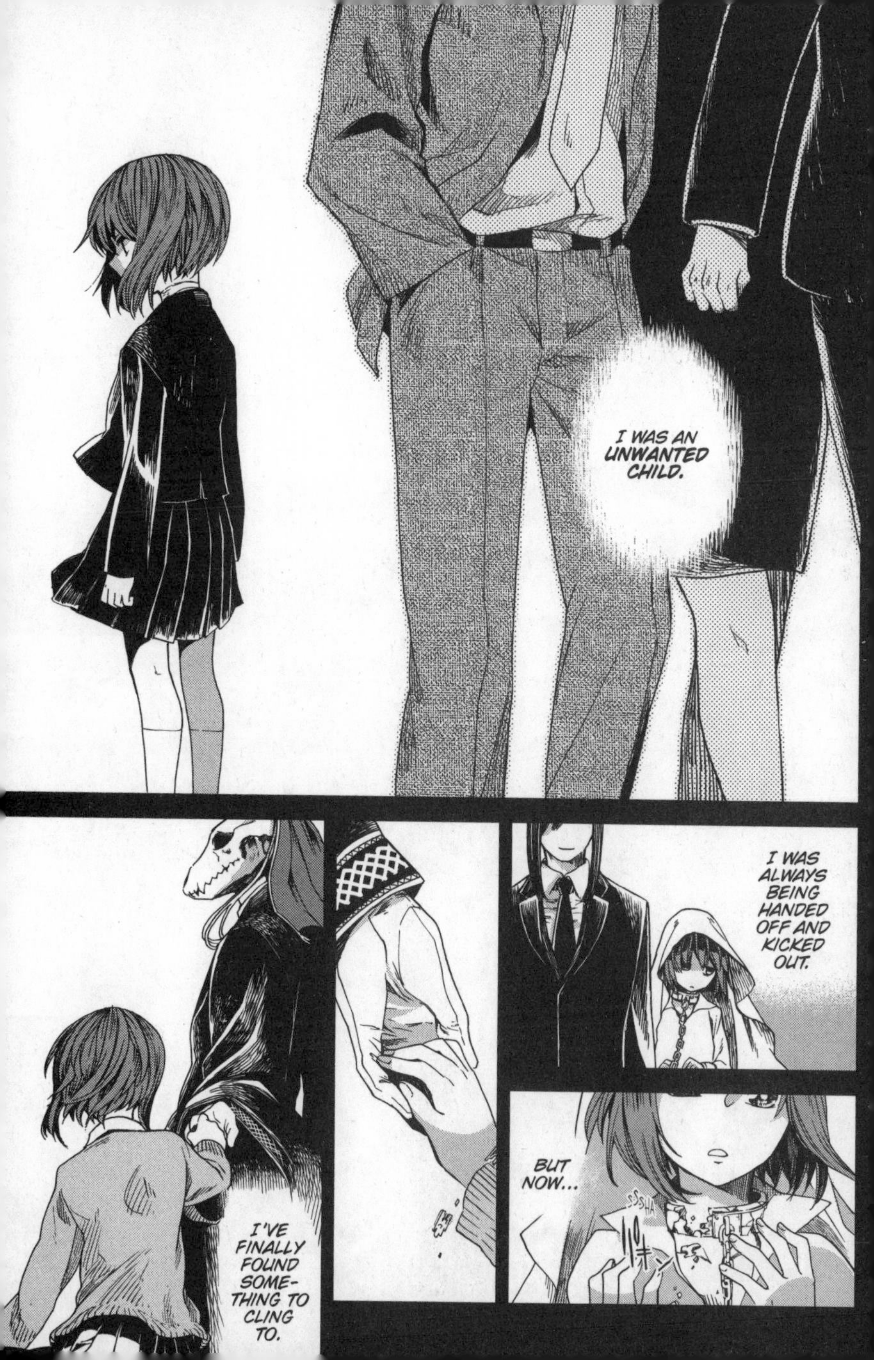
I WAS AN UNWANTED CHILD.
I WAS ALWAYS BEING HANDED OFF AND KICKED OUT.
BUT NOW...
S-S-SHA
I'VE FINALLY FOUND SOME-THING TO CLING TO.

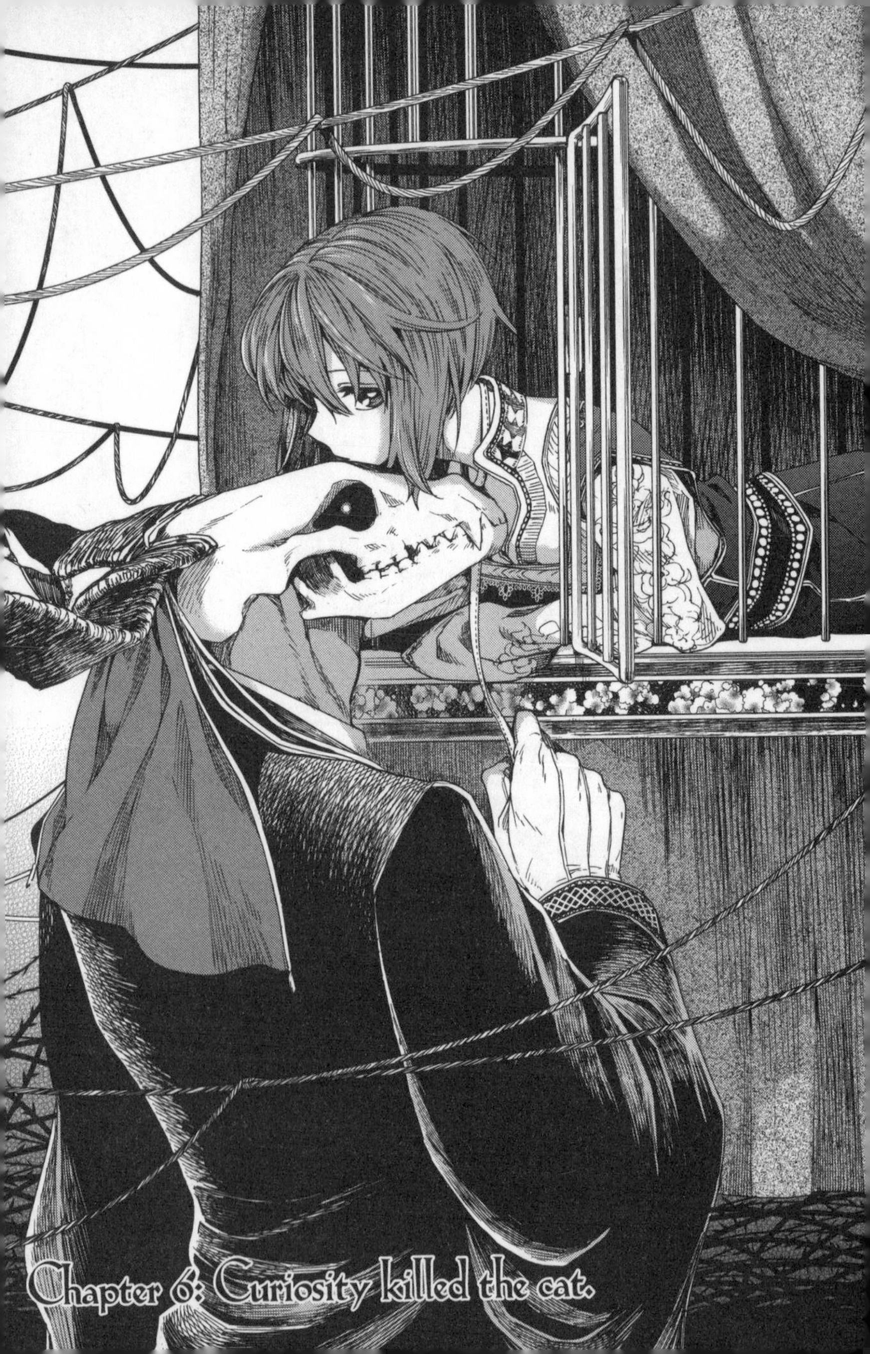
Chapter 6: Curiosity killed the cat.

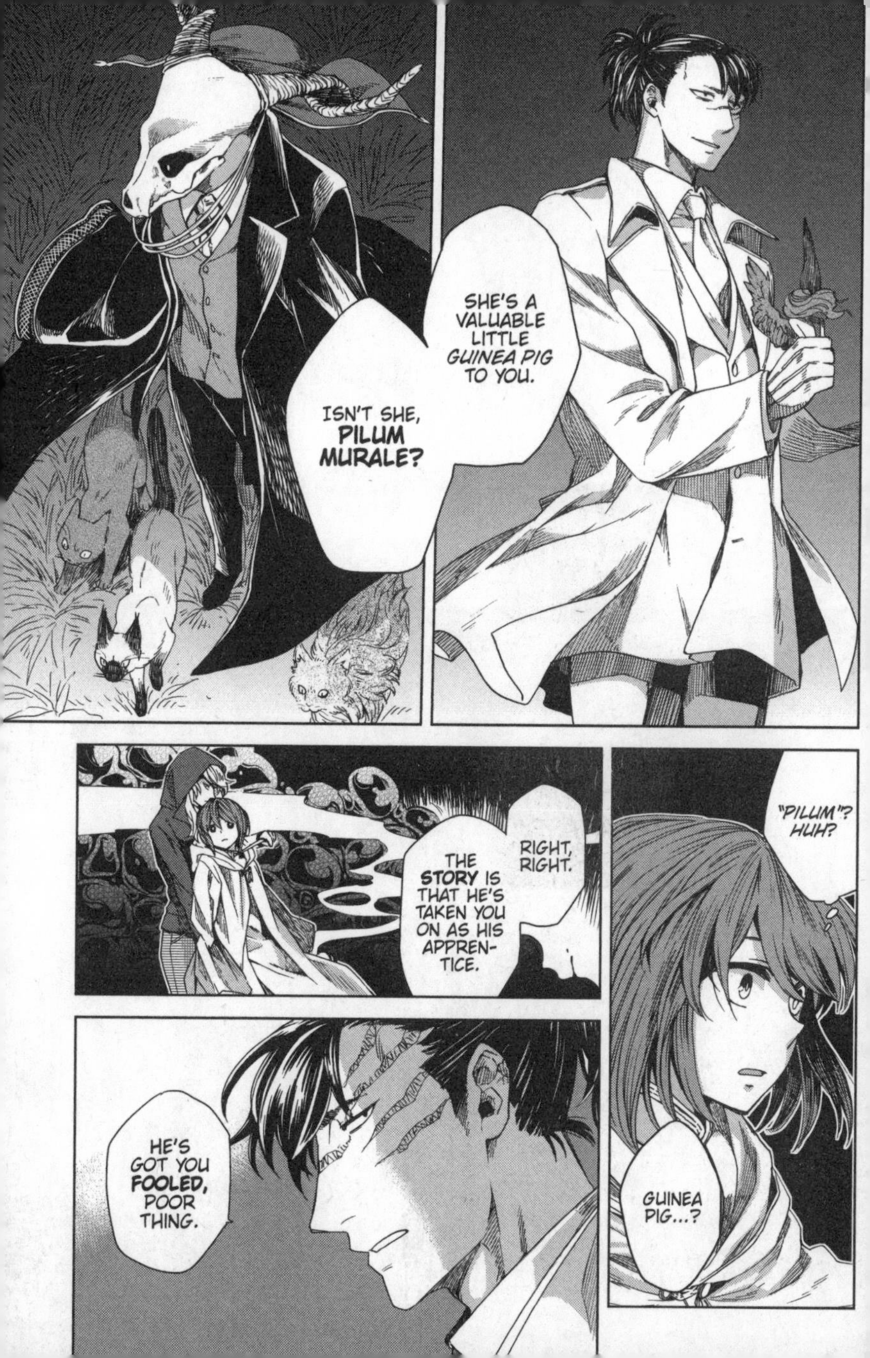
SHE'S A VALUABLE LITTLE GUINEA PIG TO YOU.
ISN'T SHE, **PILUM MURALE?**
"PILUM"? HUH?
GUINEA PIG...?
RIGHT, RIGHT.
THE **STORY** IS THAT HE'S TAKEN YOU ON AS HIS APPRENTICE.
HE'S GOT YOU **FOOLED**, POOR THING.

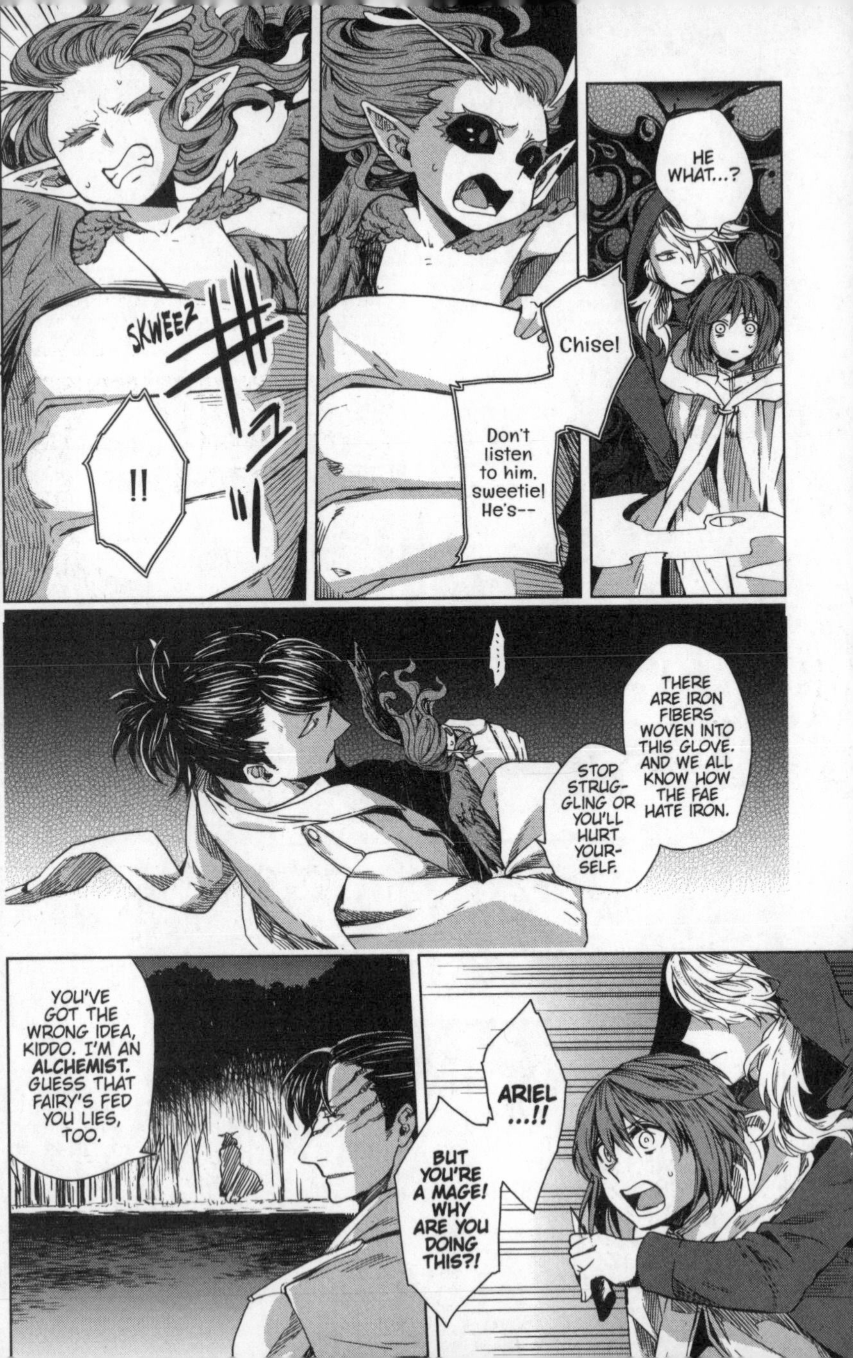
HE WHAT...?
Chise!
Don't listen to him, sweetie! He's--
SKWEEZ
!!
...!
THERE ARE IRON FIBERS WOVEN INTO THIS GLOVE. AND WE ALL KNOW HOW THE FAE HATE IRON.
STOP STRUG-GLING OR YOU'LL HURT YOUR-SELF.
ARIEL...!!
BUT YOU'RE A MAGE! WHY ARE YOU DOING THIS?!
YOU'VE GOT THE WRONG IDEA, KIDDO. I'M AN **ALCHEMIST**. GUESS THAT FAIRY'S FED YOU LIES, TOO.

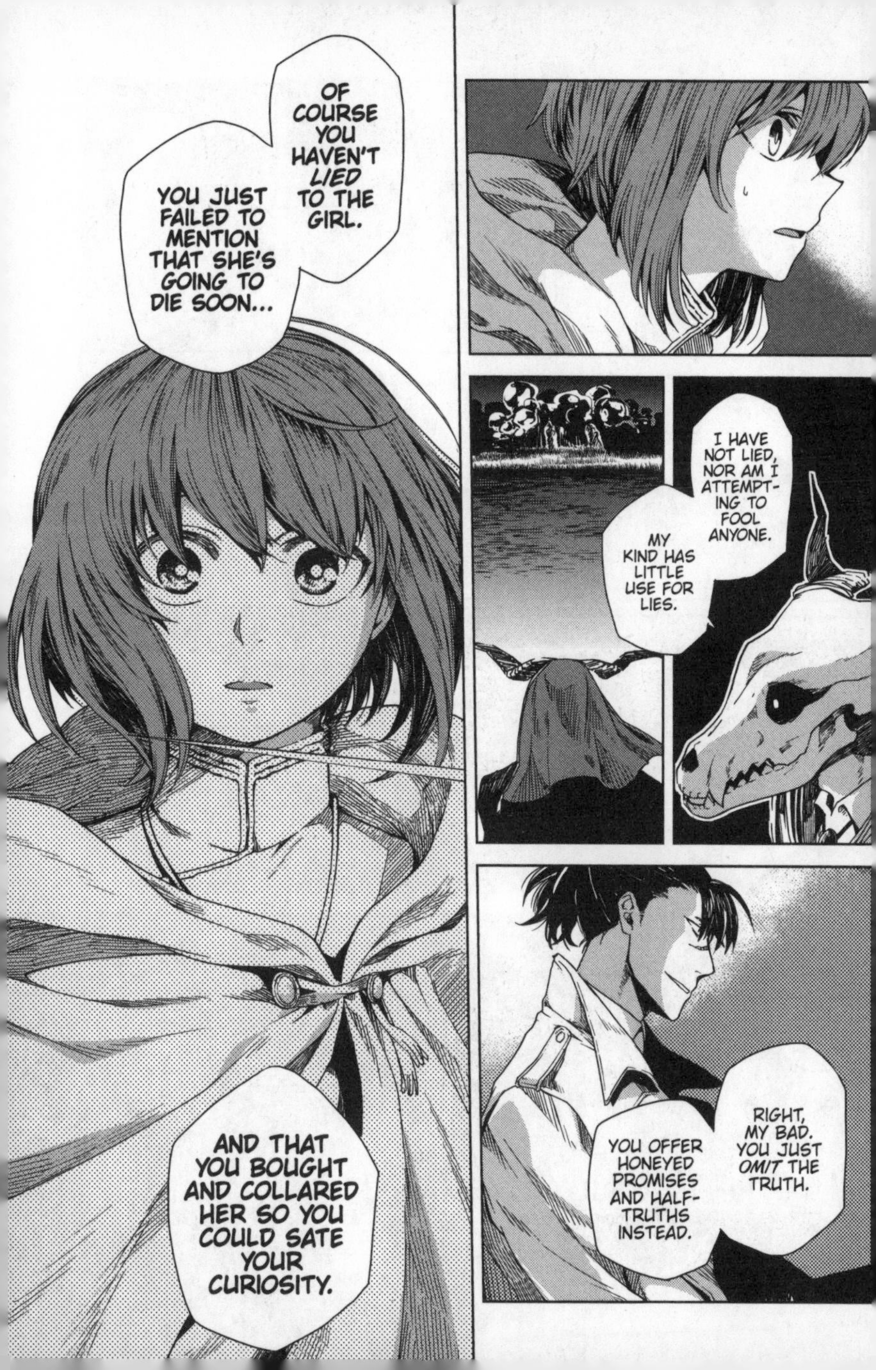
I HAVE NOT LIED, NOR AM I ATTEMPTING TO FOOL ANYONE.
MY KIND HAS LITTLE USE FOR LIES.
RIGHT, MY BAD. YOU JUST *OMIT* THE TRUTH.
YOU OFFER HONEYED PROMISES AND HALF-TRUTHS INSTEAD.
OF COURSE YOU HAVEN'T *LIED* TO THE GIRL.
YOU JUST FAILED TO MENTION THAT SHE'S GOING TO DIE SOON...
AND THAT YOU BOUGHT AND COLLARED HER SO YOU COULD SATE YOUR CURIOSITY.

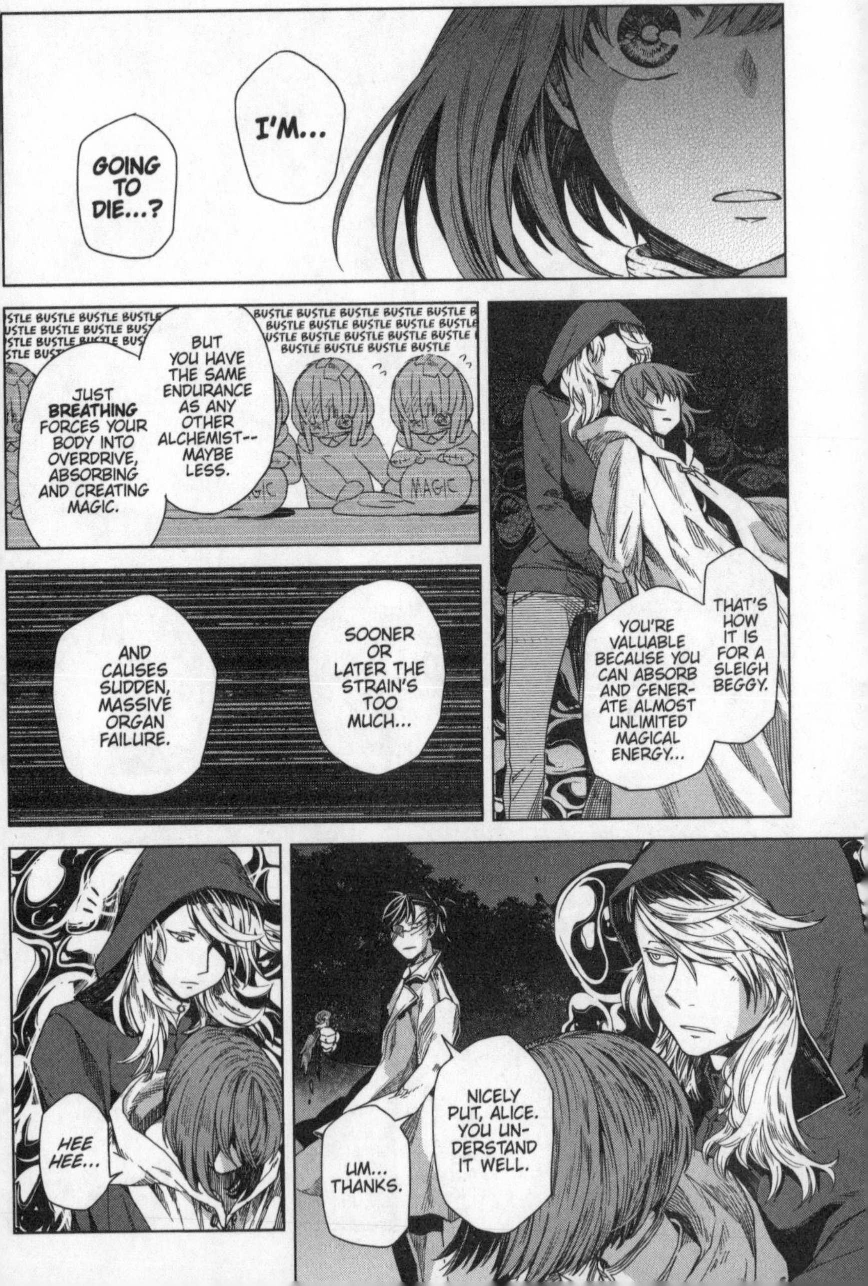
I'M...
GOING TO DIE...?
THAT'S HOW IT IS FOR A SLEIGH BEGGY.
YOU'RE VALUABLE BECAUSE YOU CAN ABSORB AND GENERATE ALMOST UNLIMITED MAGICAL ENERGY...
BUSTLE BUSTLE BUSTLE BUSTLE BUSTLE BUSTLE BUSTLE BUSTLE BUSTLE BUSTLE BUSTLE BUSTLE BUSTLE BUSTLE BUSTLE BUSTLE BUSTLE BUSTLE
BUT YOU HAVE THE SAME ENDURANCE AS ANY OTHER ALCHEMIST--MAYBE LESS.
JUST **BREATHING** FORCES YOUR BODY INTO OVERDRIVE, ABSORBING AND CREATING MAGIC.
MAGIC
SOONER OR LATER THE STRAIN'S TOO MUCH...
AND CAUSES SUDDEN, MASSIVE ORGAN FAILURE.
NICELY PUT, ALICE. YOU UNDERSTAND IT WELL.
UM... THANKS.
HEE HEE...

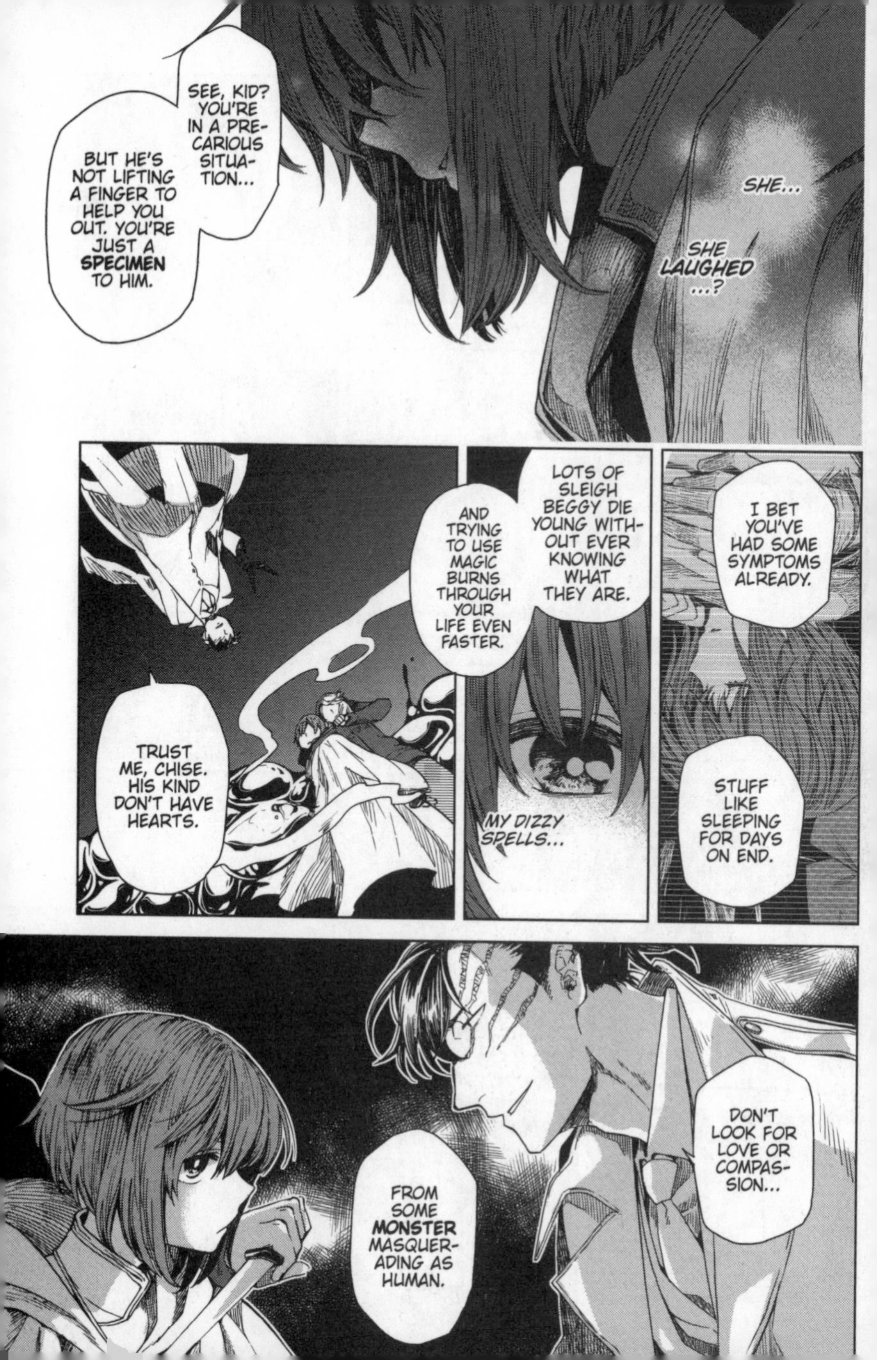
SEE, KID? YOU'RE IN A PRECARIOUS SITUATION...
BUT HE'S NOT LIFTING A FINGER TO HELP YOU OUT. YOU'RE JUST A **SPECIMEN** TO HIM.
SHE...
SHE **LAUGHED** ...?
I BET YOU'VE HAD SOME SYMPTOMS ALREADY.
STUFF LIKE SLEEPING FOR DAYS ON END.
LOTS OF SLEIGH BEGGY DIE YOUNG WITHOUT EVER KNOWING WHAT THEY ARE.
AND TRYING TO USE MAGIC BURNS THROUGH YOUR LIFE EVEN FASTER.
MY DIZZY SPELLS...
TRUST ME, CHISE. HIS KIND DON'T HAVE HEARTS.
DON'T LOOK FOR LOVE OR COMPASSION...
FROM SOME **MONSTER** MASQUERADING AS HUMAN.

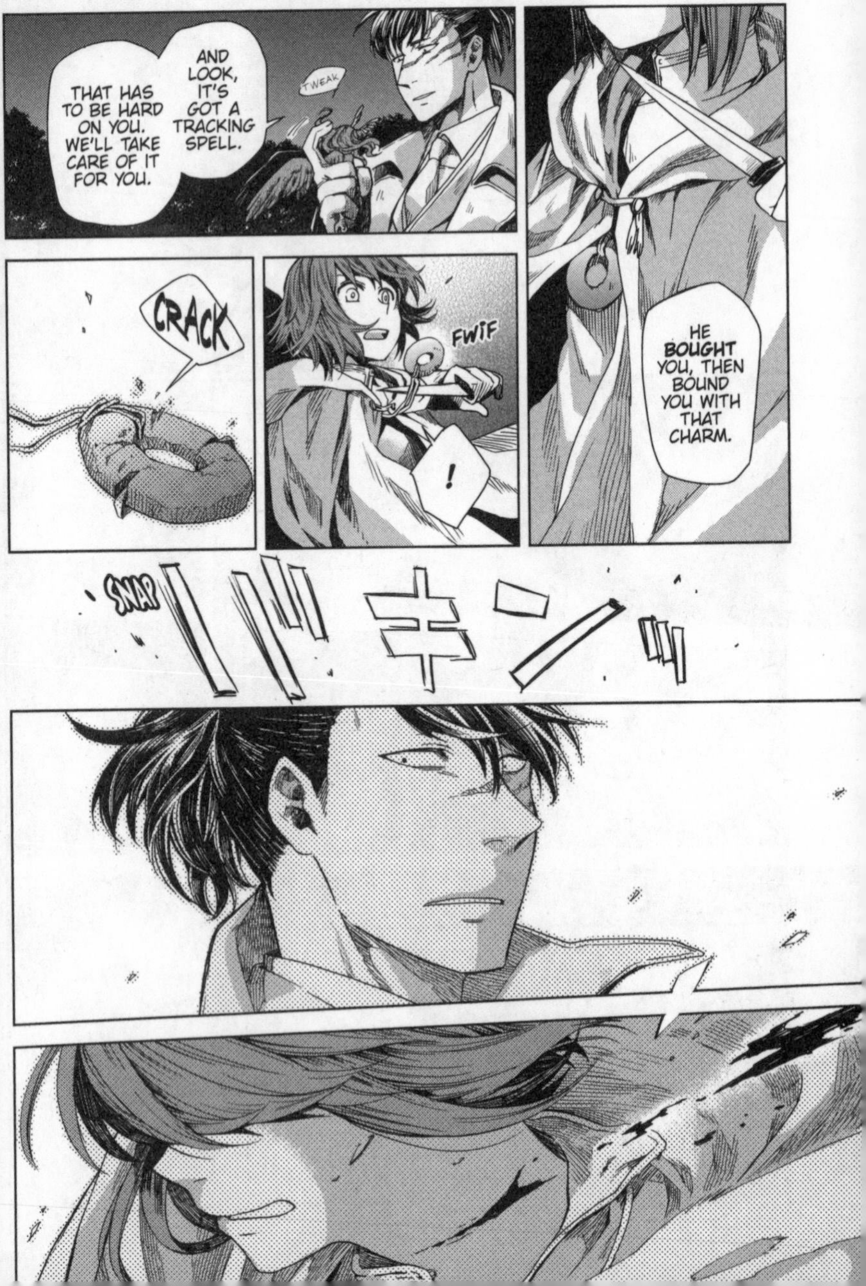
HE BOUGHT YOU, THEN BOUND YOU WITH THAT CHARM.
AND LOOK, IT'S GOT A TRACKING SPELL.
TWEAK
THAT HAS TO BE HARD ON YOU. WE'LL TAKE CARE OF IT FOR YOU.
FWIF
!
CRACK
SNAP

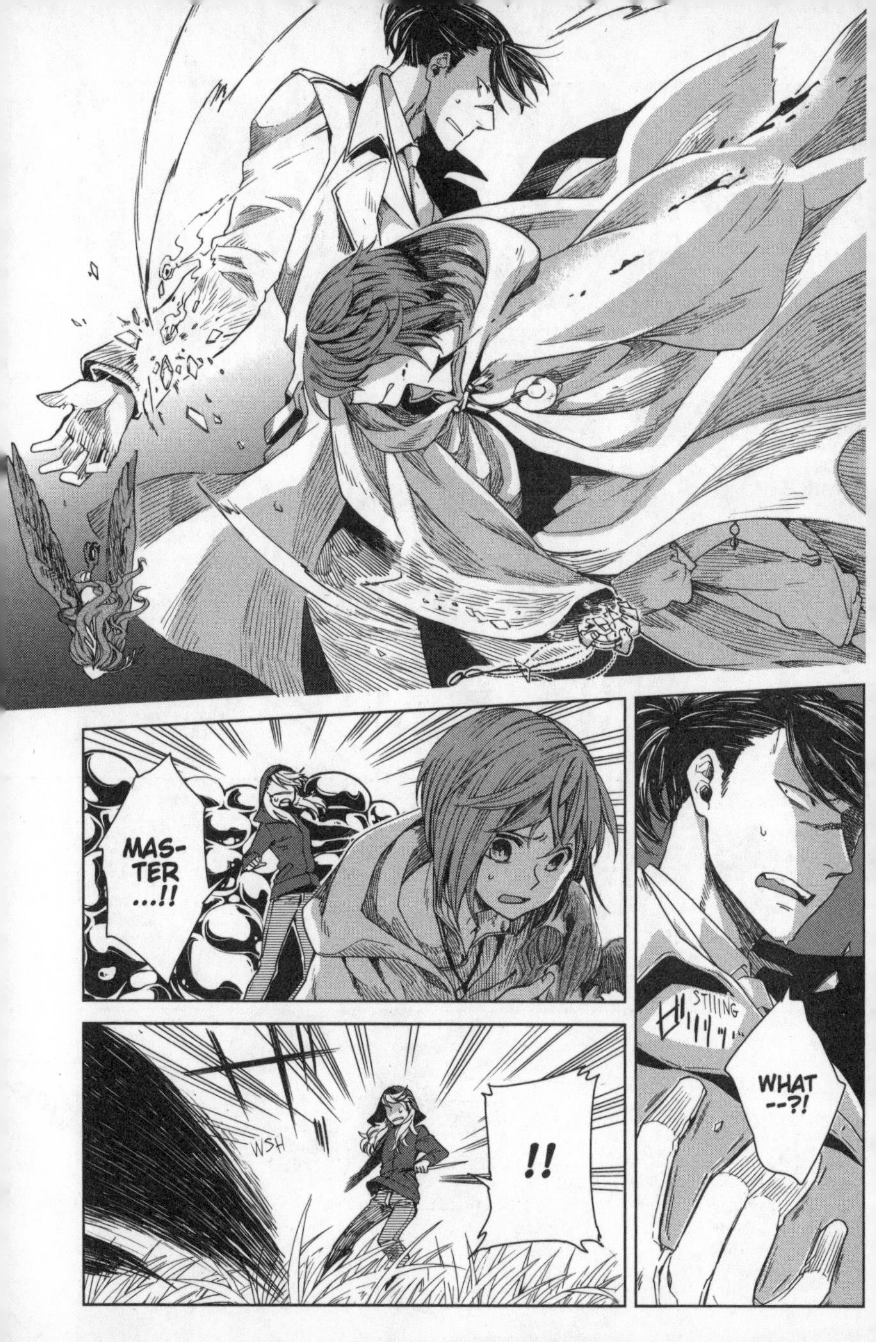
STIIING
WHAT --?!
MAS-TER ...!!
WSH
!!

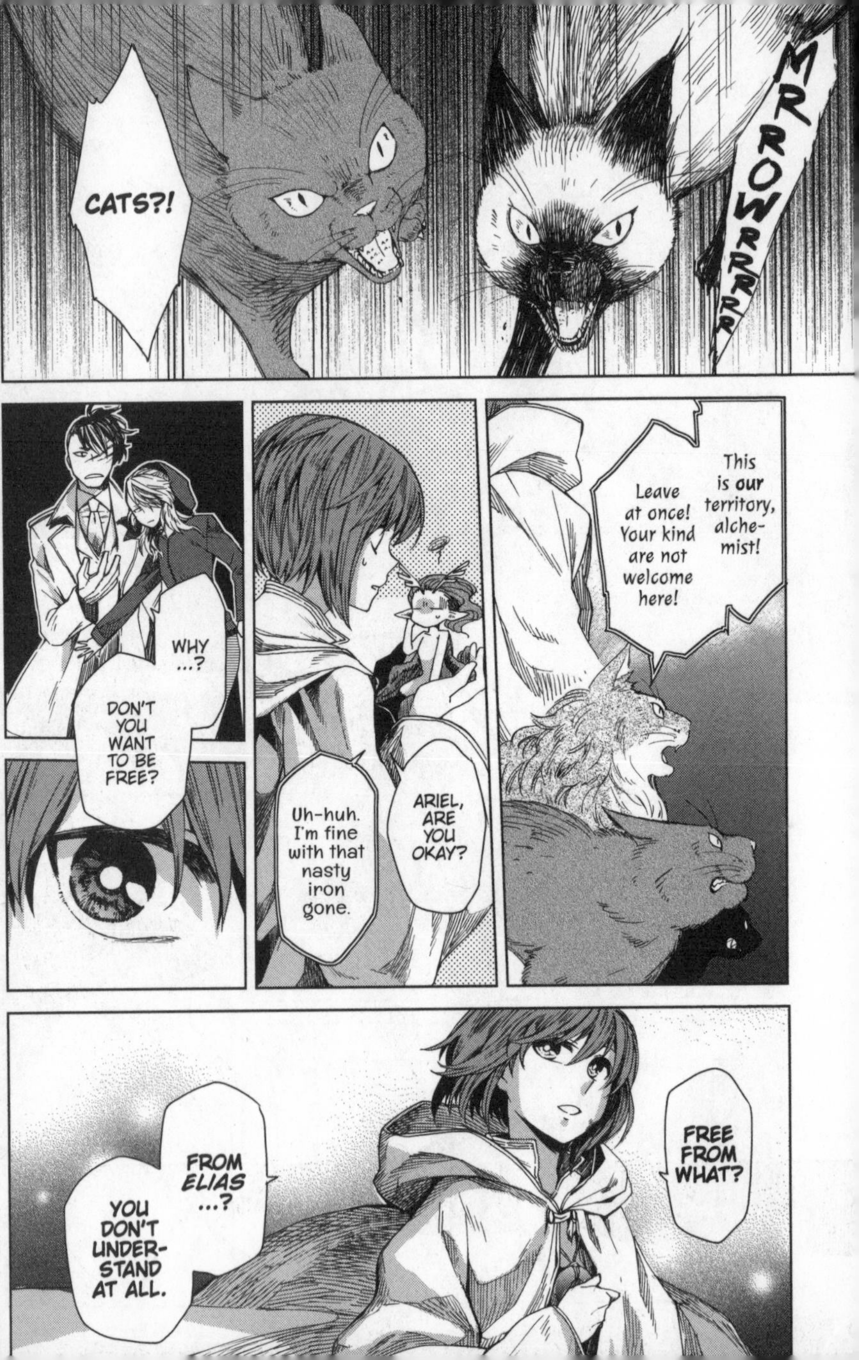
MRROWRRRR
CATS?!
This is our territory, alchemist!
Leave at once! Your kind are not welcome here!
ARIEL, ARE YOU OKAY?
Uh-huh. I'm fine with that nasty iron gone.
WHY...?
DON'T YOU WANT TO BE FREE?
FREE FROM WHAT?
FROM ELIAS...?
YOU DON'T UNDER-STAND AT ALL.

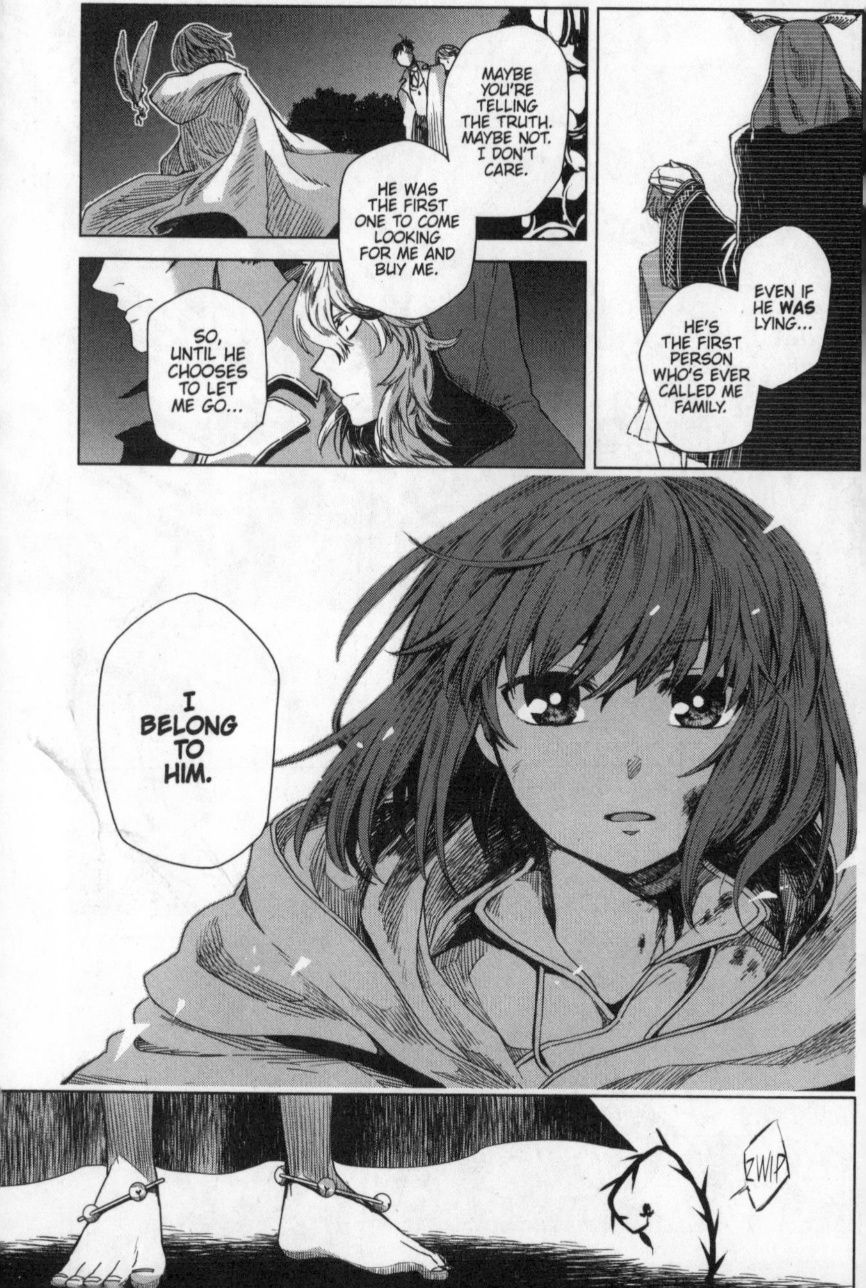
EVEN IF HE WAS LYING...
HE'S THE FIRST PERSON WHO'S EVER CALLED ME FAMILY.
MAYBE YOU'RE TELLING THE TRUTH. MAYBE NOT. I DON'T CARE.
HE WAS THE FIRST ONE TO COME LOOKING FOR ME AND BUY ME.
SO, UNTIL HE CHOOSES TO LET ME GO...
I BELONG TO HIM.
ZWIP

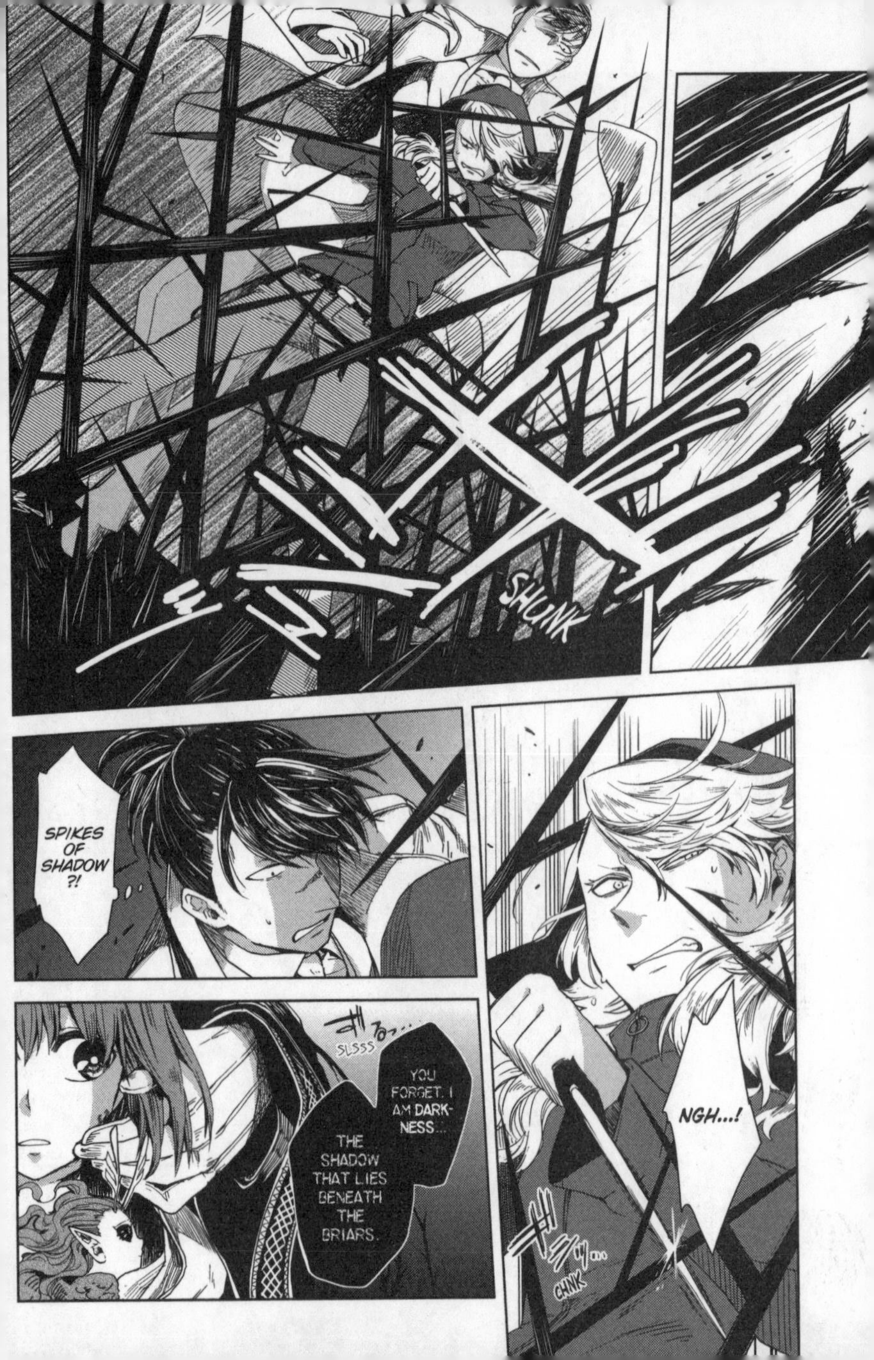
SHUNK
NGH...!
CHNK
SPIKES OF SHADOW?!
SLSSS
YOU FORGET. I AM DARKNESS...
THE SHADOW THAT LIES BENEATH THE BRIARS.

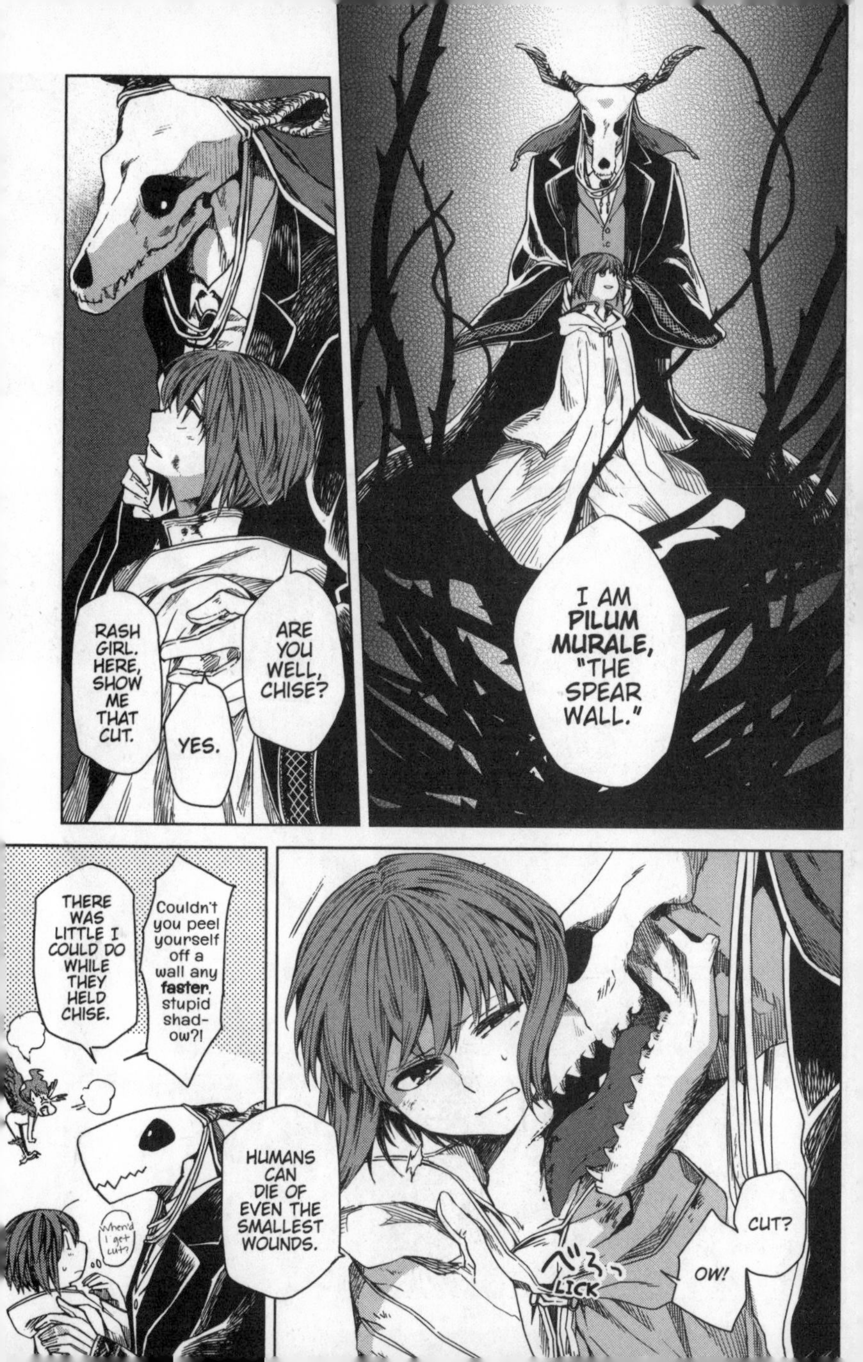
I AM PILUM MURALE, "THE SPEAR WALL."
ARE YOU WELL, CHISE?
YES.
RASH GIRL. HERE, SHOW ME THAT CUT.
CUT?
べろっ
LICK
OW!
Couldn't you peel yourself off a wall any faster, stupid shad-ow?!
THERE WAS LITTLE I COULD DO WHILE THEY HELD CHISE.
HUMANS CAN DIE OF EVEN THE SMALLEST WOUNDS.
When'd I get cut?

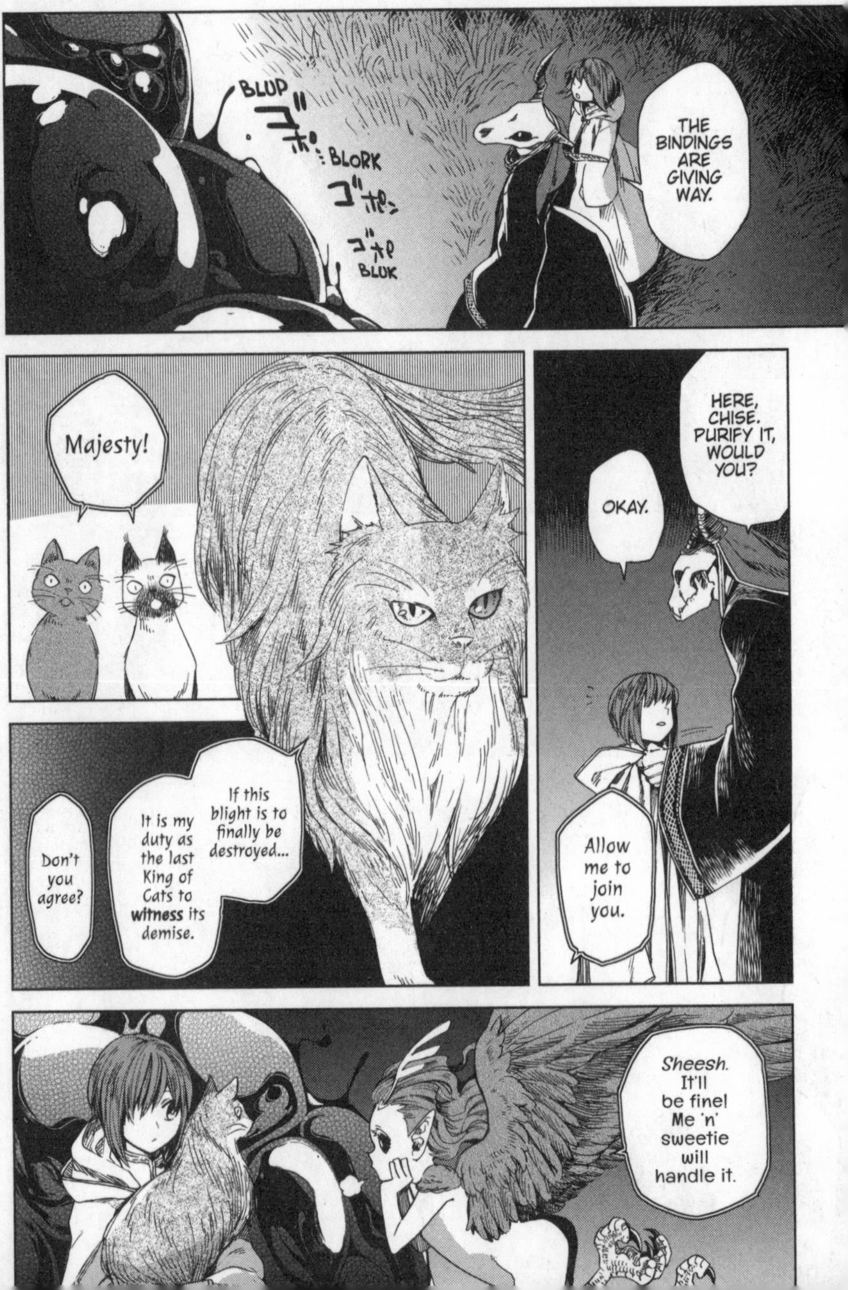
THE BINDINGS ARE GIVING WAY.
BLUP
BLORK
BLUK
HERE, CHISE. PURIFY IT, WOULD YOU?
OKAY.
Allow me to join you.
Majesty!
If this blight is to finally be destroyed...
It is my duty as the last King of Cats to **witness** its demise.
Don't you agree?
Sheesh. It'll be fine! Me 'n' sweetie will handle it.

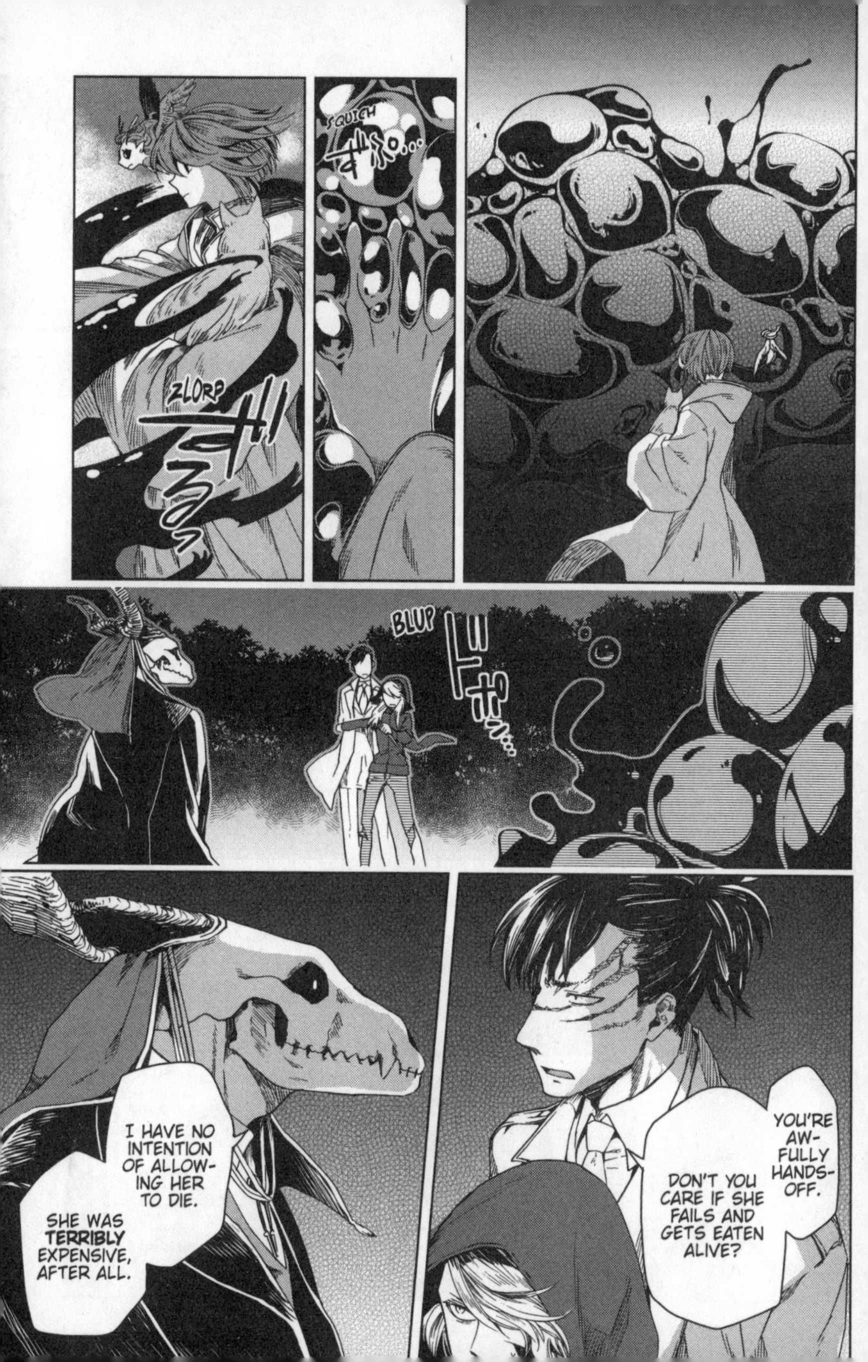
SQUICH
ZLORP
BLUP
YOU'RE AW-FULLY HANDS-OFF.
DON'T YOU CARE IF SHE FAILS AND GETS EATEN ALIVE?
I HAVE NO INTENTION OF ALLOW-ING HER TO DIE.
SHE WAS **TERRIBLY** EXPENSIVE, AFTER ALL.

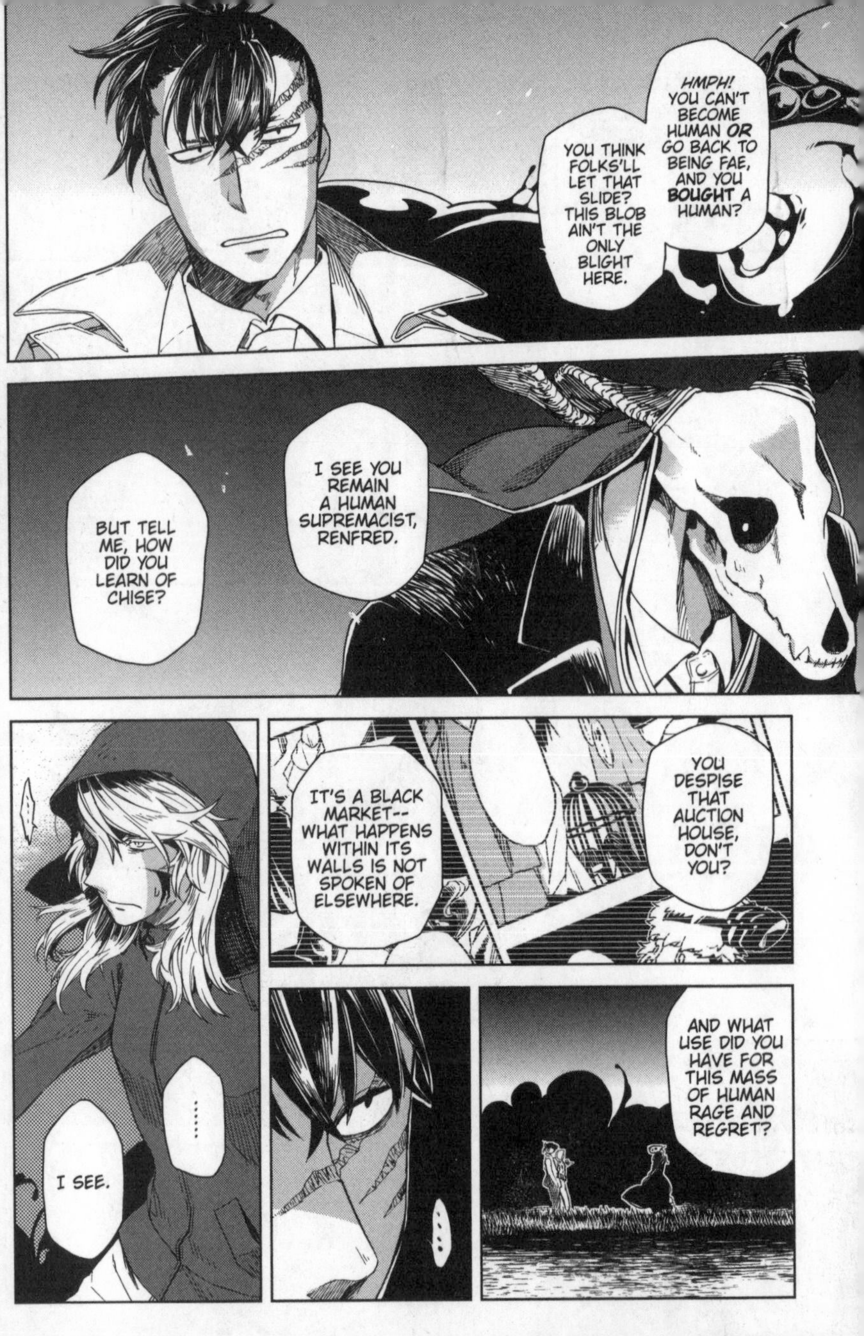
HMPH! YOU CAN'T BECOME HUMAN OR GO BACK TO BEING FAE, AND YOU BOUGHT A HUMAN?
YOU THINK FOLKS'LL LET THAT SLIDE? THIS BLOB AIN'T THE ONLY BLIGHT HERE.
I SEE YOU REMAIN A HUMAN SUPREMACIST, RENFRED.
BUT TELL ME, HOW DID YOU LEARN OF CHISE?
YOU DESPISE THAT AUCTION HOUSE, DON'T YOU?
IT'S A BLACK MARKET-- WHAT HAPPENS WITHIN ITS WALLS IS NOT SPOKEN OF ELSEWHERE.
AND WHAT USE DID YOU HAVE FOR THIS MASS OF HUMAN RAGE AND REGRET?
....
...
......
I SEE.

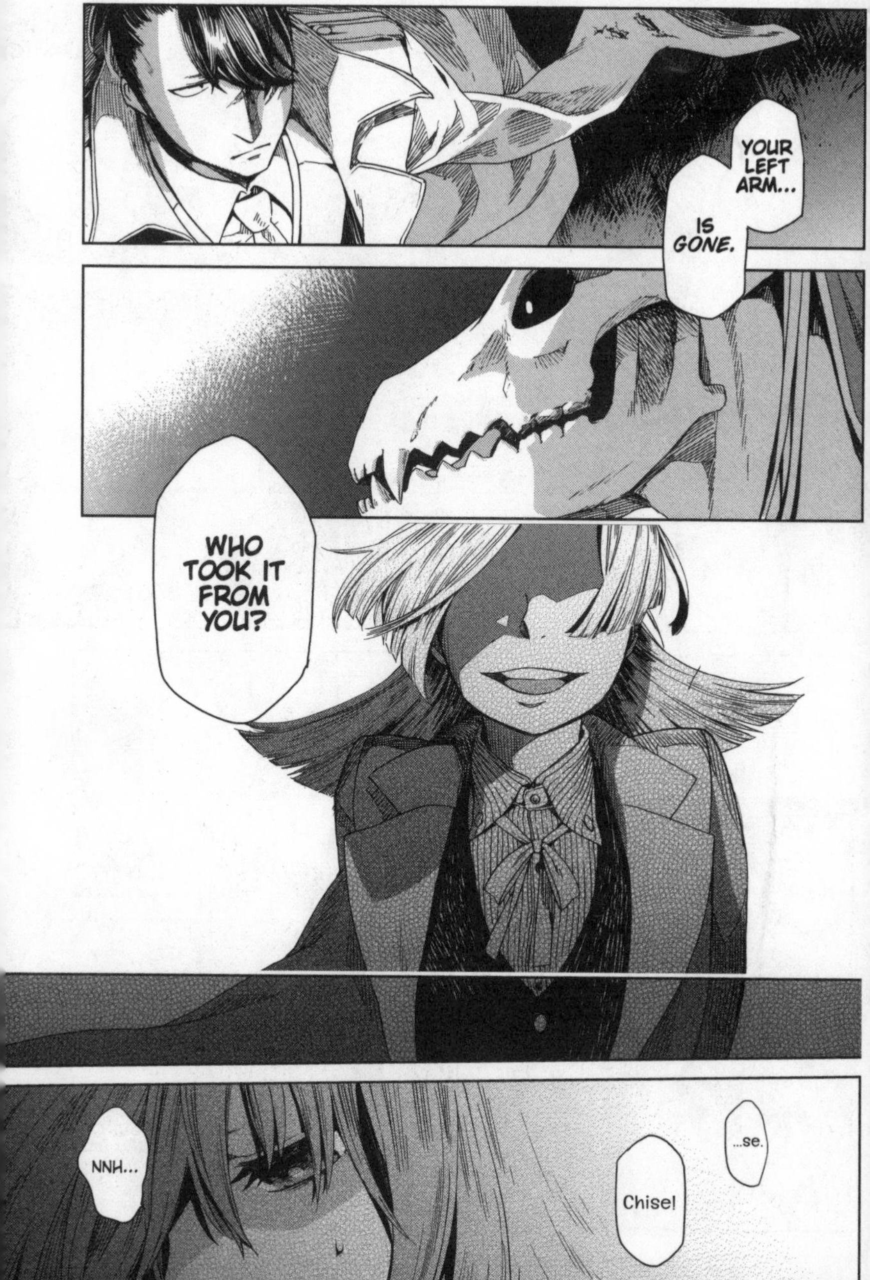
YOUR LEFT ARM...
IS GONE.
WHO TOOK IT FROM YOU?
...se.
Chise!
NNH...

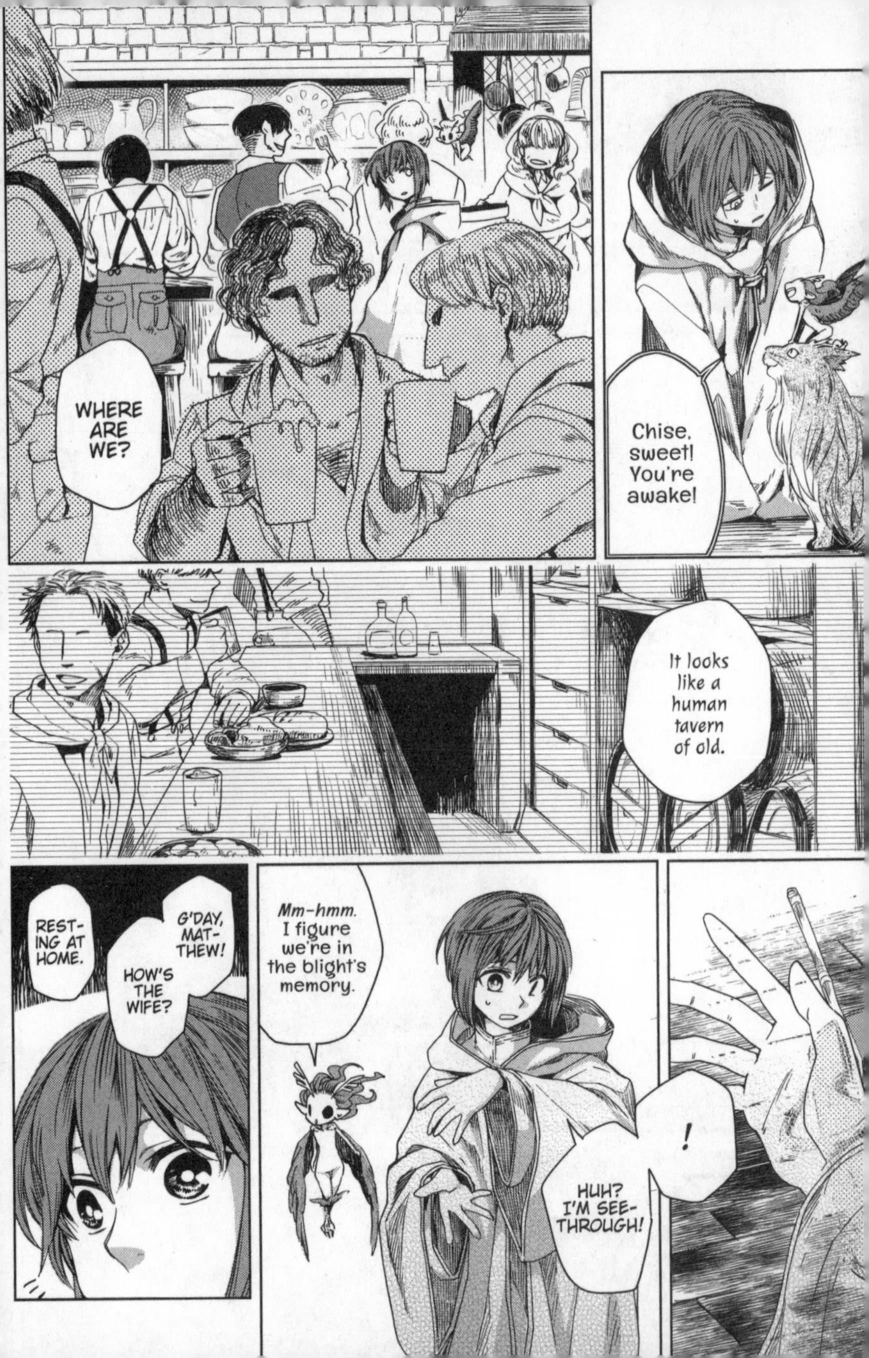
Chise, sweet! You're awake!
WHERE ARE WE?
It looks like a human tavern of old.
!
HUH? I'M SEE-THROUGH!
Mm-hmm. I figure we're in the blight's memory.
G'DAY, MAT-THEW!
HOW'S THE WIFE?
REST-ING AT HOME.

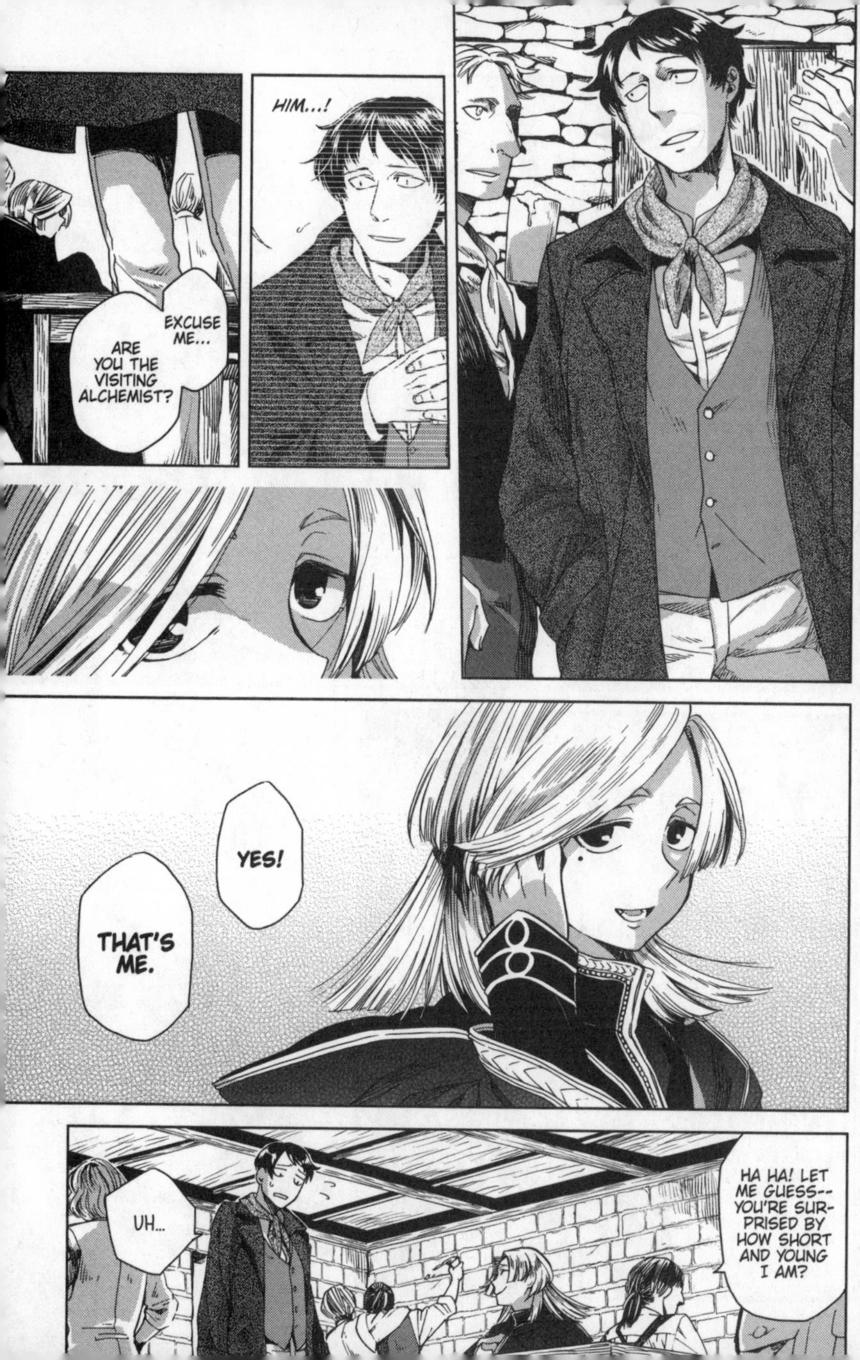
HIM...!
EXCUSE ME... ARE YOU THE VISITING ALCHEMIST?
YES!
THAT'S ME.
HA HA! LET ME GUESS-- YOU'RE SURPRISED BY HOW SHORT AND YOUNG I AM?
UH...

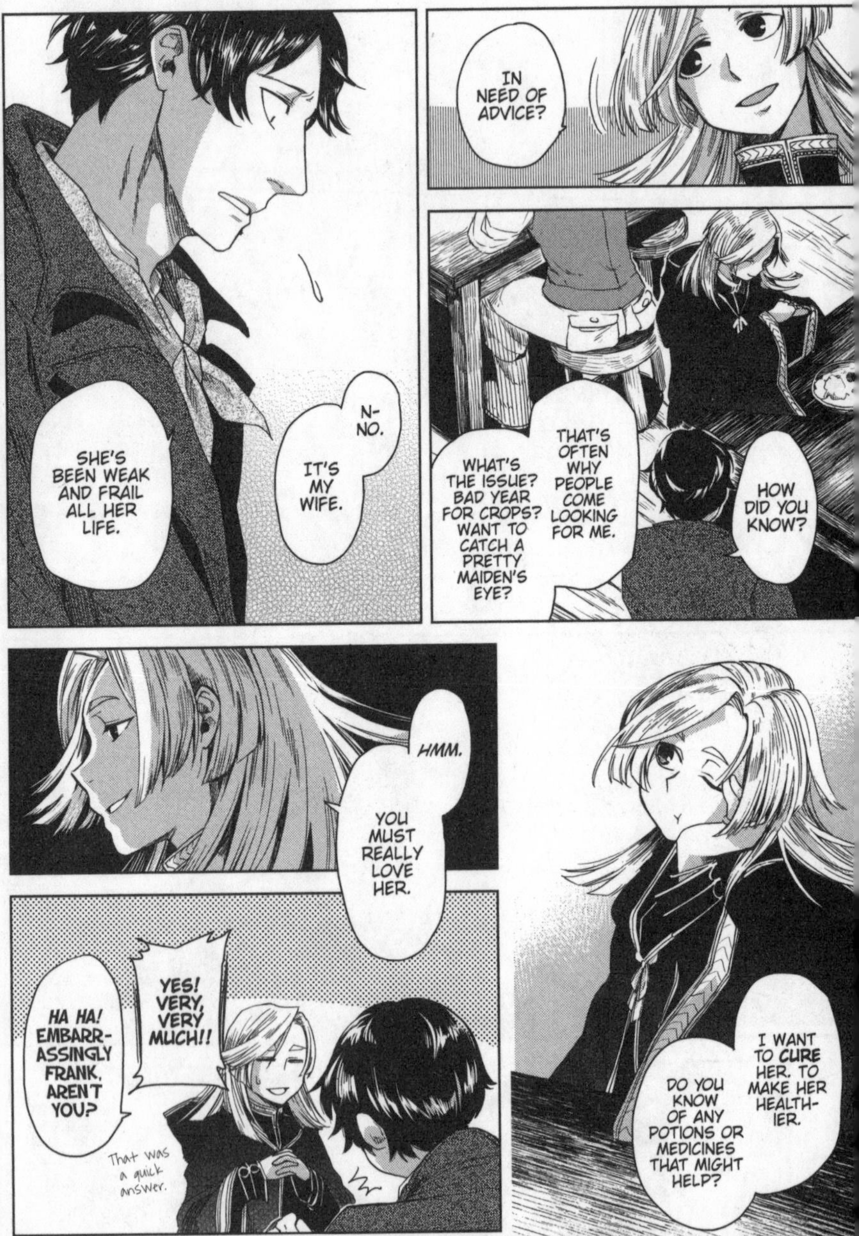
IN NEED OF ADVICE?
HOW DID YOU KNOW?
THAT'S OFTEN WHY PEOPLE COME LOOKING FOR ME.
WHAT'S THE ISSUE? BAD YEAR FOR CROPS? WANT TO CATCH A PRETTY MAIDEN'S EYE?
N-NO.
IT'S MY WIFE.
SHE'S BEEN WEAK AND FRAIL ALL HER LIFE.
I WANT TO CURE HER. TO MAKE HER HEALTHIER.
DO YOU KNOW OF ANY POTIONS OR MEDICINES THAT MIGHT HELP?
HMM.
YOU MUST REALLY LOVE HER.
YES! VERY, VERY MUCH!!
HA HA! EMBARRASSINGLY FRANK, AREN'T YOU?
That was a quick answer.

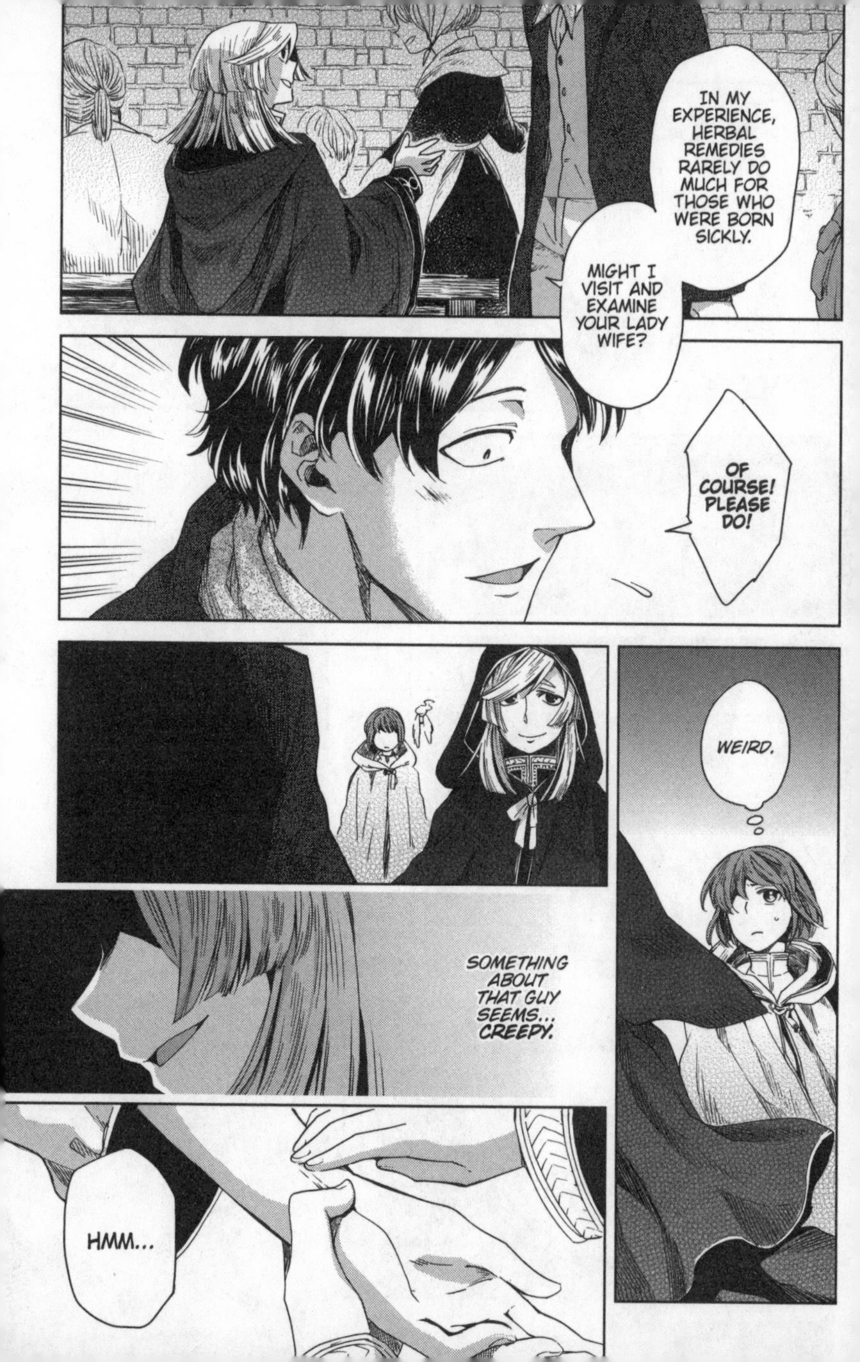
IN MY EXPERIENCE, HERBAL REMEDIES RARELY DO MUCH FOR THOSE WHO WERE BORN SICKLY.
MIGHT I VISIT AND EXAMINE YOUR LADY WIFE?
OF COURSE! PLEASE DO!
WEIRD.
SOMETHING ABOUT THAT GUY SEEMS... CREEPY.
HMM...

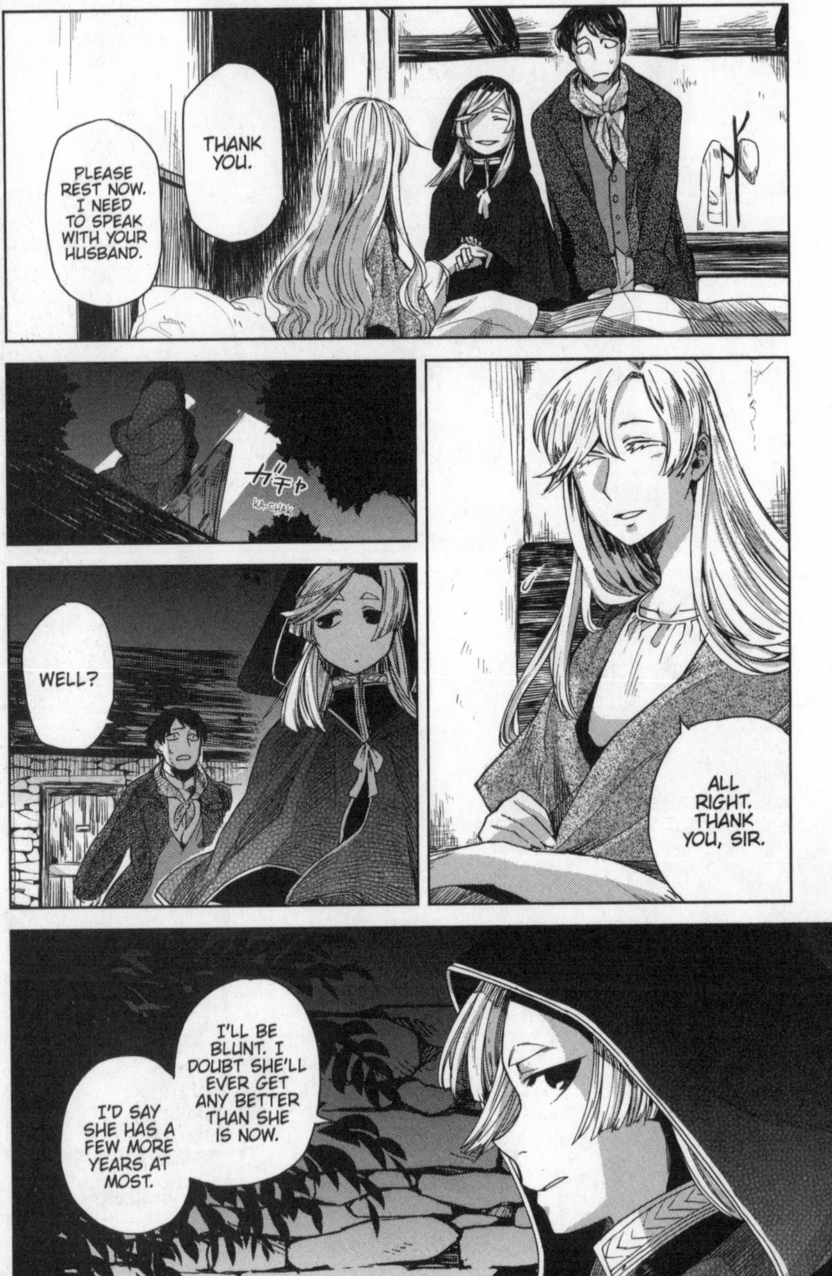
THANK YOU.
PLEASE REST NOW. I NEED TO SPEAK WITH YOUR HUSBAND.
ALL RIGHT. THANK YOU, SIR.
ガチャ
KA-CHAK
WELL?
I'LL BE BLUNT. I DOUBT SHE'LL EVER GET ANY BETTER THAN SHE IS NOW.
I'D SAY SHE HAS A FEW MORE YEARS AT MOST.

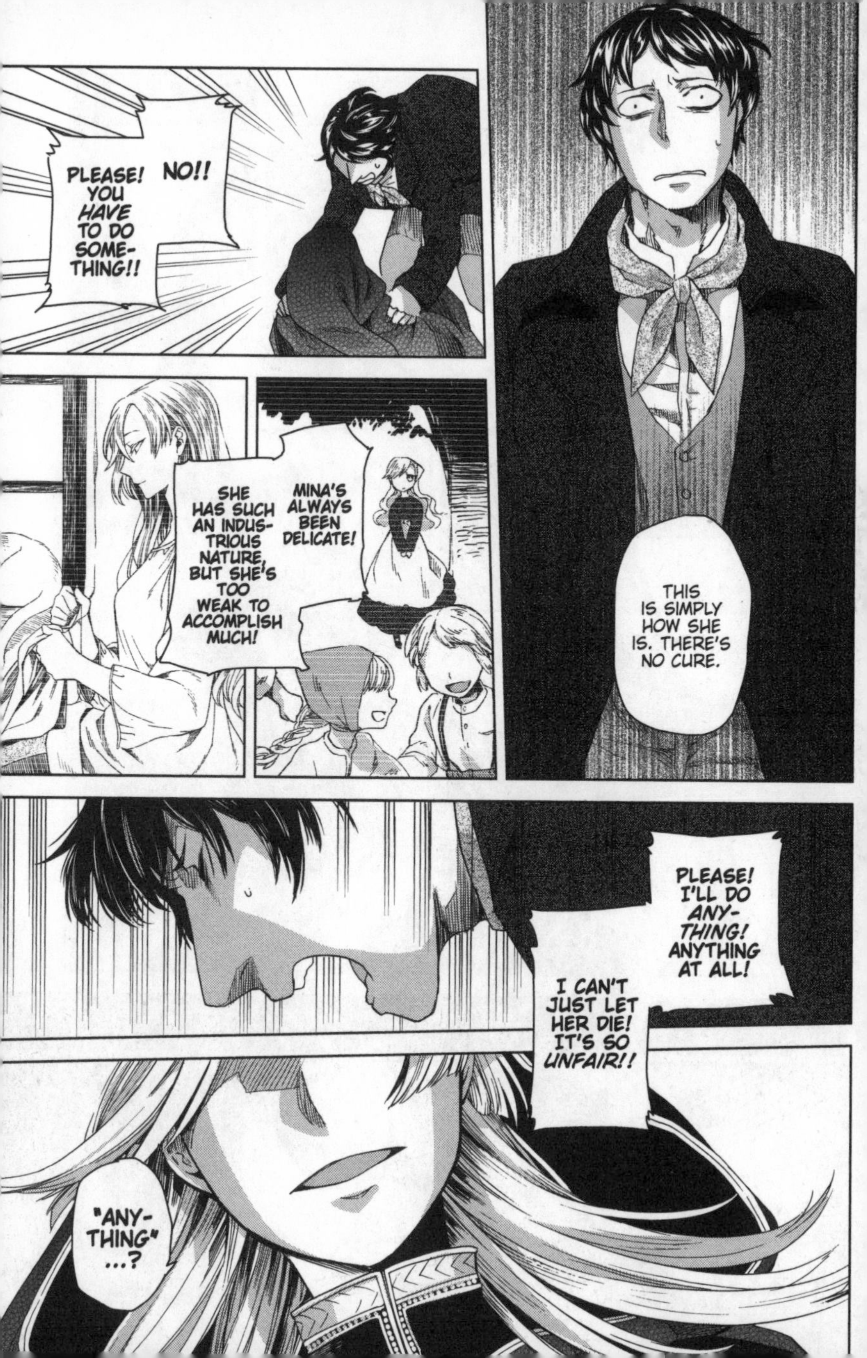
THIS IS SIMPLY HOW SHE IS. THERE'S NO CURE.
NO!!
PLEASE! YOU *HAVE* TO DO SOME-THING!!
MINA'S ALWAYS BEEN DELICATE!
SHE HAS SUCH AN INDUS-TRIOUS NATURE, BUT SHE'S TOO WEAK TO ACCOMPLISH MUCH!
PLEASE! I'LL DO *ANY-THING!* ANYTHING AT ALL!
I CAN'T JUST LET HER DIE! IT'S SO *UNFAIR!!*
"ANY-THING" ...?

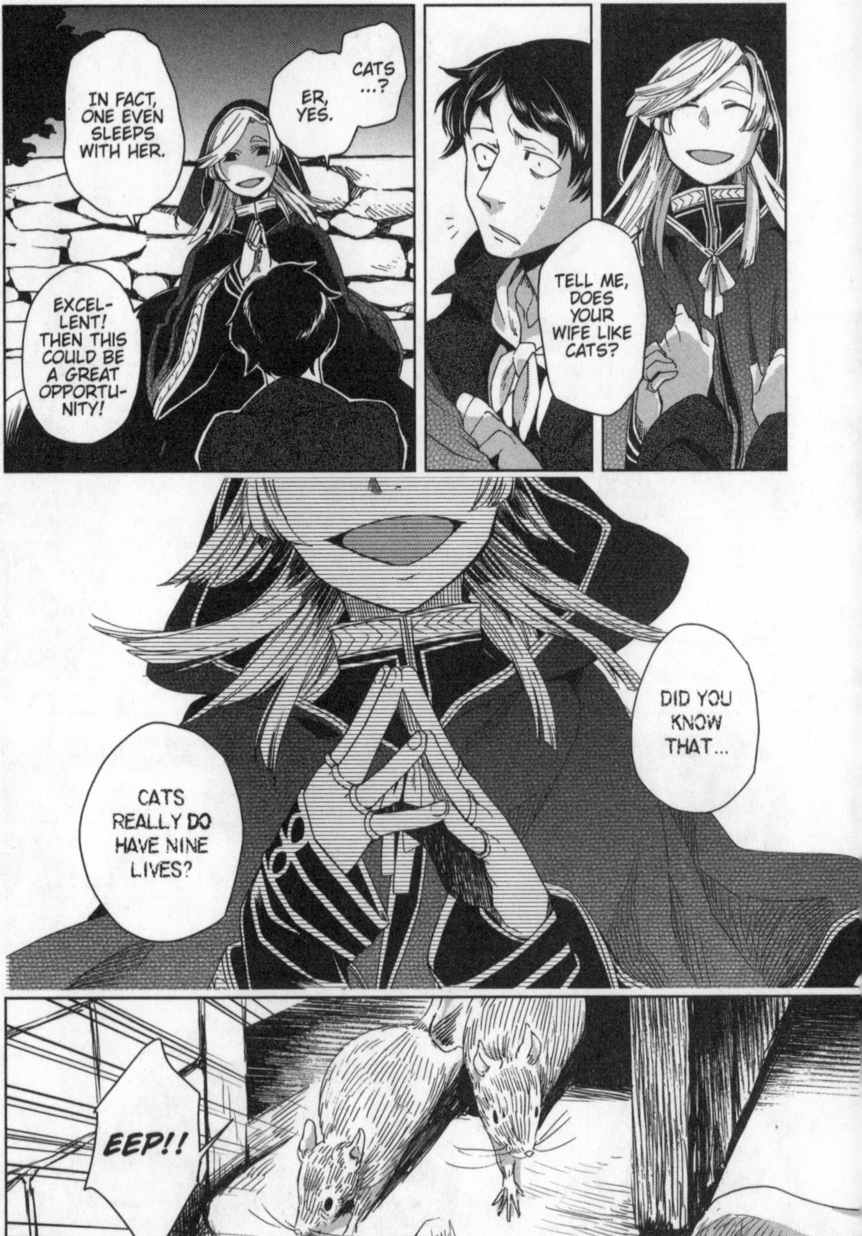
TELL ME, DOES YOUR WIFE LIKE CATS?
CATS ...?
ER, YES.
IN FACT, ONE EVEN SLEEPS WITH HER.
EXCEL-LENT! THEN THIS COULD BE A GREAT OPPORTU-NITY!
DID YOU KNOW THAT...
CATS REALLY DO HAVE NINE LIVES?
EEP!!
SQUEAK!

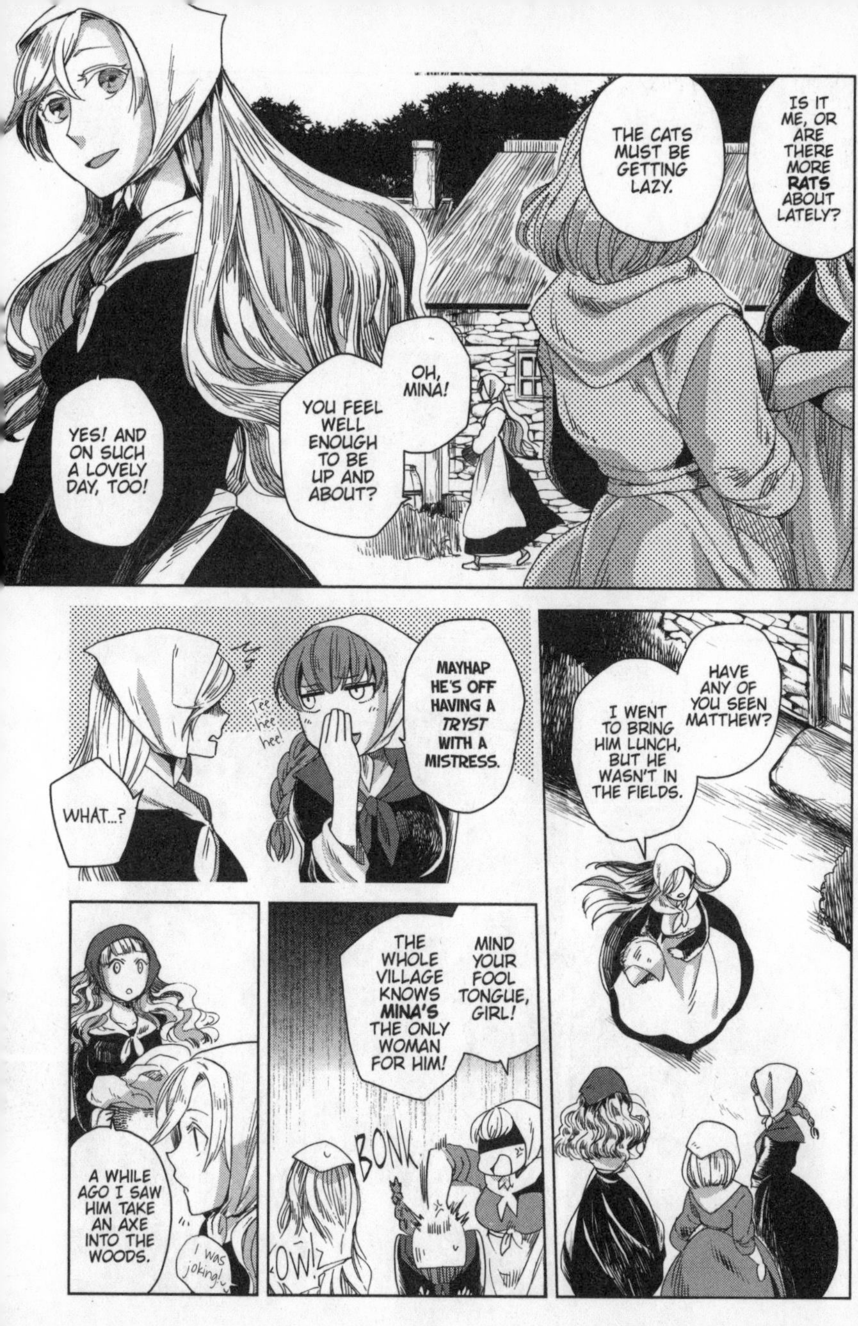
IS IT ME, OR ARE THERE MORE **RATS** ABOUT LATELY?
THE CATS MUST BE GETTING LAZY.
OH, MINA!
YOU FEEL WELL ENOUGH TO BE UP AND ABOUT?
YES! AND ON SUCH A LOVELY DAY, TOO!
HAVE ANY OF YOU SEEN MATTHEW?
I WENT TO BRING HIM LUNCH, BUT HE WASN'T IN THE FIELDS.
MAYHAP HE'S OFF HAVING A *TRYST* WITH A MISTRESS.
Tee hee hee!
WHAT...?
MIND YOUR FOOL TONGUE, GIRL!
THE WHOLE VILLAGE KNOWS **MINA'S** THE ONLY WOMAN FOR HIM!
BONK
OW!
A WHILE AGO I SAW HIM TAKE AN AXE INTO THE WOODS.
I was joking!

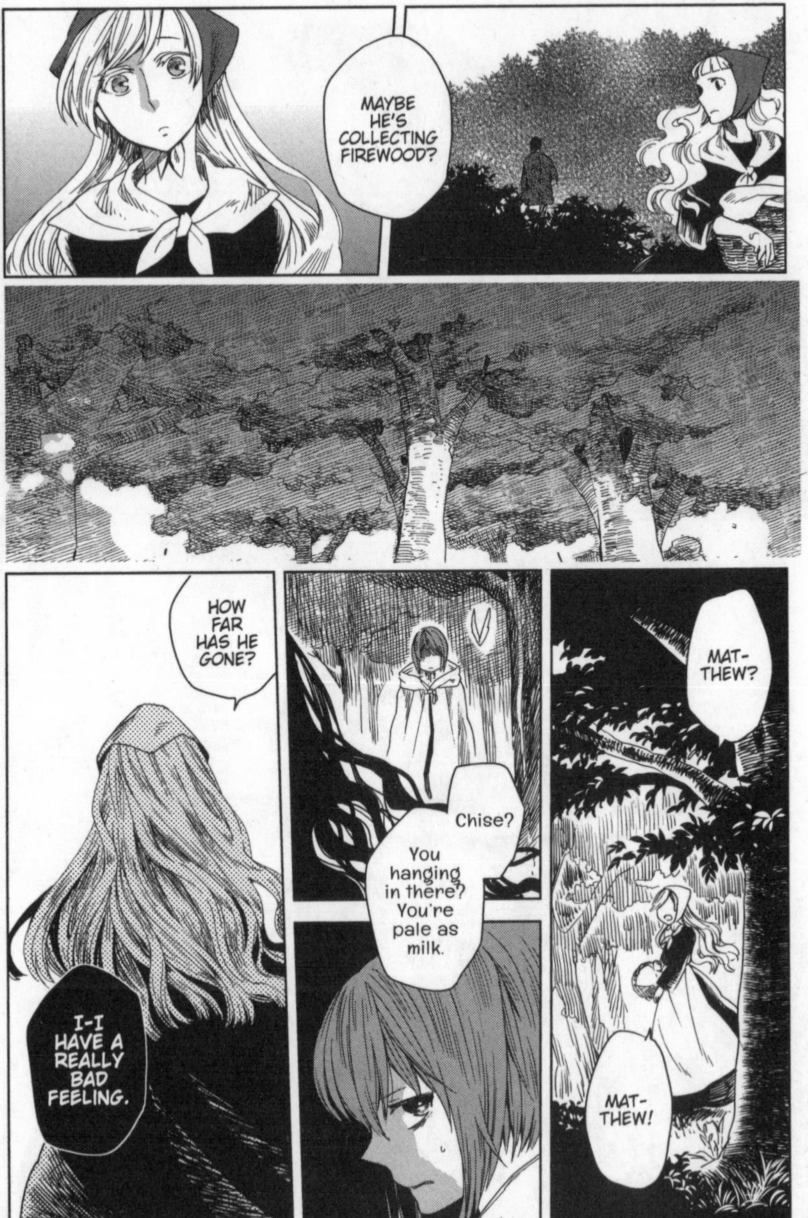
MAYBE HE'S COLLECTING FIREWOOD?
MAT-THEW?
MAT-THEW!
Chise?
You hanging in there? You're pale as milk.
HOW FAR HAS HE GONE?
I-I HAVE A REALLY BAD FEELING.

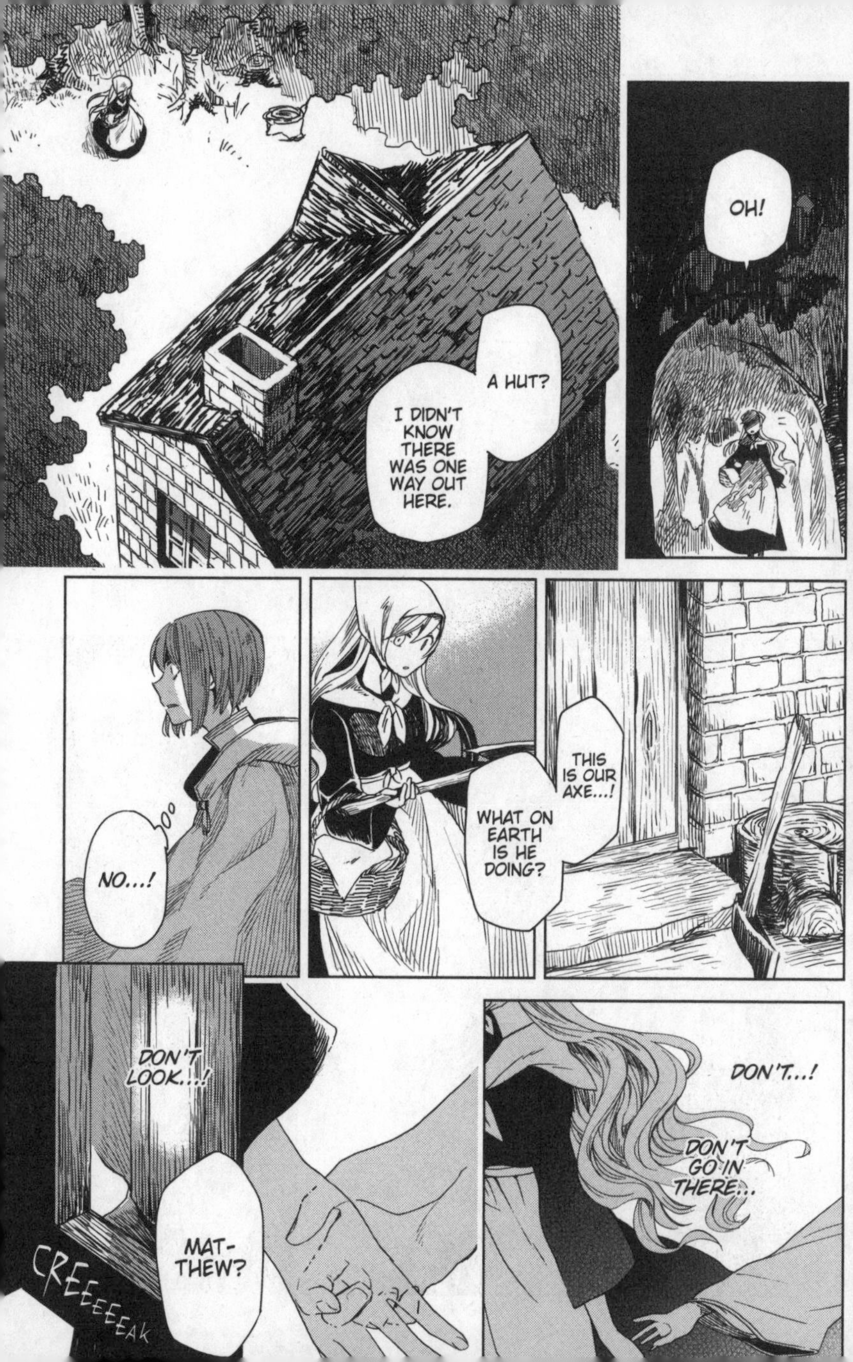
OH!
A HUT?
I DIDN'T KNOW THERE WAS ONE WAY OUT HERE.
THIS IS OUR AXE...!
WHAT ON EARTH IS HE DOING?
NO...!
DON'T...!
DON'T GO IN THERE...
DON'T LOOK...!
MAT-THEW?
CREEEEEEAK

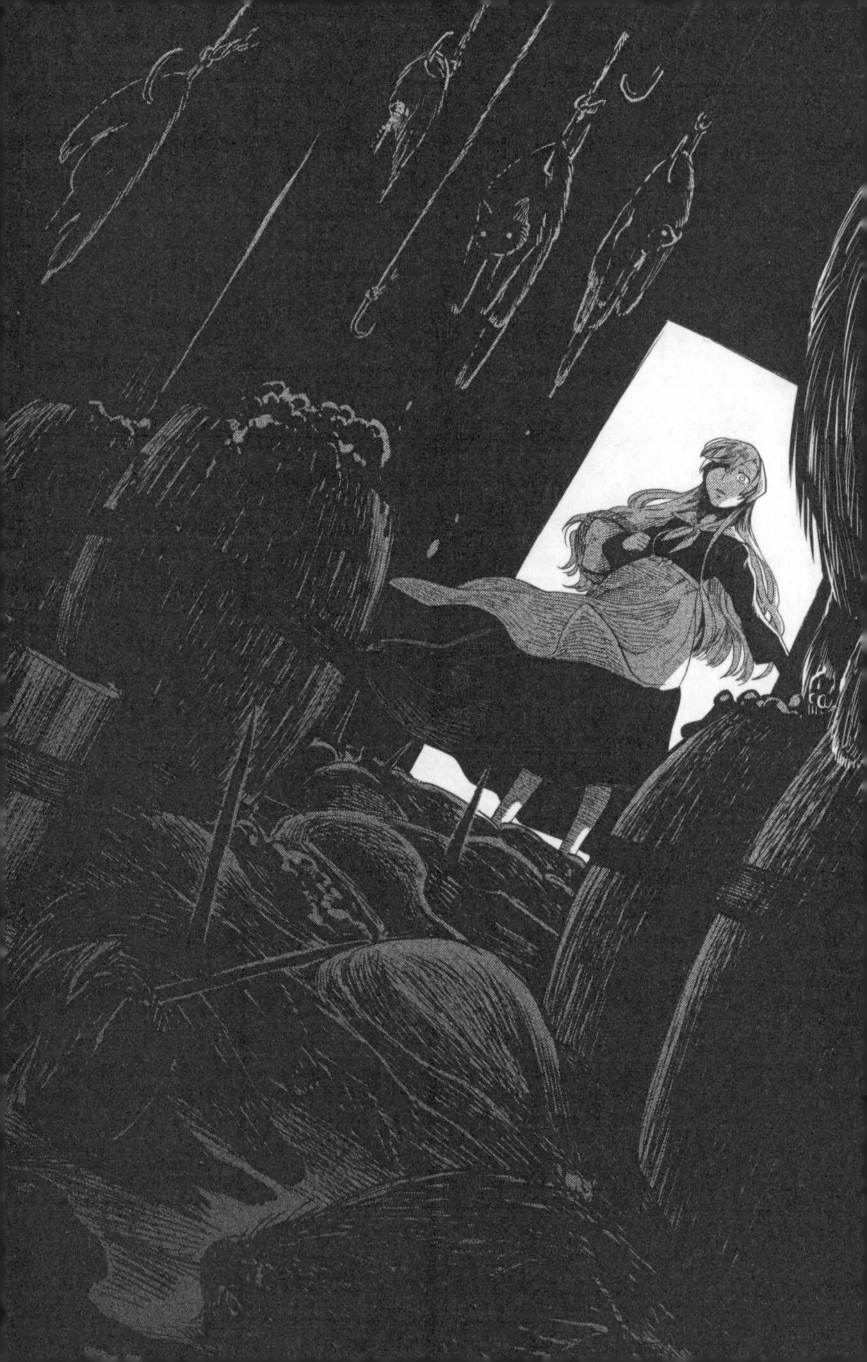

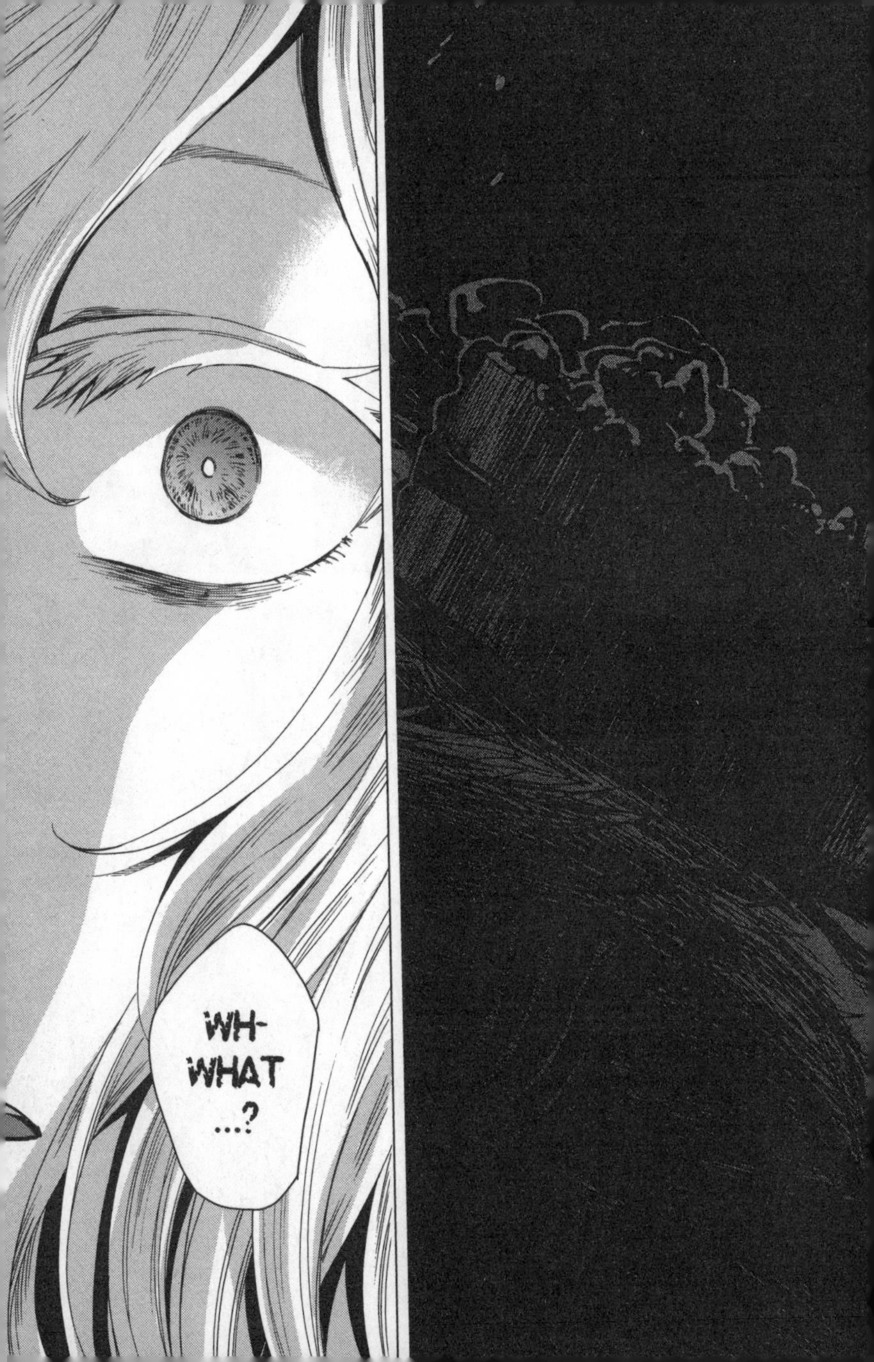
WH- WHAT ...?

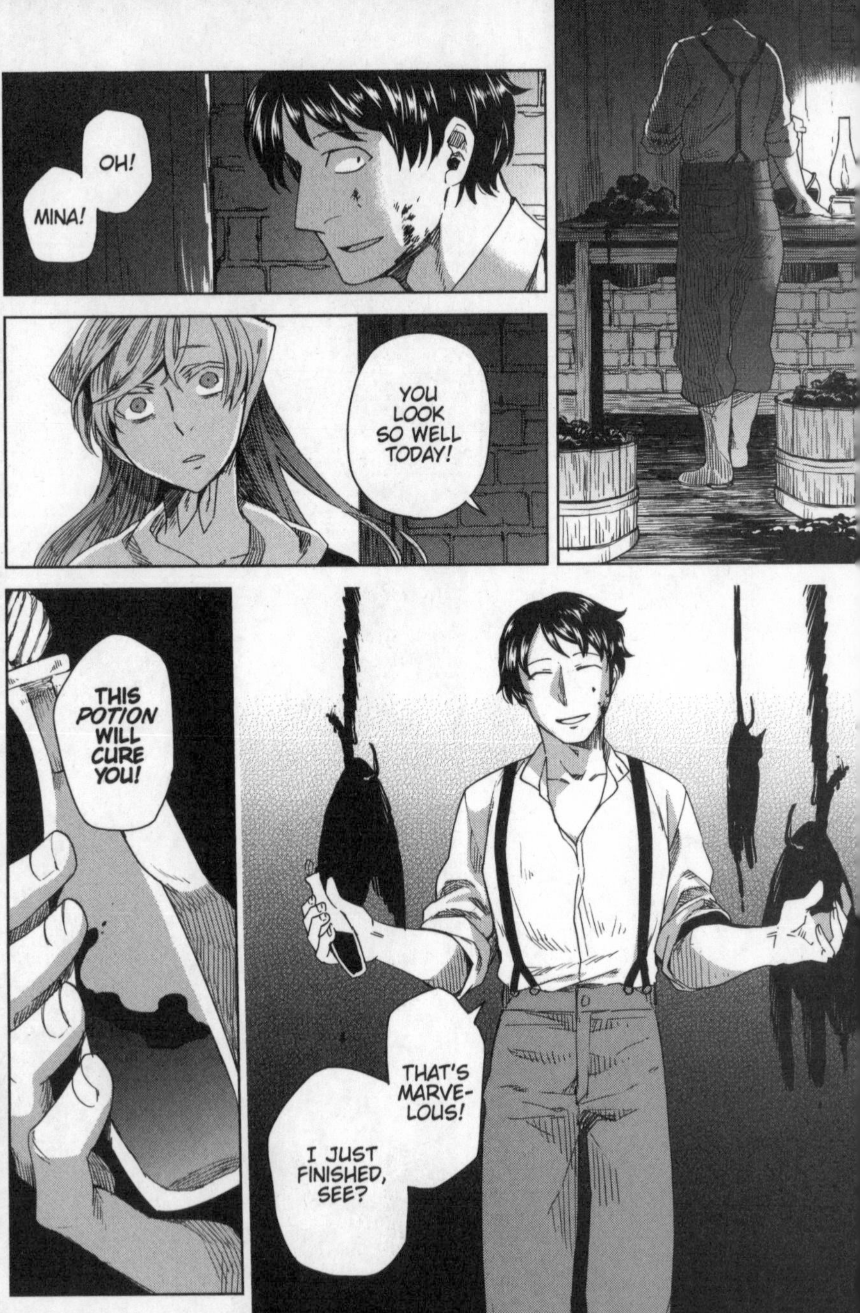
OH!
MINA!
YOU LOOK SO WELL TODAY!
THAT'S MARVE-LOUS!
I JUST FINISHED, SEE?
THIS *POTION* WILL CURE YOU!

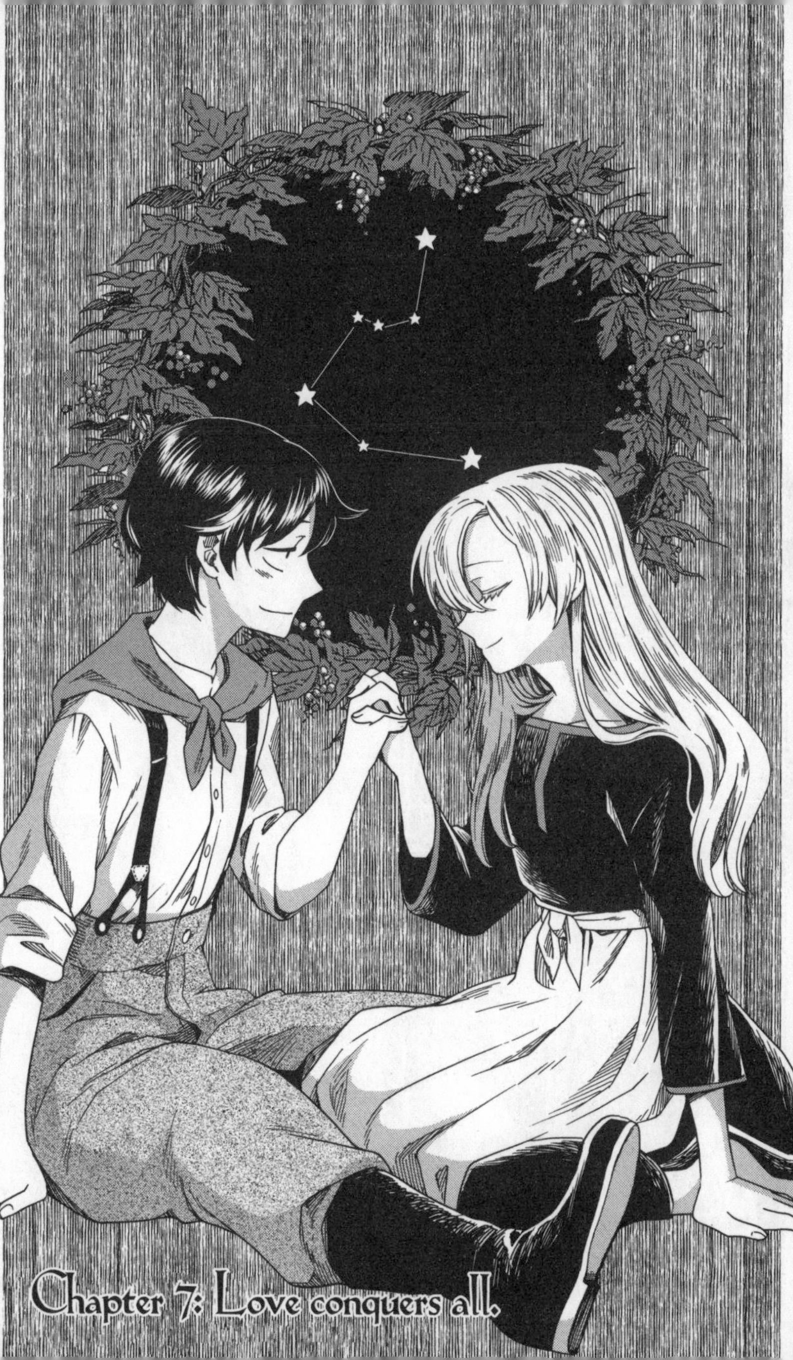
Chapter 7: Love conquers all.

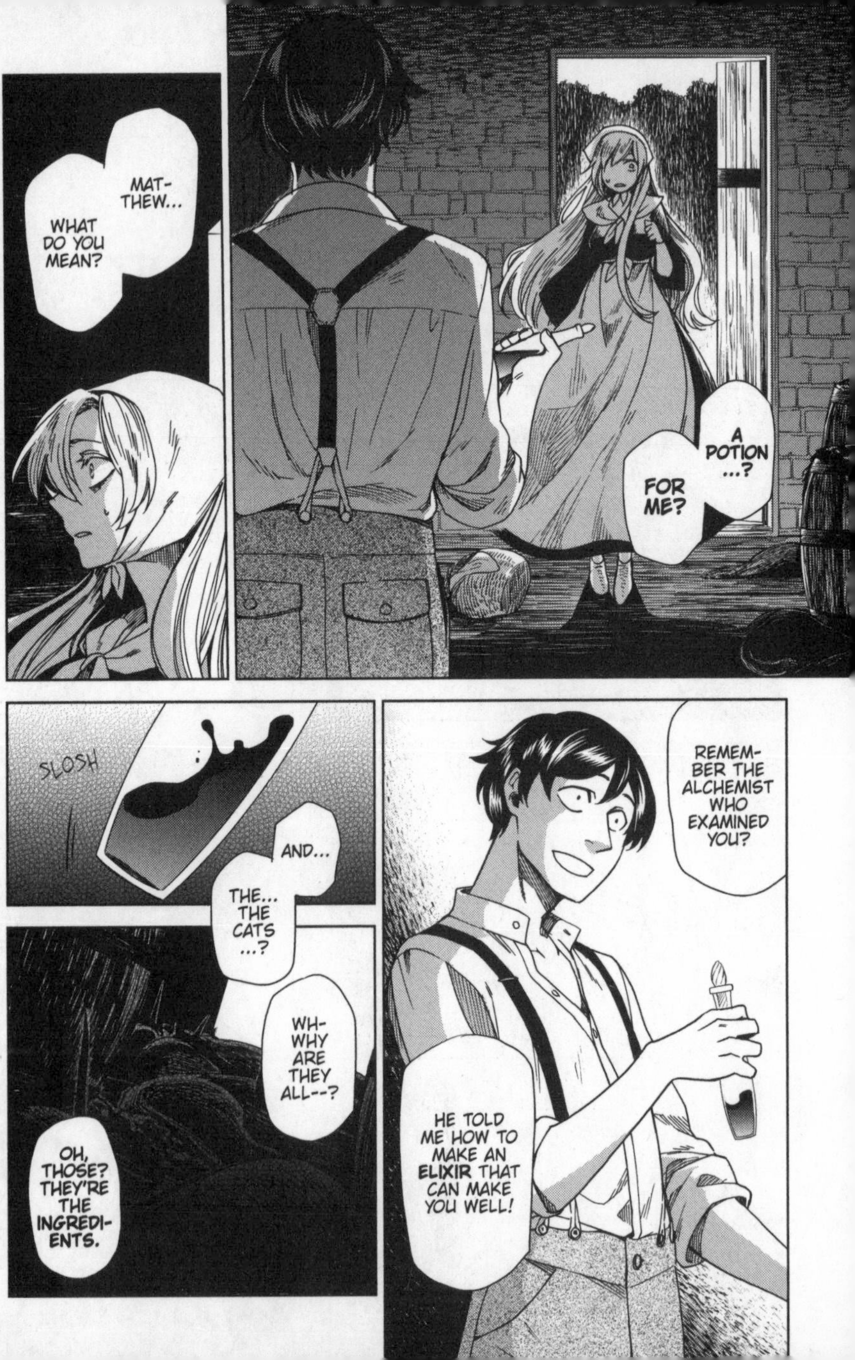
A POTION ...?
FOR ME?
MATTHEW...
WHAT DO YOU MEAN?
REMEMBER THE ALCHEMIST WHO EXAMINED YOU?
HE TOLD ME HOW TO MAKE AN ELIXIR THAT CAN MAKE YOU WELL!
SLOSH
AND...
THE... THE CATS ...?
WH-WHY ARE THEY ALL--?
OH, THOSE? THEY'RE THE INGREDIENTS.

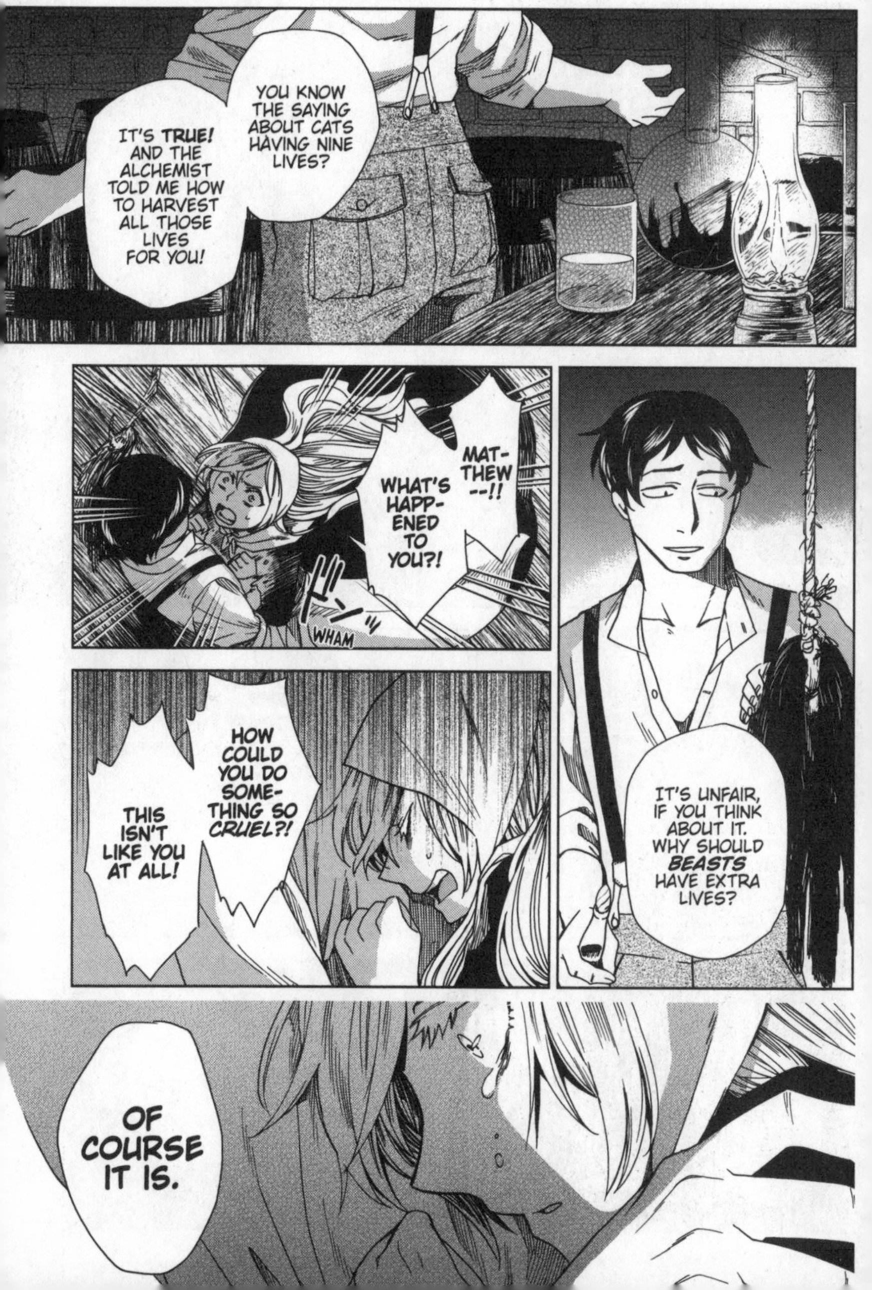
YOU KNOW THE SAYING ABOUT CATS HAVING NINE LIVES?
IT'S **TRUE!** AND THE ALCHEMIST TOLD ME HOW TO HARVEST ALL THOSE LIVES FOR YOU!
IT'S UNFAIR, IF YOU THINK ABOUT IT. WHY SHOULD ***BEASTS*** HAVE EXTRA LIVES?
MAT-THEW --!!
WHAT'S HAPP-ENED TO YOU?!
WHAM
HOW COULD YOU DO SOME-THING SO ***CRUEL?!***
THIS ISN'T LIKE YOU AT ALL!
OF COURSE IT IS.

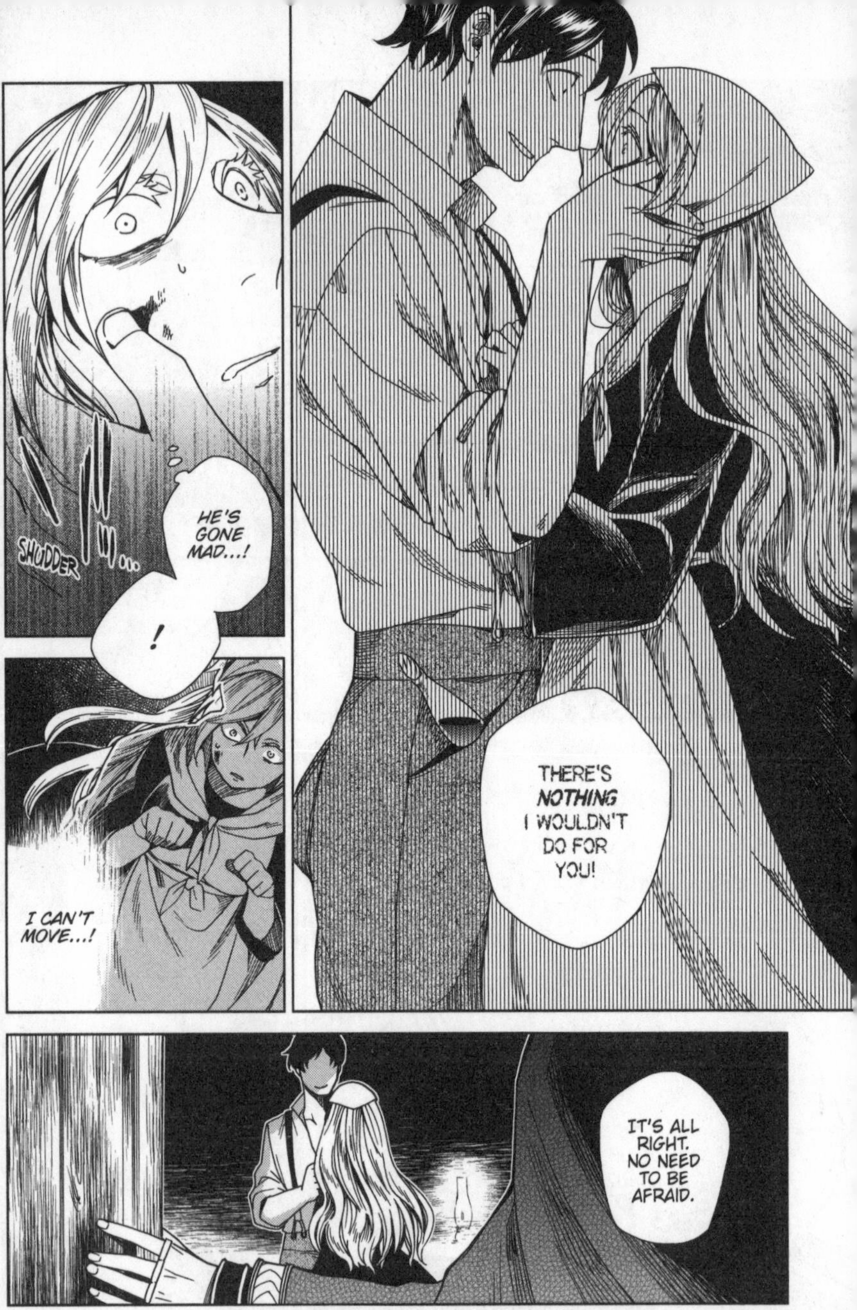
THERE'S *NOTHING* I WOULDN'T DO FOR YOU!
HE'S GONE MAD...!
SHUDDER
!
I CAN'T MOVE...!
IT'S ALL RIGHT. NO NEED TO BE AFRAID.

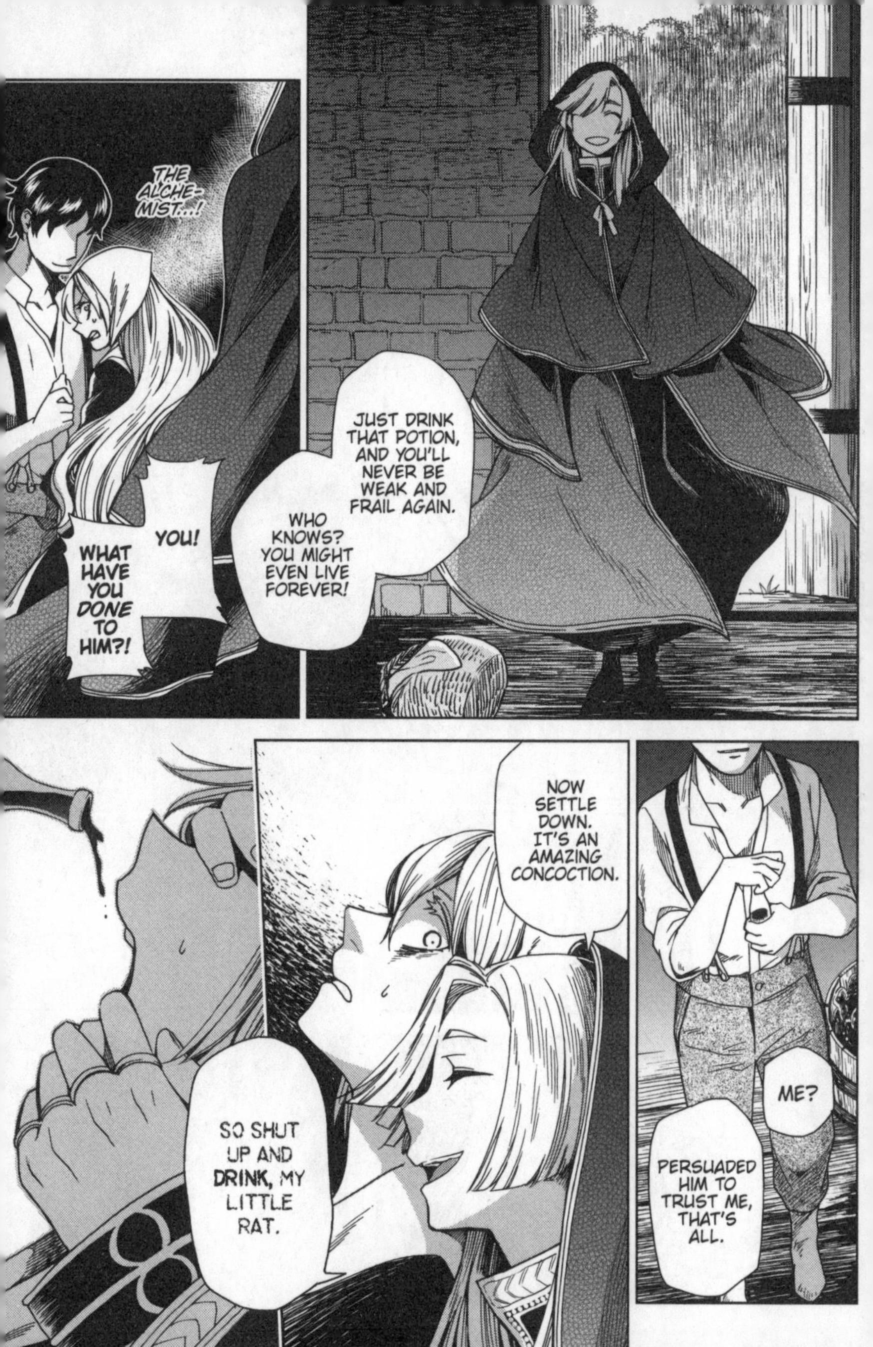
JUST DRINK THAT POTION, AND YOU'LL NEVER BE WEAK AND FRAIL AGAIN.
WHO KNOWS? YOU MIGHT EVEN LIVE FOREVER!
THE ALCHE-MIST...!
YOU!
WHAT HAVE YOU *DONE* TO HIM?!
ME?
PERSUADED HIM TO TRUST ME, THAT'S ALL.
NOW SETTLE DOWN. IT'S AN AMAZING CONCOCTION.
SO SHUT UP AND **DRINK**, MY LITTLE RAT.

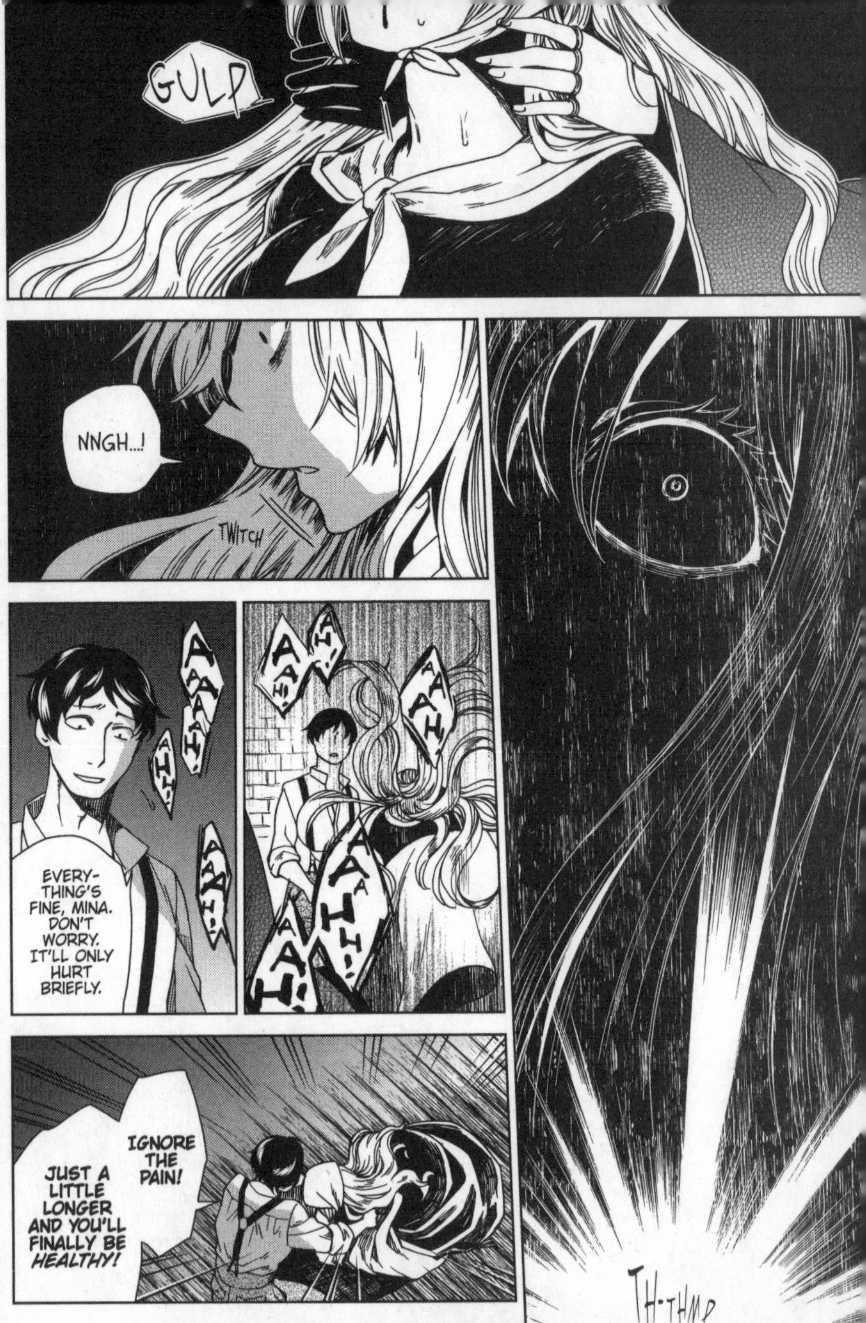
GULP
TH-THMP
NNGH...!
TWITCH
AAH!
AAH!
AAAH!
AAH!
AAAAH!
AH!
AAAH!
EVERY-THING'S FINE, MINA. DON'T WORRY. IT'LL ONLY HURT BRIEFLY.
IGNORE THE PAIN!
JUST A LITTLE LONGER AND YOU'LL FINALLY BE *HEALTHY*!

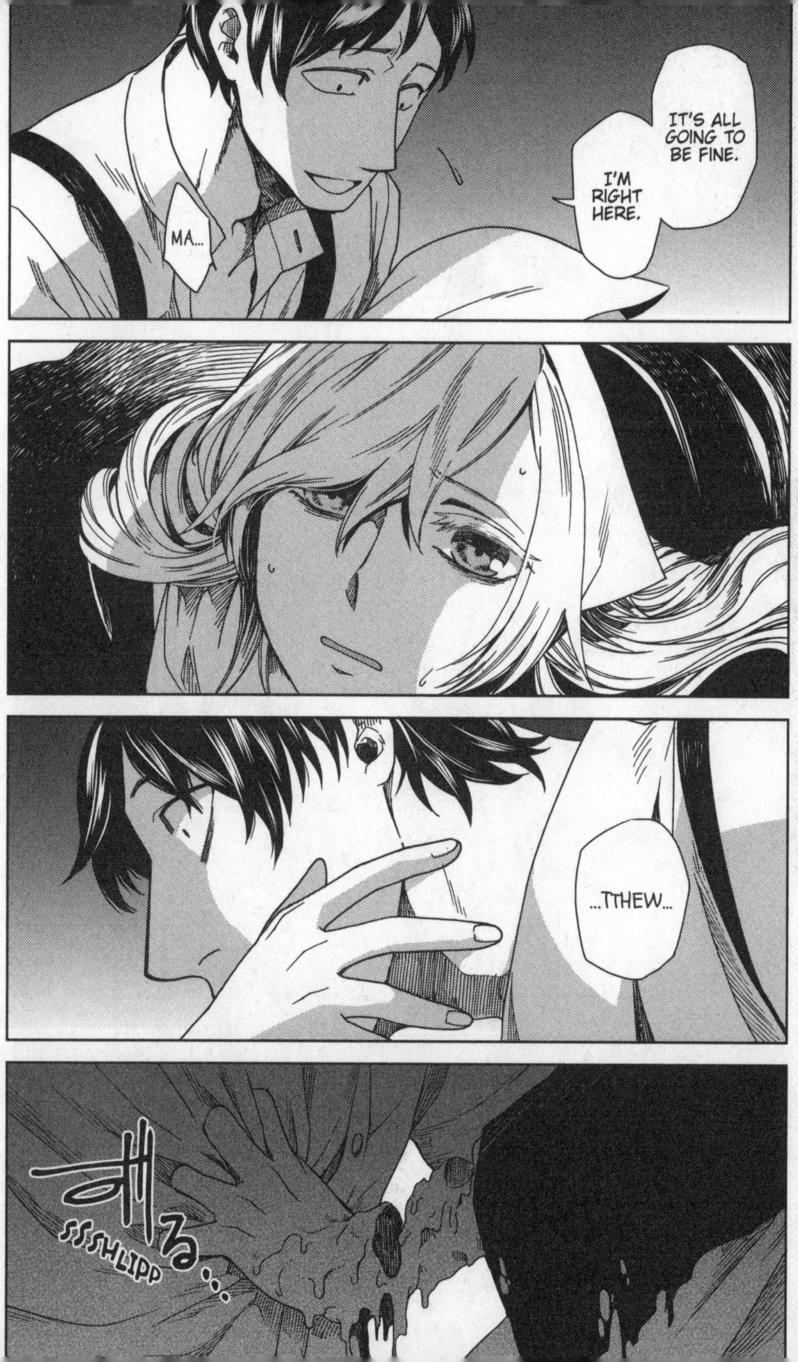
IT'S ALL GOING TO BE FINE.
I'M RIGHT HERE.
MA...
...TTHEW...
ずる…
SSSHLIPP

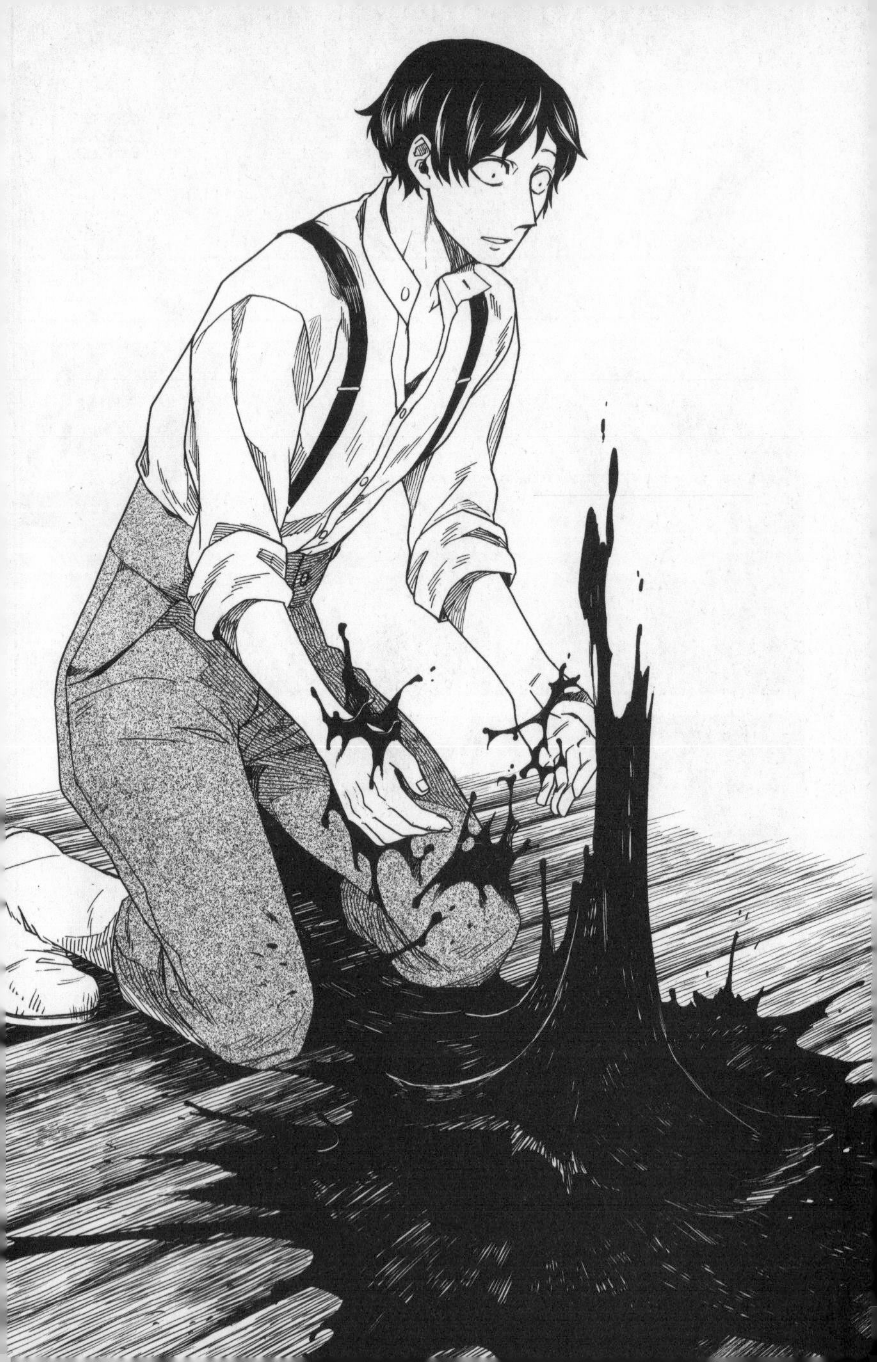

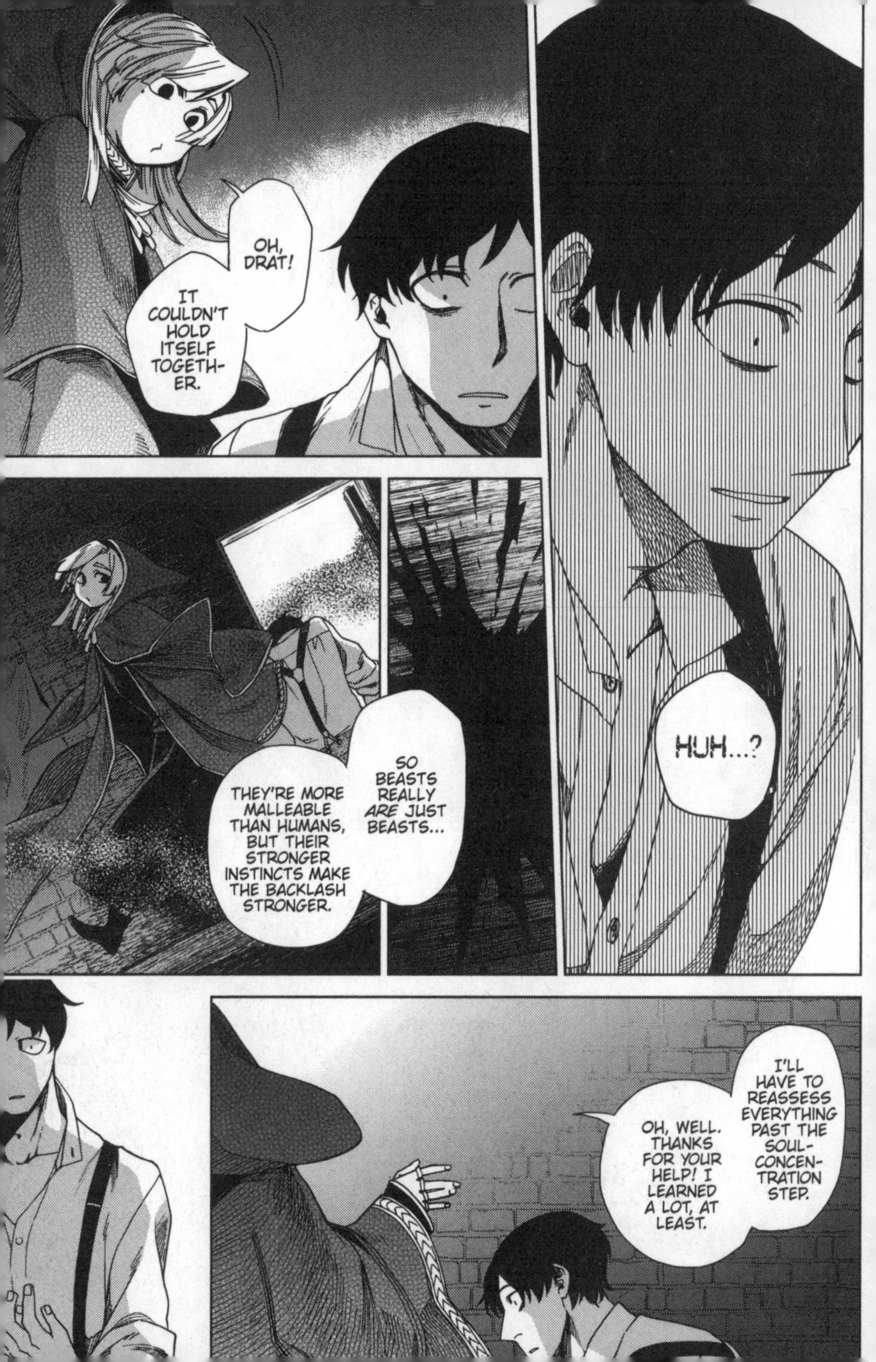
HUH...?
OH, DRAT!
IT COULDN'T HOLD ITSELF TOGETH-ER.
SO BEASTS REALLY *ARE* JUST BEASTS...
THEY'RE MORE MALLEABLE THAN HUMANS, BUT THEIR STRONGER INSTINCTS MAKE THE BACKLASH STRONGER.
I'LL HAVE TO REASSESS EVERYTHING PAST THE SOUL-CONCEN-TRATION STEP.
OH, WELL. THANKS FOR YOUR HELP! I LEARNED A LOT, AT LEAST.

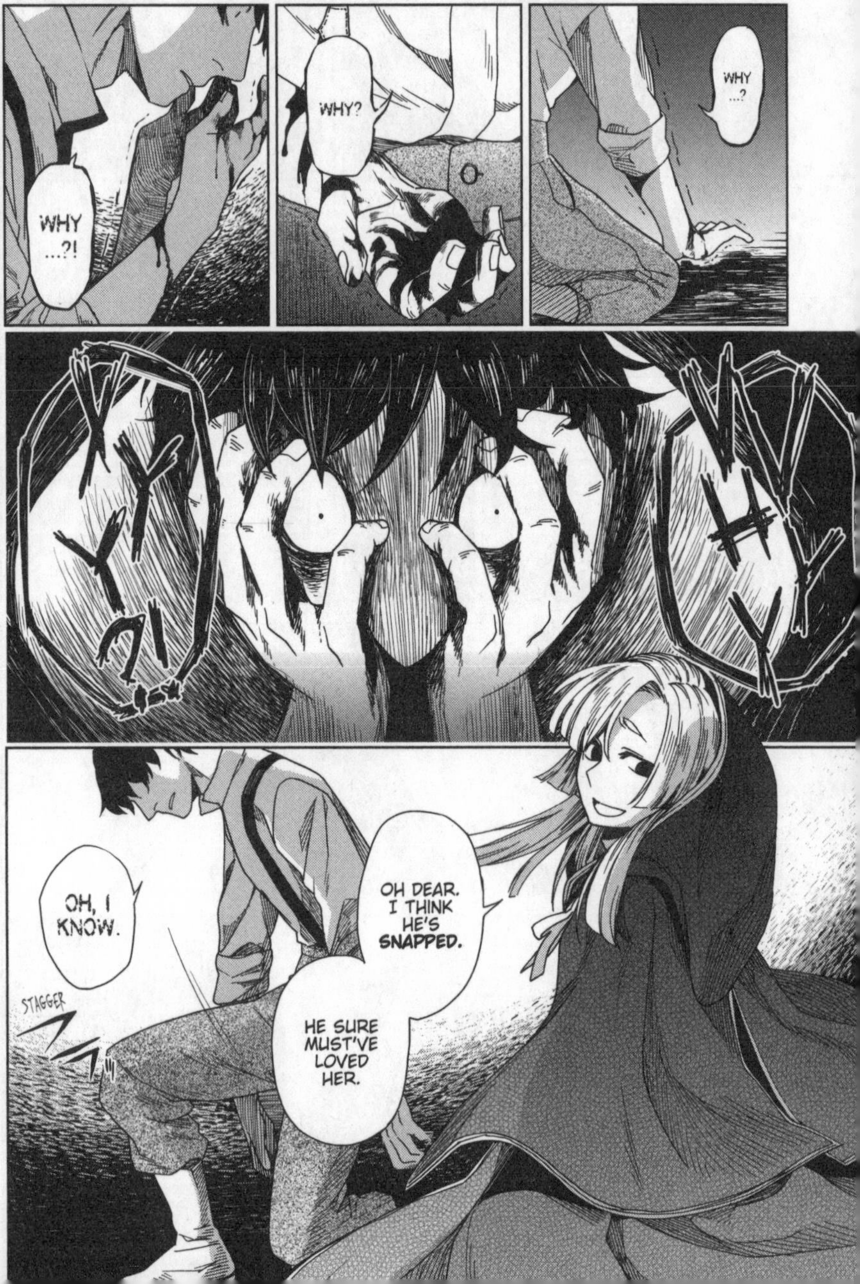
WHY ...?
WHY?
WHY ...?!
WHYY
YYYY?!
OH DEAR. I THINK HE'S **SNAPPED.**
HE SURE MUST'VE LOVED HER.
OH, I KNOW.
STAGGER

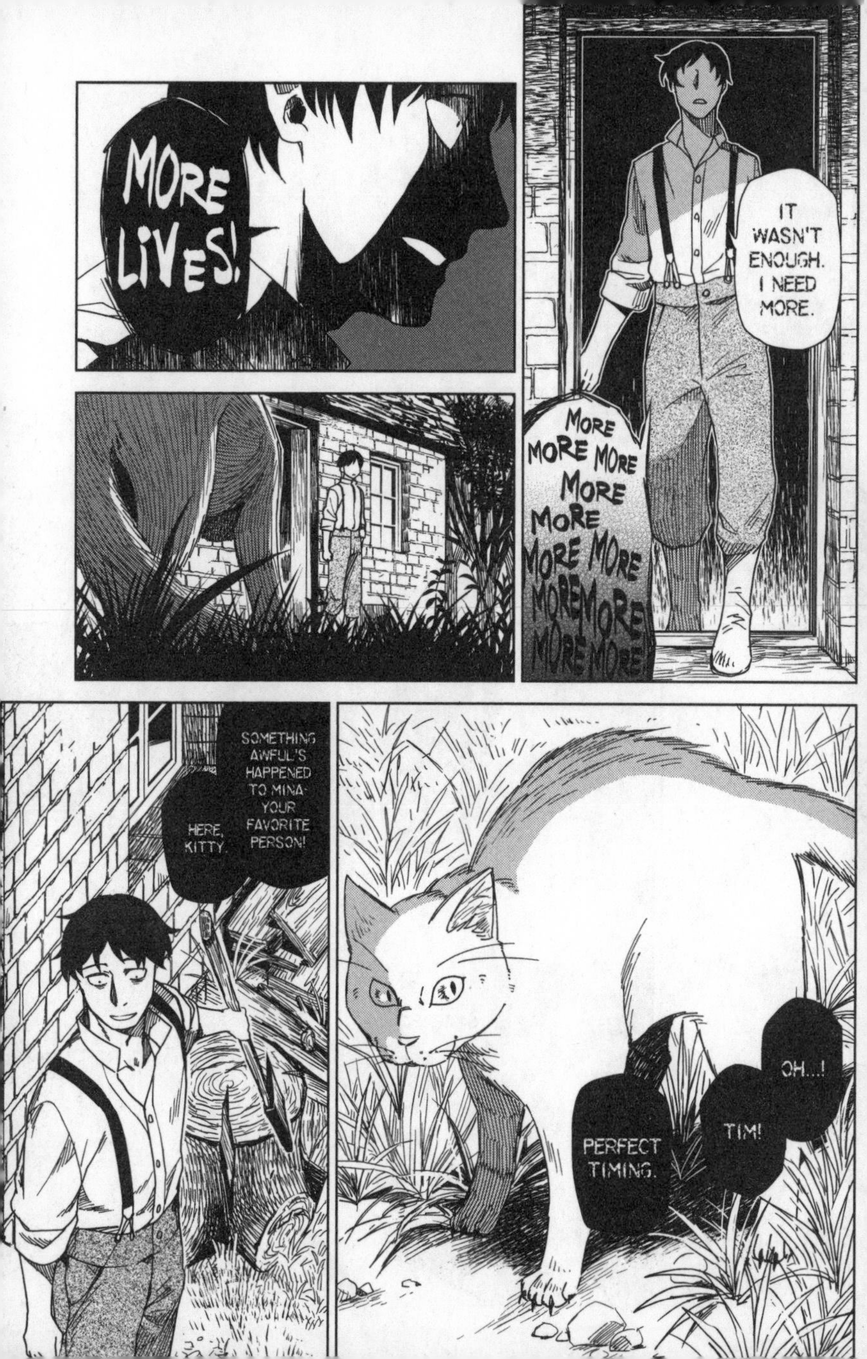
IT WASN'T ENOUGH. I NEED MORE.
MORE MORE MORE MORE MORE MORE MORE MORE MORE MORE MORE MORE
MORE LIVES!
OH...!
TIM!
PERFECT TIMING.
SOMETHING AWFUL'S HAPPENED TO MINA- YOUR FAVORITE PERSON!
HERE, KITTY.

COME HERE...

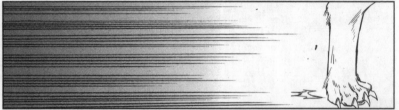

You are no longer human.

THUD

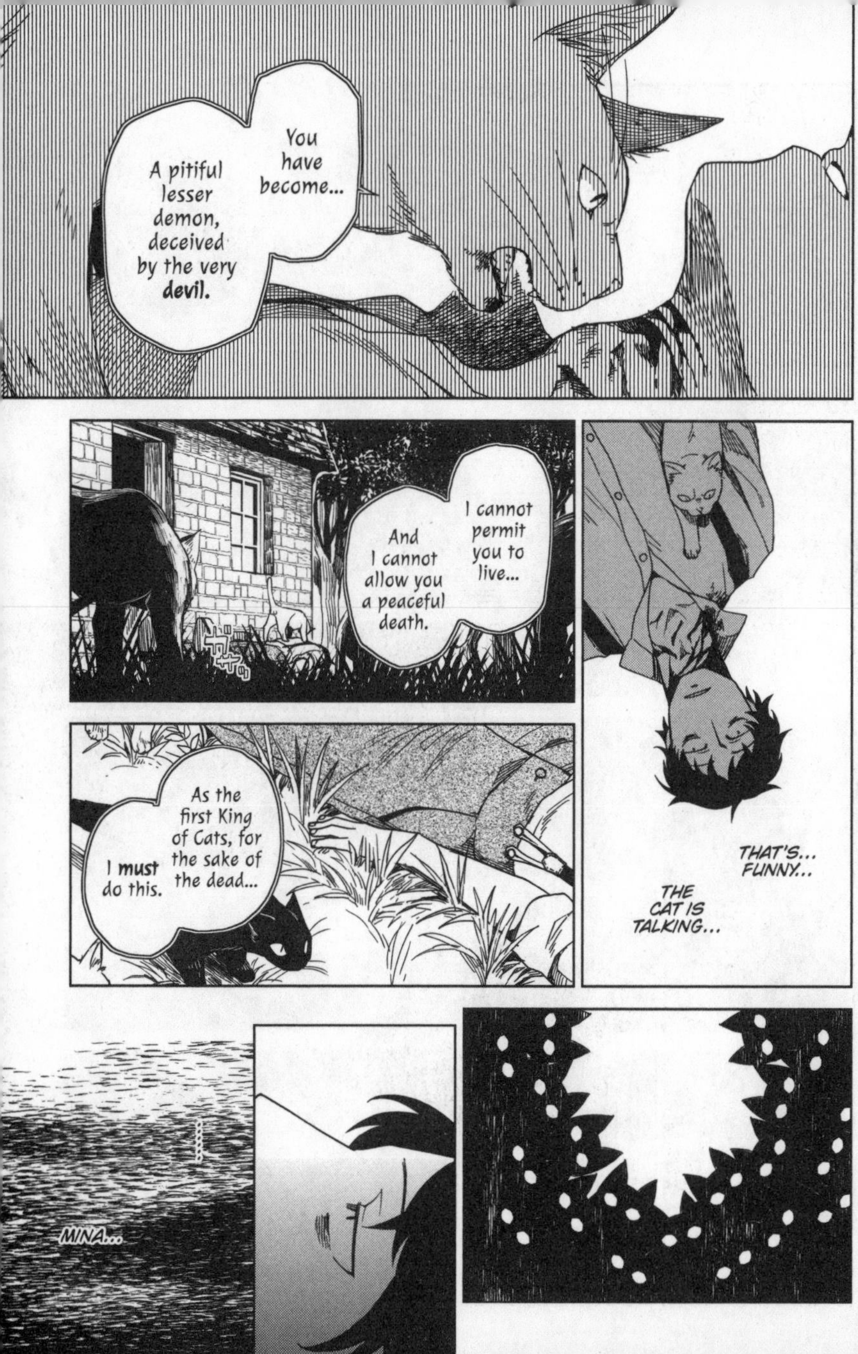
You have become...
A pitiful lesser demon, deceived by the very **devil.**
THAT'S... FUNNY...
THE CAT IS TALKING...
I cannot permit you to live...
And I cannot allow you a peaceful death.
ガサッ
As the first King of Cats, for the sake of the dead...
I **must** do this.
MINA...

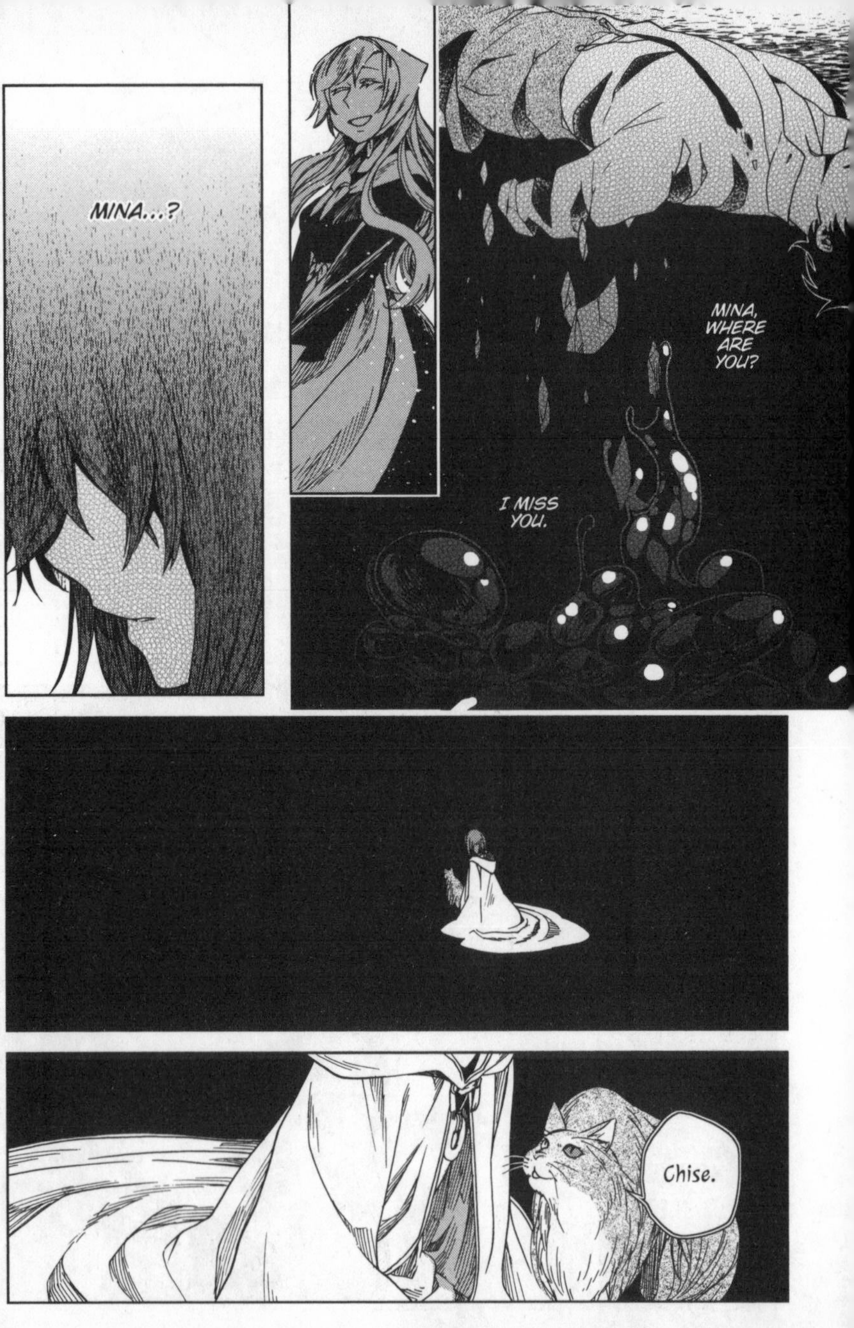
MINA, WHERE ARE YOU?
I MISS YOU.
MINA...?
Chise.

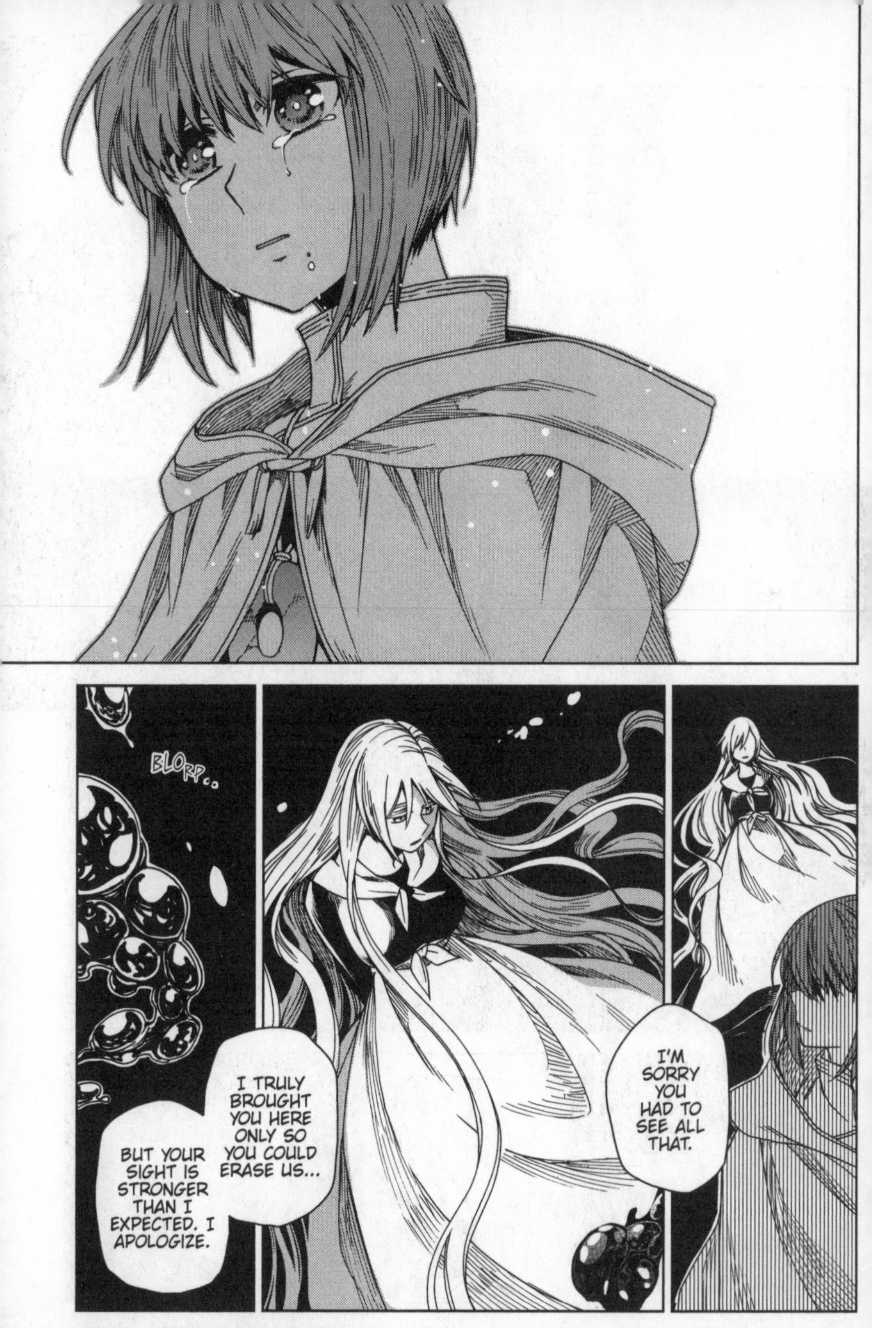
I'M SORRY YOU HAD TO SEE ALL THAT.
I TRULY BROUGHT YOU HERE ONLY SO YOU COULD ERASE US...
BUT YOUR SIGHT IS STRONGER THAN I EXPECTED. I APOLOGIZE.
BLORP...

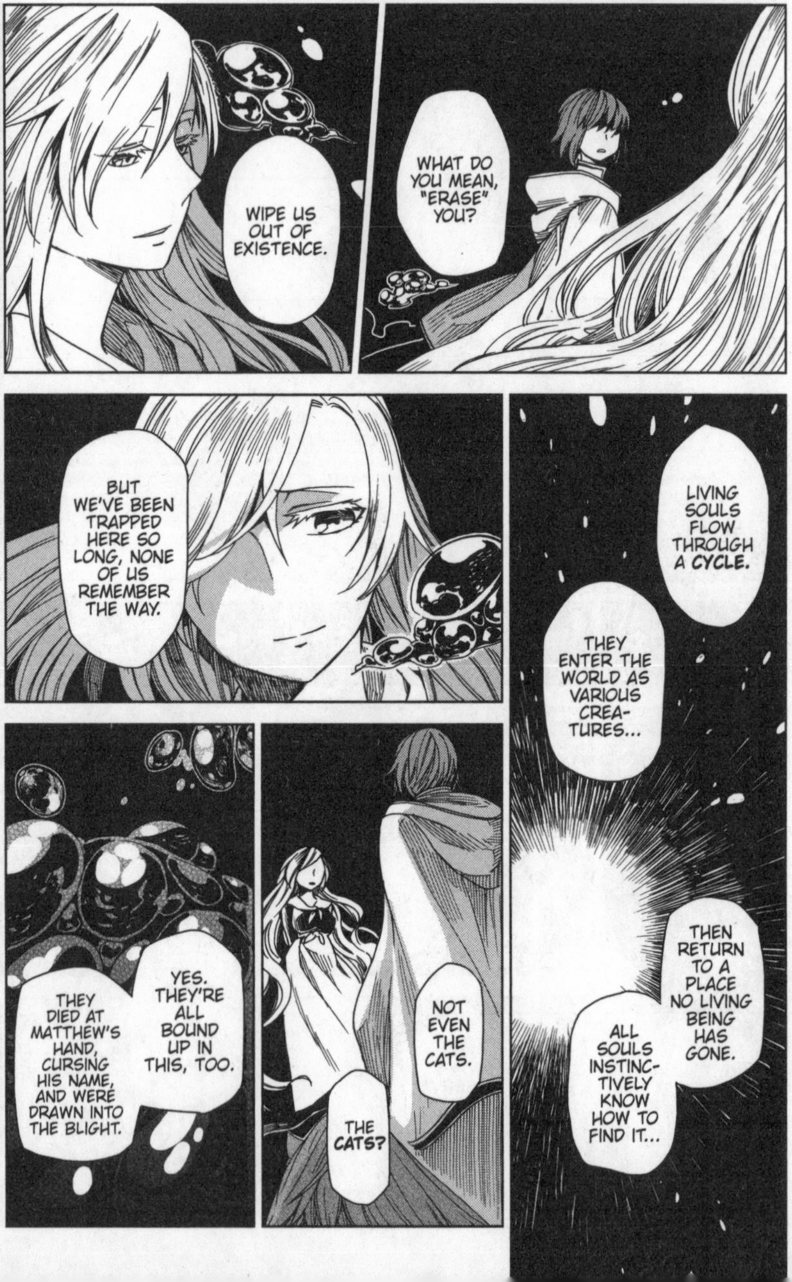
WHAT DO YOU MEAN, "ERASE" YOU?
WIPE US OUT OF EXISTENCE.
LIVING SOULS FLOW THROUGH A **CYCLE.**
THEY ENTER THE WORLD AS VARIOUS CREA-TURES...
THEN RETURN TO A PLACE NO LIVING BEING HAS GONE.
ALL SOULS INSTINC-TIVELY KNOW HOW TO FIND IT...
BUT WE'VE BEEN TRAPPED HERE SO LONG, NONE OF US REMEMBER THE WAY.
NOT EVEN THE CATS.
THE **CATS?**
YES. THEY'RE ALL BOUND UP IN THIS, TOO.
THEY DIED AT MATTHEW'S HAND, CURSING HIS NAME, AND WERE DRAWN INTO THE BLIGHT.

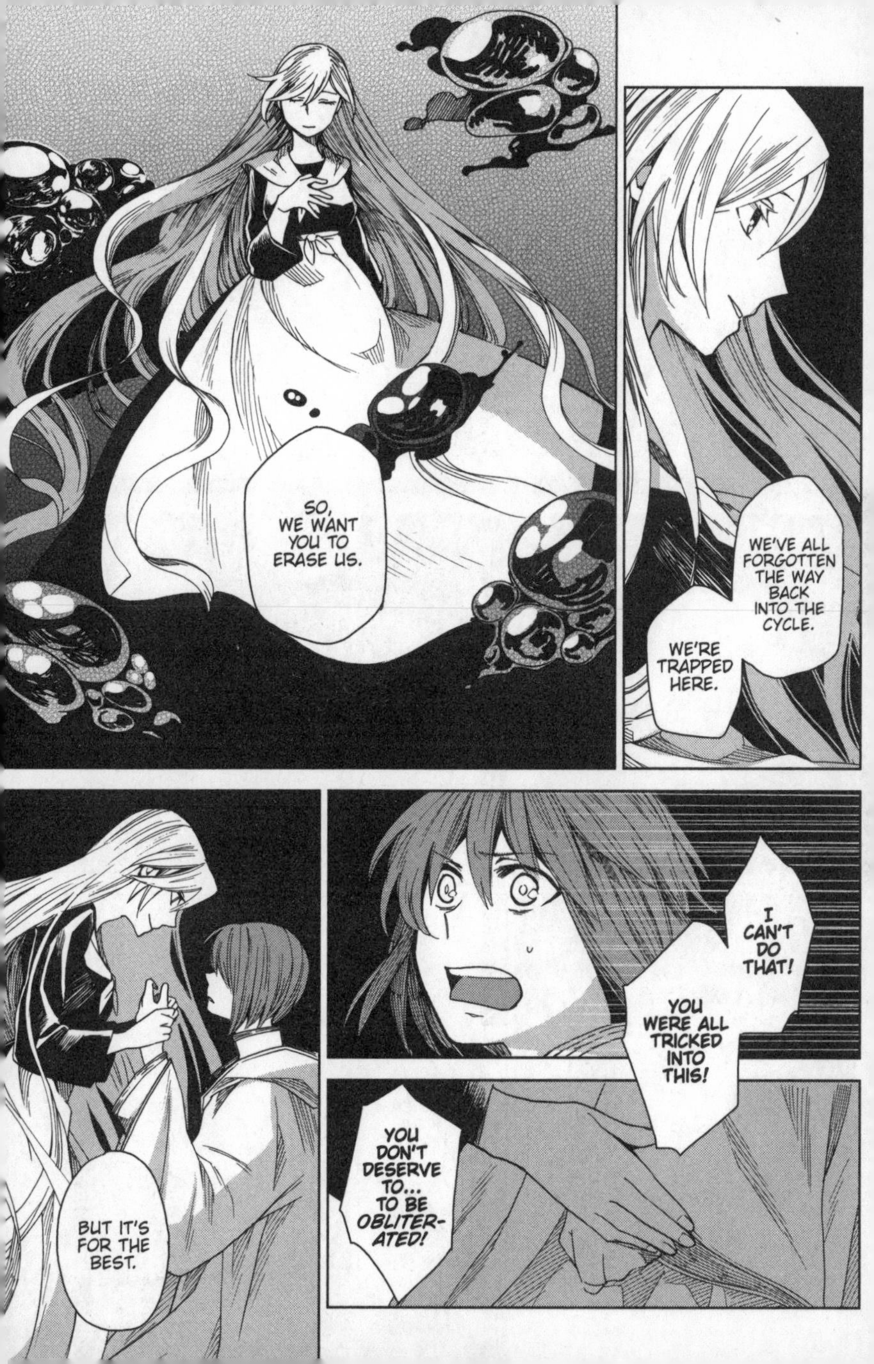
WE'VE ALL FORGOTTEN THE WAY BACK INTO THE CYCLE.
WE'RE TRAPPED HERE.
SO, WE WANT YOU TO ERASE US.
I CAN'T DO THAT!
YOU WERE ALL TRICKED INTO THIS!
YOU DON'T DESERVE TO... TO BE OBLITERATED!
BUT IT'S FOR THE BEST.

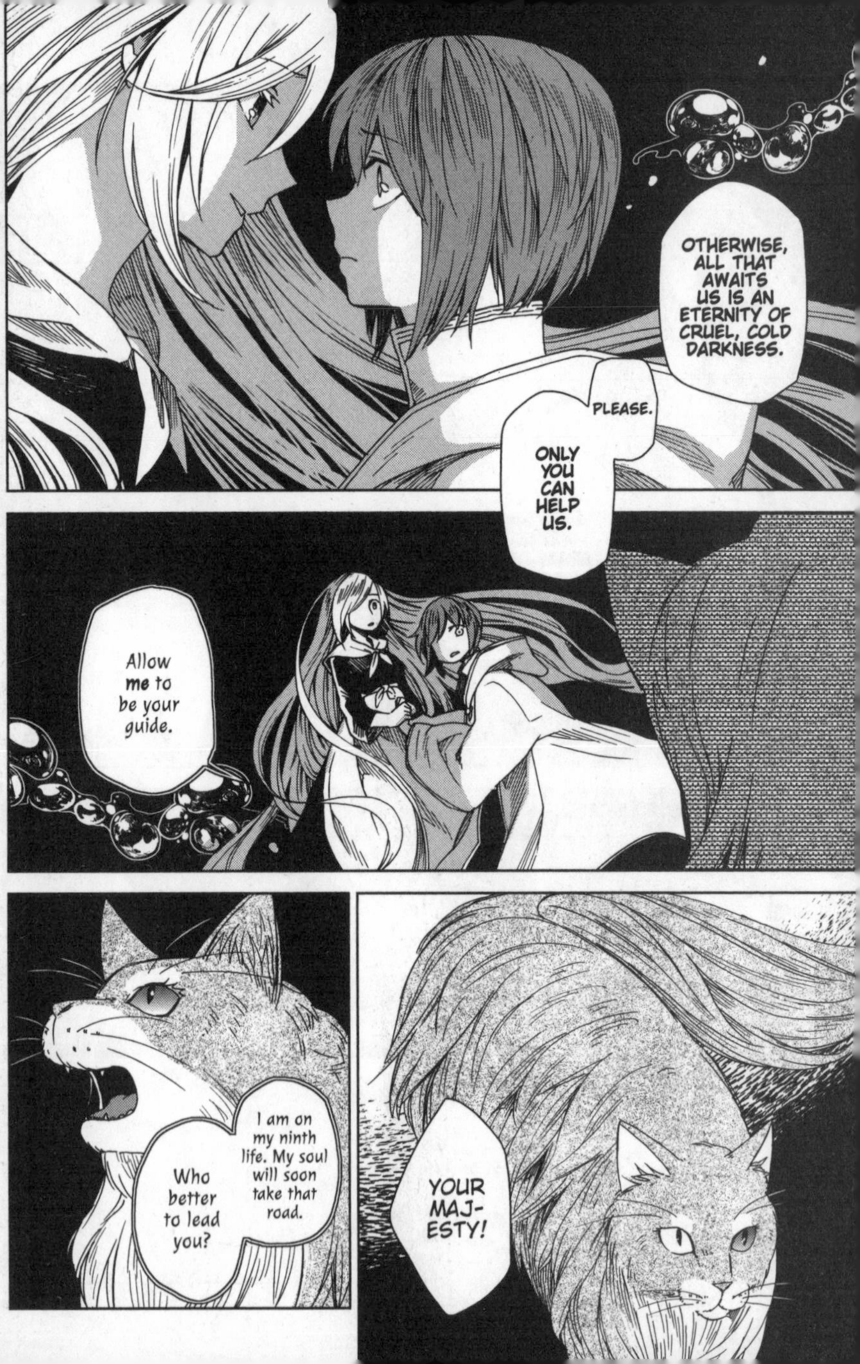
OTHERWISE, ALL THAT AWAITS US IS AN ETERNITY OF CRUEL, COLD DARKNESS.
PLEASE.
ONLY YOU CAN HELP US.
Allow me to be your guide.
YOUR MAJ-ESTY!
I am on my ninth life. My soul will soon take that road.
Who better to lead you?

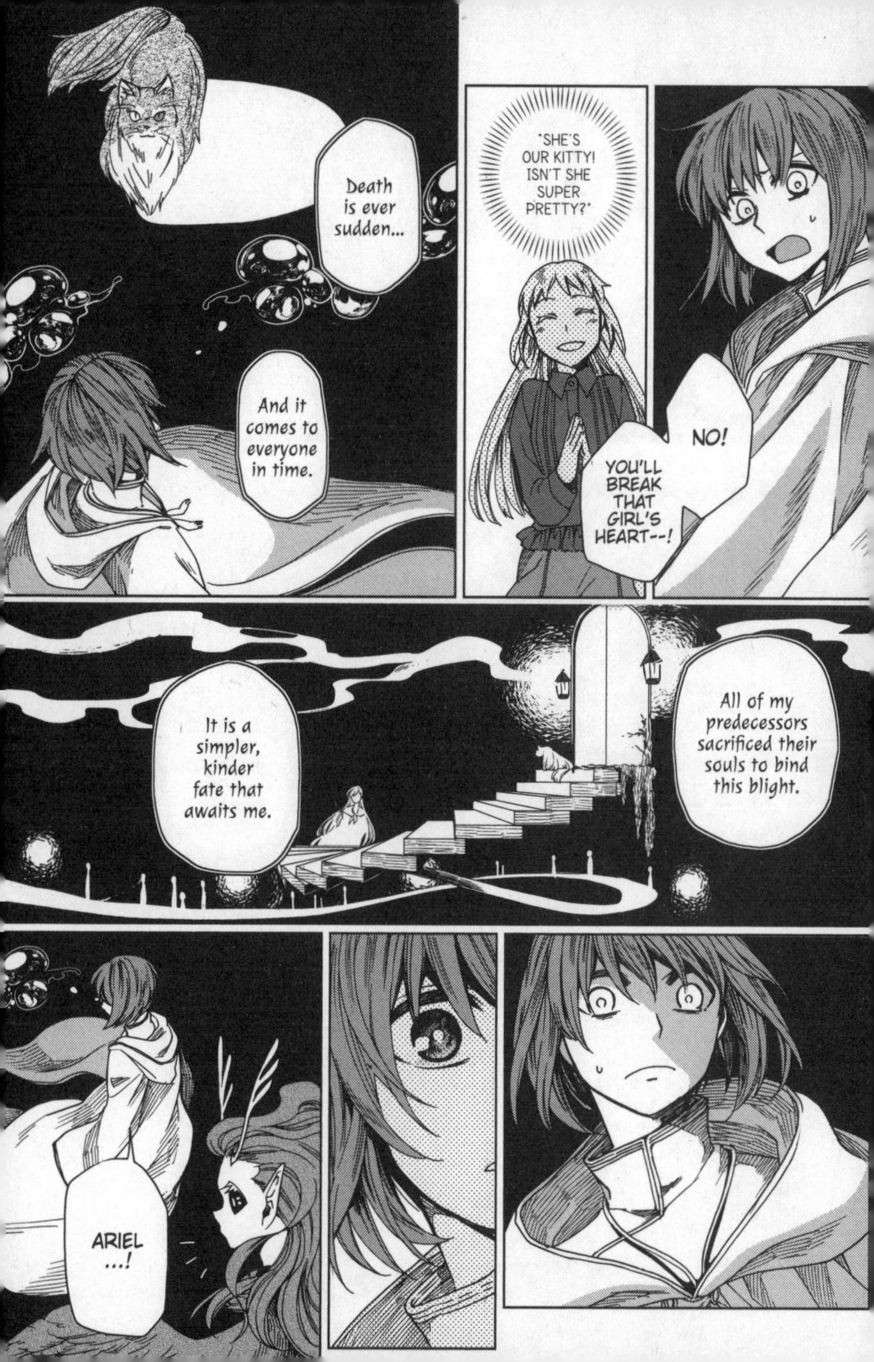
NO!
YOU'LL BREAK THAT GIRL'S HEART--!
"SHE'S OUR KITTY! ISN'T SHE SUPER PRETTY?"
Death is ever sudden...
And it comes to everyone in time.
All of my predecessors sacrificed their souls to bind this blight.
It is a simpler, kinder fate that awaits me.
ARIEL ...!

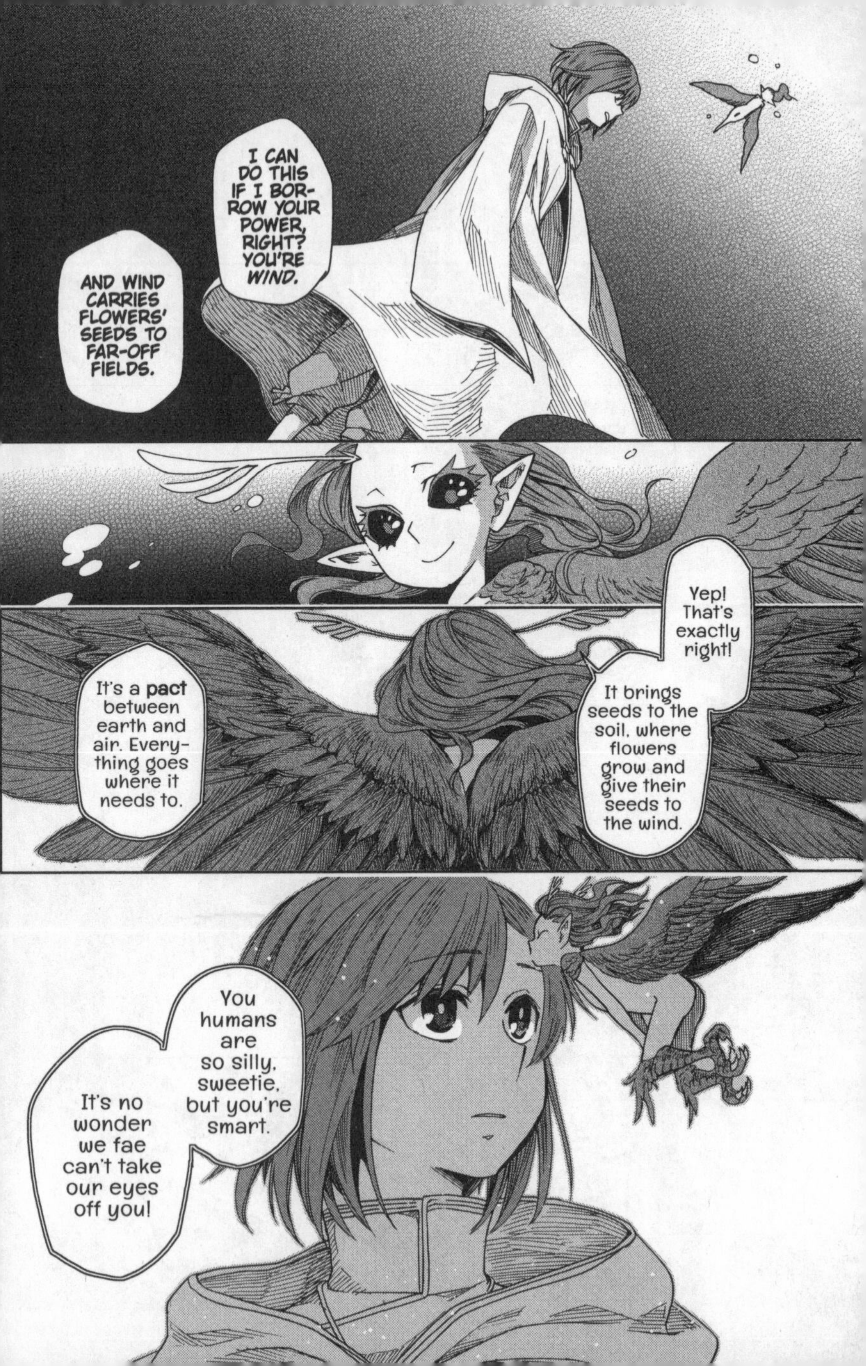
I CAN DO THIS IF I BOR-ROW YOUR POWER, RIGHT? YOU'RE *WIND.*
AND WIND CARRIES FLOWERS' SEEDS TO FAR-OFF FIELDS.
Yep! That's exactly right!
It brings seeds to the soil, where flowers grow and give their seeds to the wind.
It's a **pact** between earth and air. Every-thing goes where it needs to.
You humans are so silly, sweetie, but you're smart.
It's no wonder we fae can't take our eyes off you!

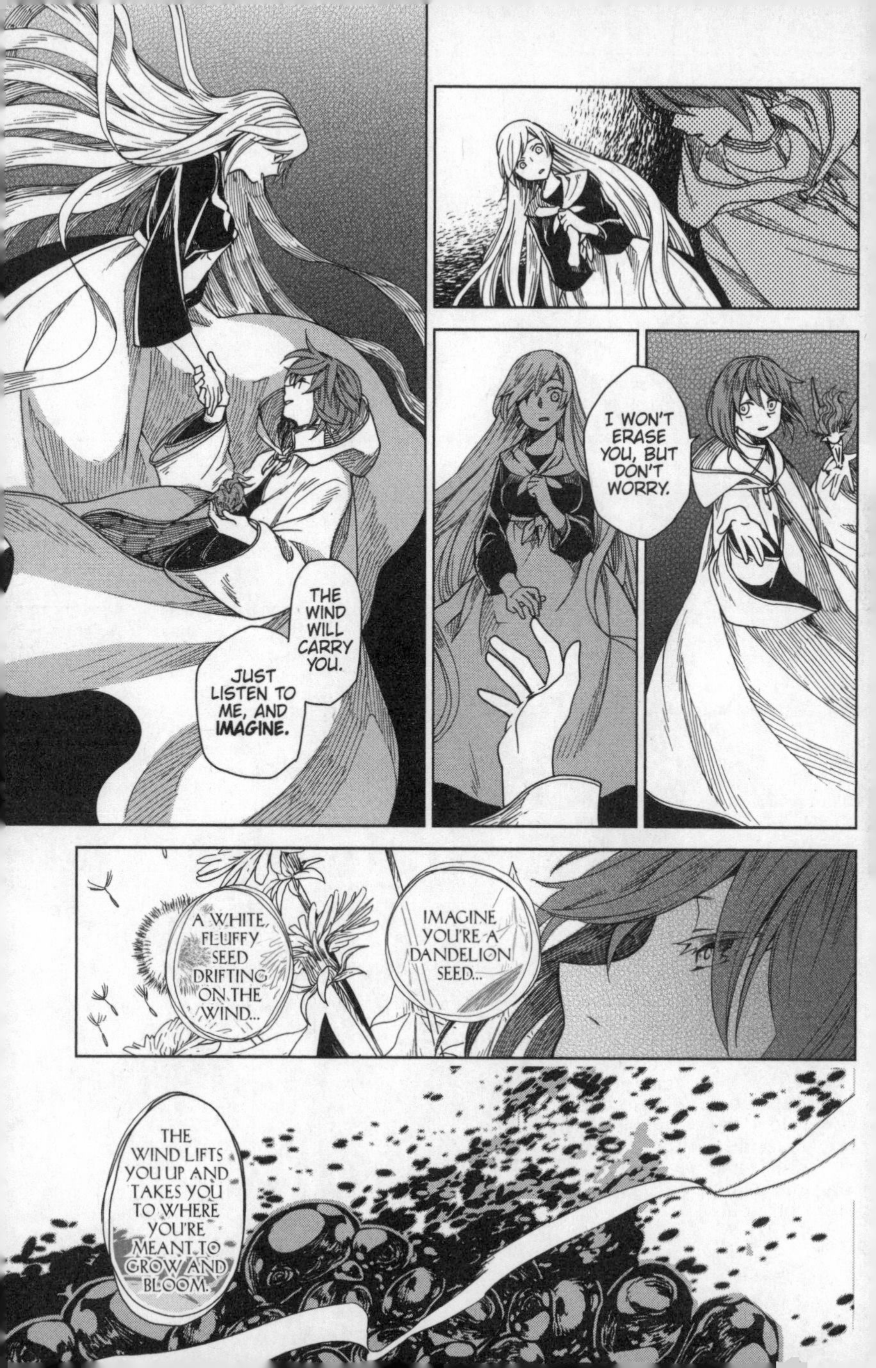
I WON'T ERASE YOU, BUT DON'T WORRY.
THE WIND WILL CARRY YOU.
JUST LISTEN TO ME, AND IMAGINE.
IMAGINE YOU'RE A DANDELION SEED...
A WHITE, FLUFFY SEED DRIFTING ON THE WIND...
THE WIND LIFTS YOU UP AND TAKES YOU TO WHERE YOU'RE MEANT TO GROW AND BLOOM.

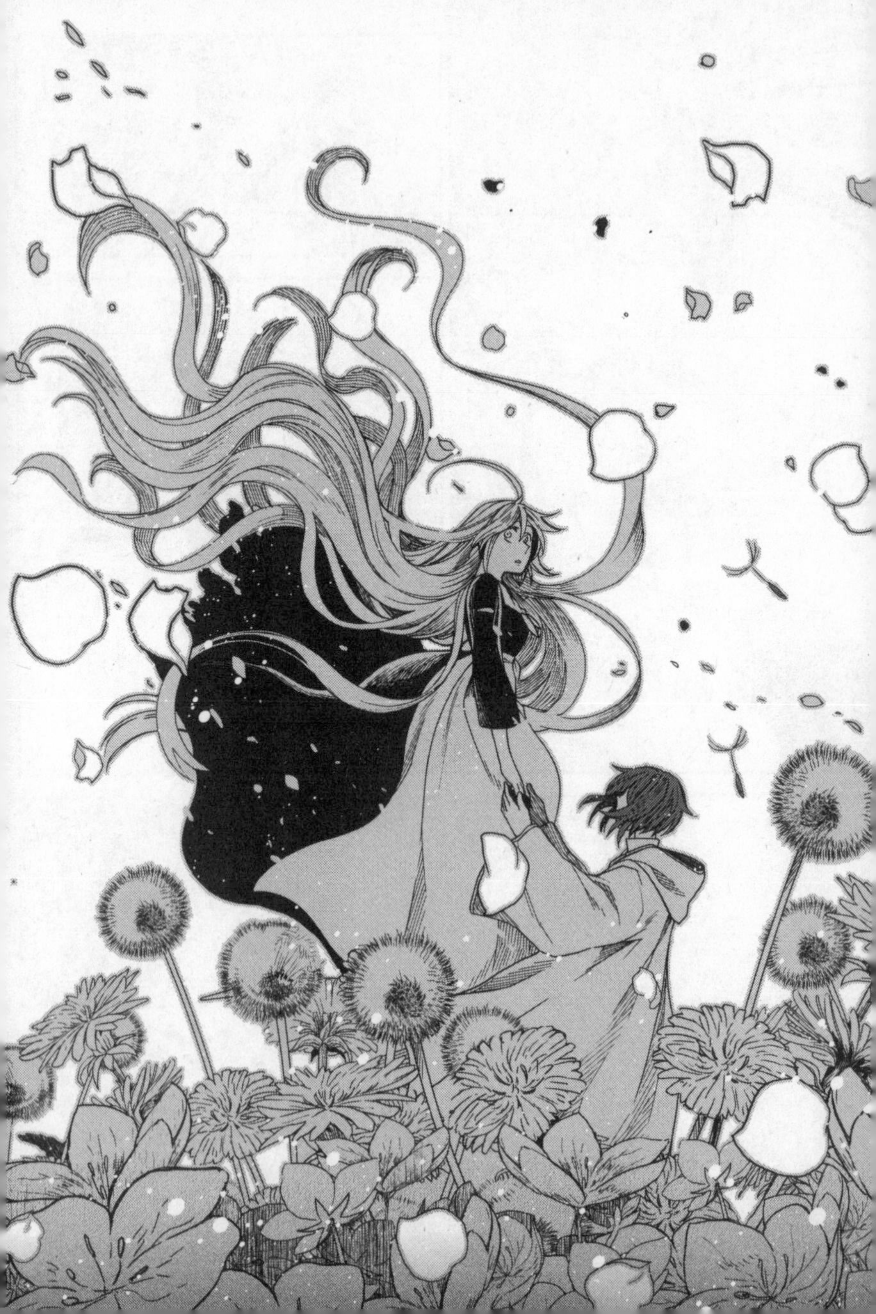

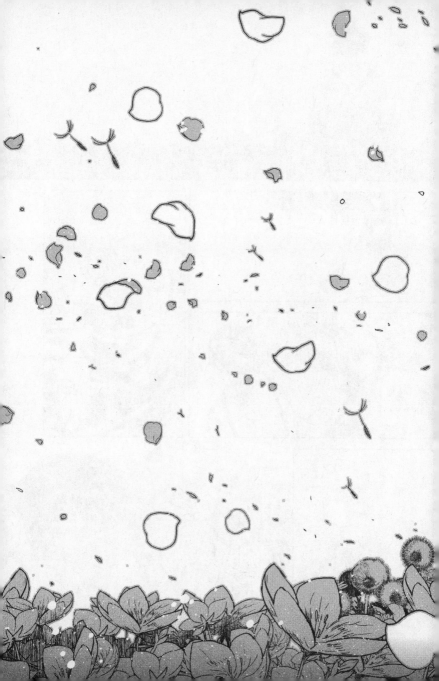

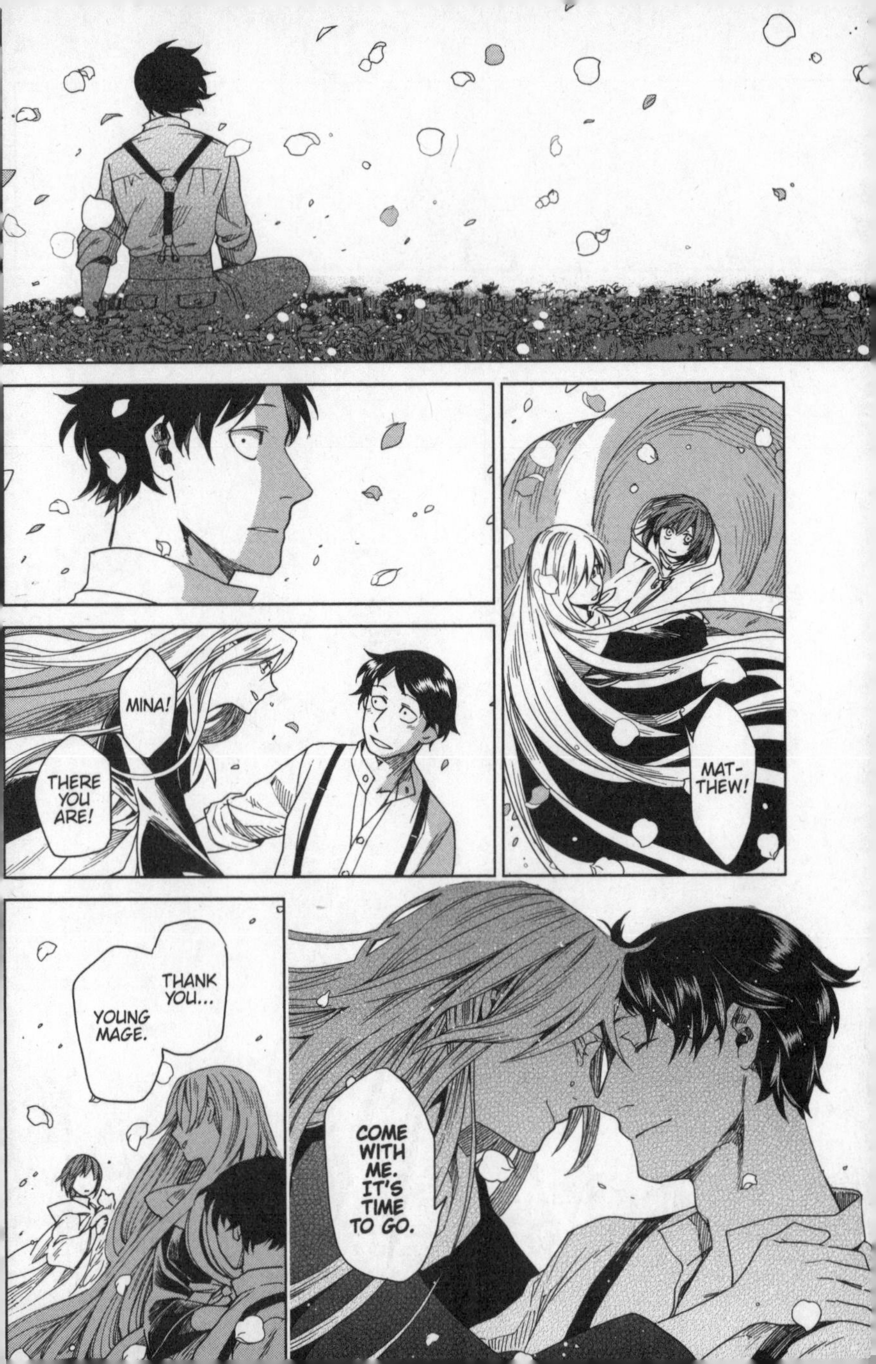
MAT-THEW!
MINA!
THERE YOU ARE!
COME WITH ME. IT'S TIME TO GO.
THANK YOU... YOUNG MAGE.

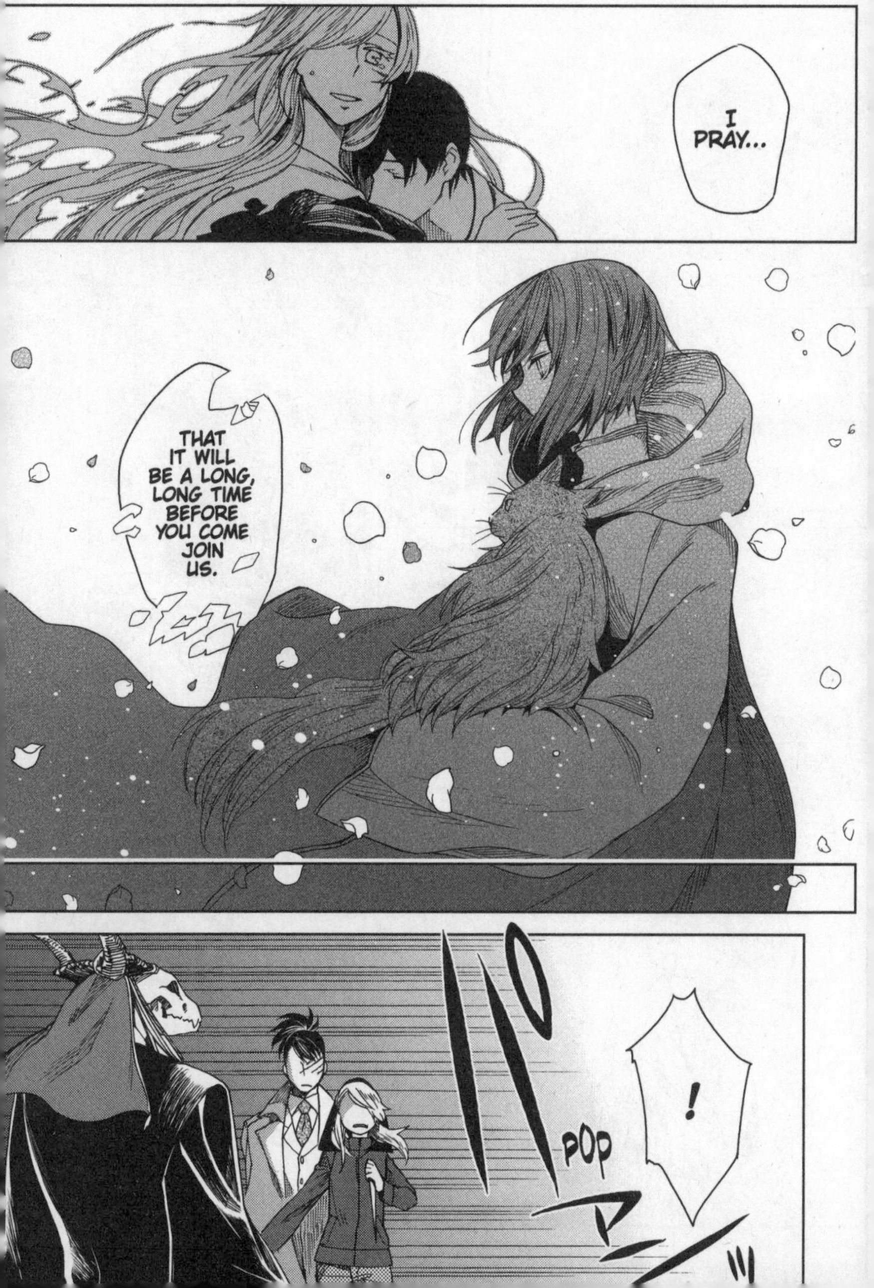
I PRAY...
THAT IT WILL BE A LONG, LONG TIME BEFORE YOU COME JOIN US.
!
POP

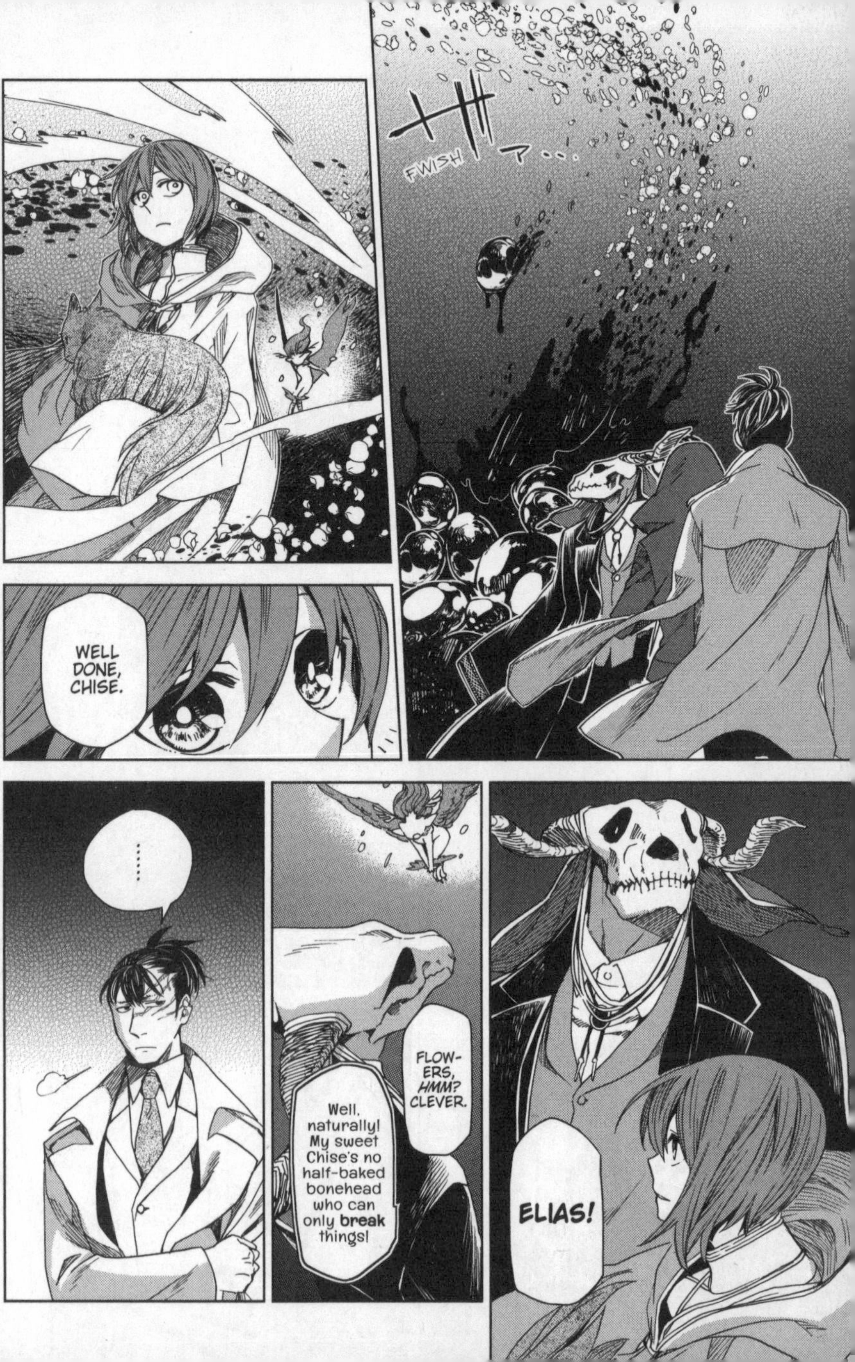
FWISH
WELL DONE, CHISE.
ELIAS!
FLOWERS, HMM? CLEVER.
Well, naturally! My sweet Chise's no half-baked bonehead who can only **break** things!
……

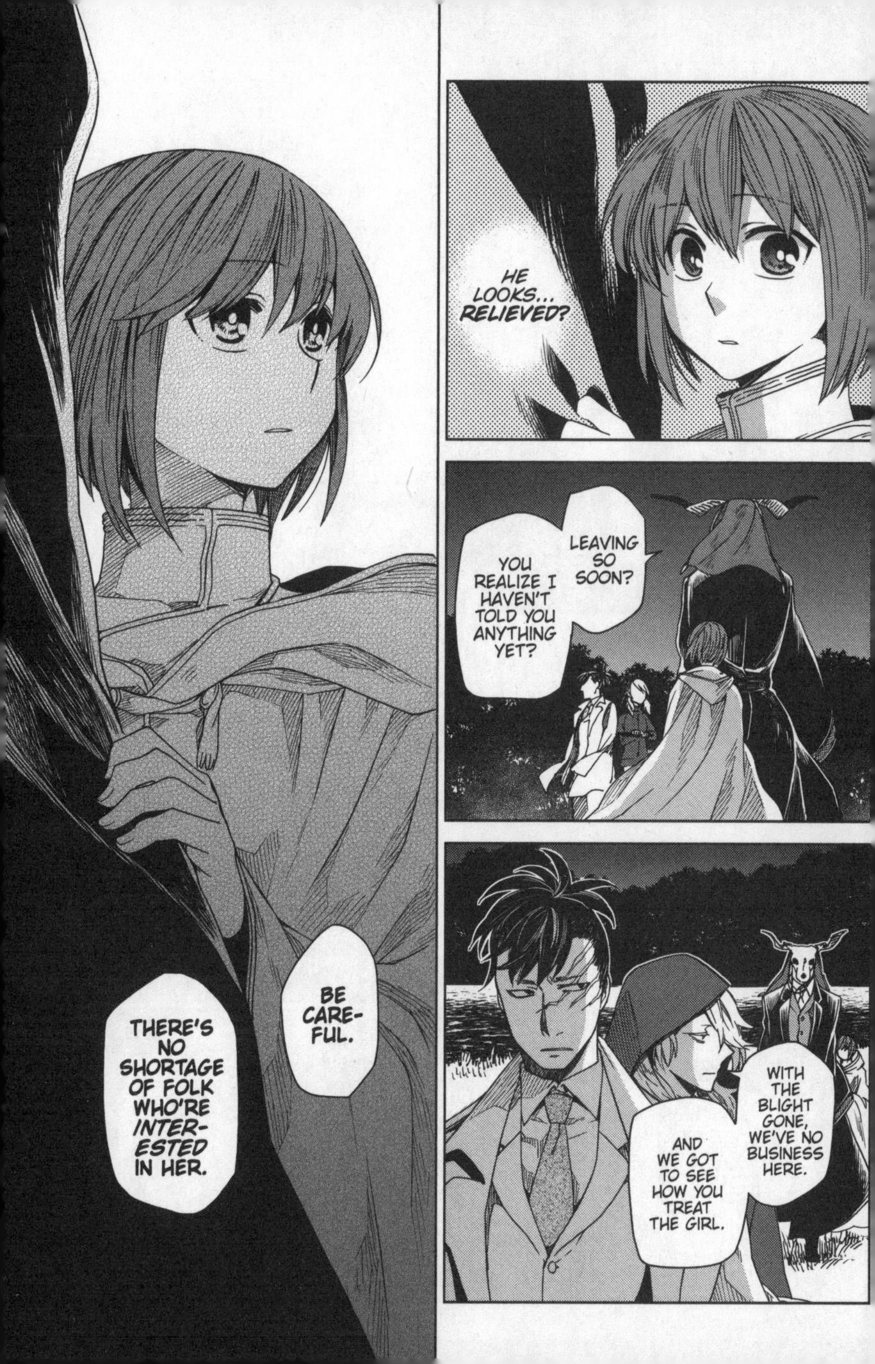
HE LOOKS... RELIEVED?
LEAVING SO SOON?
YOU REALIZE I HAVEN'T TOLD YOU ANYTHING YET?
WITH THE BLIGHT GONE, WE'VE NO BUSINESS HERE.
AND WE GOT TO SEE HOW YOU TREAT THE GIRL.
BE CAREFUL.
THERE'S NO SHORTAGE OF FOLK WHO'RE *INTERESTED* IN HER.

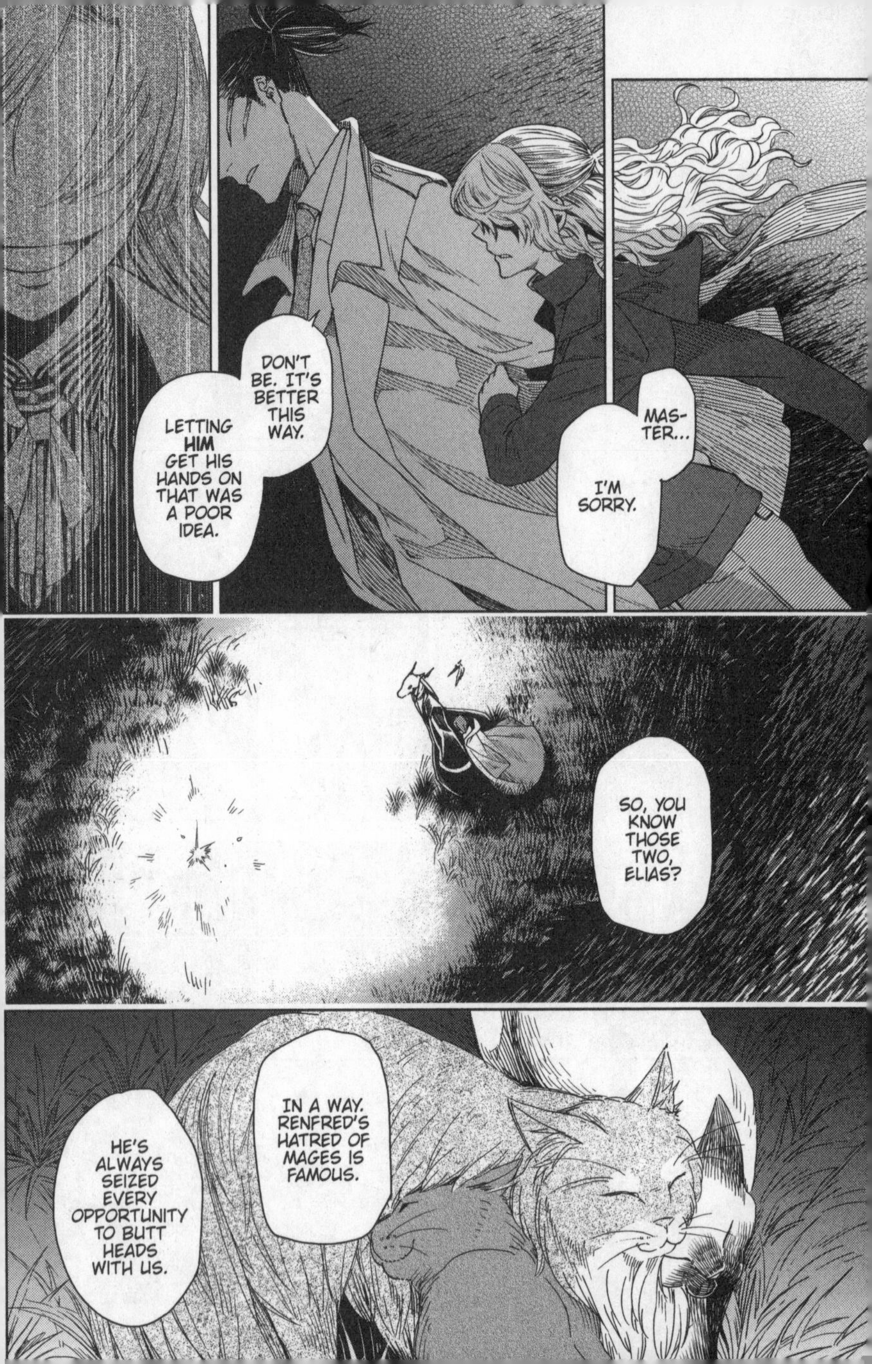
MAS-TER...
I'M SORRY.
DON'T BE. IT'S BETTER THIS WAY.
LETTING **HIM** GET HIS HANDS ON THAT WAS A POOR IDEA.
SO, YOU KNOW THOSE TWO, ELIAS?
IN A WAY. RENFRED'S HATRED OF MAGES IS FAMOUS.
HE'S ALWAYS SEIZED EVERY OPPORTUNITY TO BUTT HEADS WITH US.

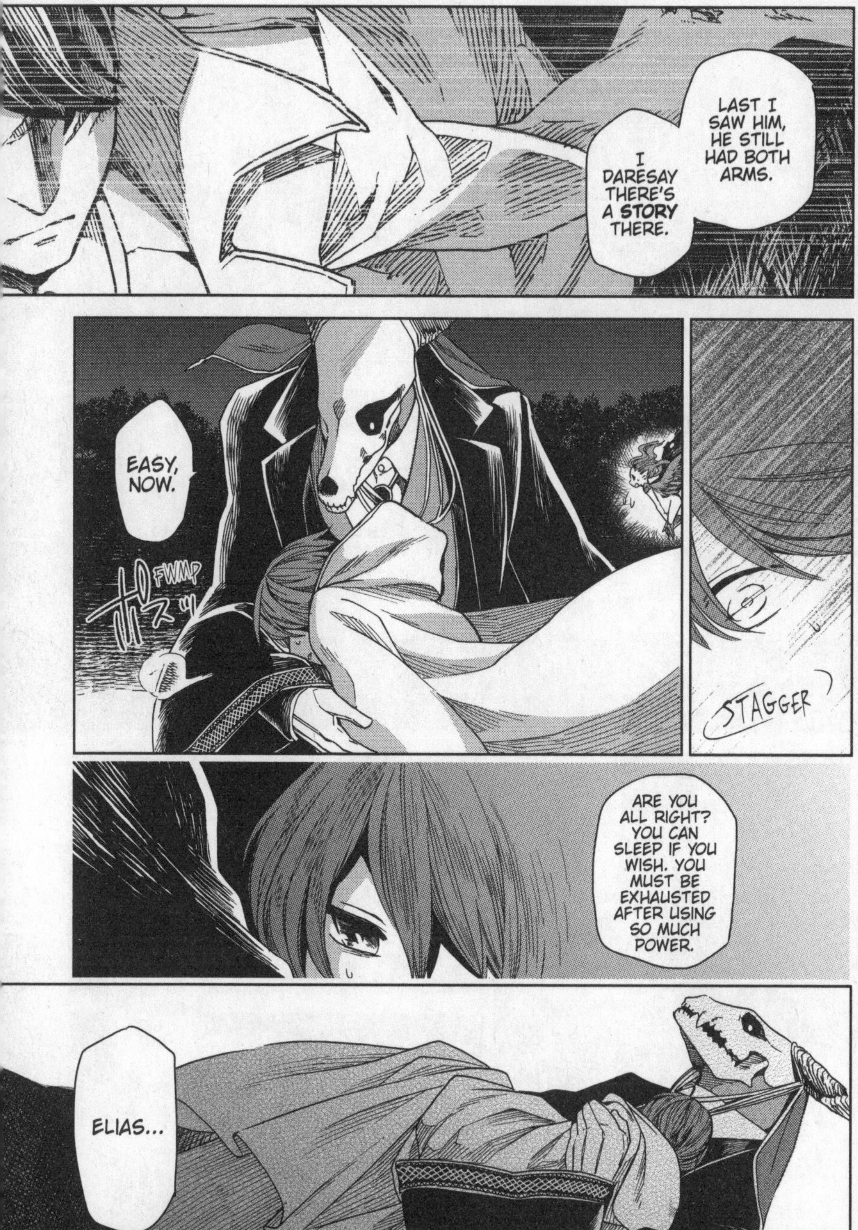
LAST I SAW HIM, HE STILL HAD BOTH ARMS.
I DARESAY THERE'S A **STORY** THERE.
STAGGER
EASY, NOW.
FWMP
ARE YOU ALL RIGHT? YOU CAN SLEEP IF YOU WISH. YOU MUST BE EXHAUSTED AFTER USING SO MUCH POWER.
ELIAS...

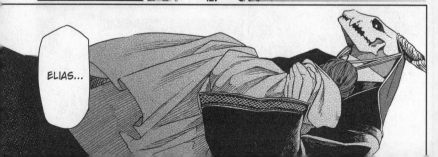

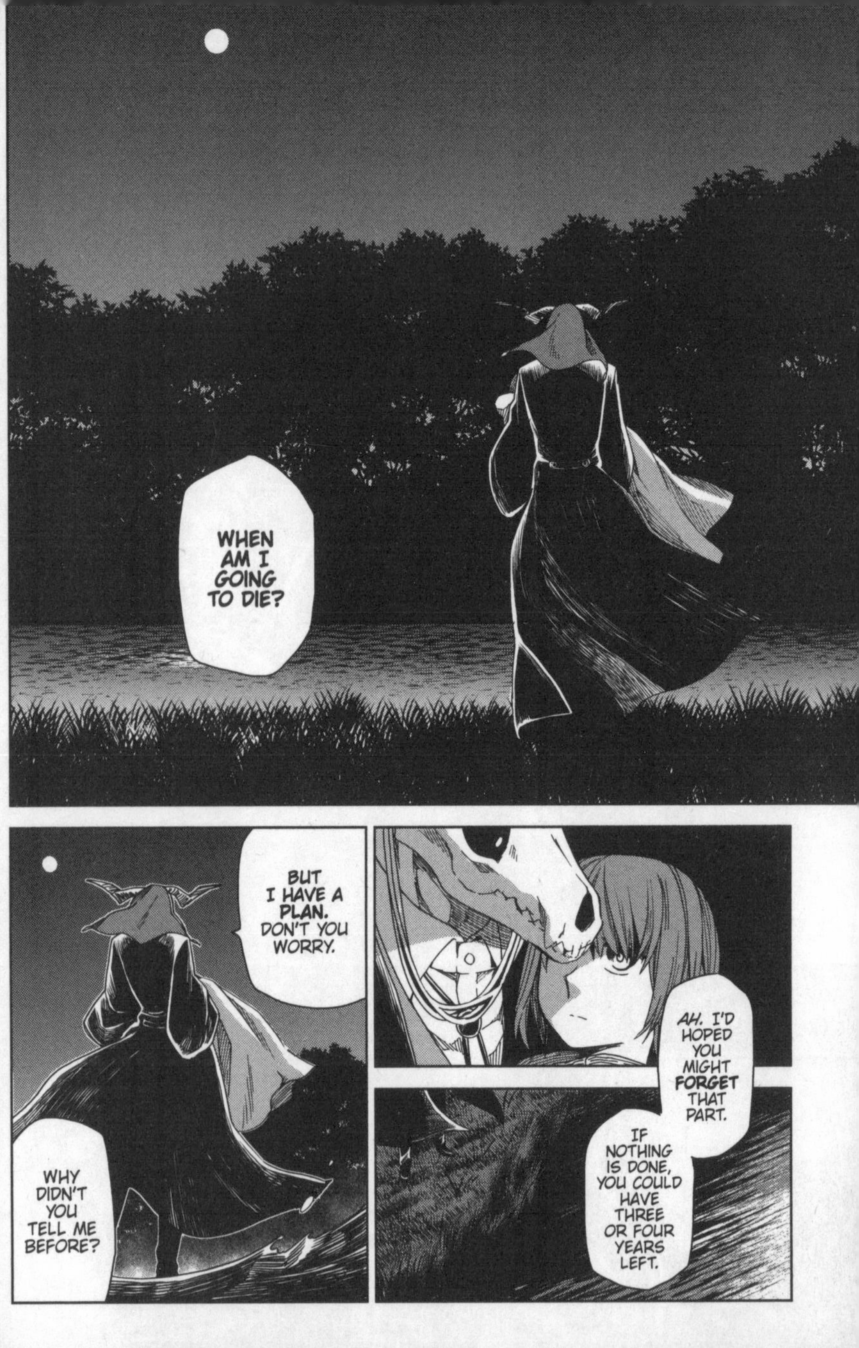
WHEN AM I GOING TO DIE?
AH. I'D HOPED YOU MIGHT **FORGET** THAT PART.
IF NOTHING IS DONE, YOU COULD HAVE THREE OR FOUR YEARS LEFT.
BUT I HAVE A **PLAN.** DON'T YOU WORRY.
WHY DIDN'T YOU TELL ME BEFORE?

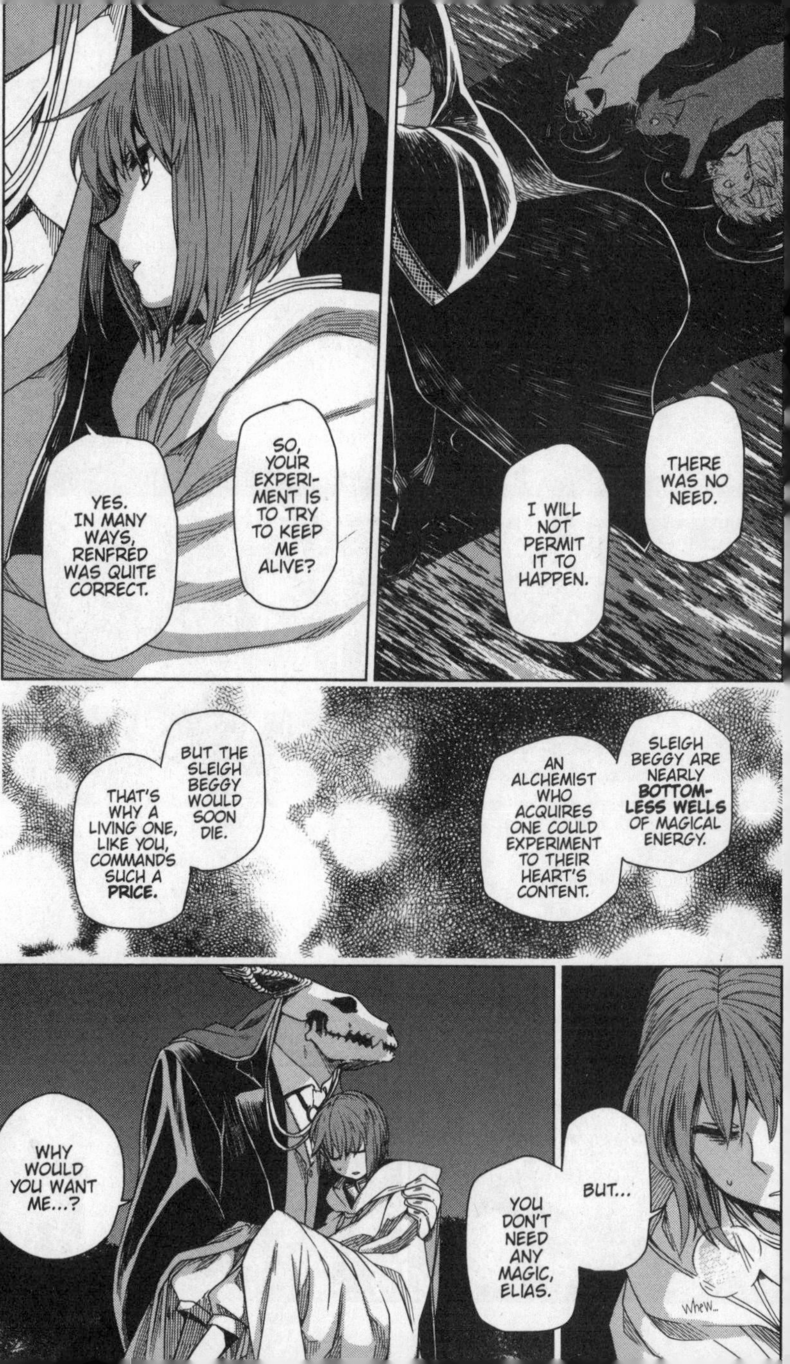
THERE WAS NO NEED.
I WILL NOT PERMIT IT TO HAPPEN.
SO, YOUR EXPERIMENT IS TO TRY TO KEEP ME ALIVE?
YES. IN MANY WAYS, RENFRED WAS QUITE CORRECT.
SLEIGH BEGGY ARE NEARLY BOTTOMLESS WELLS OF MAGICAL ENERGY.
AN ALCHEMIST WHO ACQUIRES ONE COULD EXPERIMENT TO THEIR HEART'S CONTENT.
BUT THE SLEIGH BEGGY WOULD SOON DIE.
THAT'S WHY A LIVING ONE, LIKE YOU, COMMANDS SUCH A PRICE.
BUT...
YOU DON'T NEED ANY MAGIC, ELIAS.
Whew...
WHY WOULD YOU WANT ME...?

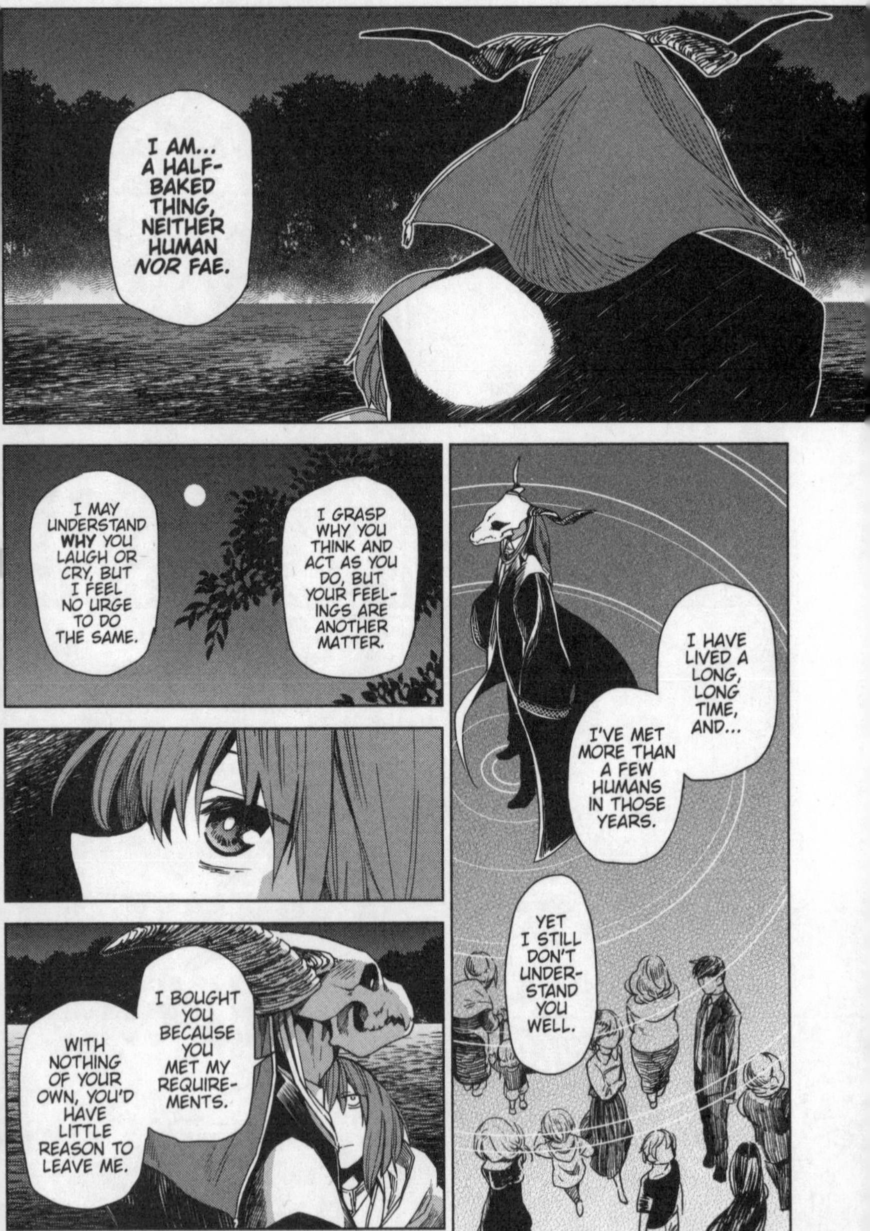
I AM... A HALF-BAKED THING, NEITHER HUMAN NOR FAE.
I HAVE LIVED A LONG, LONG TIME, AND...
I'VE MET MORE THAN A FEW HUMANS IN THOSE YEARS.
YET I STILL DON'T UNDERSTAND YOU WELL.
I GRASP WHY YOU THINK AND ACT AS YOU DO, BUT YOUR FEELINGS ARE ANOTHER MATTER.
I MAY UNDERSTAND **WHY** YOU LAUGH OR CRY, BUT I FEEL NO URGE TO DO THE SAME.
I BOUGHT YOU BECAUSE YOU MET MY REQUIREMENTS.
WITH NOTHING OF YOUR OWN, YOU'D HAVE LITTLE REASON TO LEAVE ME.

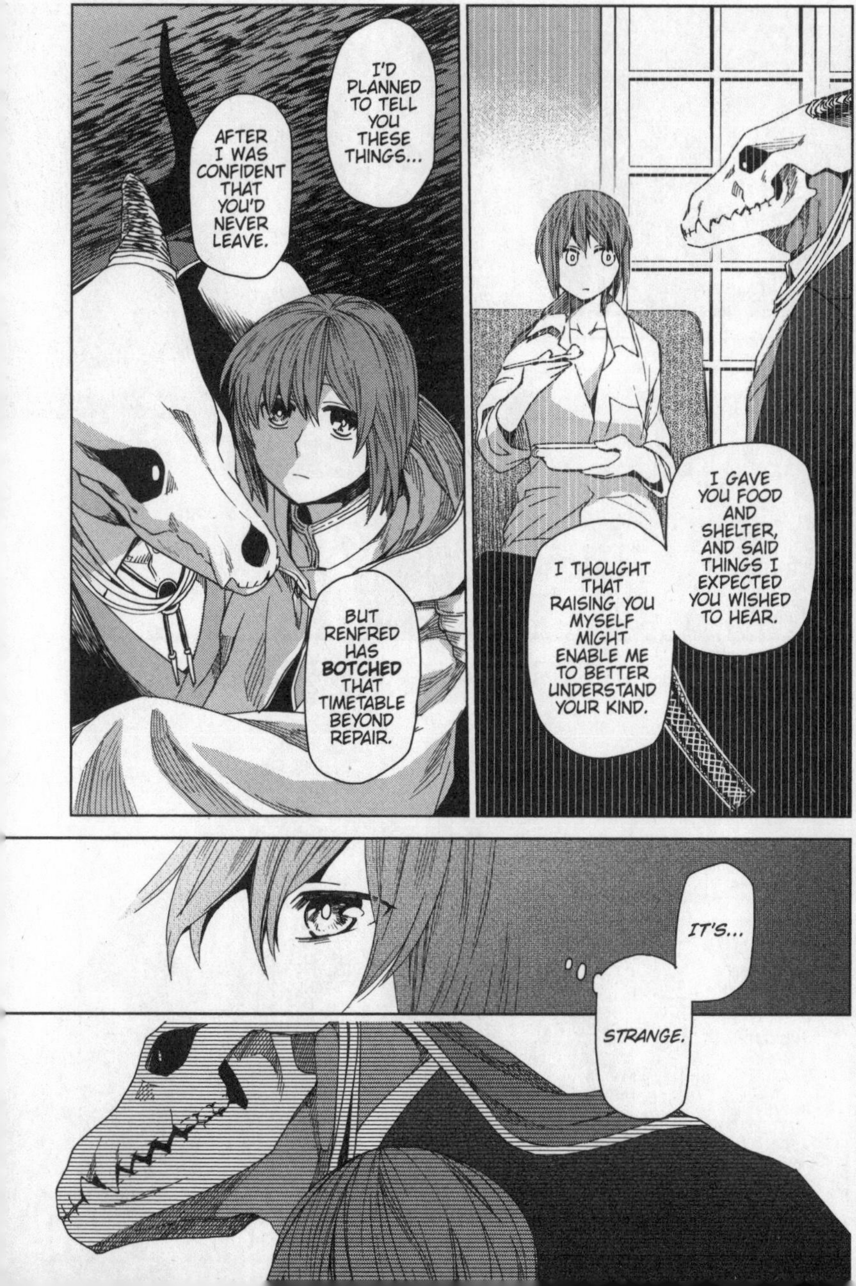
I GAVE YOU FOOD AND SHELTER, AND SAID THINGS I EXPECTED YOU WISHED TO HEAR.
I THOUGHT THAT RAISING YOU MYSELF MIGHT ENABLE ME TO BETTER UNDERSTAND YOUR KIND.
I'D PLANNED TO TELL YOU THESE THINGS...
AFTER I WAS CONFIDENT THAT YOU'D NEVER LEAVE.
BUT RENFRED HAS **BOTCHED** THAT TIMETABLE BEYOND REPAIR.
IT'S...
STRANGE.

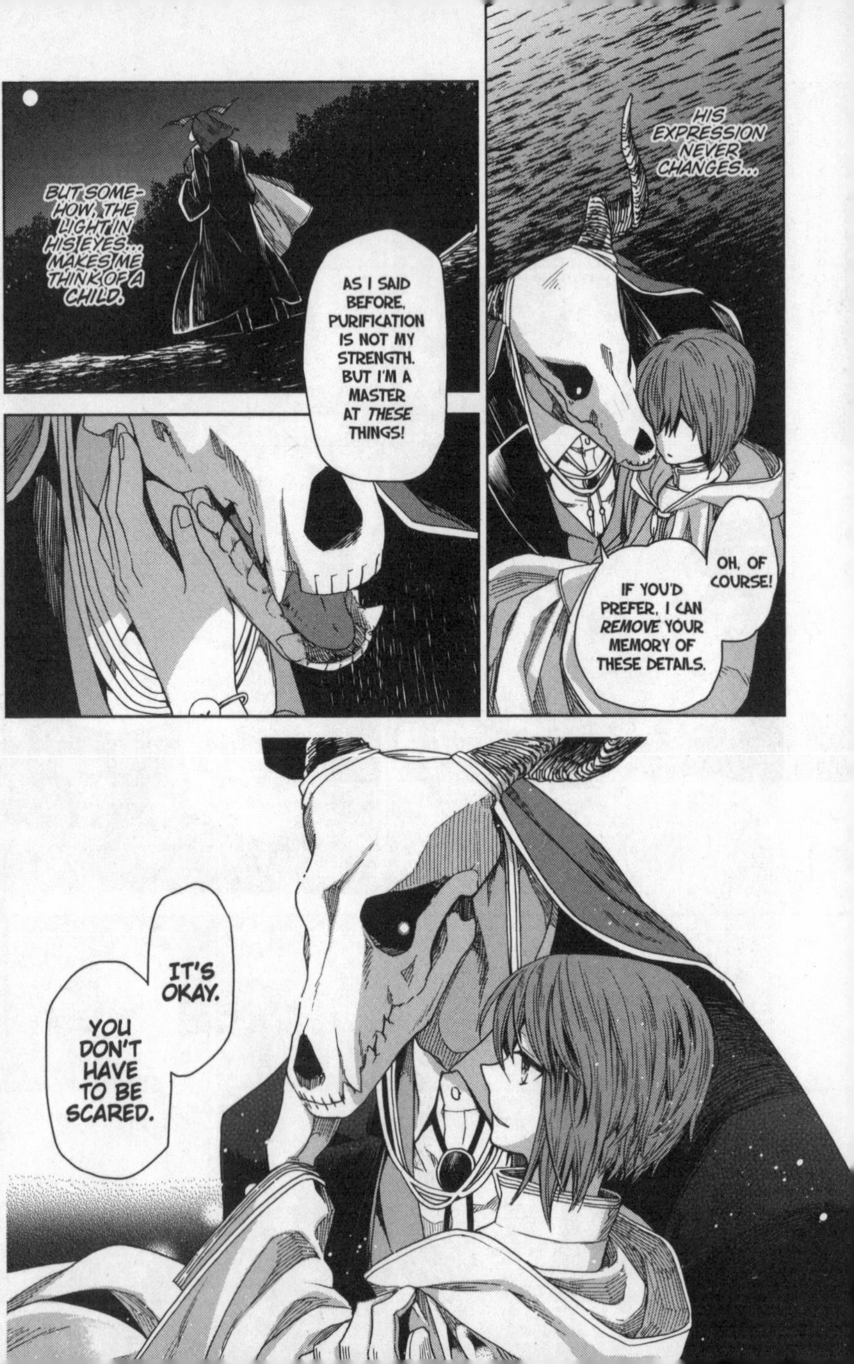
HIS EXPRESSION NEVER CHANGES...
OH, OF COURSE!
IF YOU'D PREFER, I CAN *REMOVE* YOUR MEMORY OF THESE DETAILS.
BUT SOMEHOW, THE LIGHT IN HIS EYES... MAKES ME THINK OF A CHILD.
AS I SAID BEFORE, PURIFICATION IS NOT MY STRENGTH. BUT I'M A MASTER AT *THESE* THINGS!
IT'S OKAY.
YOU DON'T HAVE TO BE SCARED.

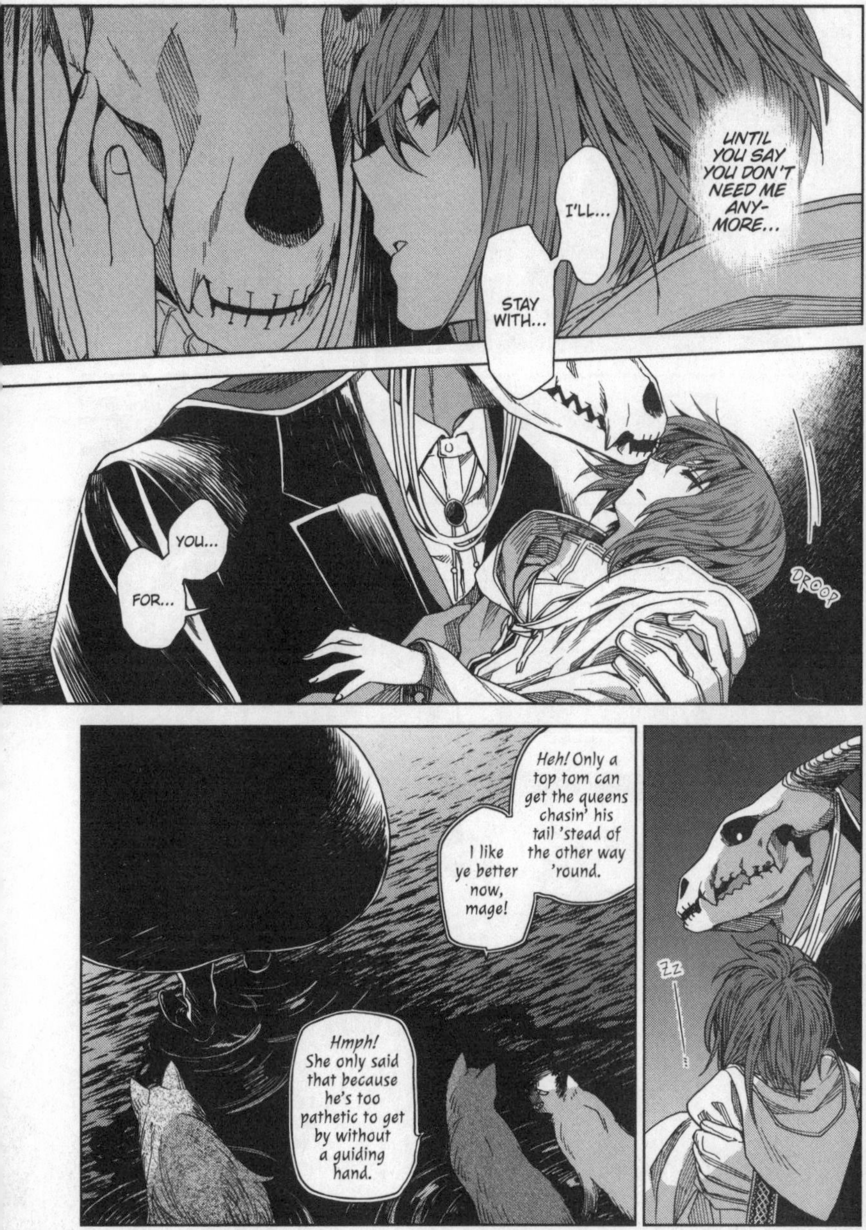
UNTIL YOU SAY YOU DON'T NEED ME ANYMORE...
I'LL...
STAY WITH...
DROOP
YOU...
FOR...
ZZ
Heh! Only a top tom can get the queens chasin' his tail 'stead of the other way 'round.
I like ye better now, mage!
Hmph! She only said that because he's too pathetic to get by without a guiding hand.

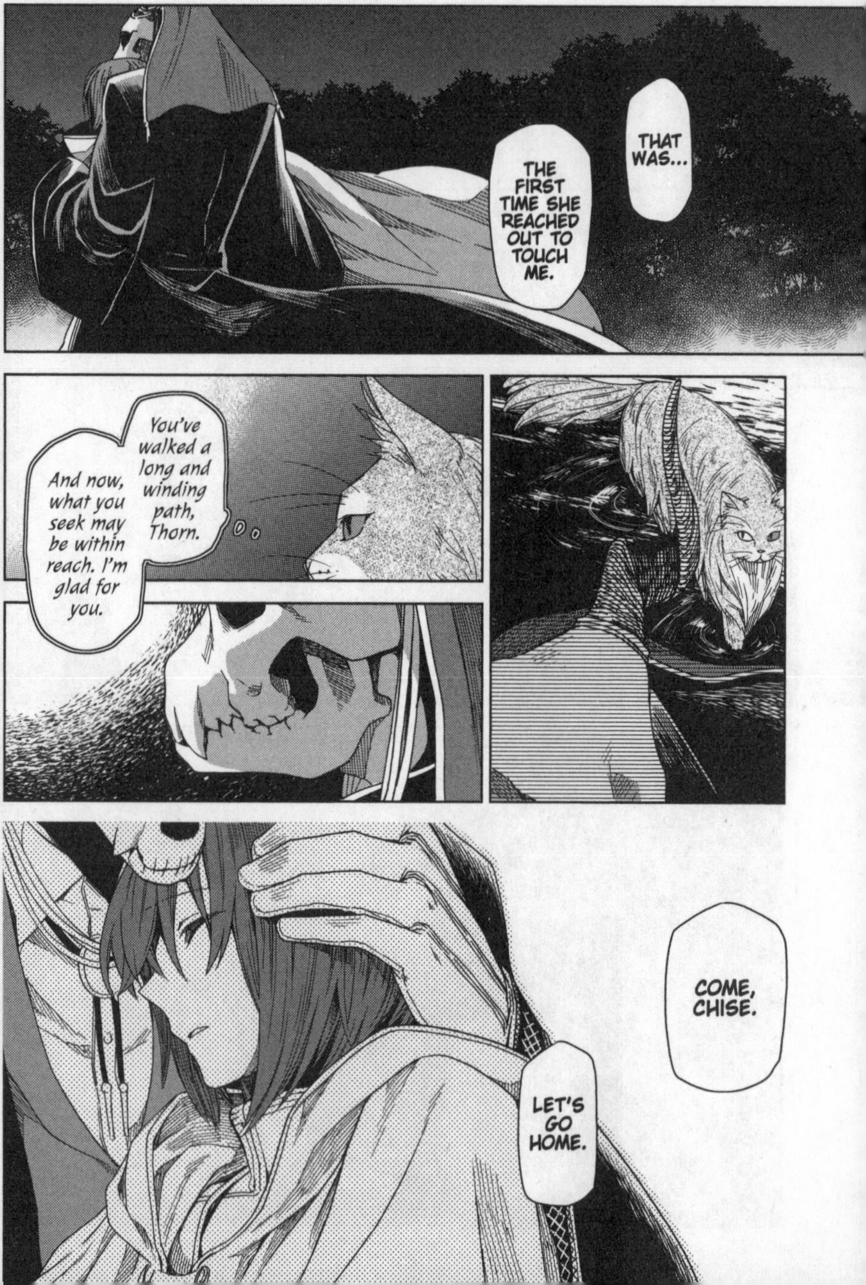
THAT WAS...
THE FIRST TIME SHE REACHED OUT TO TOUCH ME.
You've walked a long and winding path, Thorn.
And now, what you seek may be within reach. I'm glad for you.
COME, CHISE.
LET'S GO HOME.

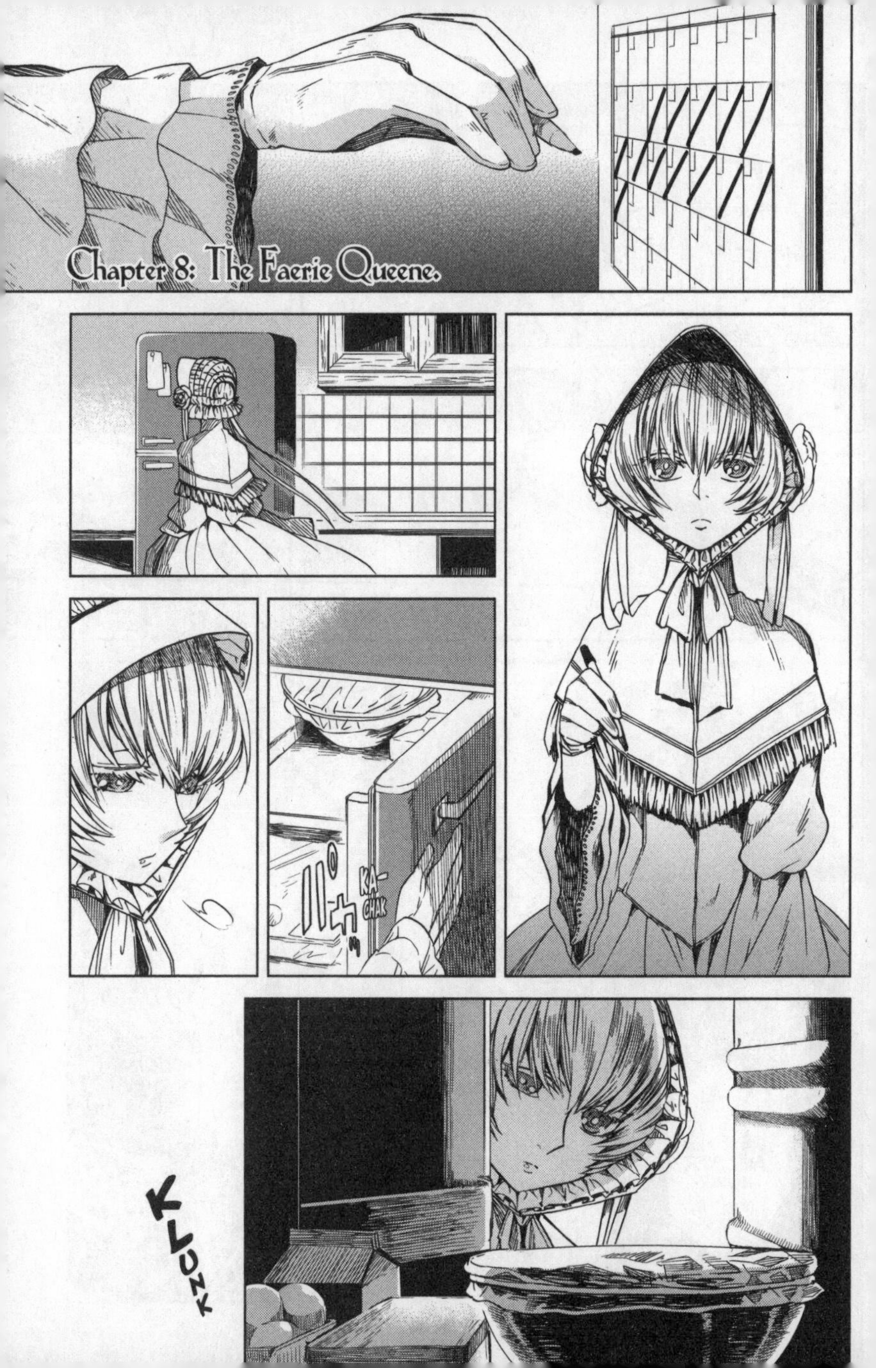
Chapter 8: The Faerie Queene.
KA-CHAK
KLUNK

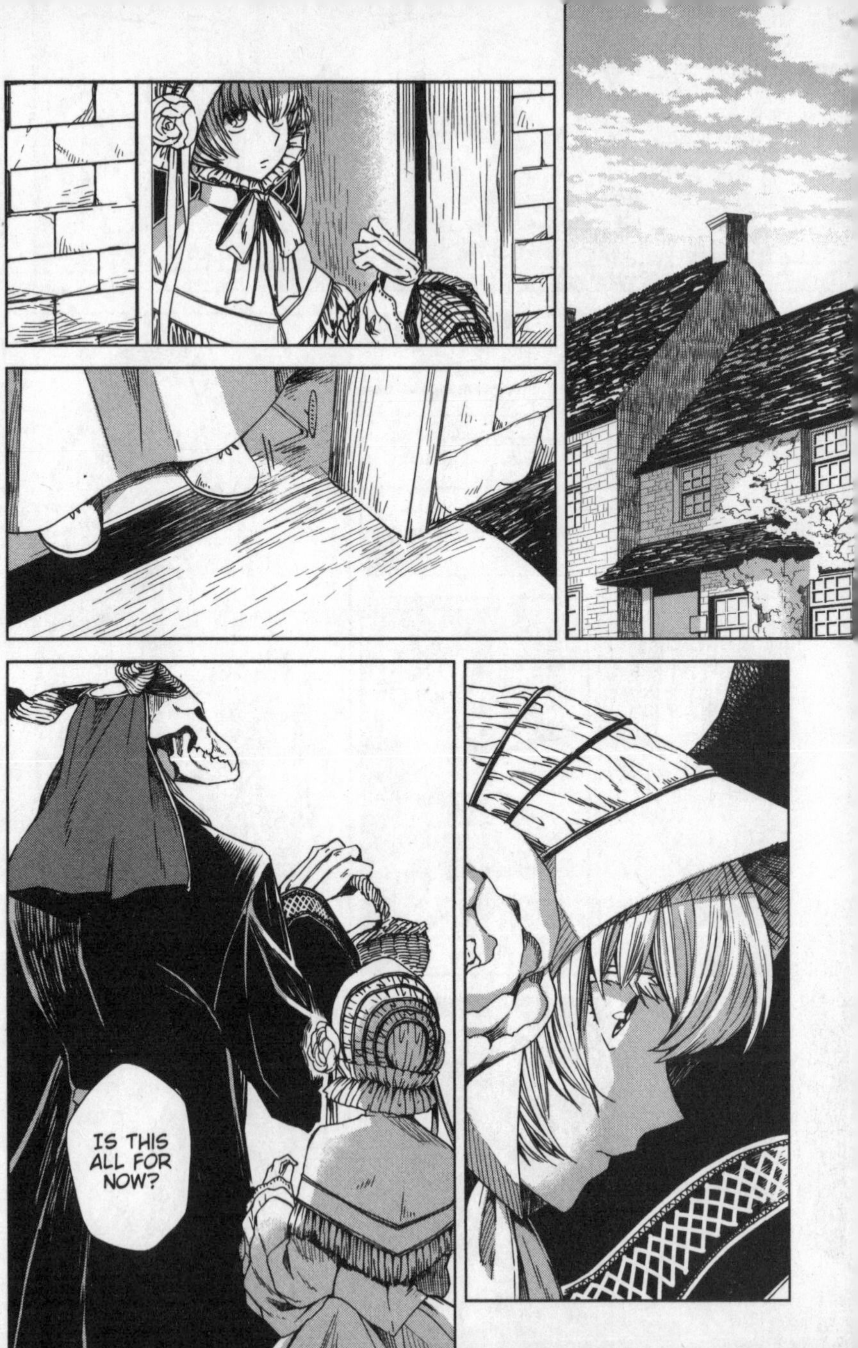
IS THIS ALL FOR NOW?

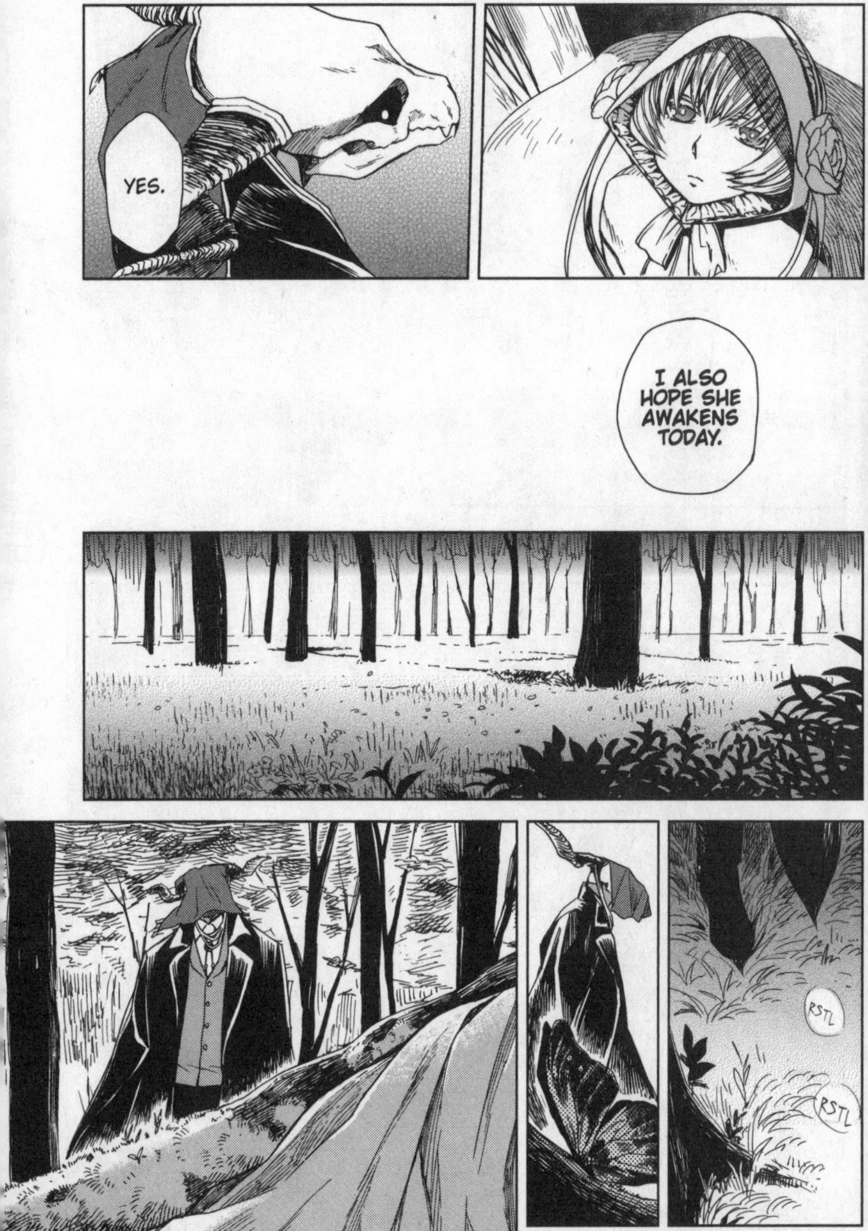
YES.
I ALSO HOPE SHE AWAKENS TODAY.
RSTL
RSTL

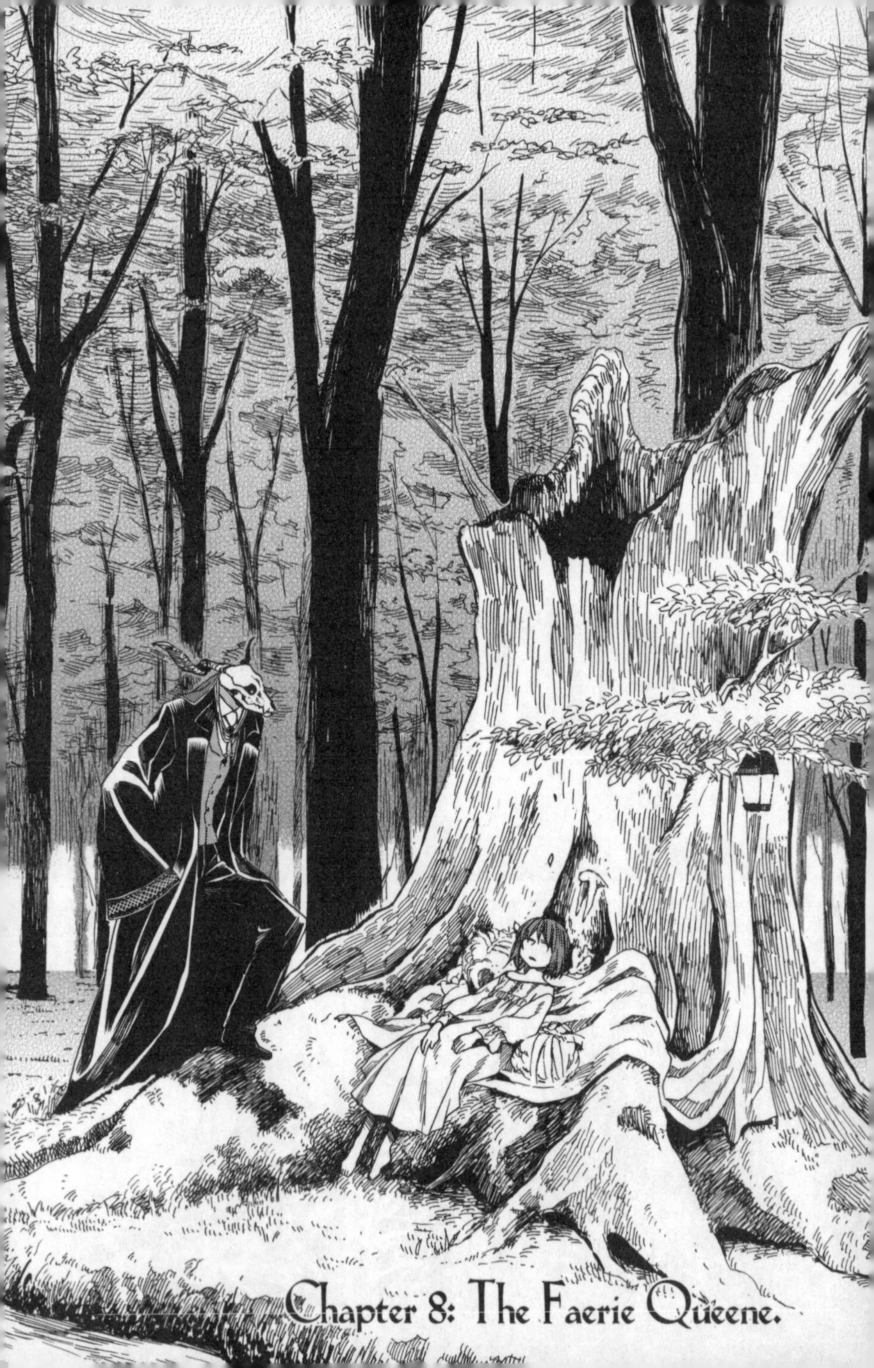

Chapter 8: The Faerie Queene.

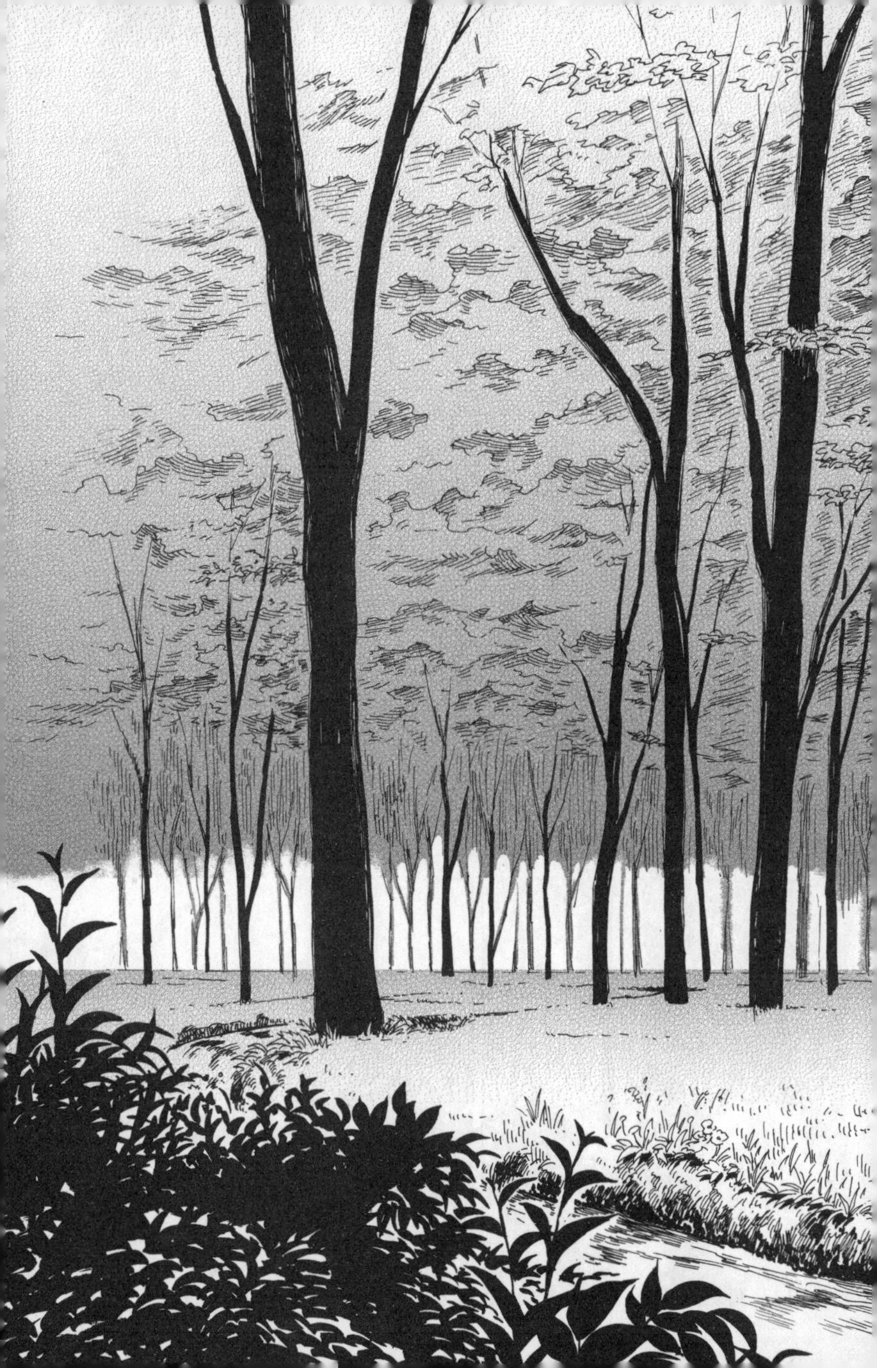

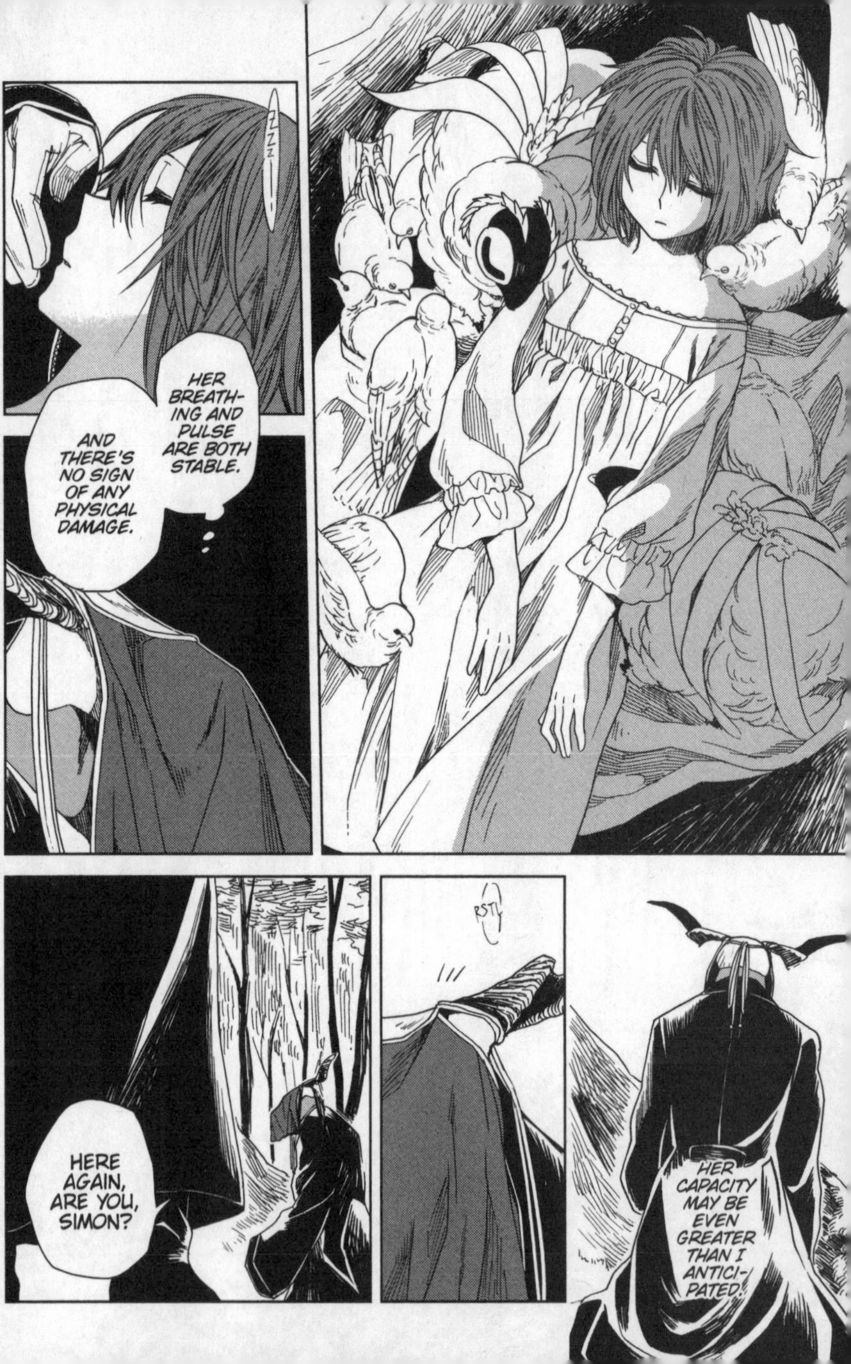
ZZZ...
HER BREATHING AND PULSE ARE BOTH STABLE.
AND THERE'S NO SIGN OF ANY PHYSICAL DAMAGE.
HER CAPACITY MAY BE EVEN GREATER THAN I ANTICIPATED.
RSTL
HERE AGAIN, ARE YOU, SIMON?

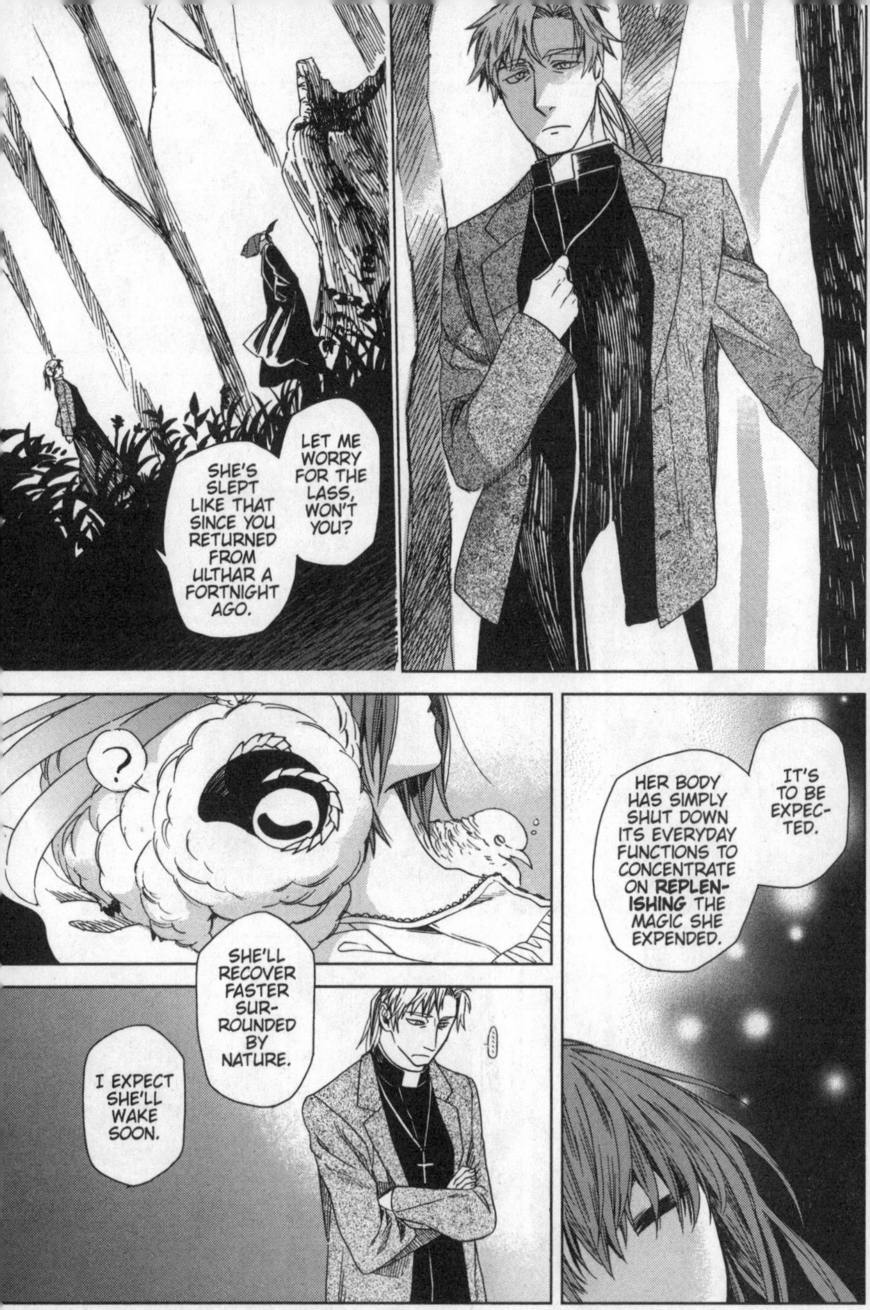
LET ME WORRY FOR THE LASS, WON'T YOU?
SHE'S SLEPT LIKE THAT SINCE YOU RETURNED FROM ULTHAR A FORTNIGHT AGO.
IT'S TO BE EXPECTED.
HER BODY HAS SIMPLY SHUT DOWN ITS EVERYDAY FUNCTIONS TO CONCENTRATE ON **REPLENISHING** THE MAGIC SHE EXPENDED.
?
SHE'LL RECOVER FASTER SURROUNDED BY NATURE.
I EXPECT SHE'LL WAKE SOON.

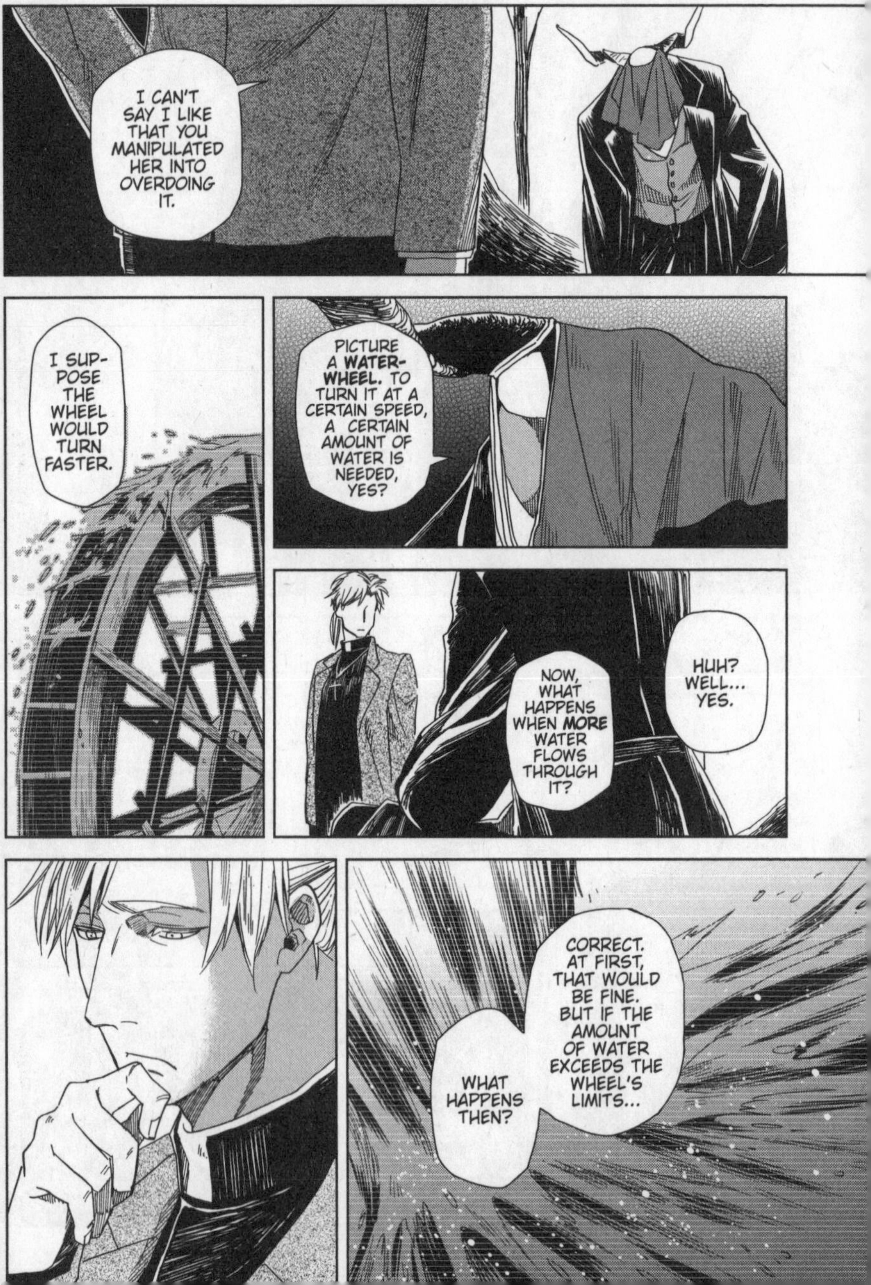
I CAN'T SAY I LIKE THAT YOU MANIPULATED HER INTO OVERDOING IT.
PICTURE A **WATER-WHEEL.** TO TURN IT AT A CERTAIN SPEED, A CERTAIN AMOUNT OF WATER IS NEEDED, YES?
HUH? WELL... YES.
NOW, WHAT HAPPENS WHEN **MORE** WATER FLOWS THROUGH IT?
I SUPPOSE THE WHEEL WOULD TURN FASTER.
CORRECT. AT FIRST, THAT WOULD BE FINE. BUT IF THE AMOUNT OF WATER EXCEEDS THE WHEEL'S LIMITS...
WHAT HAPPENS THEN?

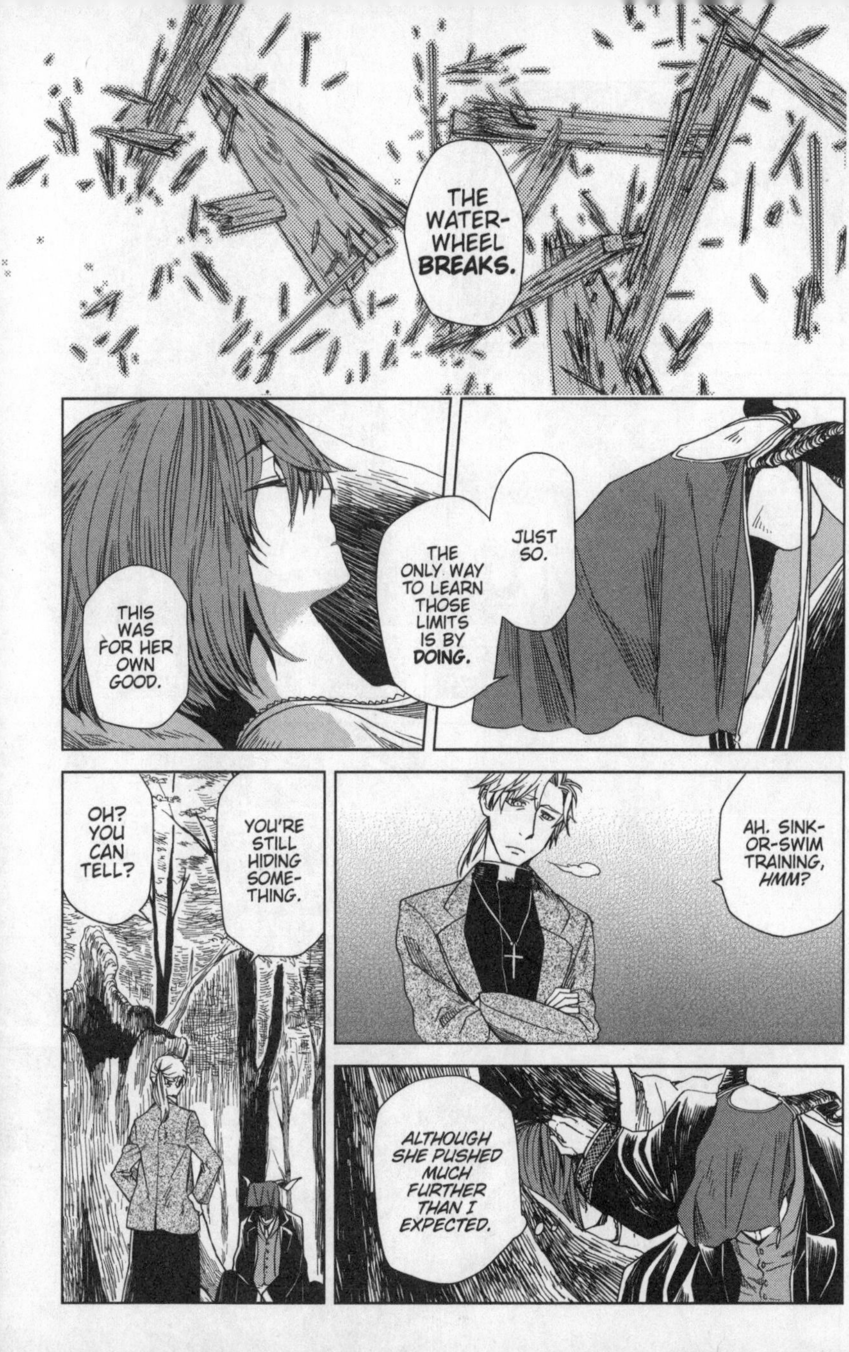
THE WATER-WHEEL **BREAKS.**
JUST SO.
THE ONLY WAY TO LEARN THOSE LIMITS IS BY **DOING.**
THIS WAS FOR HER OWN GOOD.
AH. SINK-OR-SWIM TRAINING, *HMM?*
ALTHOUGH SHE PUSHED MUCH FURTHER THAN I EXPECTED.
YOU'RE STILL HIDING SOME-THING.
OH? YOU CAN TELL?

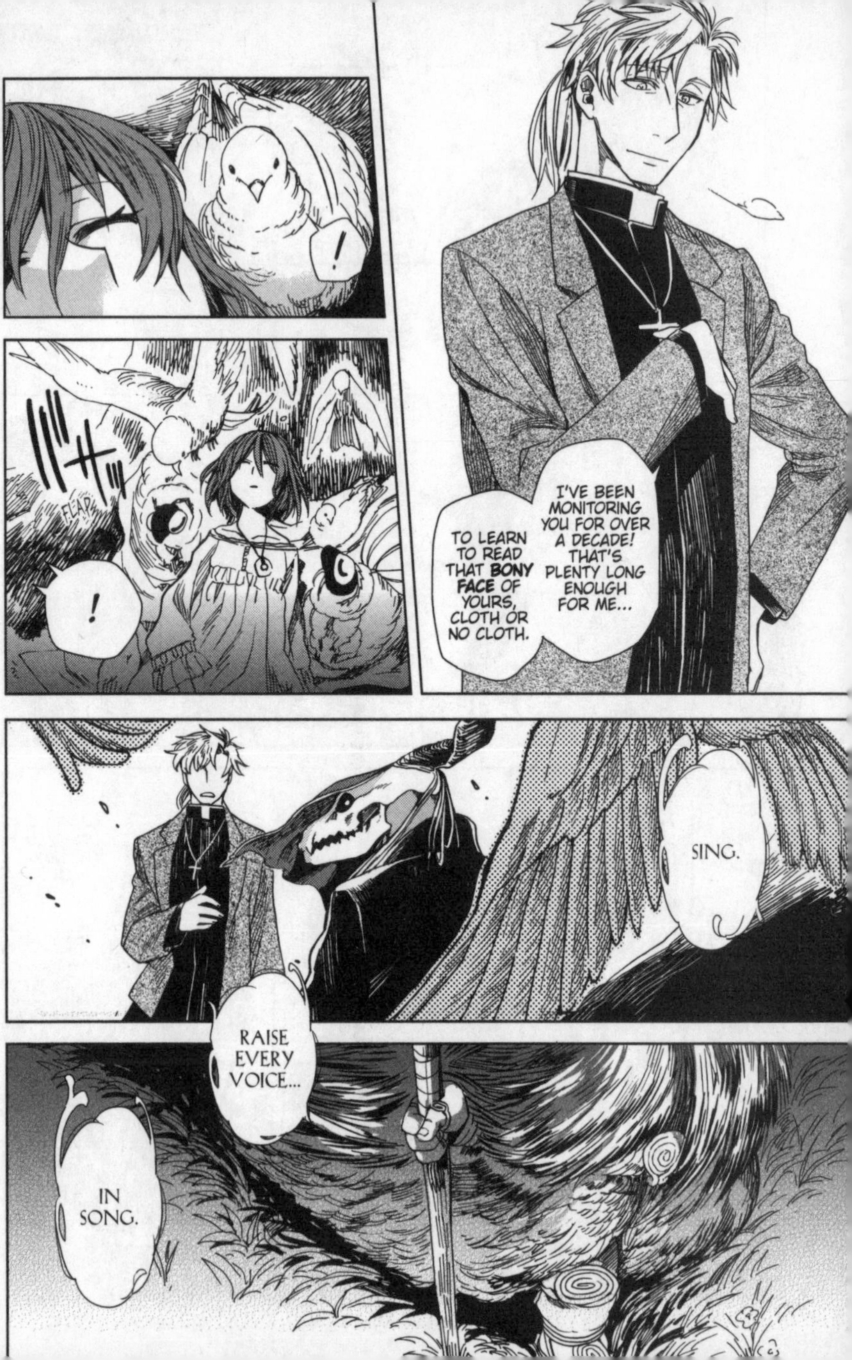
I'VE BEEN MONITORING YOU FOR OVER A DECADE! THAT'S PLENTY LONG ENOUGH FOR ME...
TO LEARN TO READ THAT **BONY FACE** OF YOURS, CLOTH OR NO CLOTH.
!
FLAP
!
SING.
RAISE EVERY VOICE...
IN SONG.

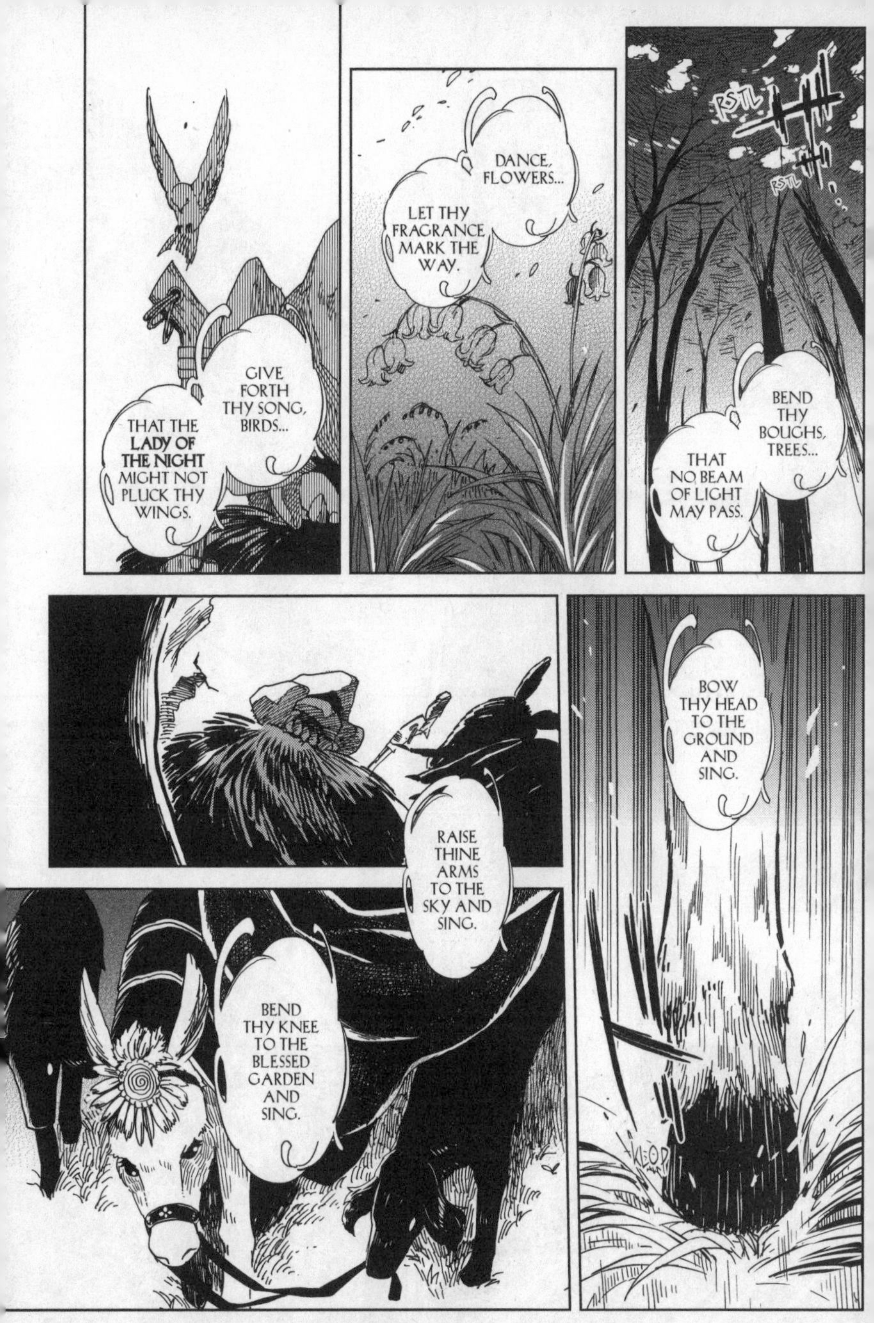
RSTL
RSTL
BEND THY BOUGHS, TREES...
THAT NO BEAM OF LIGHT MAY PASS.
DANCE, FLOWERS...
LET THY FRAGRANCE MARK THE WAY.
GIVE FORTH THY SONG, BIRDS...
THAT THE **LADY OF THE NIGHT** MIGHT NOT PLUCK THY WINGS.
BOW THY HEAD TO THE GROUND AND SING.
RAISE THINE ARMS TO THE SKY AND SING.
BEND THY KNEE TO THE BLESSED GARDEN AND SING.

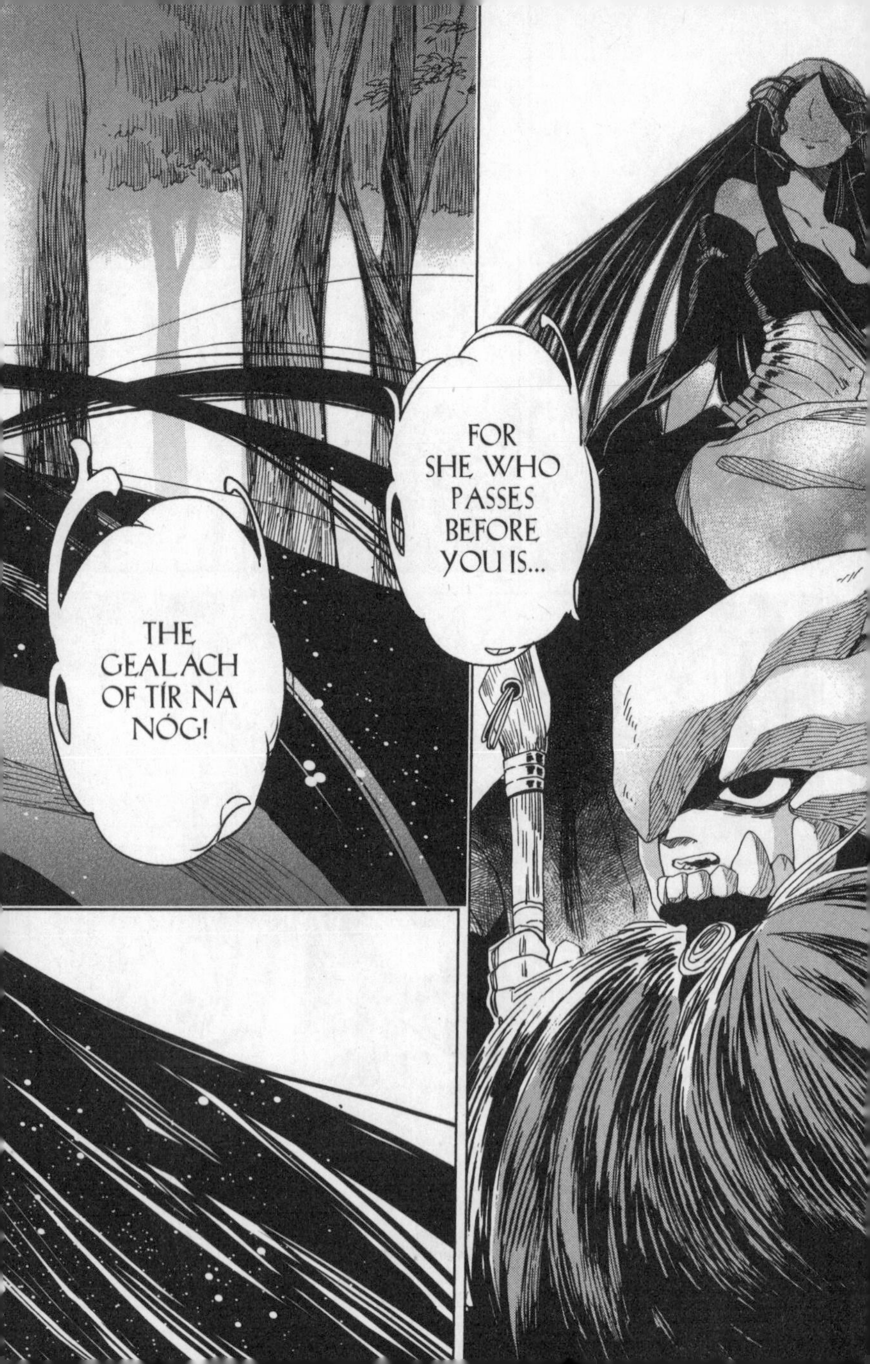
FOR SHE WHO PASSES BEFORE YOU IS...
THE GEALACH OF TÍR NA NÓG!

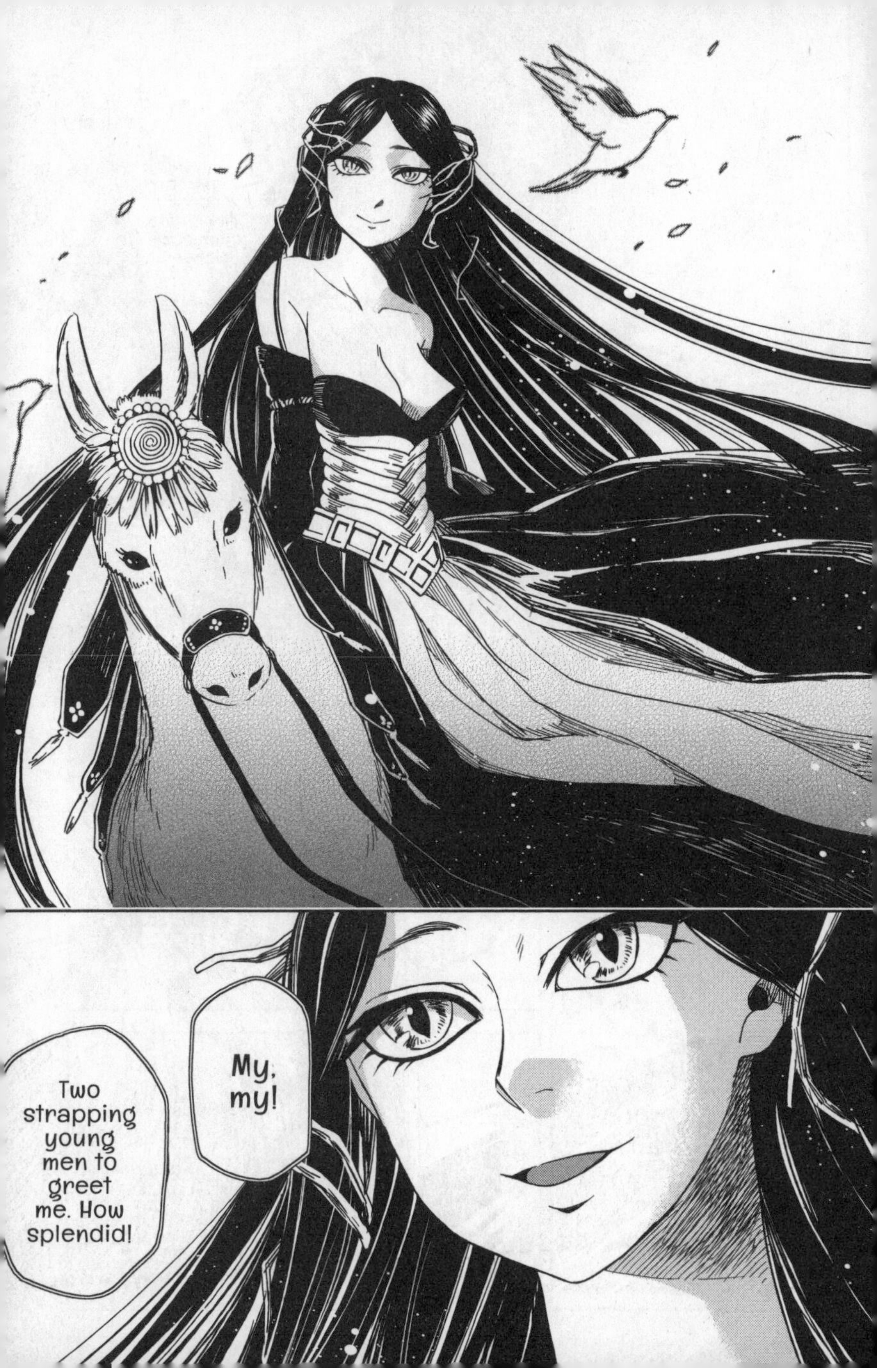
My, my!
Two strapping young men to greet me. How splendid!

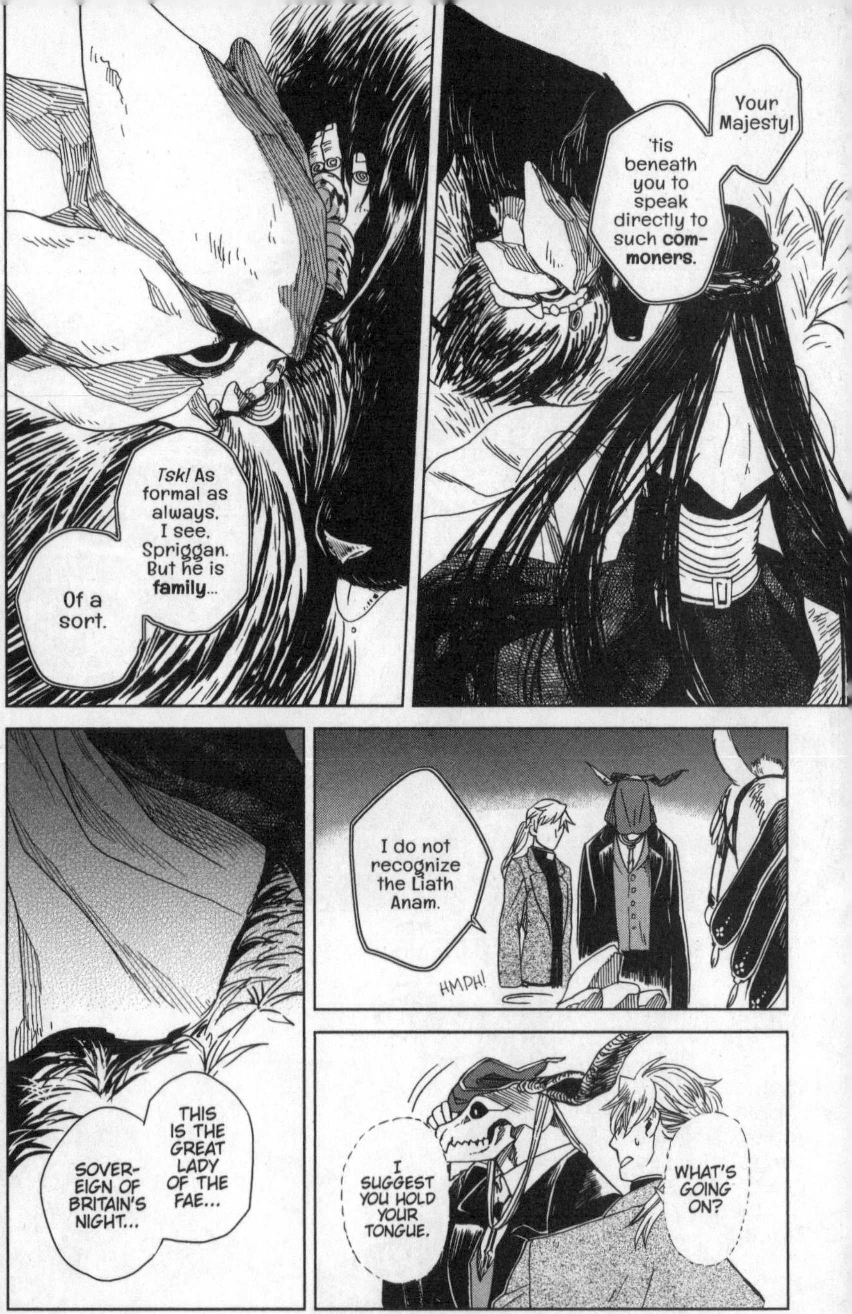
Your Majesty!
'tis beneath you to speak directly to such **commoners.**
Tsk! As formal as always, I see, Spriggan. But he is **family**...
Of a sort.
I do not recognize the Liath Anam.
HMPH!
WHAT'S GOING ON?
I SUGGEST YOU HOLD YOUR TONGUE.
THIS IS THE GREAT LADY OF THE FAE...
SOVEREIGN OF BRITAIN'S NIGHT...

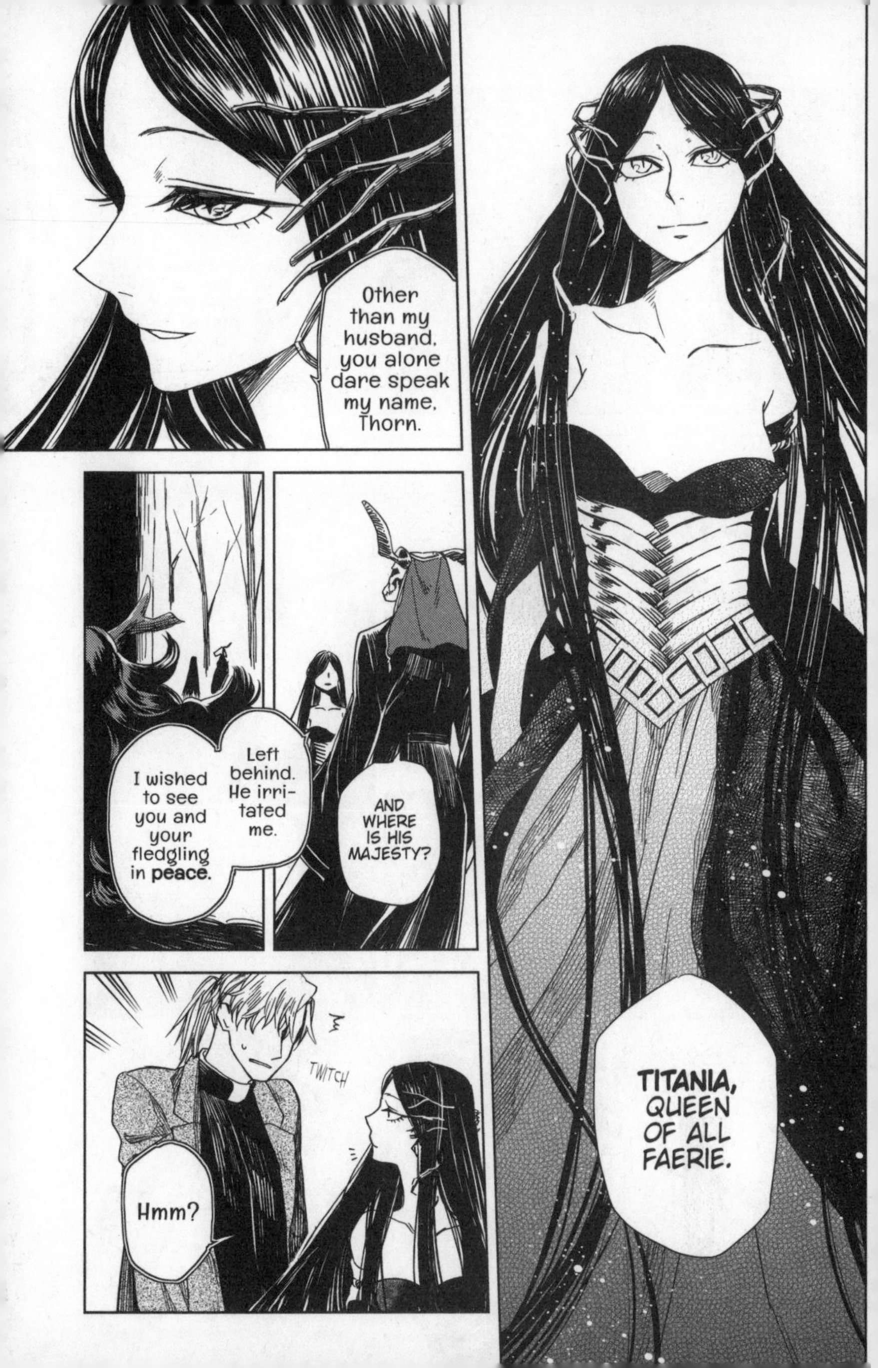
TITANIA, QUEEN OF ALL FAERIE.
Other than my husband, you alone dare speak my name, Thorn.
AND WHERE IS HIS MAJESTY?
Left behind. He irri-tated me.
I wished to see you and your fledgling in **peace**.
TWITCH
Hmm?

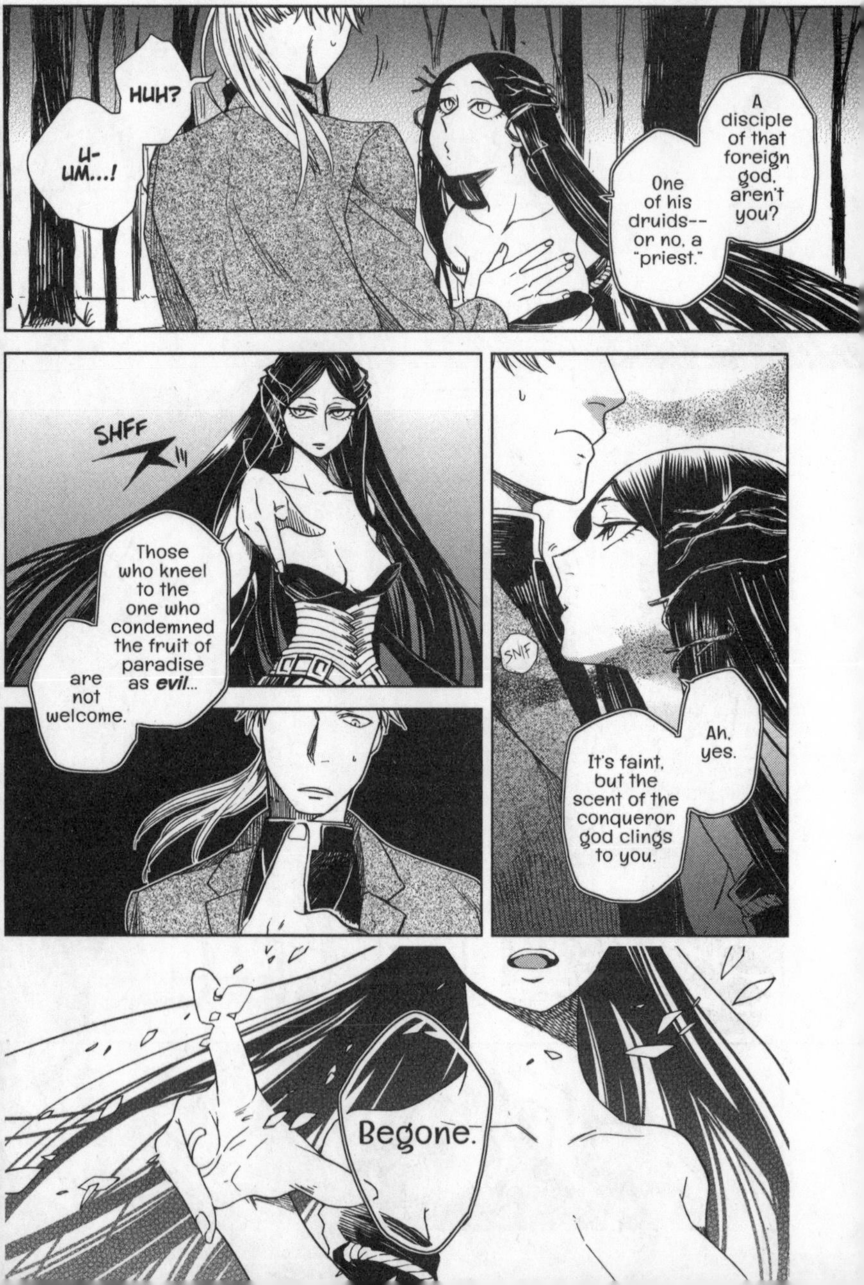
A disciple of that foreign god, aren't you?
One of his druids--or no, a "priest."
HUH?
U-UM...!
Ah, yes.
It's faint, but the scent of the conqueror god clings to you.
SNIF
SHFF
Those who kneel to the one who condemned the fruit of paradise as *evil*...
are not welcome.
Begone.

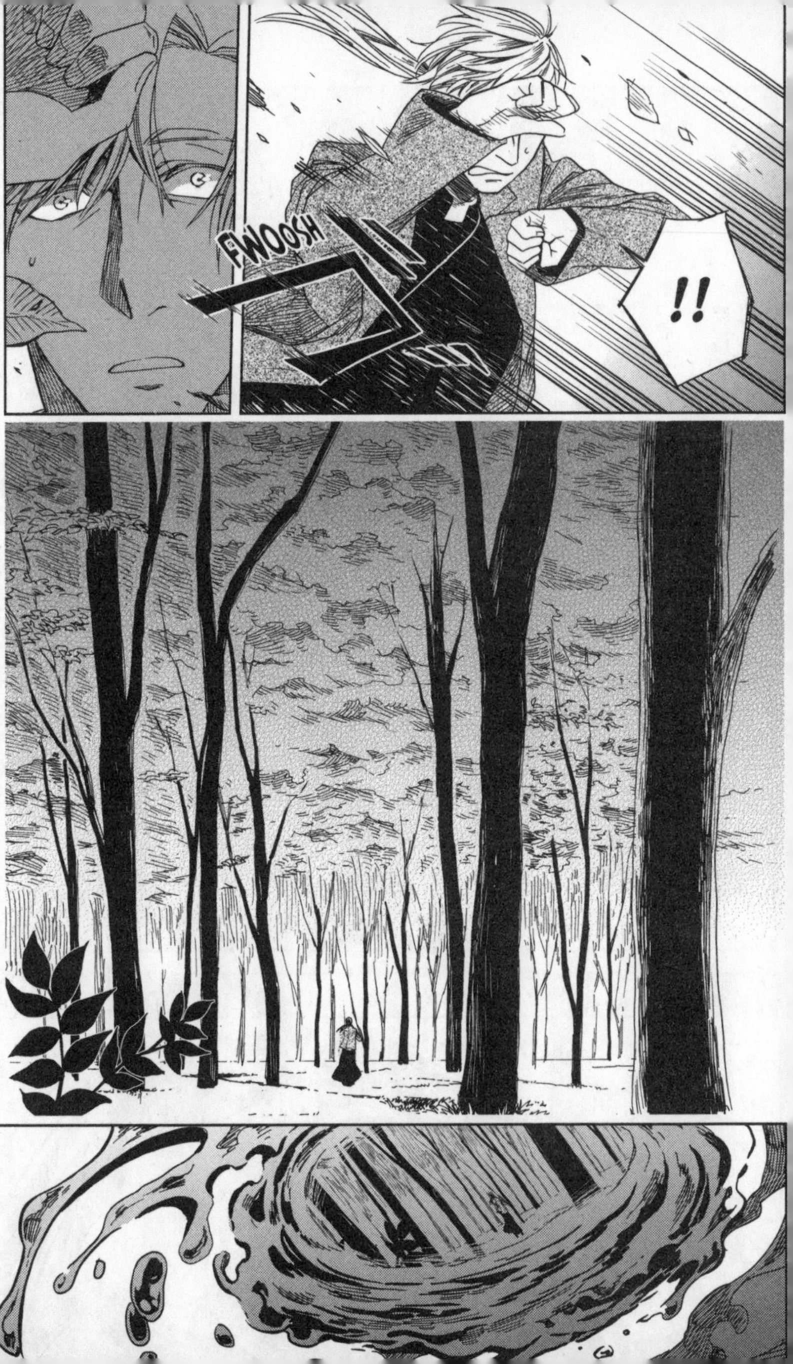
!!
FWOOSH

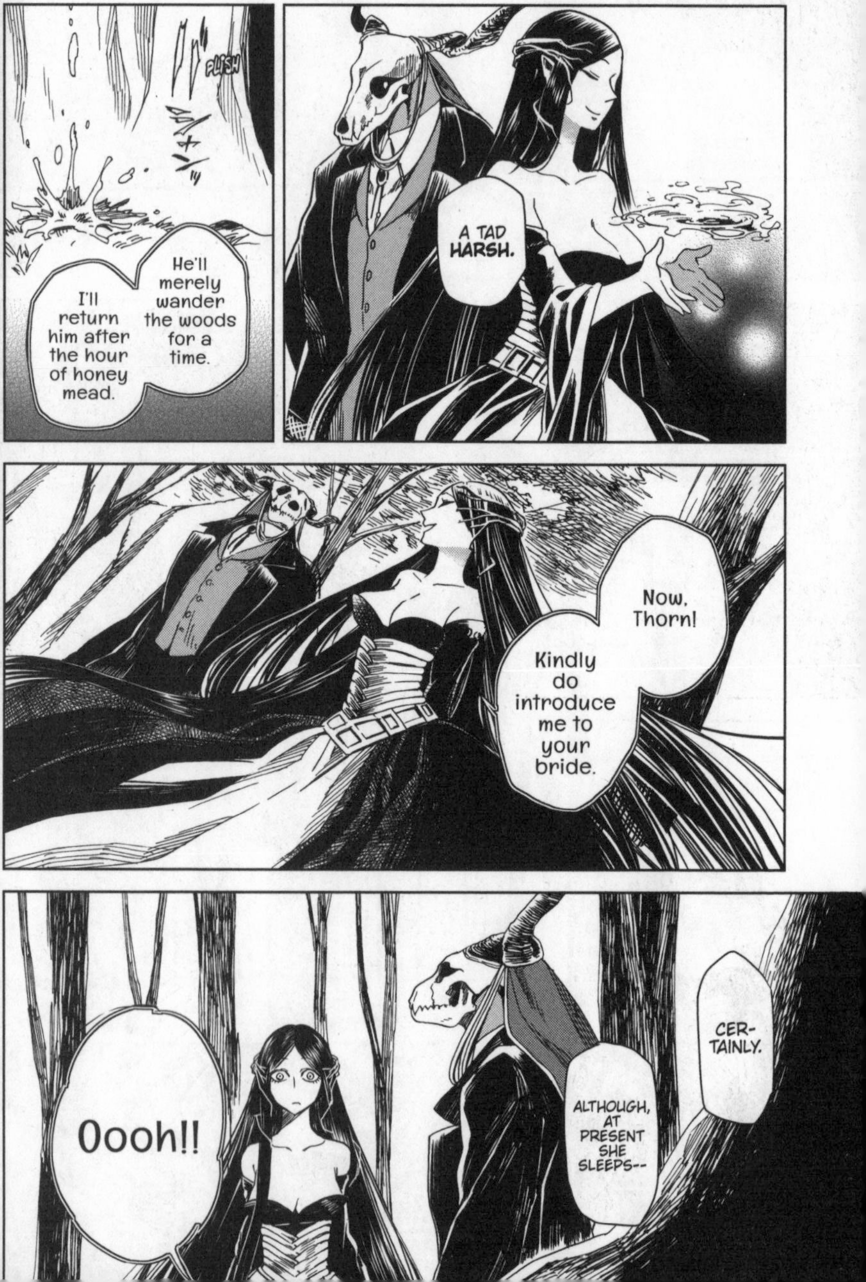
A TAD HARSH.
PLISH
He'll merely wander the woods for a time.
I'll return him after the hour of honey mead.
Now, Thorn!
Kindly do introduce me to your bride.
CERTAINLY.
ALTHOUGH, AT PRESENT SHE SLEEPS--
Oooh!!

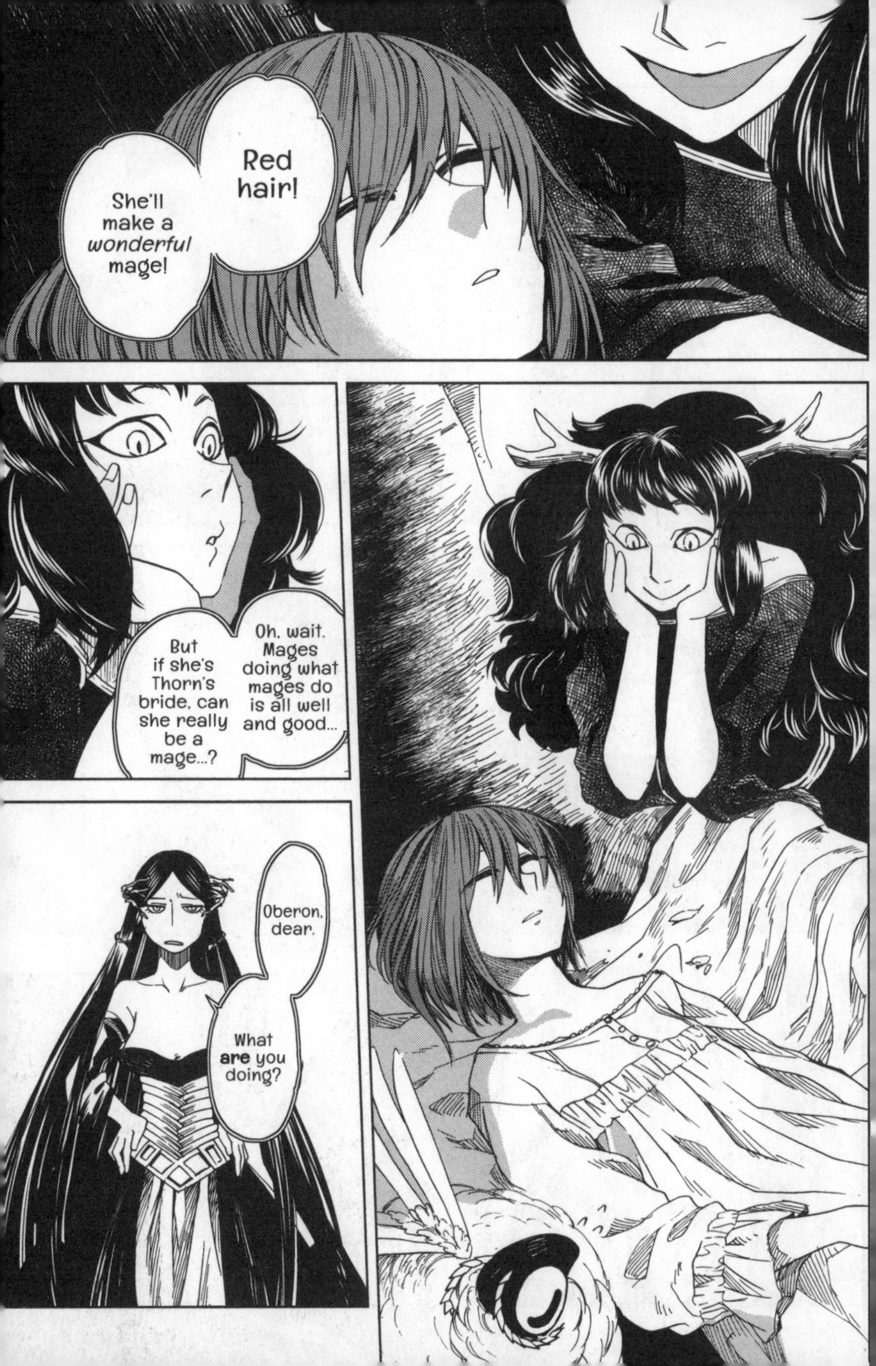
Red hair!
She'll make a *wonderful* mage!
Oh, wait. Mages doing what mages do is all well and good...
But if she's Thorn's bride, can she really be a mage...?
Oberon, dear.
What **are** you doing?

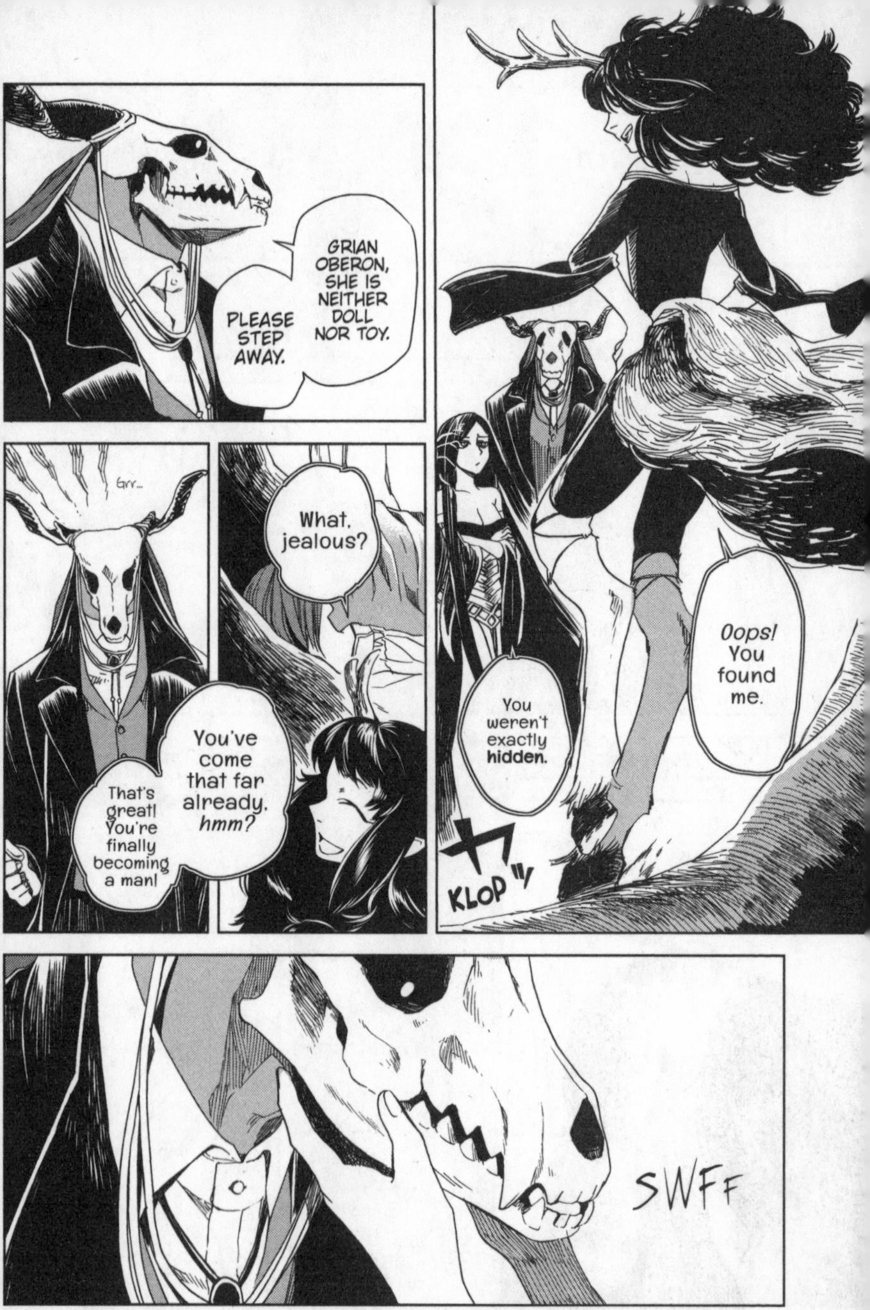
Oops! You found me.
You weren't exactly **hidden.**
KLOP
GRIAN OBERON, SHE IS NEITHER DOLL NOR TOY.
PLEASE STEP AWAY.
What, jealous?
You've come that far already, *hmm?*
That's great! You're finally becoming a man!
Grr...
SWFF

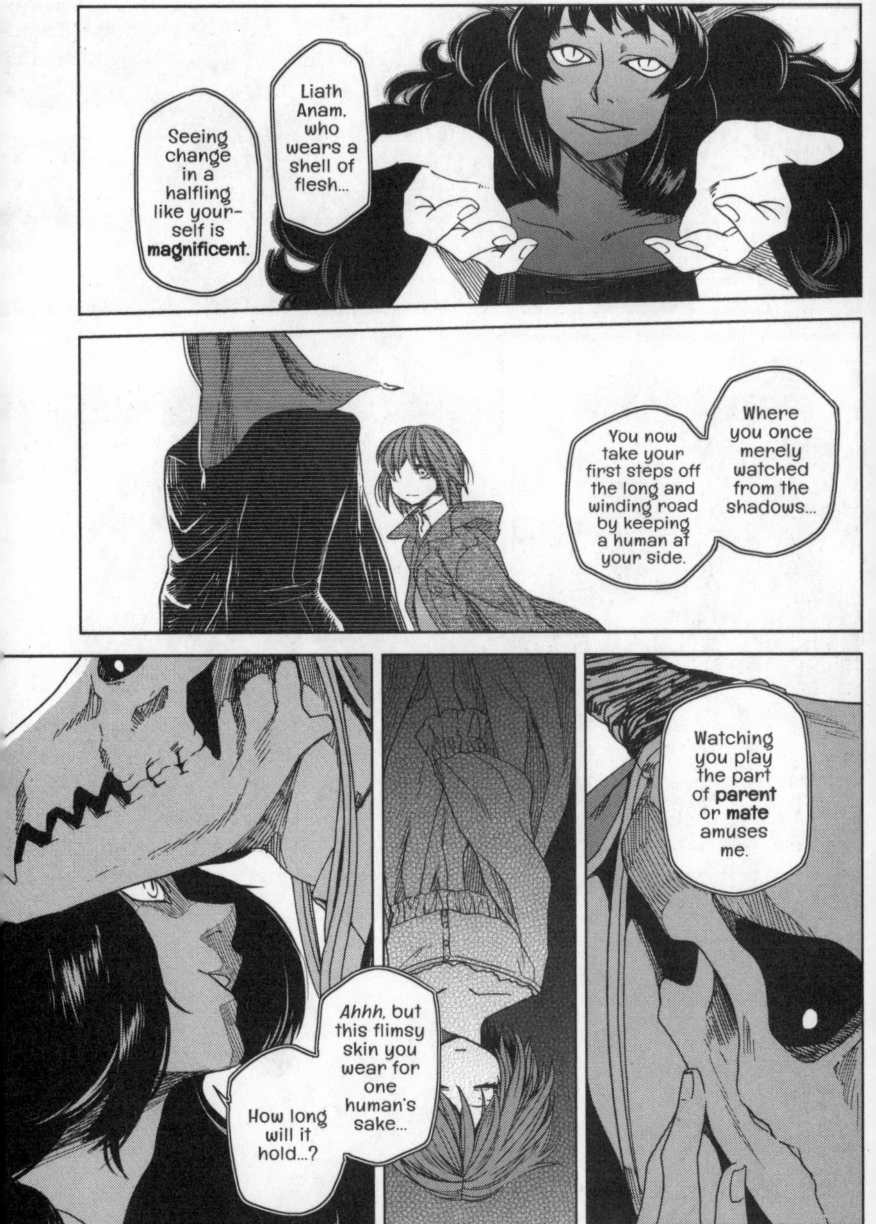
Liath Anam, who wears a shell of flesh...
Seeing change in a halfling like yourself is **magnificent.**
Where you once merely watched from the shadows...
You now take your first steps off the long and winding road by keeping a human at your side.
Watching you play the part of **parent** or **mate** amuses me.
Ahhh, but this flimsy skin you wear for one human's sake...
How long will it hold...?

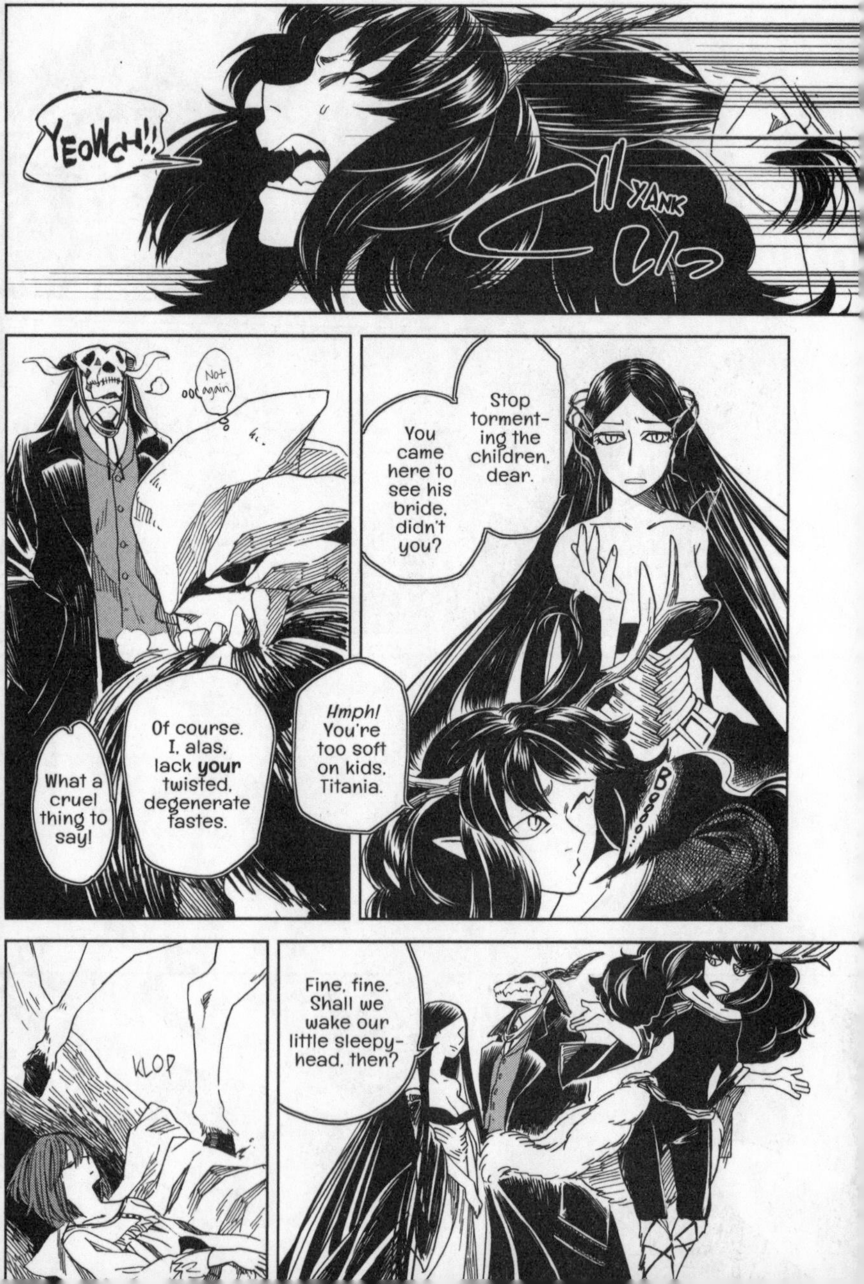
YEOWCH!!
YANK
Stop torment-ing the children, dear.
You came here to see his bride, didn't you?
Hmph! You're too soft on kids, Titania.
Booo...
Not again.
Of course. I, alas, lack **your** twisted, degenerate tastes.
What a cruel thing to say!
Fine, fine. Shall we wake our little sleepy-head, then?
KLOP

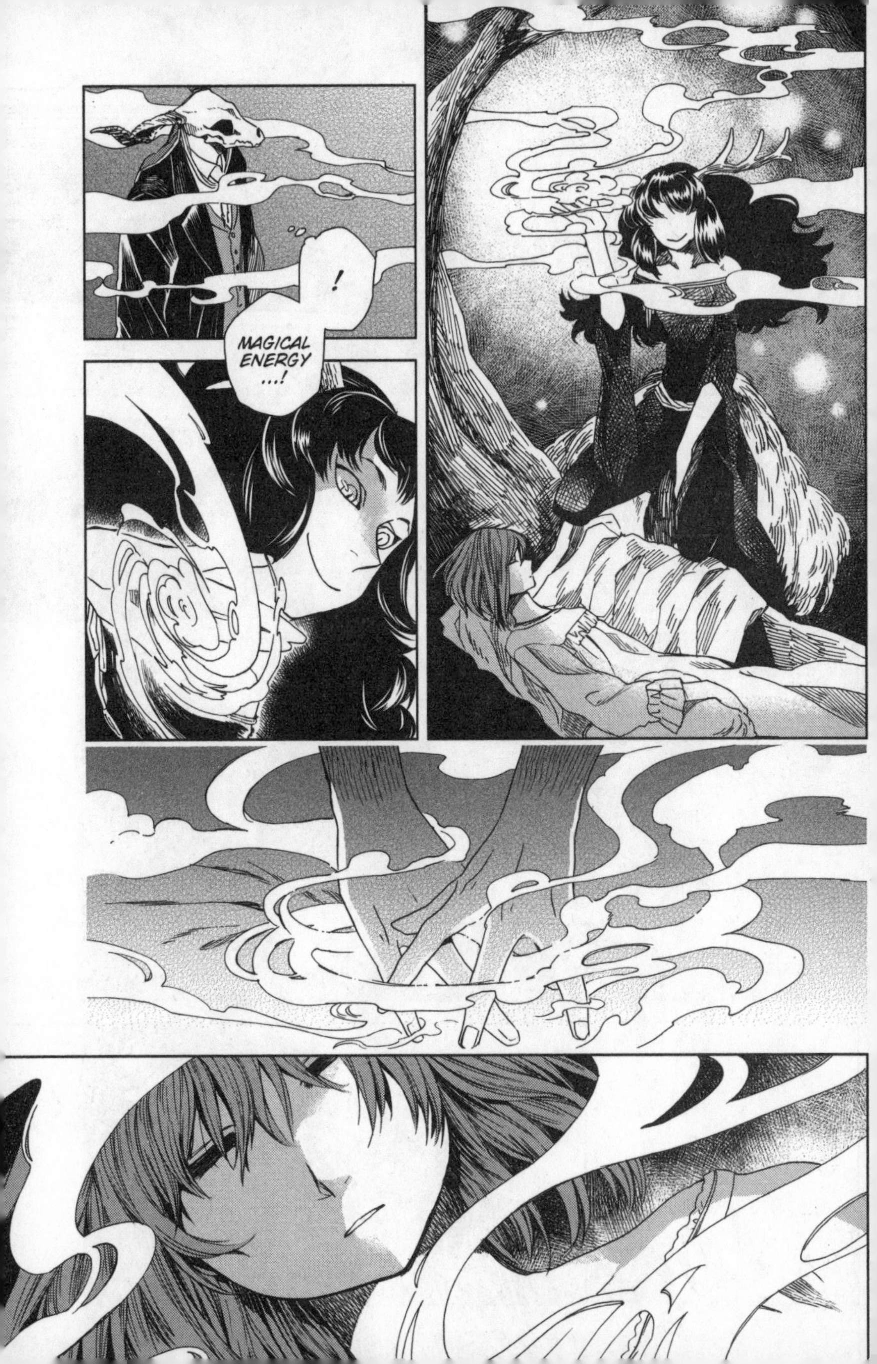
!
MAGICAL ENERGY ...!

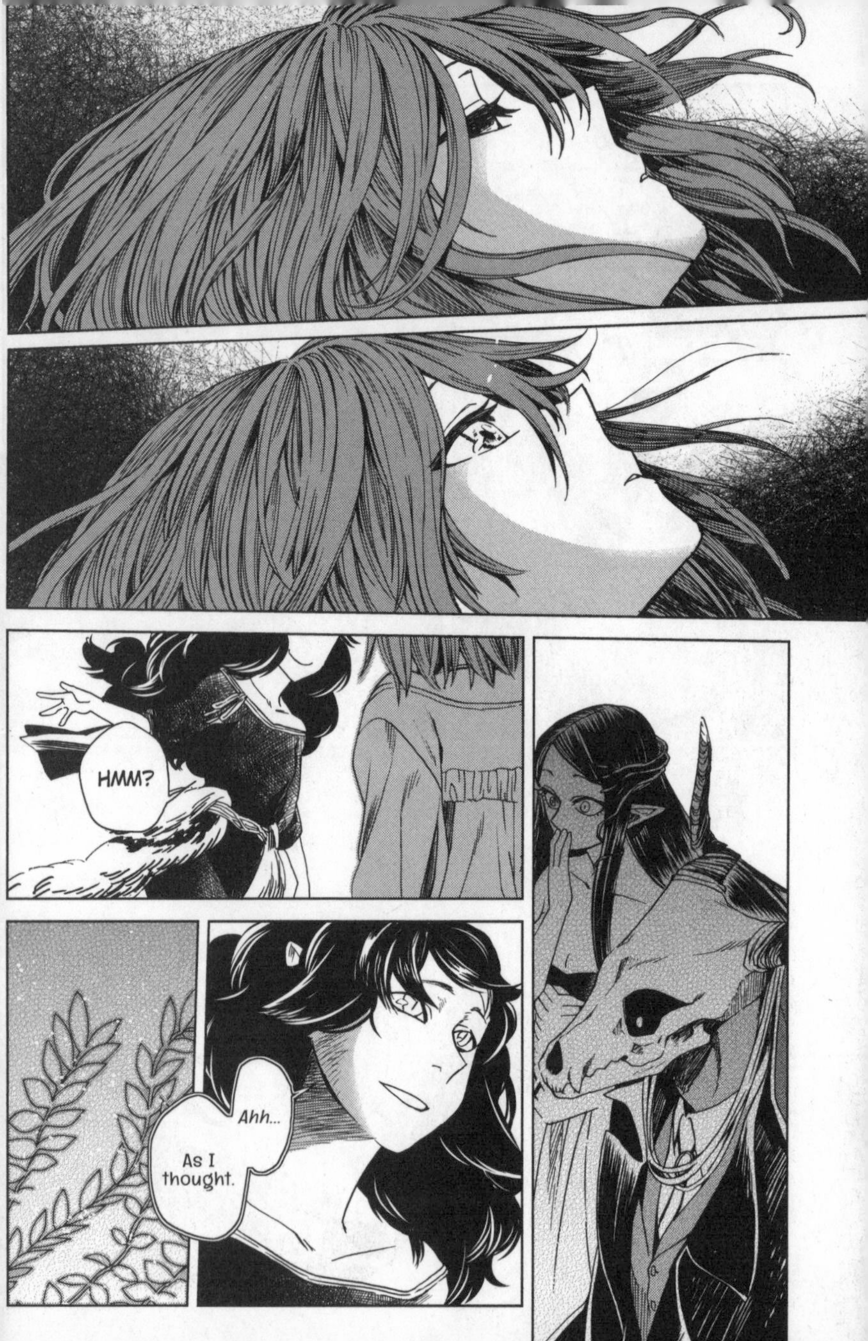
HMM?
Ahh...
As I thought.

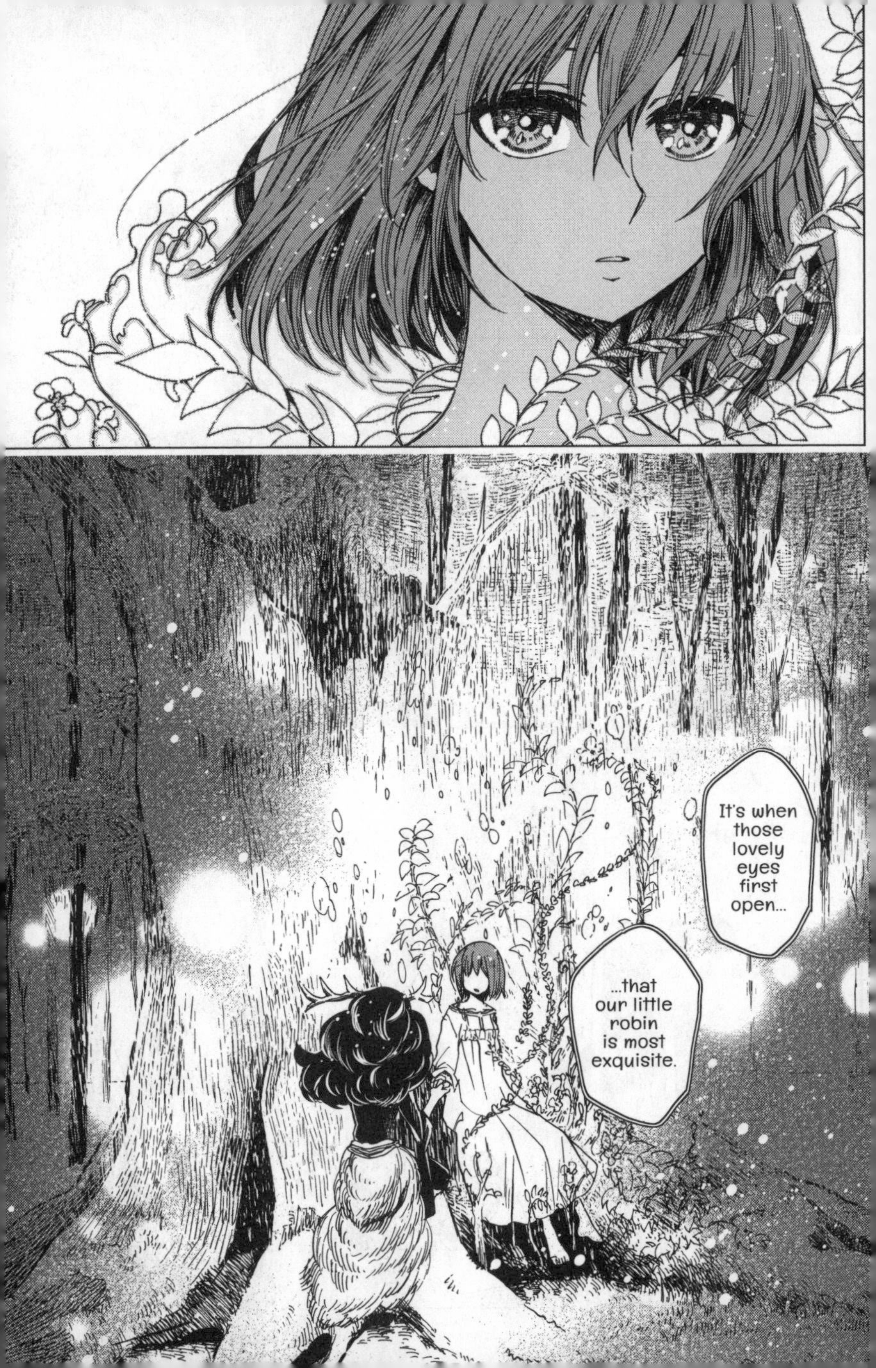
It's when those lovely eyes first open...
...that our little robin is most exquisite.

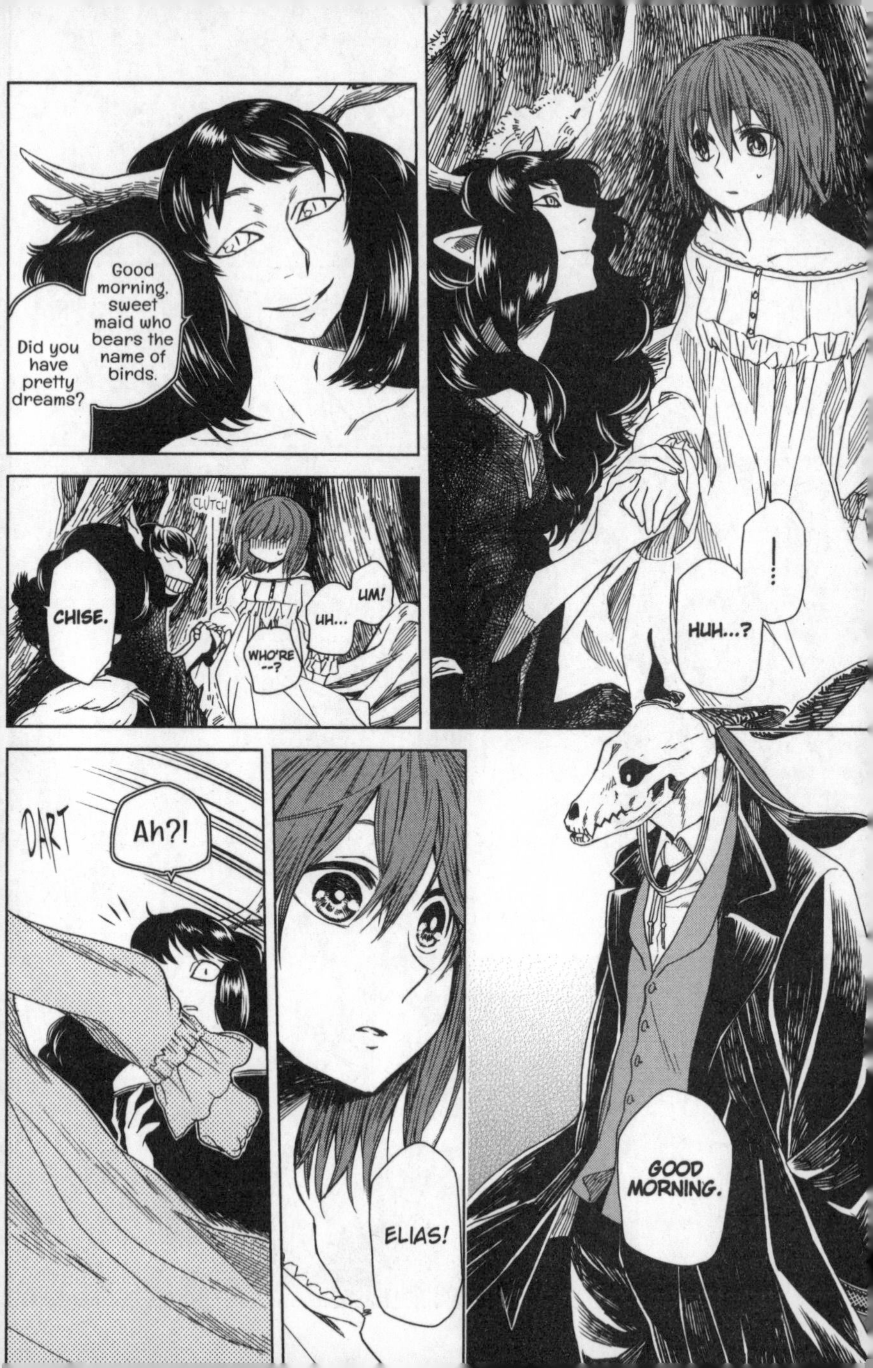
!...
HUH...?
Good morning, sweet maid who bears the name of birds.
Did you have pretty dreams?
CLUTCH
UM!
UH...
WHO'RE --?
CHISE.
GOOD MORNING.
ELIAS!
DART
Ah?!

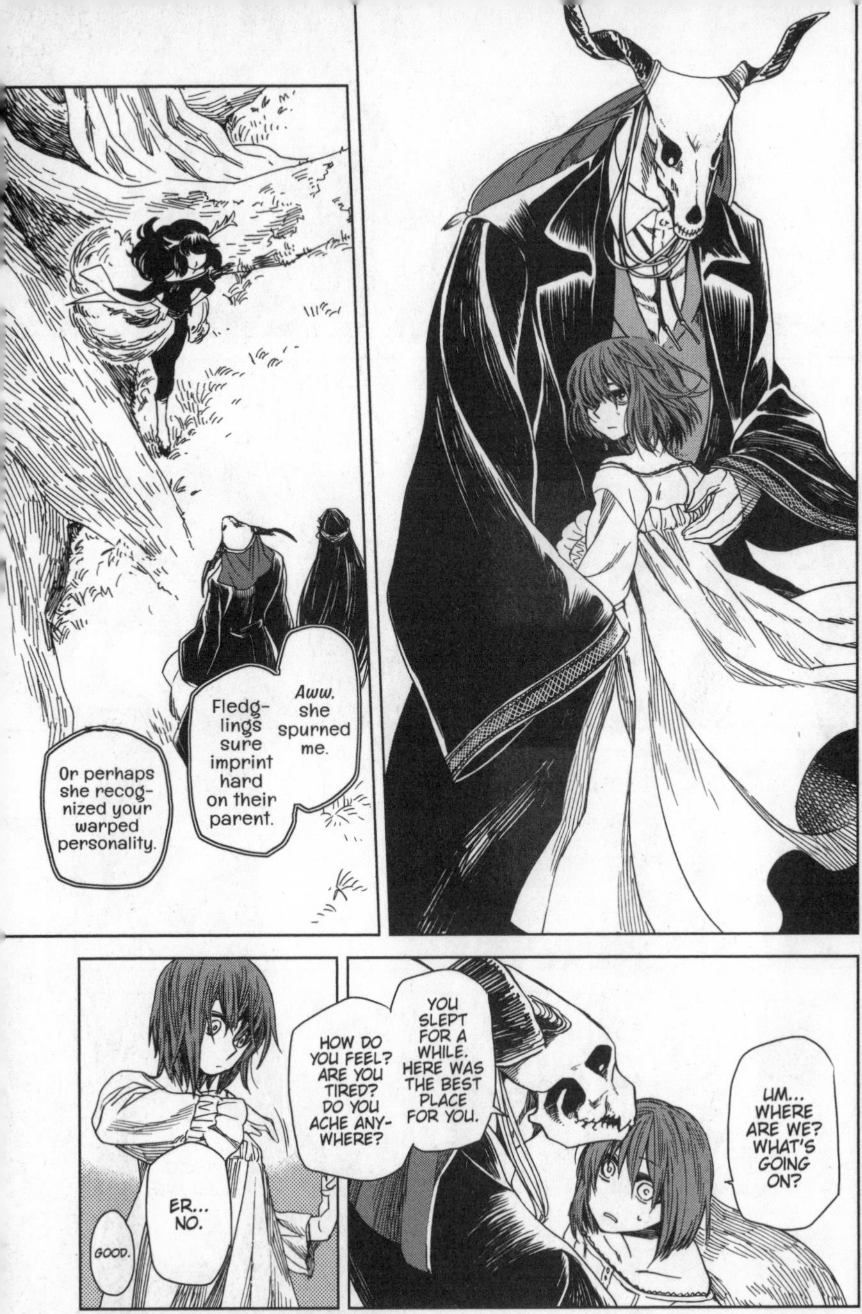
Aww, she spurned me.
Fledglings sure imprint hard on their parent.
Or perhaps she recognized your warped personality.
UM... WHERE ARE WE? WHAT'S GOING ON?
YOU SLEPT FOR A WHILE. HERE WAS THE BEST PLACE FOR YOU.
HOW DO YOU FEEL? ARE YOU TIRED? DO YOU ACHE ANYWHERE?
ER... NO.
GOOD.

I do apologize for startling you, sweetling.

SWFF

SPROING

I am queen of the fae who reside within Albion, and thus all of Tír na nÓg.

It's a pleasure to meet you. I am **Titania**.

And I'm her hubby, **Oberon!** Good to meetcha!

AND *TIR NA NÓG* IS THE **FAERIE KINGDOM**.

ALBION IS THE ANCIENT NAME FOR THE BRITISH ISLES.

"ALBION"? "TIR" WHAT...?

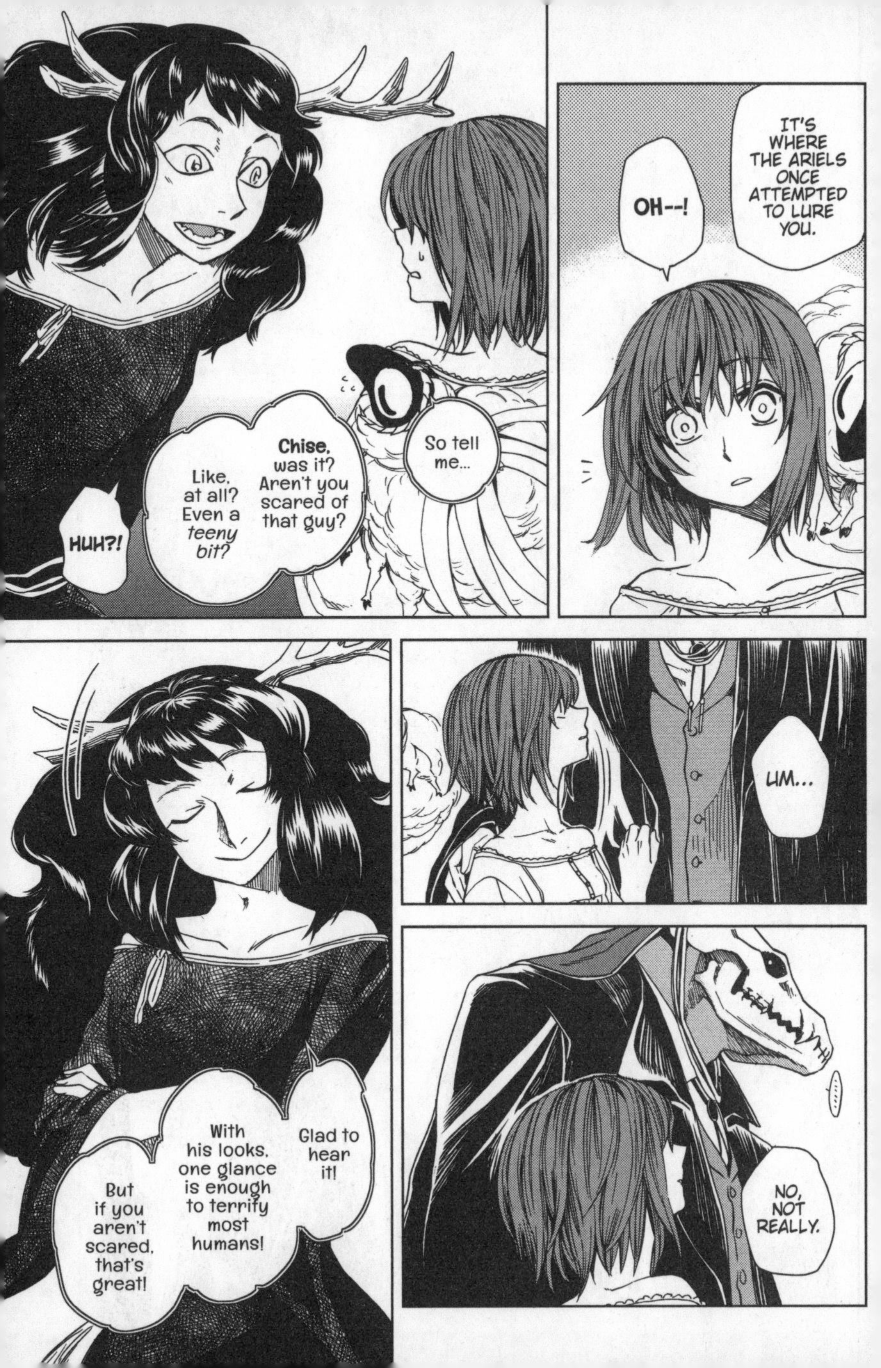
IT'S WHERE THE ARIELS ONCE ATTEMPTED TO LURE YOU.
OH--!
So tell me...
Chise, was it? Aren't you scared of that guy?
Like, at all? Even a *teeny* bit?
HUH?!
UM...
......
NO, NOT REALLY.
Glad to hear it!
With his looks, one glance is enough to terrify most humans!
But if you aren't scared, that's great!

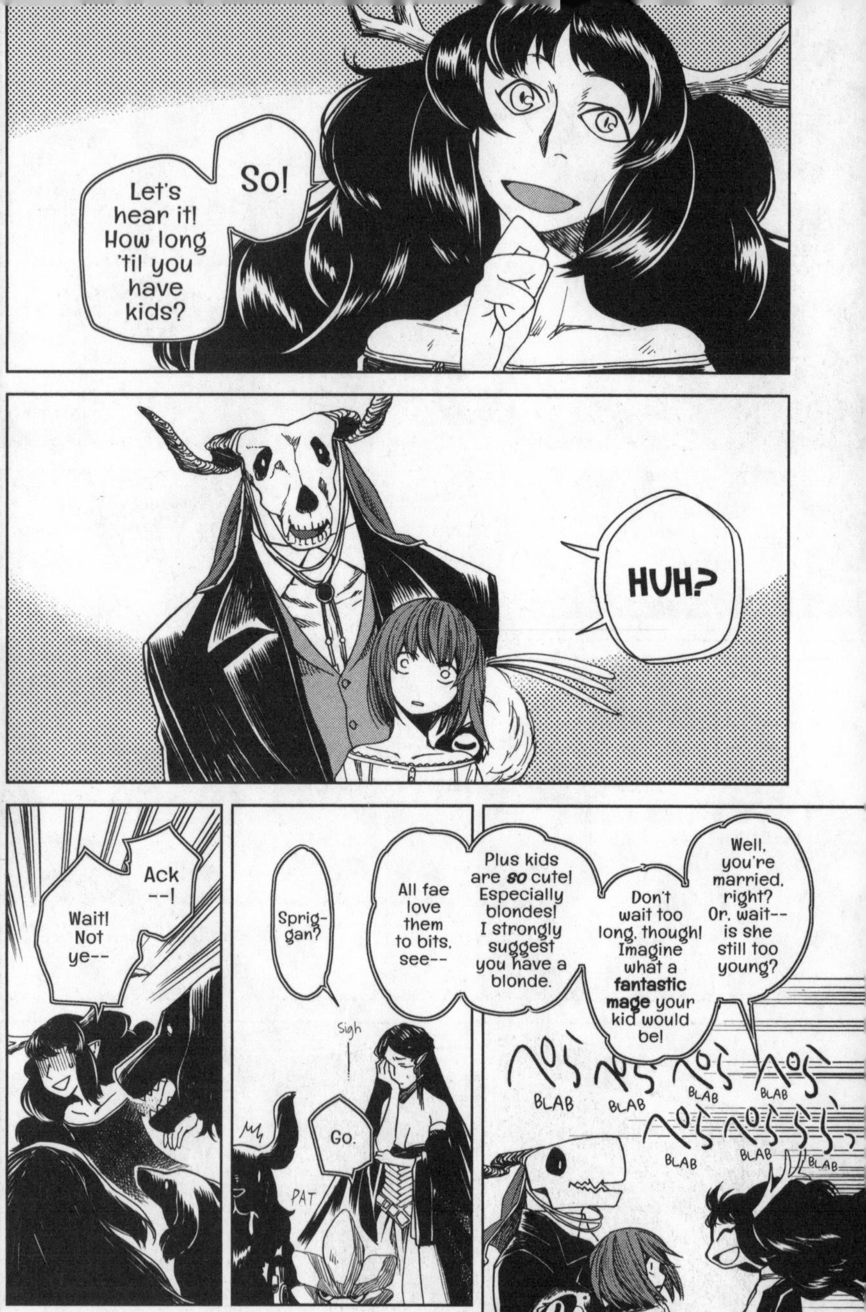
So!
Let's hear it! How long 'til you have kids?
HUH?
Well, you're married, right? Or, wait-- is she still too young?
Don't wait too long, though! Imagine what a **fantastic mage** your kid would be!
Plus kids are ***so*** cute! Especially blondes! I strongly suggest you have a blonde.
All fae love them to bits, see--
BLAB BLAB BLAB BLAB
BLAB BLAB BLAB
Sprig-gan?
Sigh
Go.
PAT
Ack--!
Wait! Not ye--

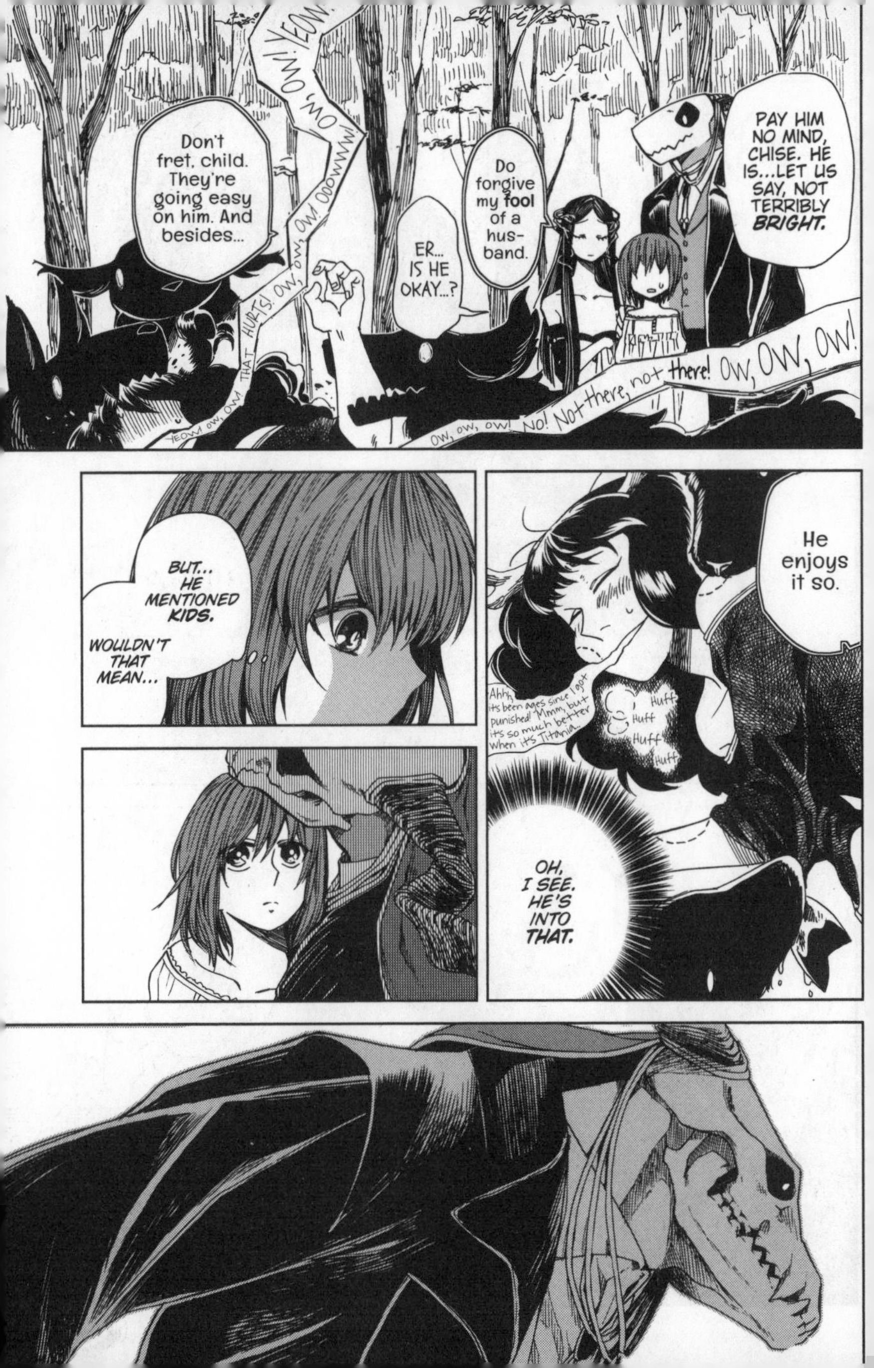
PAY HIM NO MIND, CHISE. HE IS...LET US SAY, NOT TERRIBLY BRIGHT.
Do forgive my fool of a hus-band.
ER... IS HE OKAY...?
Don't fret, child. They're going easy on him. And besides...
YEOW! ow, ow, ow! THAT HURTS! OW, OW, OW! OOOWWW! OW, OW, YEOW! YEOW!
ow, ow, ow! NO! Not there, not there! Ow, Ow, Ow!
He enjoys it so.
Ahhh, it's been ages since I got punished! Mmm, but it's so much better when it's Titania...
Huff Huff Huff Huff
OH, I SEE. HE'S INTO THAT.
BUT... HE MENTIONED KIDS.
WOULDN'T THAT MEAN...

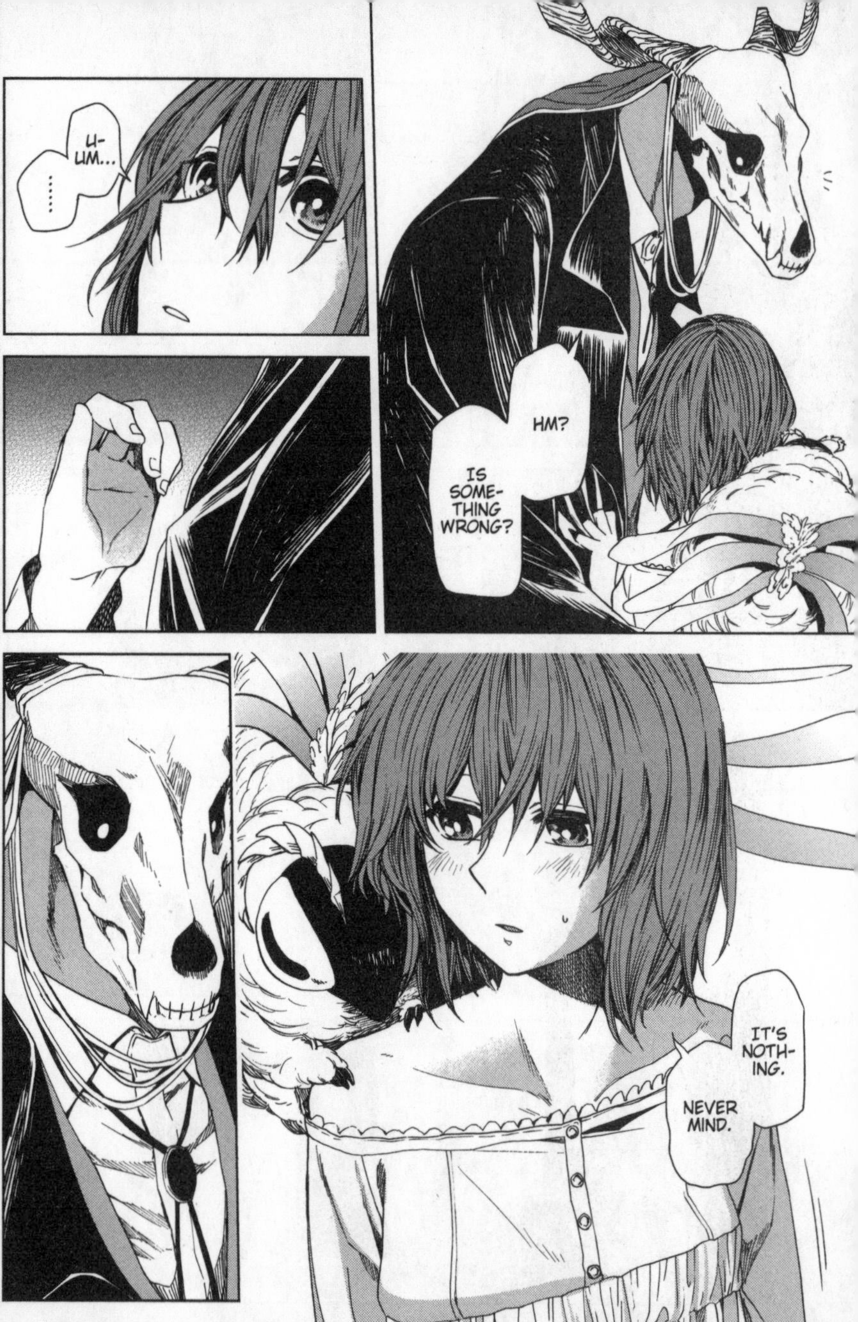
HM?
IS SOMETHING WRONG?
U-UM...
......
IT'S NOTHING.
NEVER MIND.

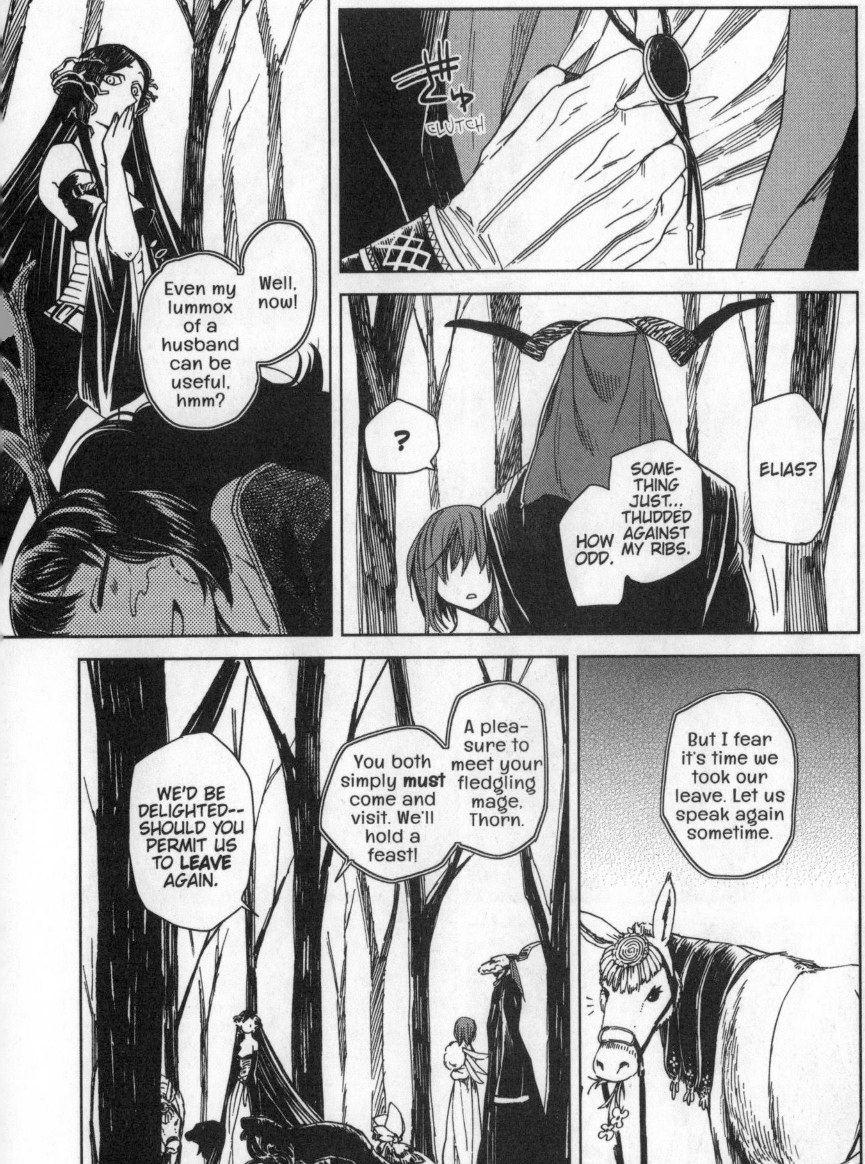
ぎゅ
CLUTCH
ELIAS?
SOMETHING JUST... THUDDED AGAINST MY RIBS. HOW ODD.
?
Well, now!
Even my lummox of a husband can be useful, hmm?
But I fear it's time we took our leave. Let us speak again sometime.
A pleasure to meet your fledgling mage, Thorn.
You both simply **must** come and visit. We'll hold a feast!
WE'D BE DELIGHTED-- SHOULD YOU PERMIT US TO **LEAVE** AGAIN.

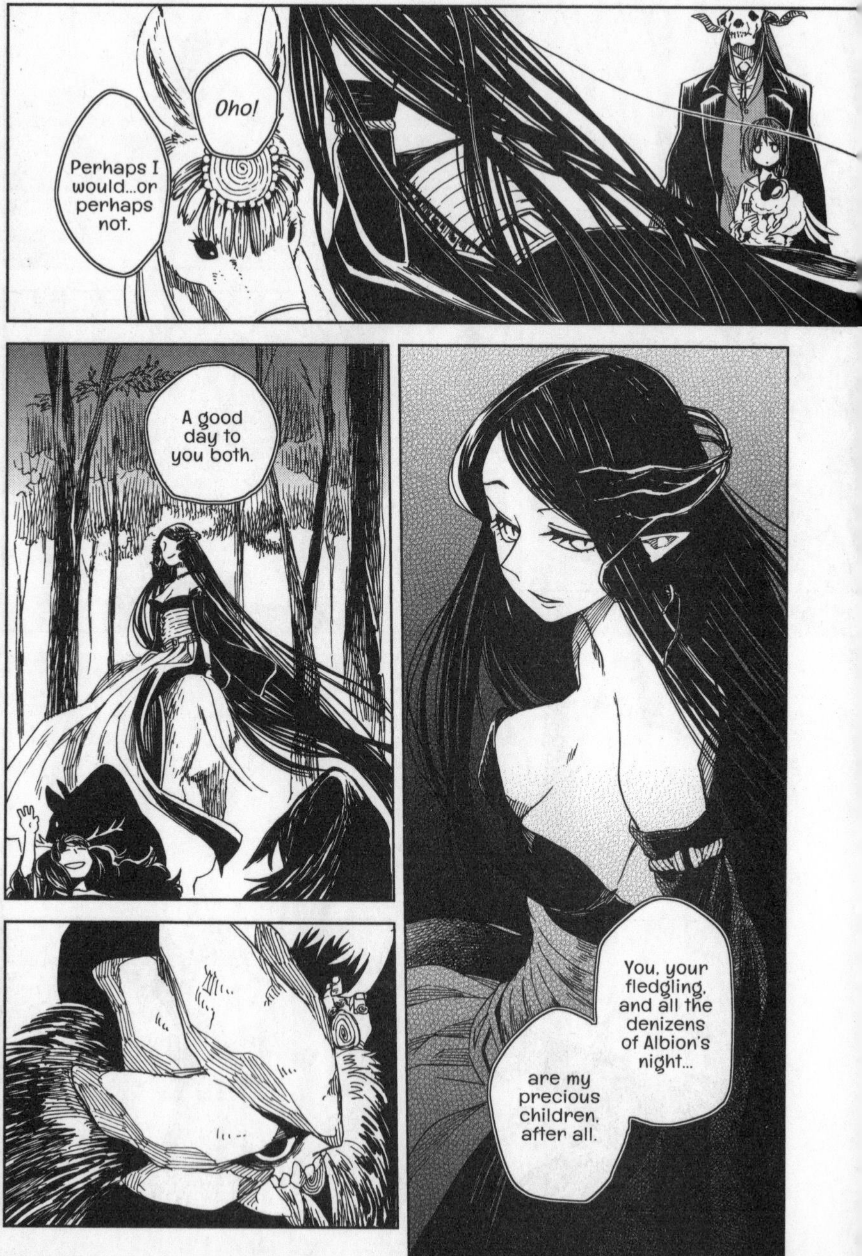
Oho!
Perhaps I would...or perhaps not.
You, your fledgling, and all the denizens of Albion's night...
are my precious children, after all.
A good day to you both.

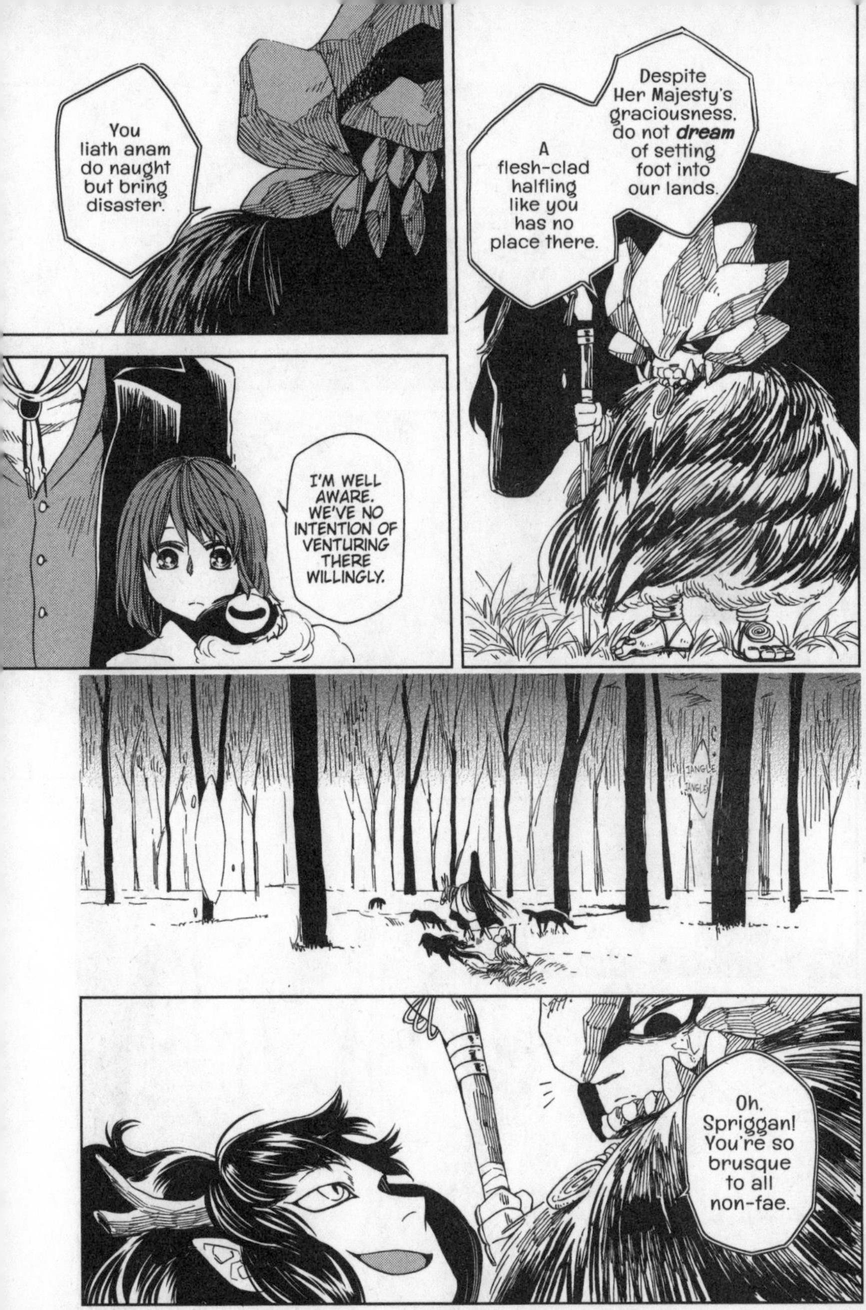
Despite Her Majesty's graciousness, do not **dream** of setting foot into our lands.
A flesh-clad halfling like you has no place there.
You liath anam do naught but bring disaster.
I'M WELL AWARE. WE'VE NO INTENTION OF VENTURING THERE WILLINGLY.
JANGLE
JANGLE
Oh, Spriggan! You're so brusque to all non-fae.

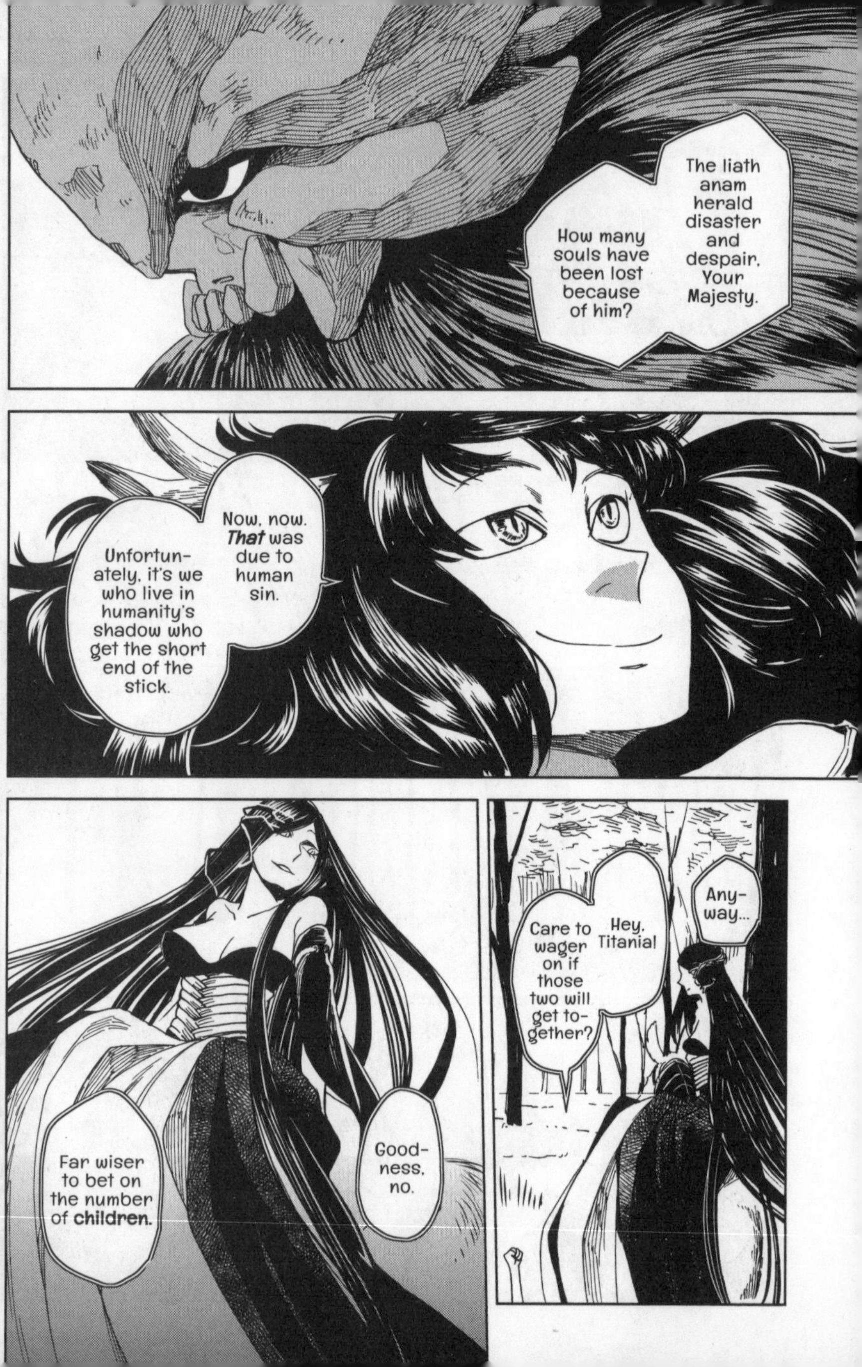
The liath anam herald disaster and despair, Your Majesty.
How many souls have been lost because of him?
Now, now. *That* was due to human sin.
Unfortunately, it's we who live in humanity's shadow who get the short end of the stick.
Anyway...
Hey, Titania!
Care to wager on if those two will get together?
Goodness, no.
Far wiser to bet on the number of **children.**

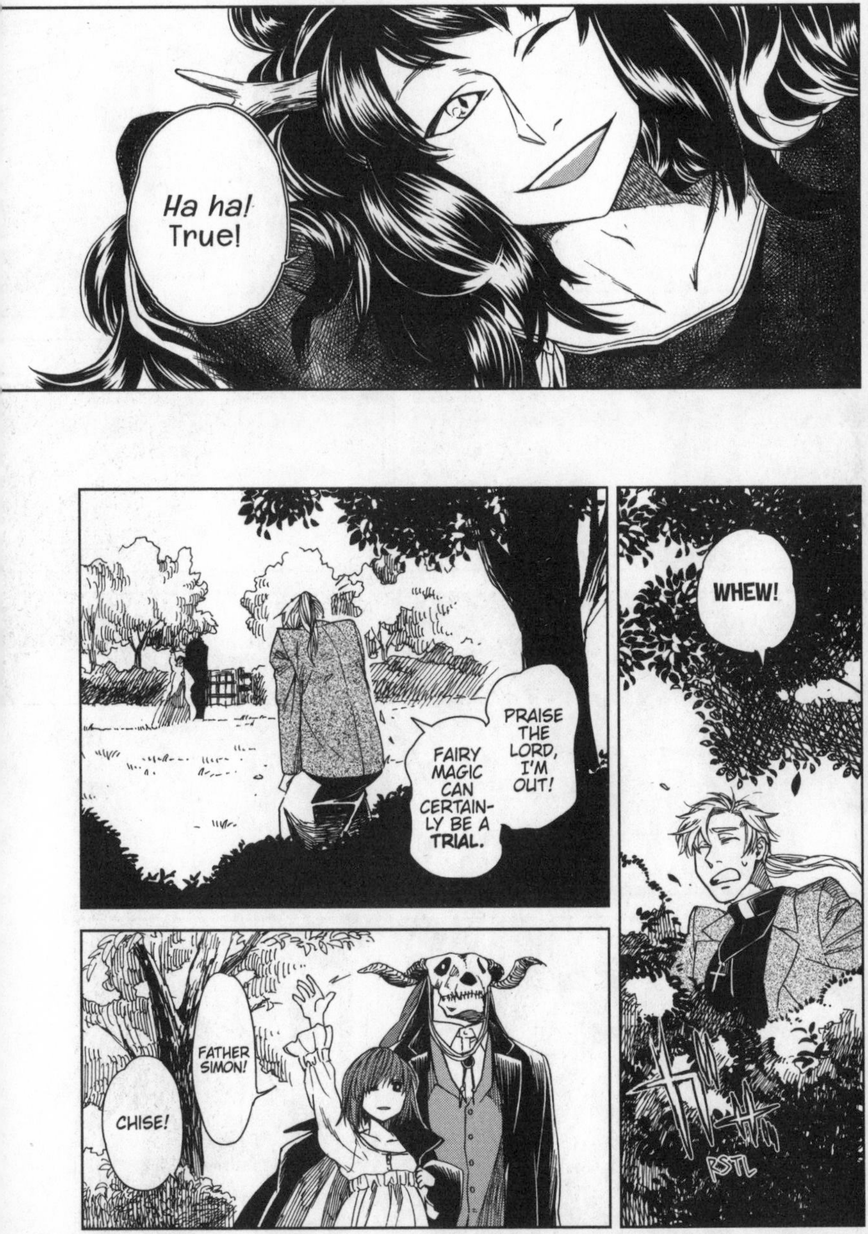
Ha ha! True!
WHEW!
RSTL
PRAISE THE LORD, I'M OUT!
FAIRY MAGIC CAN CERTAINLY BE A TRIAL.
FATHER SIMON!
CHISE!

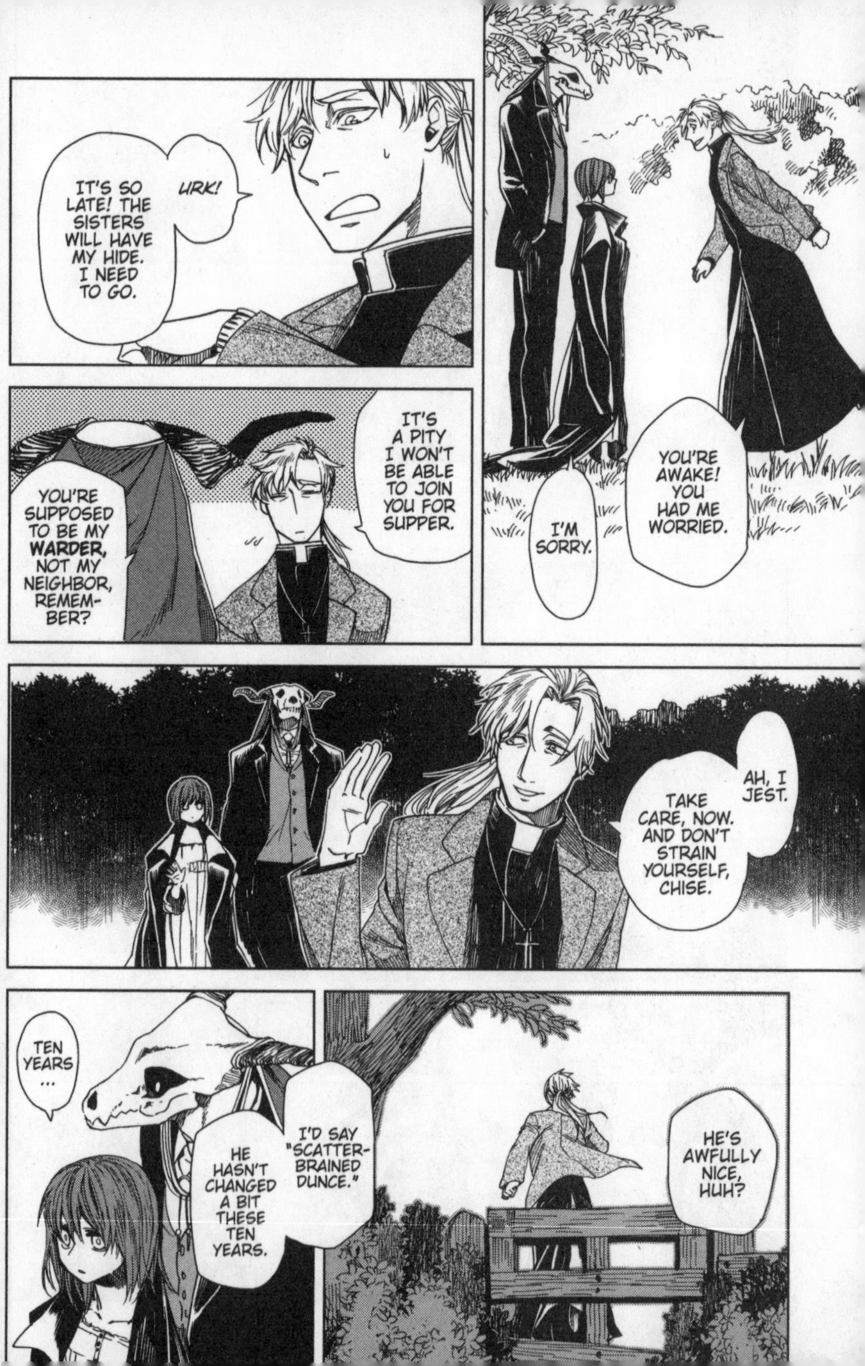
YOU'RE AWAKE! YOU HAD ME WORRIED.
I'M SORRY.
URK!
IT'S SO LATE! THE SISTERS WILL HAVE MY HIDE. I NEED TO GO.
IT'S A PITY I WON'T BE ABLE TO JOIN YOU FOR SUPPER.
YOU'RE SUPPOSED TO BE MY **WARDER,** NOT MY NEIGHBOR, REMEMBER?
AH, I JEST.
TAKE CARE, NOW. AND DON'T STRAIN YOURSELF, CHISE.
HE'S AWFULLY NICE, HUH?
I'D SAY "SCATTER-BRAINED DUNCE."
HE HASN'T CHANGED A BIT THESE TEN YEARS.
TEN YEARS...

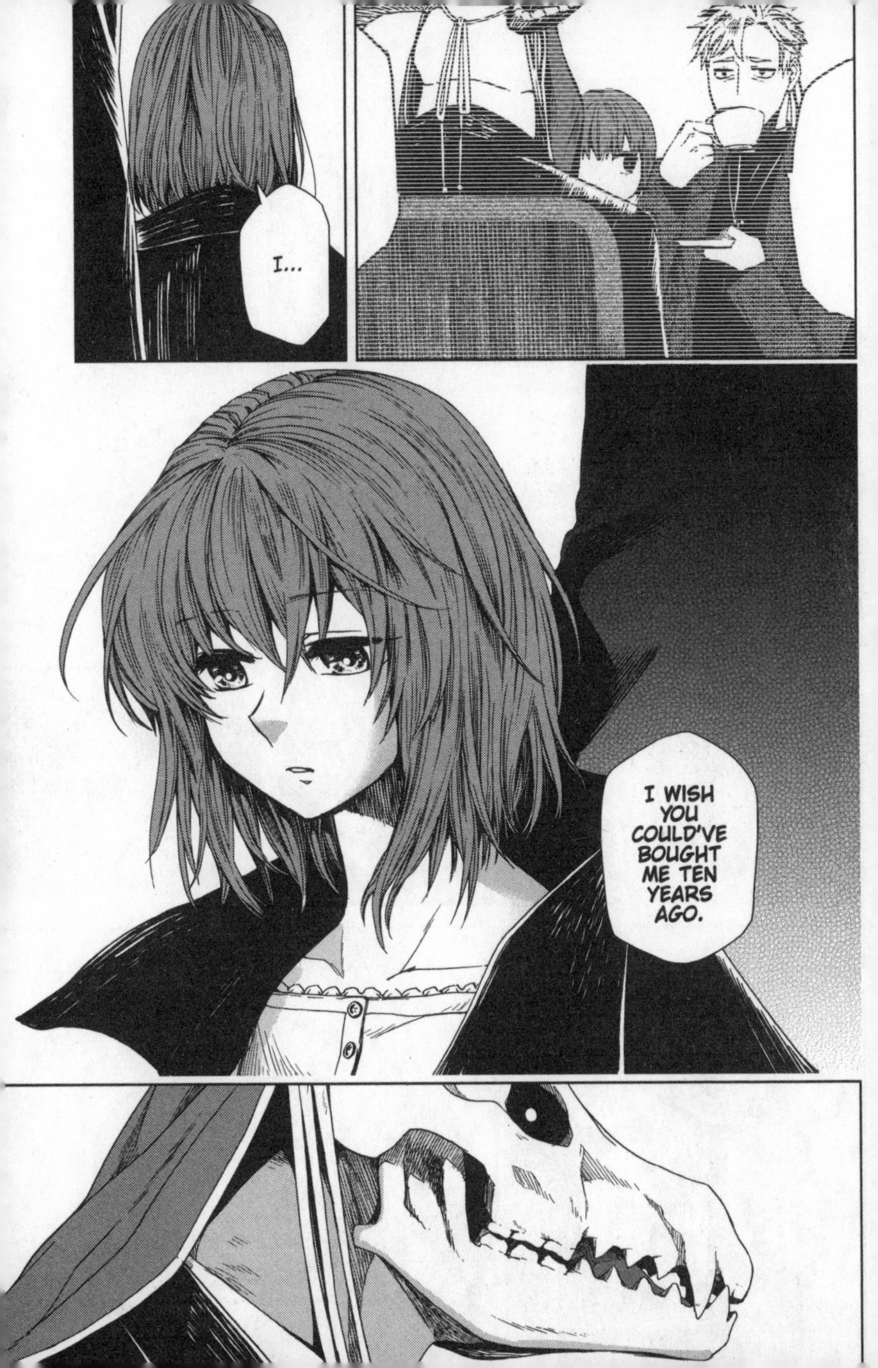
I...
I WISH YOU COULD'VE BOUGHT ME TEN YEARS AGO.

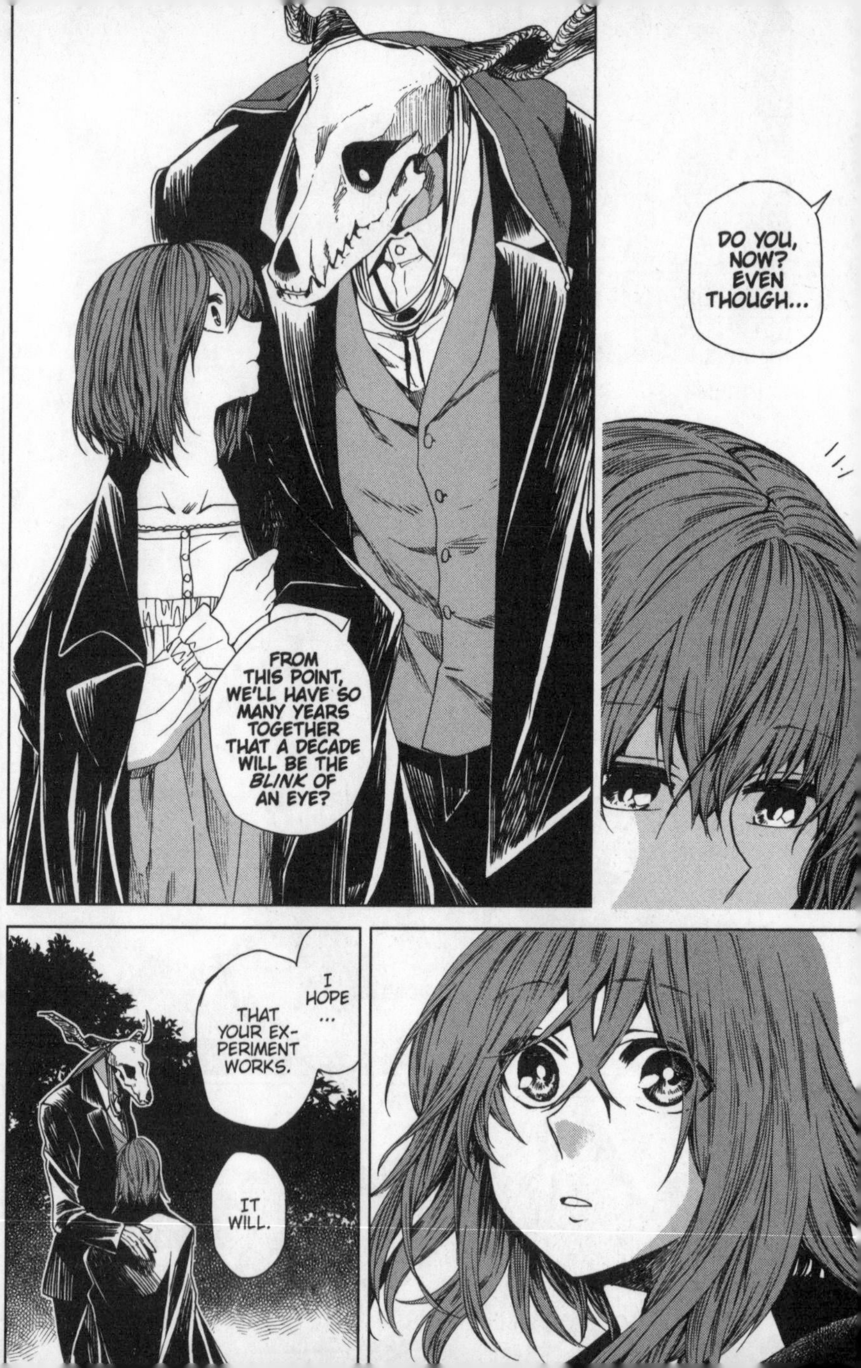

DO YOU, NOW? EVEN THOUGH...
FROM THIS POINT, WE'LL HAVE SO MANY YEARS TOGETHER THAT A DECADE WILL BE THE *BLINK* OF AN EYE?
I HOPE...
THAT YOUR EX-PERIMENT WORKS.
IT WILL.

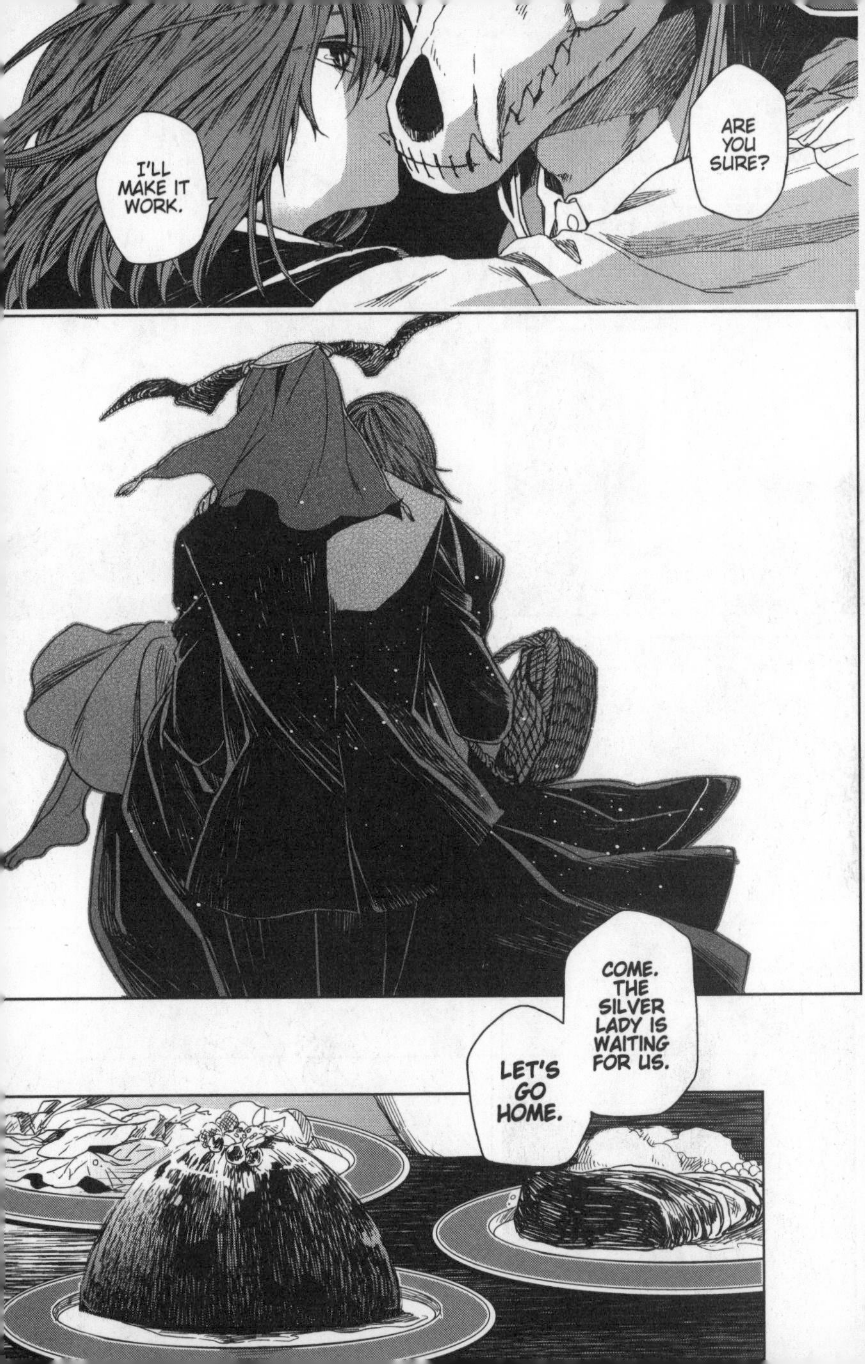
ARE YOU SURE?
I'LL MAKE IT WORK.
COME. THE SILVER LADY IS WAITING FOR US.
LET'S GO HOME.

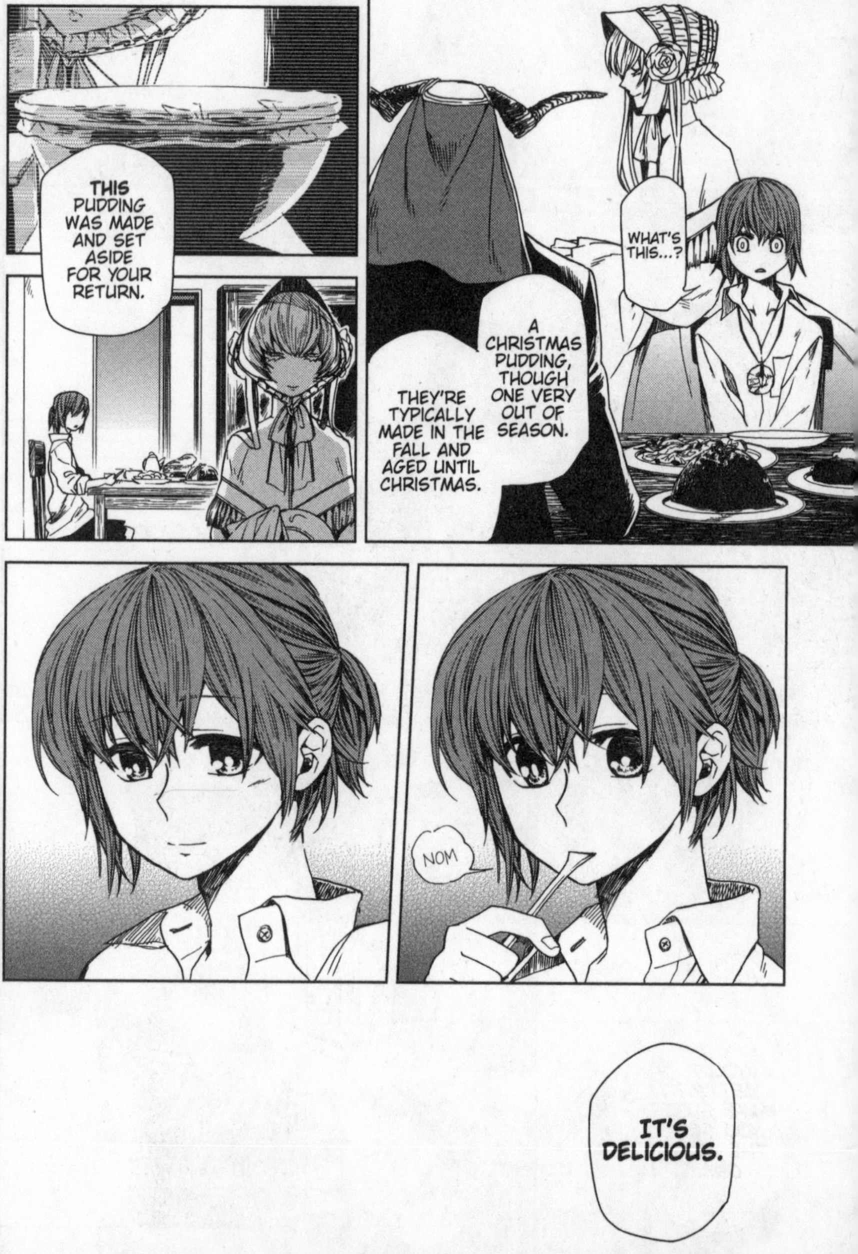
WHAT'S THIS...?
A CHRISTMAS PUDDING, THOUGH ONE VERY OUT OF SEASON.
THEY'RE TYPICALLY MADE IN THE FALL AND AGED UNTIL CHRISTMAS.
THIS PUDDING WAS MADE AND SET ASIDE FOR YOUR RETURN.
NOM
IT'S DELICIOUS.

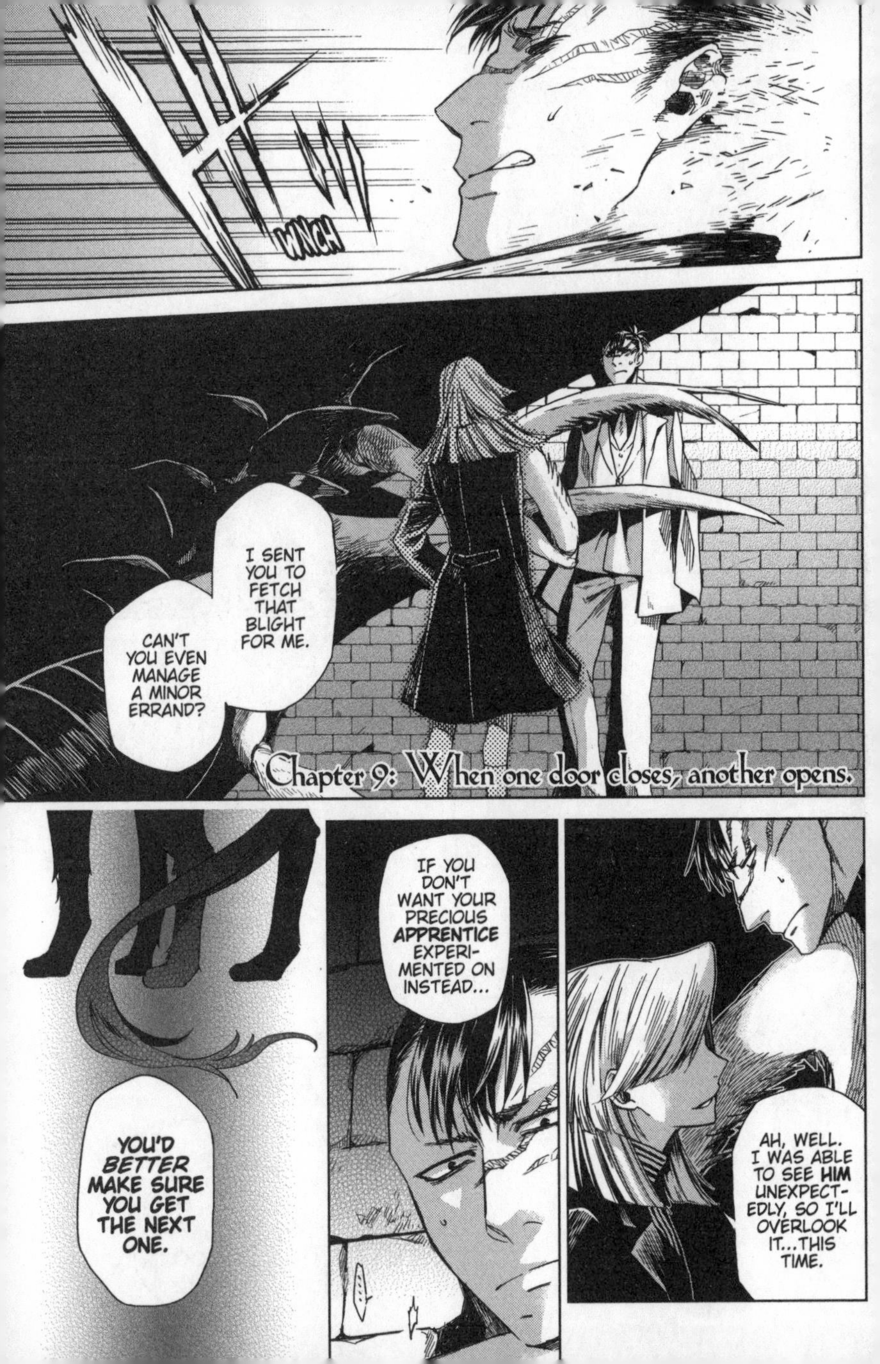
WINCH
I SENT YOU TO FETCH THAT BLIGHT FOR ME.
CAN'T YOU EVEN MANAGE A MINOR ERRAND?
Chapter 9: When one door closes, another opens.
AH, WELL. I WAS ABLE TO SEE **HIM** UNEXPECTEDLY, SO I'LL OVERLOOK IT...THIS TIME.
IF YOU DON'T WANT YOUR PRECIOUS **APPRENTICE** EXPERIMENTED ON INSTEAD...
...
YOU'D *BETTER* MAKE SURE YOU GET THE NEXT ONE.

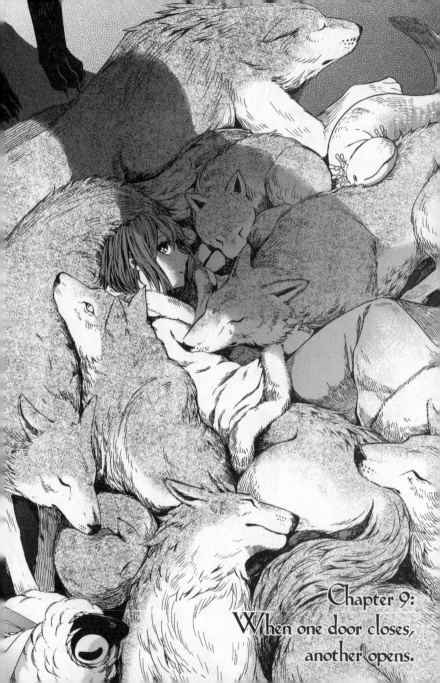

Chapter 9:
When one door closes,
another opens.

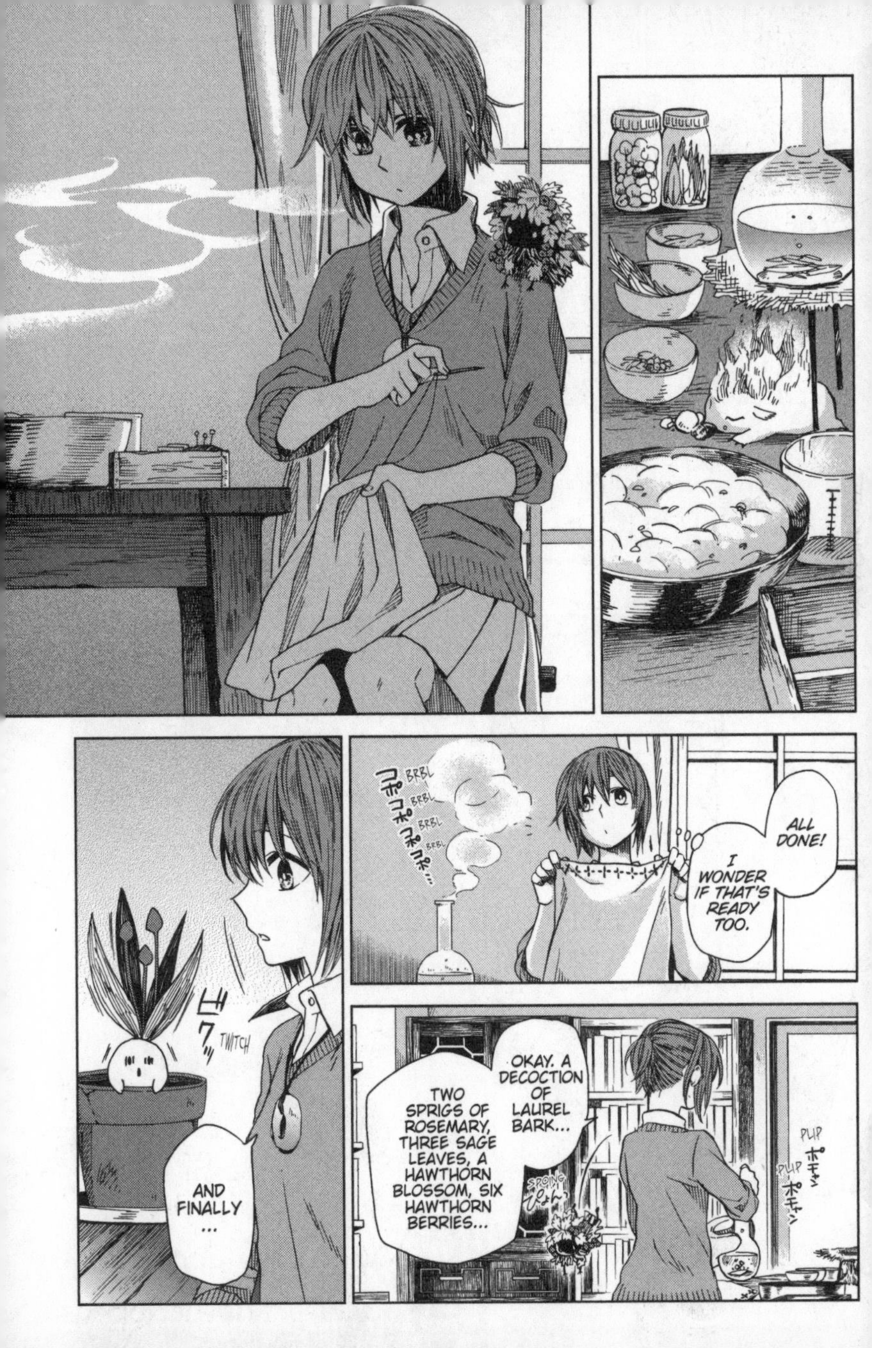
ALL DONE!
I WONDER IF THAT'S READY TOO.
BRBL BRBL BRBL BRBL
PLIP PLIP
OKAY. A DECOCTION OF LAUREL BARK...
TWO SPRIGS OF ROSEMARY, THREE SAGE LEAVES, A HAWTHORN BLOSSOM, SIX HAWTHORN BERRIES...
SPOING
TWITCH
AND FINALLY ...

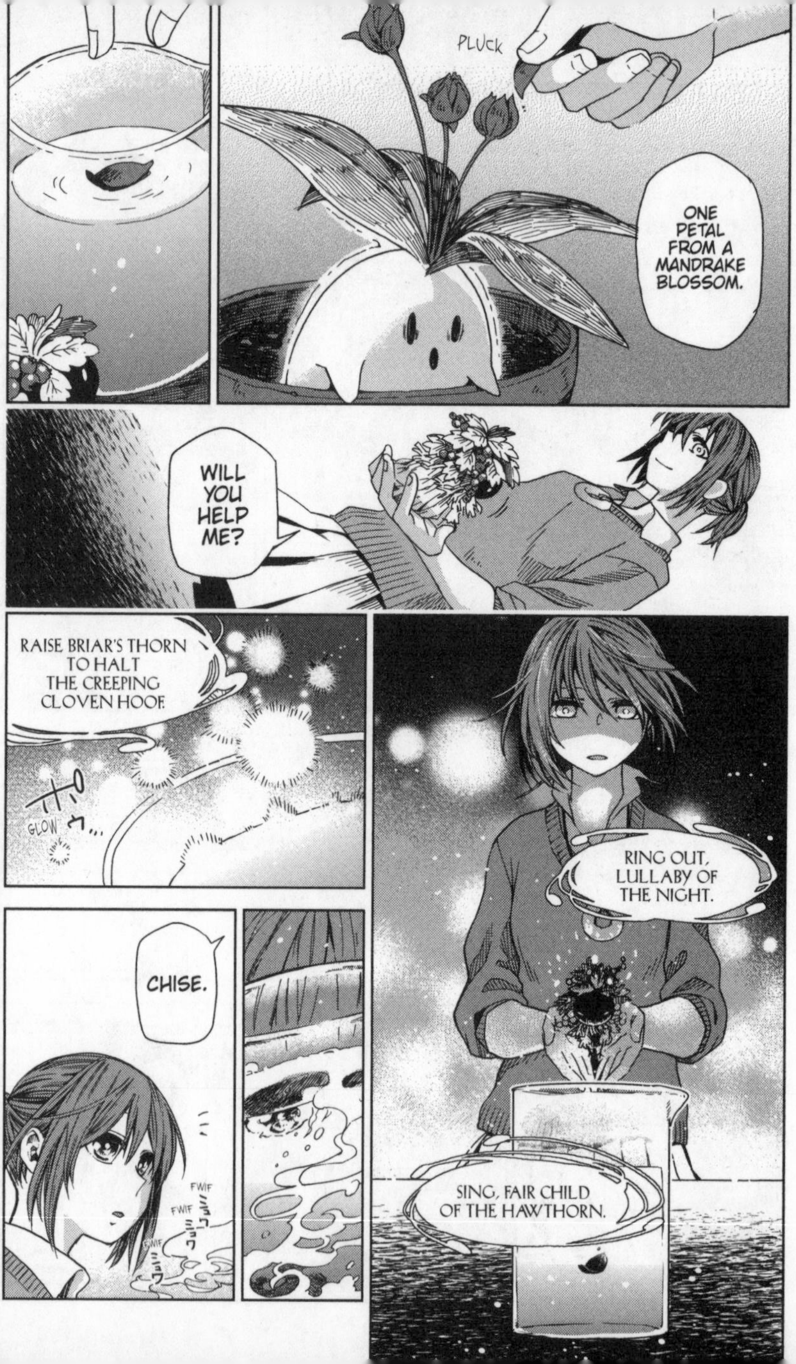
PLUCK
ONE PETAL FROM A MANDRAKE BLOSSOM.
WILL YOU HELP ME?
RING OUT, LULLABY OF THE NIGHT.
SING, FAIR CHILD OF THE HAWTHORN.
RAISE BRIAR'S THORN TO HALT THE CREEPING CLOVEN HOOF.
GLOW
CHISE.
FWIF
FWIF
FWIF

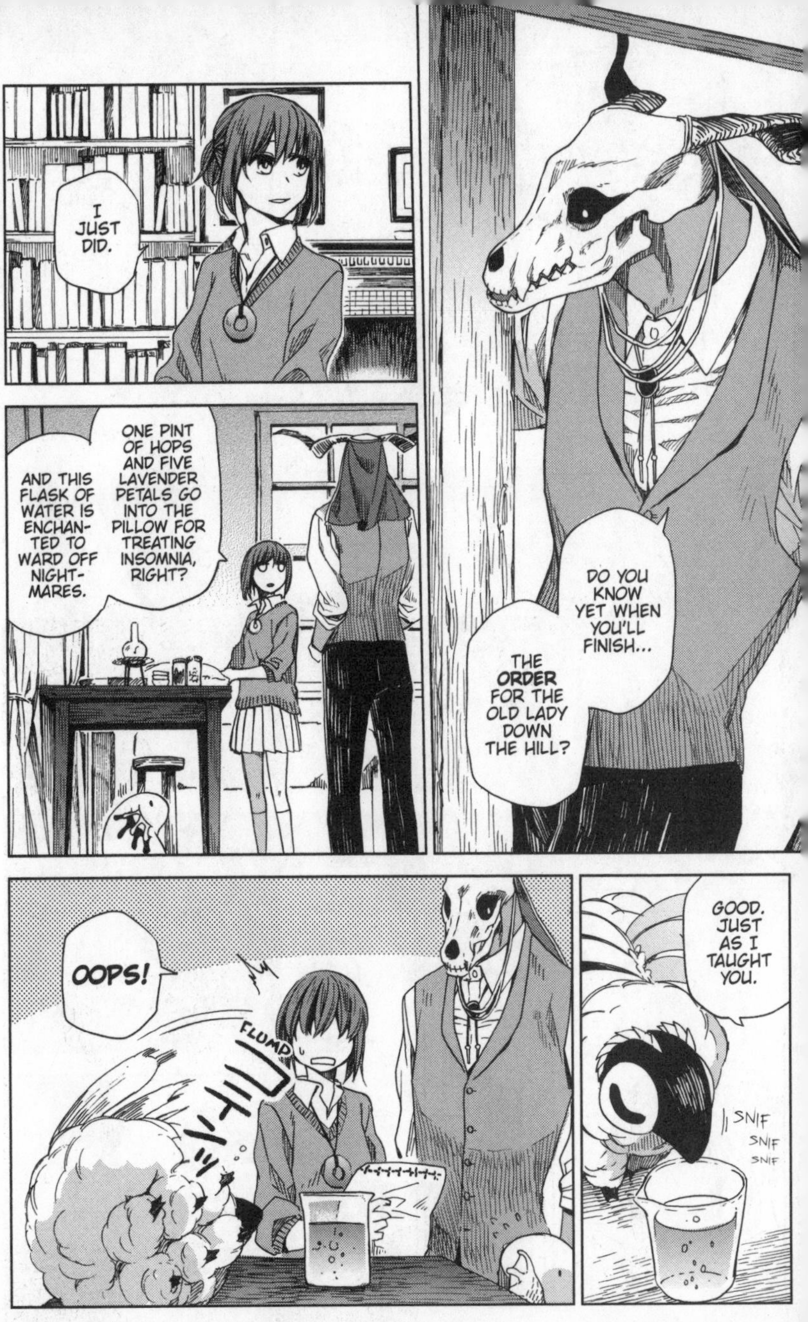
DO YOU KNOW YET WHEN YOU'LL FINISH...
THE **ORDER** FOR THE OLD LADY DOWN THE HILL?
I JUST DID.
ONE PINT OF HOPS AND FIVE LAVENDER PETALS GO INTO THE PILLOW FOR TREATING INSOMNIA, RIGHT?
AND THIS FLASK OF WATER IS ENCHANTED TO WARD OFF NIGHTMARES.
GOOD. JUST AS I TAUGHT YOU.
SNIF
SNIF
SNIF
OOPS!
FLUMP

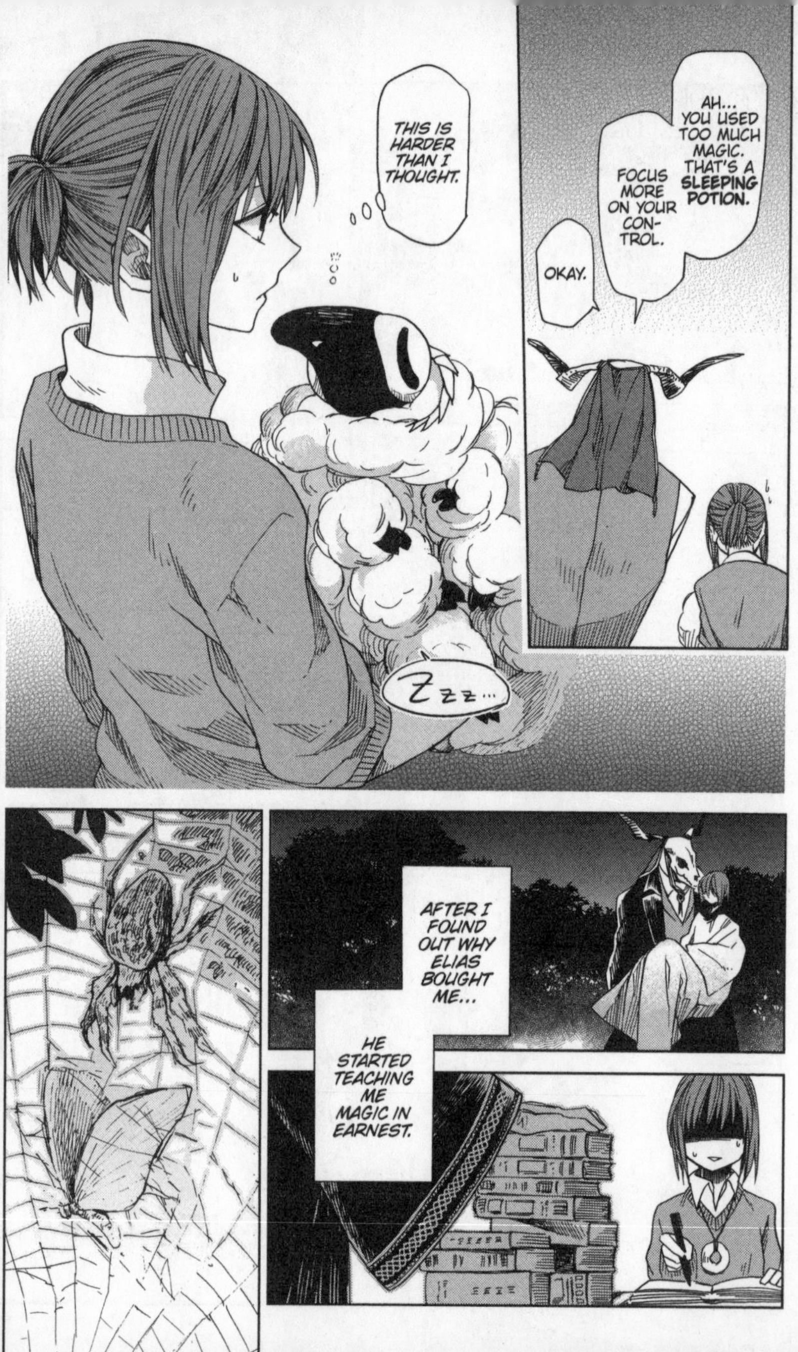
AH... YOU USED TOO MUCH MAGIC. THAT'S A SLEEPING POTION.
FOCUS MORE ON YOUR CONTROL.
OKAY.
THIS IS HARDER THAN I THOUGHT.
Zzz...
AFTER I FOUND OUT WHY ELIAS BOUGHT ME...
HE STARTED TEACHING ME MAGIC IN EARNEST.

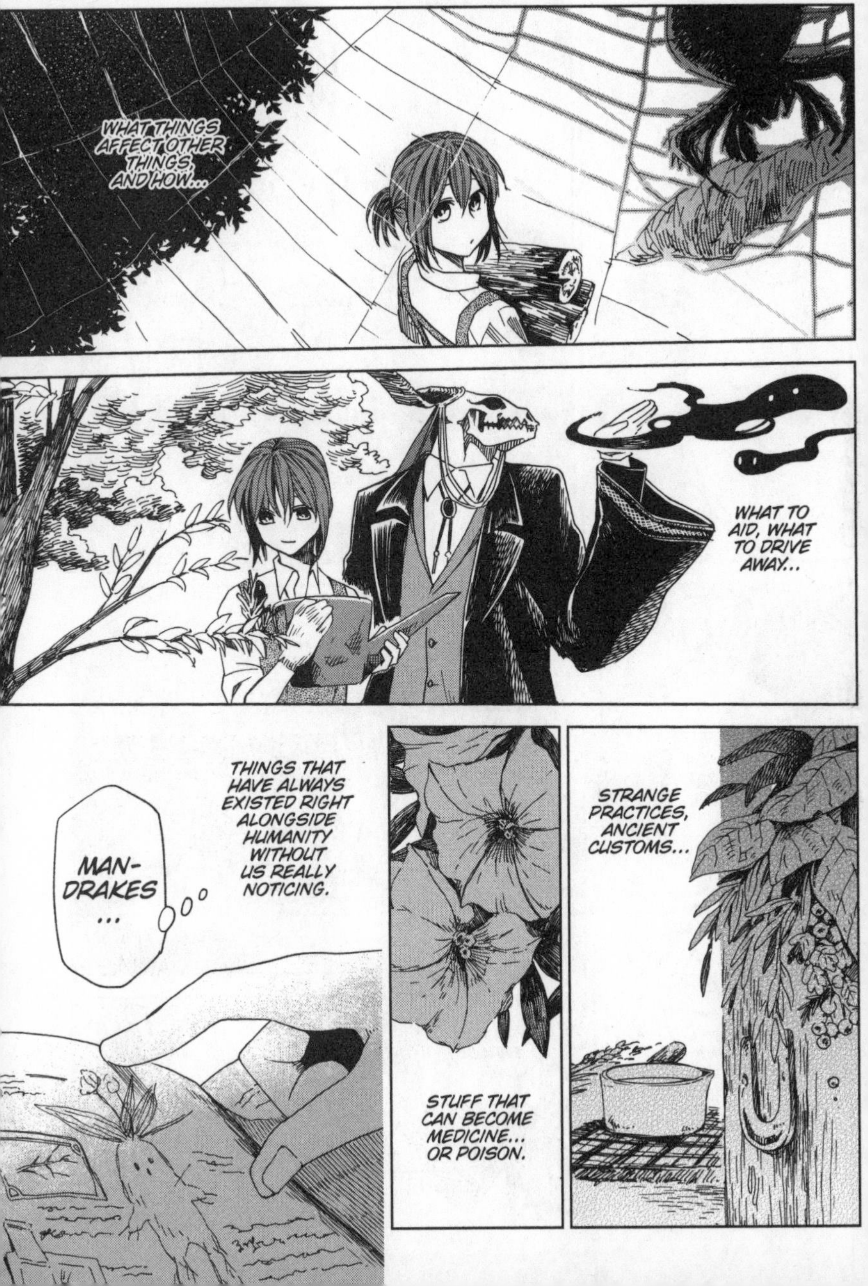
WHAT THINGS AFFECT OTHER THINGS, AND HOW...
WHAT TO AID, WHAT TO DRIVE AWAY...
STRANGE PRACTICES, ANCIENT CUSTOMS...
STUFF THAT CAN BECOME MEDICINE... OR POISON.
THINGS THAT HAVE ALWAYS EXISTED RIGHT ALONGSIDE HUMANITY WITHOUT US REALLY NOTICING.
MAN-DRAKES...

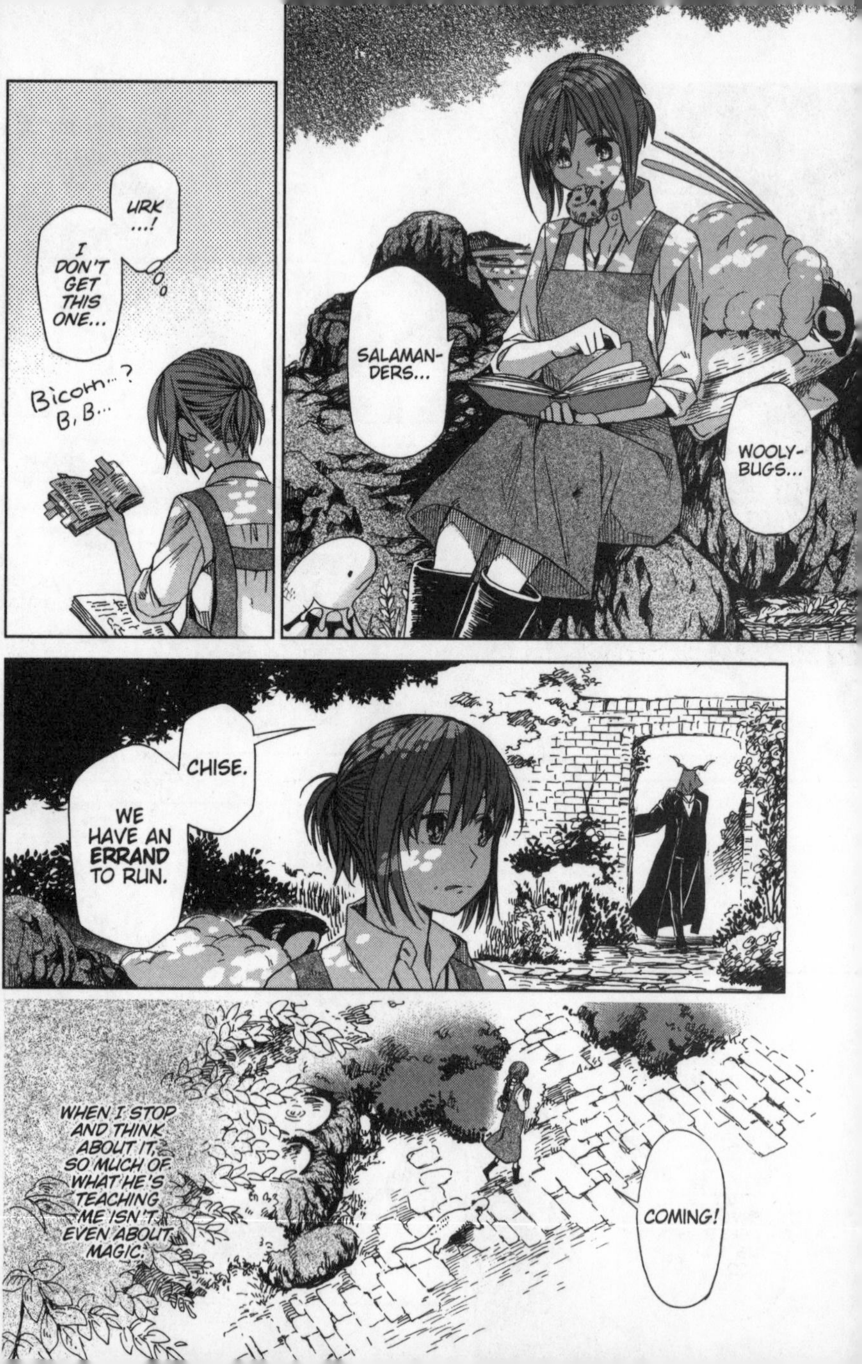
SALAMANDERS...
WOOLY-BUGS...
URK ...! I DON'T GET THIS ONE...
Bicorn...? B, B...
CHISE.
WE HAVE AN ERRAND TO RUN.
COMING!
WHEN I STOP AND THINK ABOUT IT, SO MUCH OF WHAT HE'S TEACHING ME ISN'T EVEN ABOUT MAGIC.

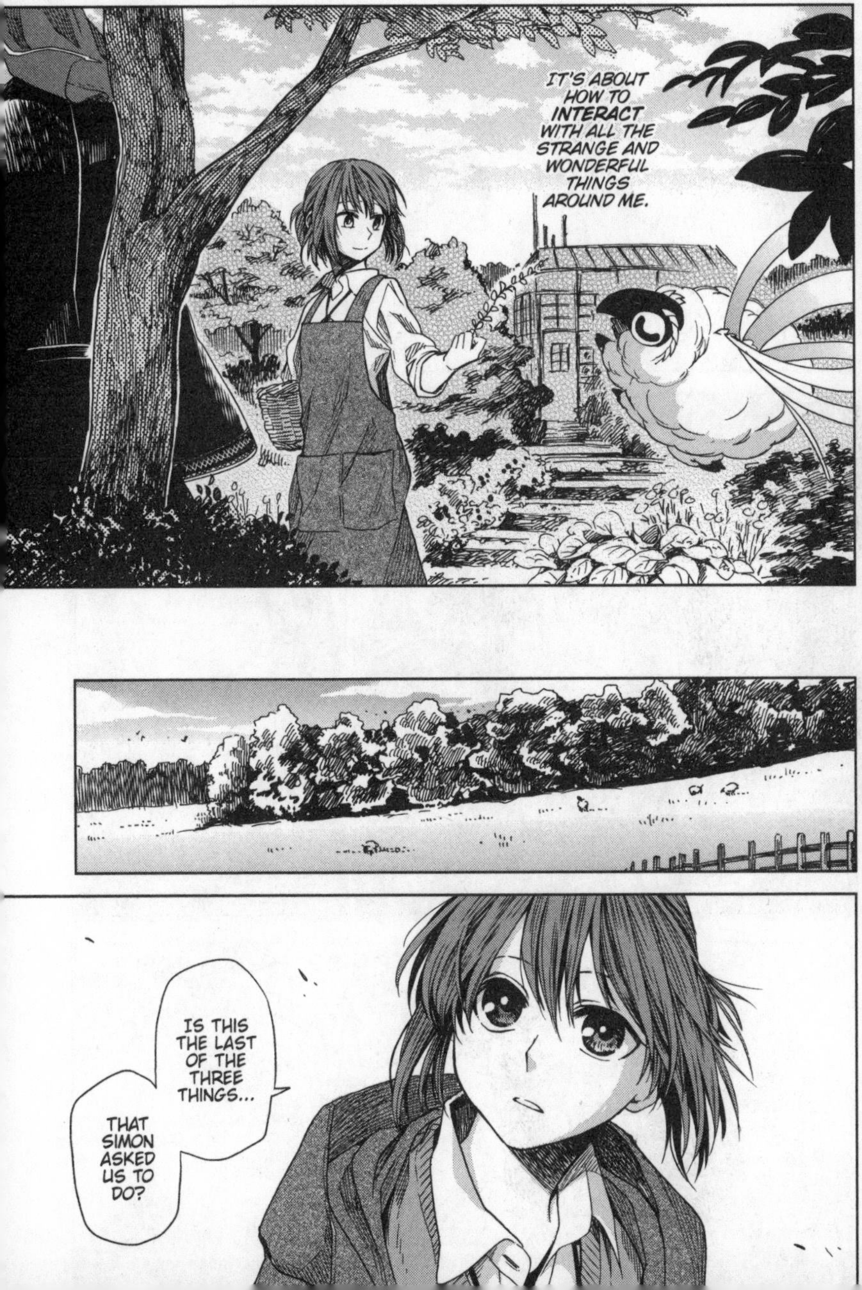
IT'S ABOUT HOW TO INTERACT WITH ALL THE STRANGE AND WONDERFUL THINGS AROUND ME.
IS THIS THE LAST OF THE THREE THINGS...
THAT SIMON ASKED US TO DO?

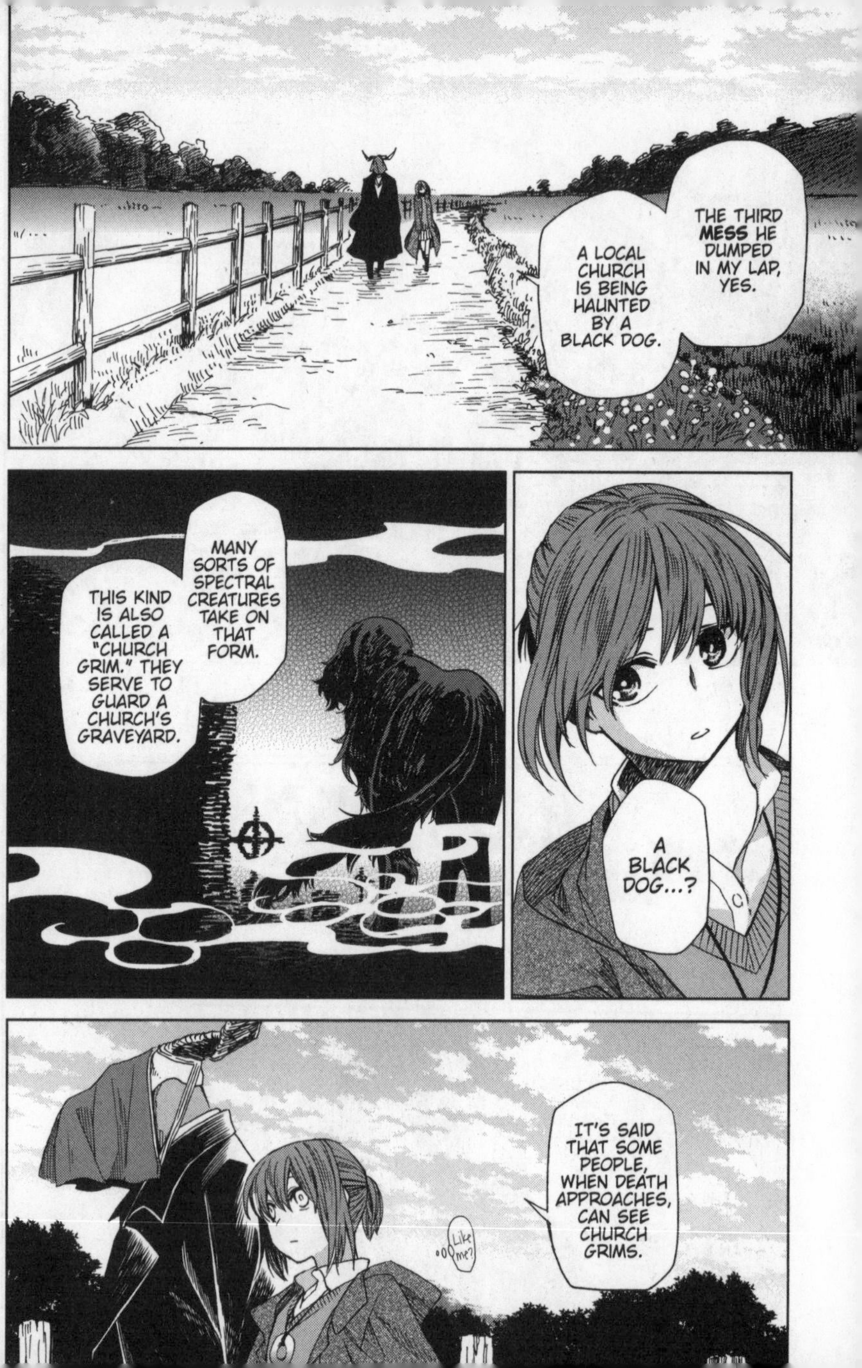
THE THIRD MESS HE DUMPED IN MY LAP, YES.
A LOCAL CHURCH IS BEING HAUNTED BY A BLACK DOG.
A BLACK DOG...?
MANY SORTS OF SPECTRAL CREATURES TAKE ON THAT FORM.
THIS KIND IS ALSO CALLED A "CHURCH GRIM." THEY SERVE TO GUARD A CHURCH'S GRAVEYARD.
IT'S SAID THAT SOME PEOPLE, WHEN DEATH APPROACHES, CAN SEE CHURCH GRIMS.
Like me?

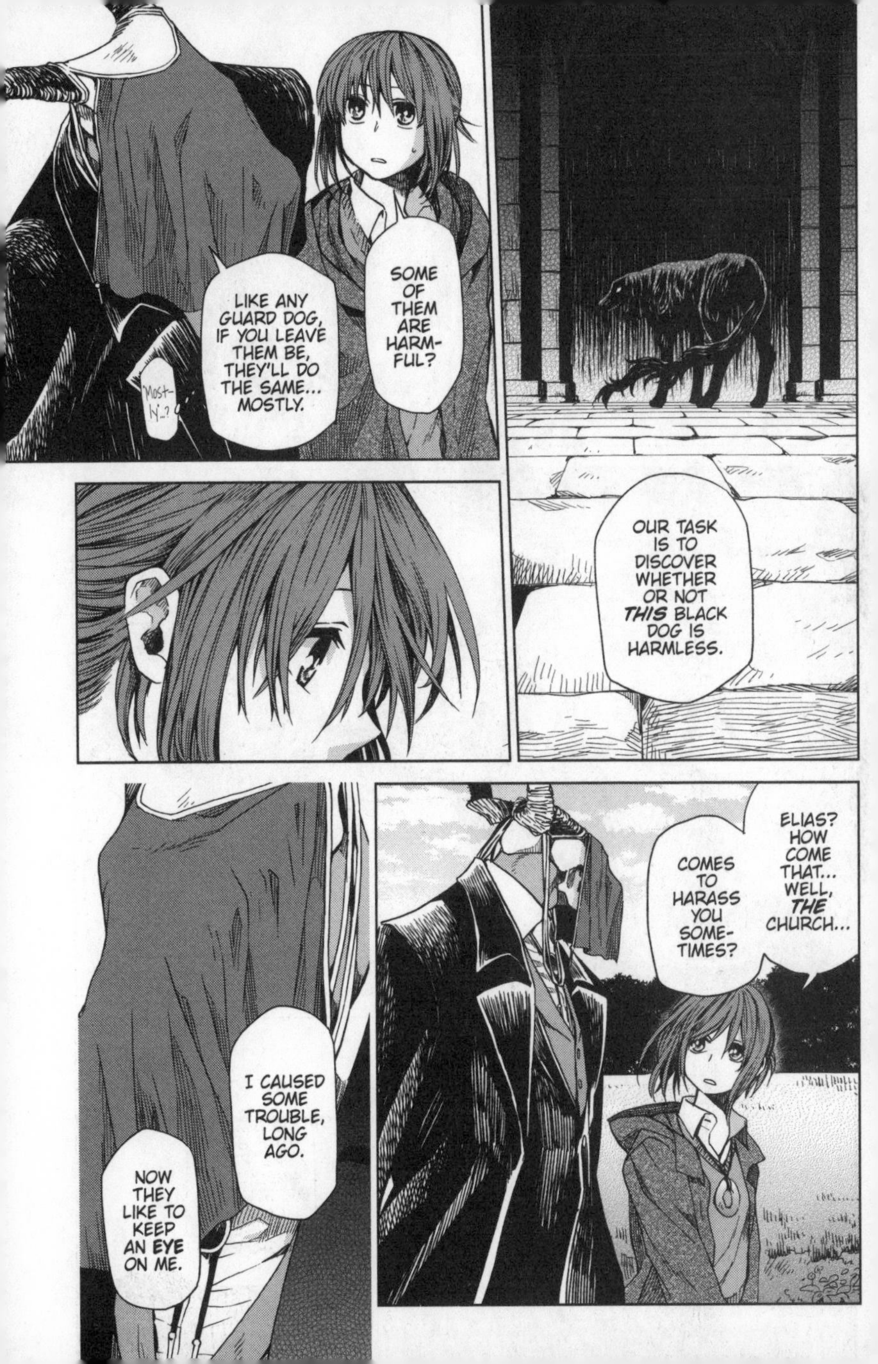
OUR TASK IS TO DISCOVER WHETHER OR NOT *THIS* BLACK DOG IS HARMLESS.
SOME OF THEM ARE HARMFUL?
LIKE ANY GUARD DOG, IF YOU LEAVE THEM BE, THEY'LL DO THE SAME... MOSTLY.
Most-ly...?
ELIAS? HOW COME THAT... WELL, *THE* CHURCH...
COMES TO HARASS YOU SOMETIMES?
I CAUSED SOME TROUBLE, LONG AGO.
NOW THEY LIKE TO KEEP AN EYE ON ME.

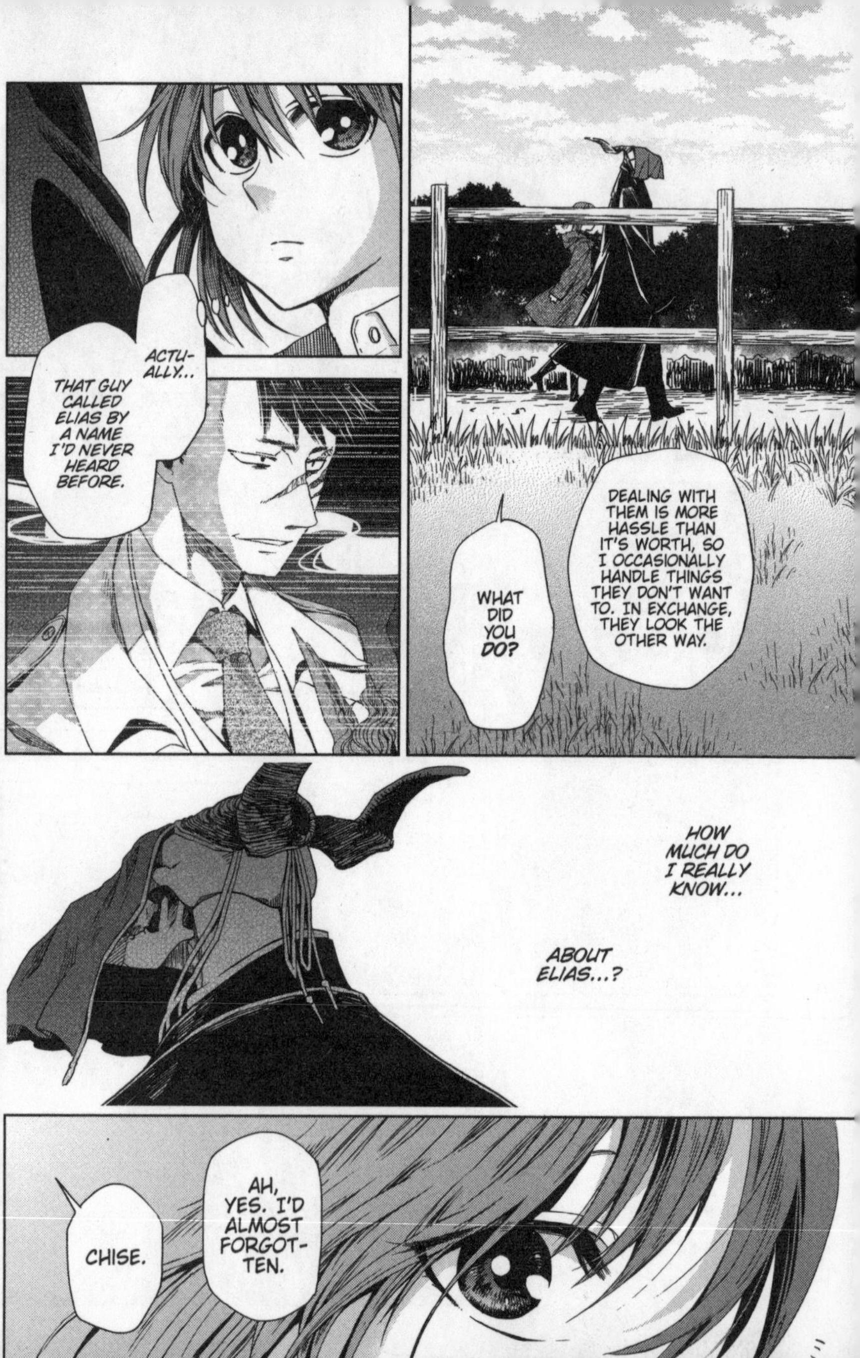
DEALING WITH THEM IS MORE HASSLE THAN IT'S WORTH, SO I OCCASIONALLY HANDLE THINGS THEY DON'T WANT TO. IN EXCHANGE, THEY LOOK THE OTHER WAY.
WHAT DID YOU *DO?*
ACTU-ALLY...
THAT GUY CALLED ELIAS BY A NAME I'D NEVER HEARD BEFORE.
HOW MUCH DO I REALLY KNOW...
ABOUT ELIAS...?
AH, YES. I'D ALMOST FORGOT-TEN.
CHISE.

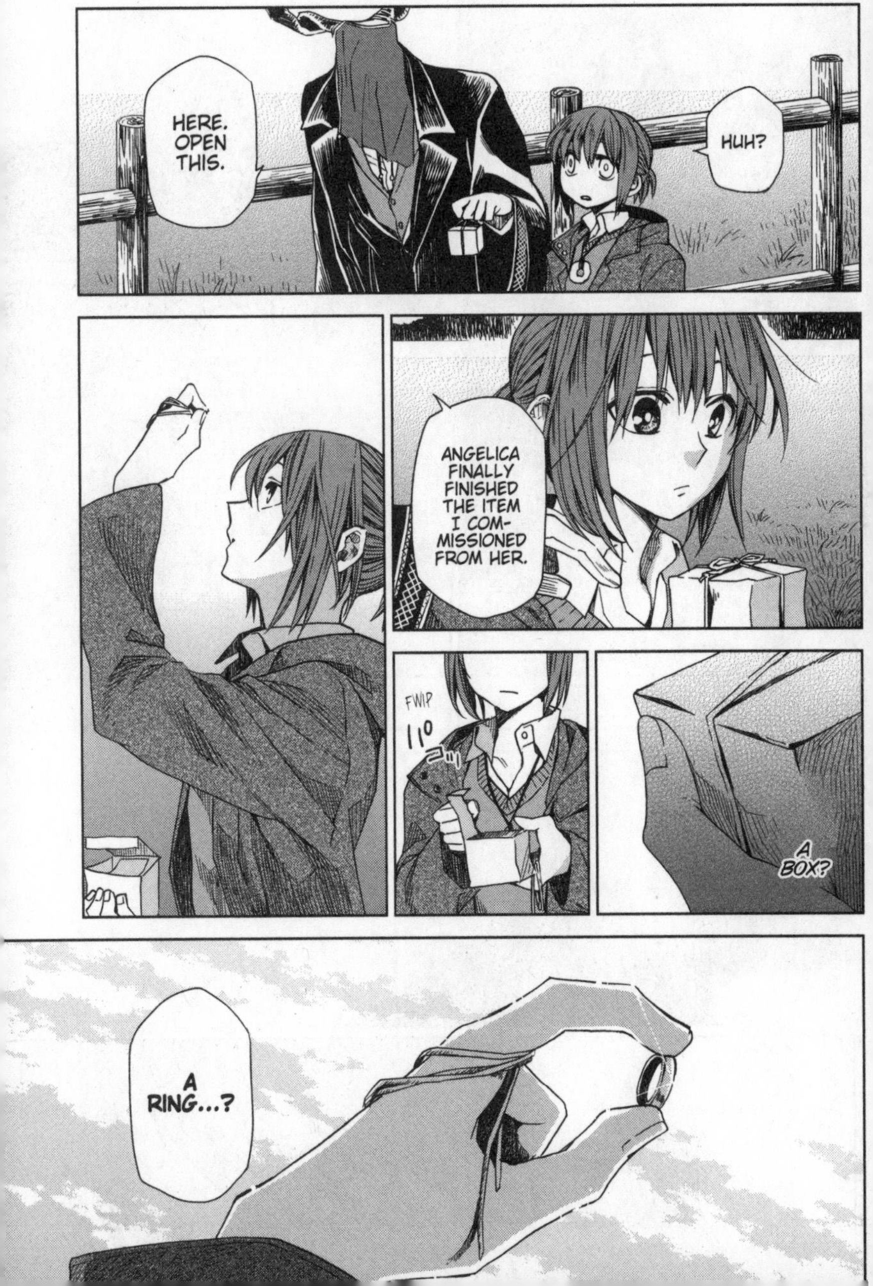
HUH?
HERE. OPEN THIS.
ANGELICA FINALLY FINISHED THE ITEM I COM- MISSIONED FROM HER.
A BOX?
FWIP
A RING...?

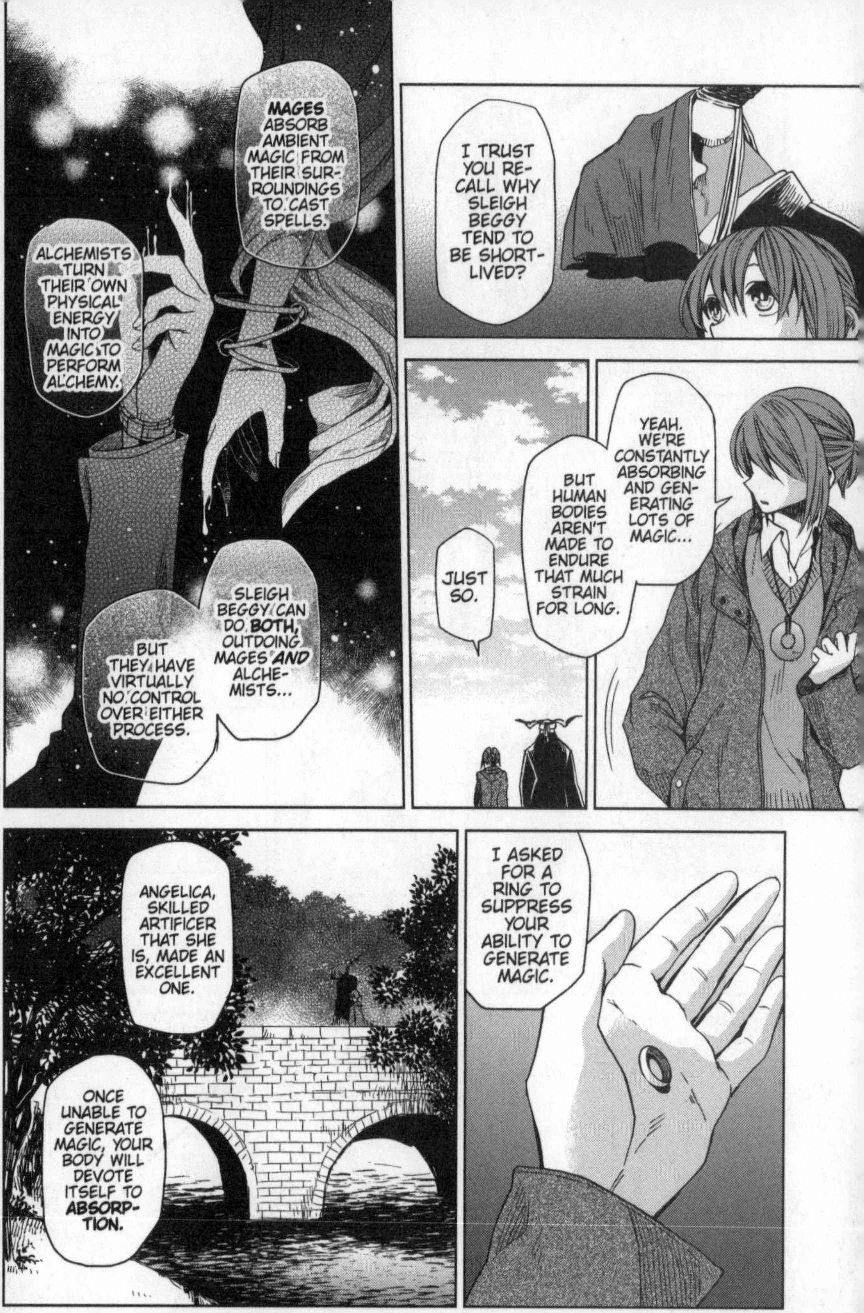
I TRUST YOU RECALL WHY SLEIGH BEGGY TEND TO BE SHORT-LIVED?
YEAH. WE'RE CONSTANTLY ABSORBING AND GENERATING LOTS OF MAGIC...
BUT HUMAN BODIES AREN'T MADE TO ENDURE THAT MUCH STRAIN FOR LONG.
JUST SO.
MAGES ABSORB AMBIENT MAGIC FROM THEIR SURROUNDINGS TO CAST SPELLS.
ALCHEMISTS TURN THEIR OWN PHYSICAL ENERGY INTO MAGIC TO PERFORM ALCHEMY.
SLEIGH BEGGY CAN DO BOTH, OUTDOING MAGES AND ALCHEMISTS...
BUT THEY HAVE VIRTUALLY NO CONTROL OVER EITHER PROCESS.
I ASKED FOR A RING TO SUPPRESS YOUR ABILITY TO GENERATE MAGIC.
ANGELICA, SKILLED ARTIFICER THAT SHE IS, MADE AN EXCELLENT ONE.
ONCE UNABLE TO GENERATE MAGIC, YOUR BODY WILL DEVOTE ITSELF TO ABSORPTION.

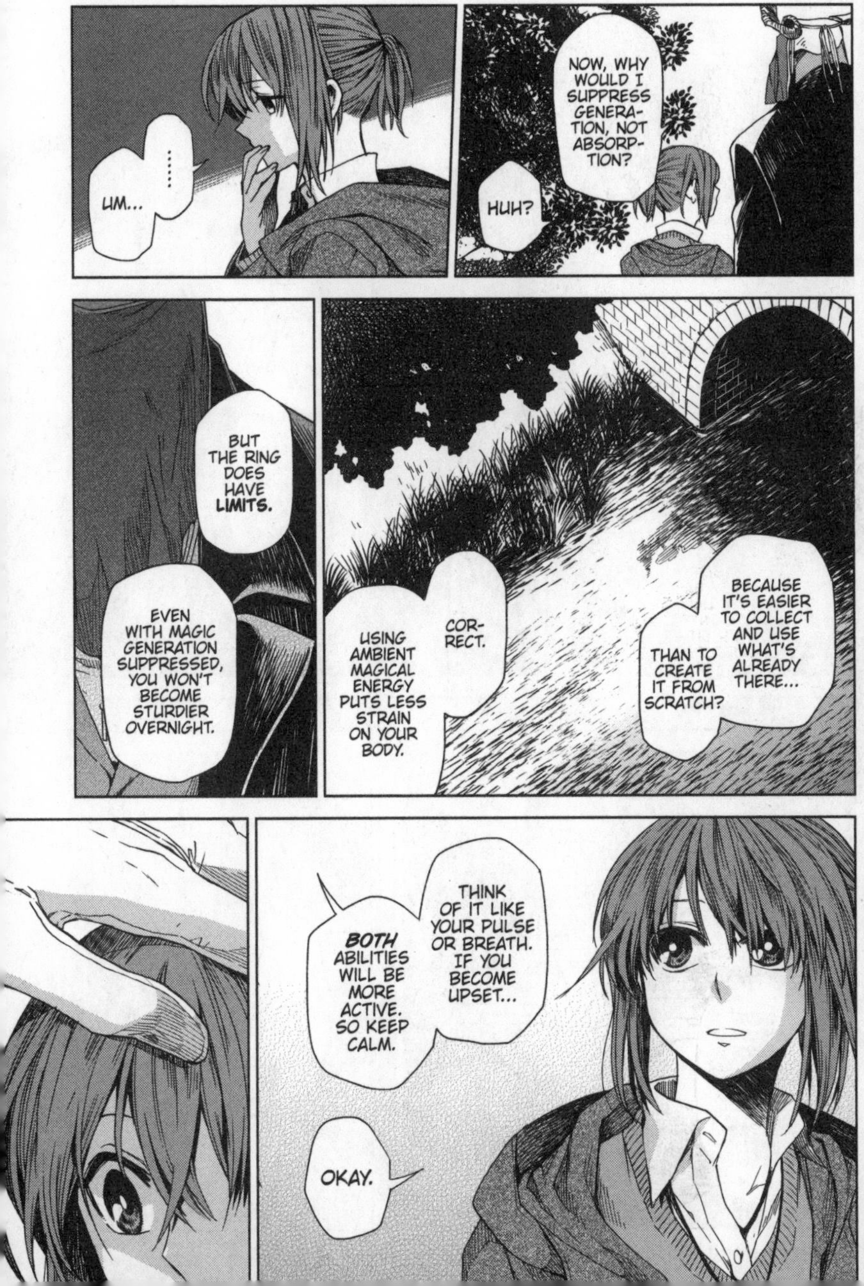
NOW, WHY WOULD I SUPPRESS GENERATION, NOT ABSORPTION?
HUH?
......
UM...
BECAUSE IT'S EASIER TO COLLECT AND USE WHAT'S ALREADY THERE...
THAN TO CREATE IT FROM SCRATCH?
CORRECT.
USING AMBIENT MAGICAL ENERGY PUTS LESS STRAIN ON YOUR BODY.
BUT THE RING DOES HAVE **LIMITS.**
EVEN WITH MAGIC GENERATION SUPPRESSED, YOU WON'T BECOME STURDIER OVERNIGHT.
THINK OF IT LIKE YOUR PULSE OR BREATH. IF YOU BECOME UPSET...
BOTH ABILITIES WILL BE MORE ACTIVE. SO KEEP CALM.
OKAY.

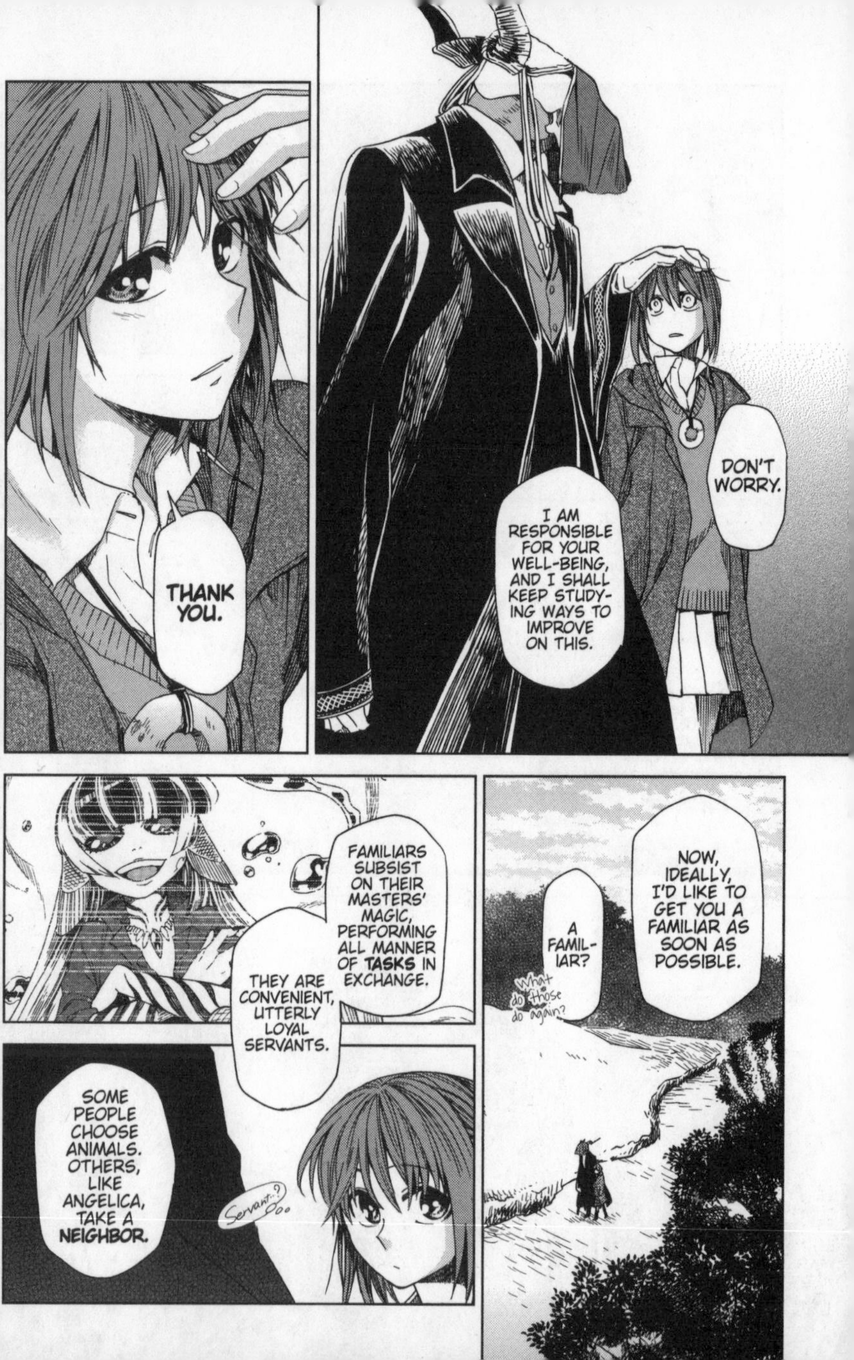
DON'T WORRY.
I AM RESPONSIBLE FOR YOUR WELL-BEING, AND I SHALL KEEP STUDYING WAYS TO IMPROVE ON THIS.
THANK YOU.
NOW, IDEALLY, I'D LIKE TO GET YOU A FAMILIAR AS SOON AS POSSIBLE.
A FAMILIAR?
What do those do again?
FAMILIARS SUBSIST ON THEIR MASTERS' MAGIC, PERFORMING ALL MANNER OF TASKS IN EXCHANGE.
THEY ARE CONVENIENT, UTTERLY LOYAL SERVANTS.
SOME PEOPLE CHOOSE ANIMALS. OTHERS, LIKE ANGELICA, TAKE A NEIGHBOR.
Servant...?

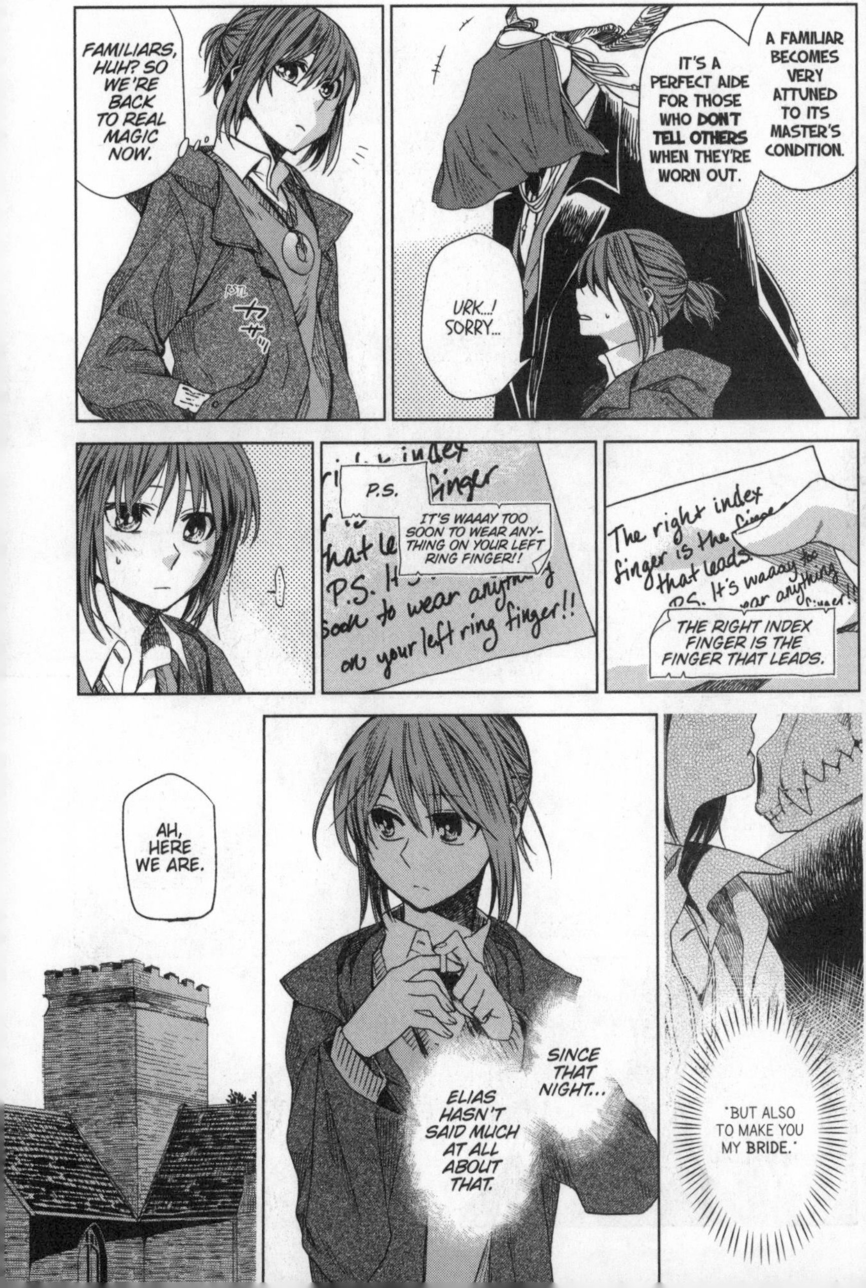
A FAMILIAR BECOMES VERY ATTUNED TO ITS MASTER'S CONDITION.
IT'S A PERFECT AIDE FOR THOSE WHO DON'T TELL OTHERS WHEN THEY'RE WORN OUT.
URK...! SORRY...
FAMILIARS, HUH? SO WE'RE BACK TO REAL MAGIC NOW.
THE RIGHT INDEX FINGER IS THE FINGER THAT LEADS.
P.S.
IT'S WAAAY TOO SOON TO WEAR ANYTHING ON YOUR LEFT RING FINGER!!
...
"BUT ALSO TO MAKE YOU MY BRIDE."
SINCE THAT NIGHT...
ELIAS HASN'T SAID MUCH AT ALL ABOUT THAT.
AH, HERE WE ARE.

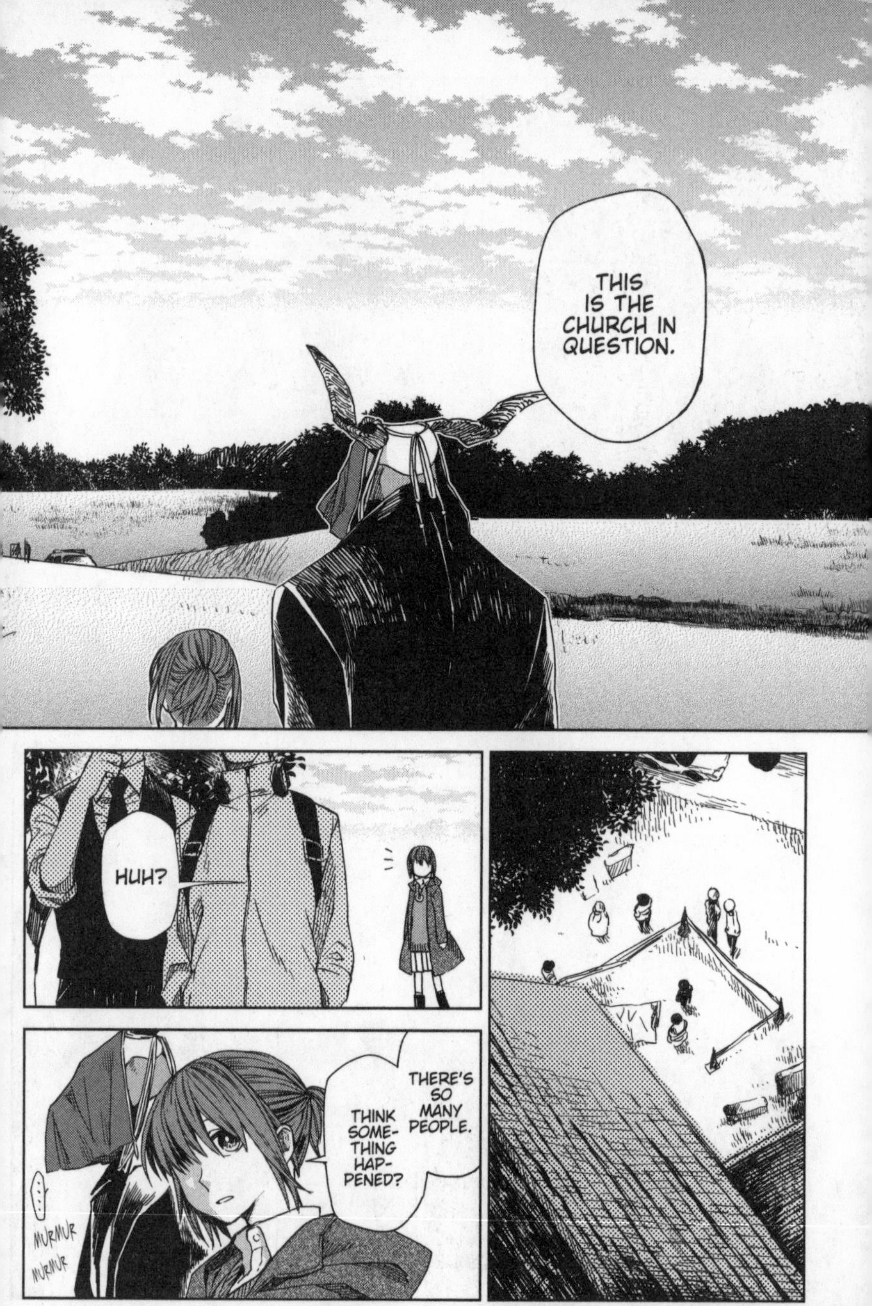
THIS IS THE CHURCH IN QUESTION.
HUH?
THERE'S SO MANY PEOPLE.
THINK SOMETHING HAPPENED?
...!
MURMUR
MURMUR

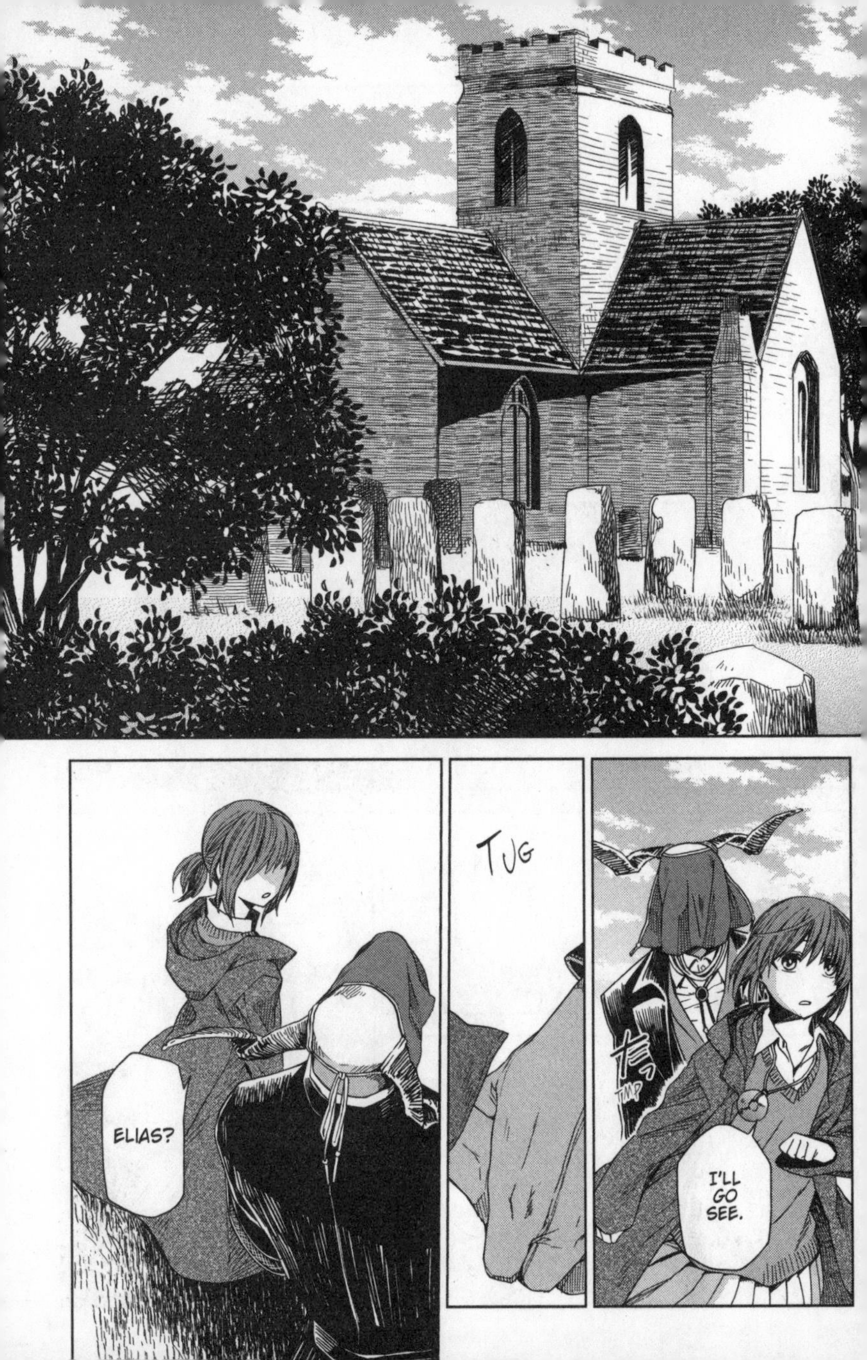
TMP
I'LL GO SEE.
TUG
ELIAS?

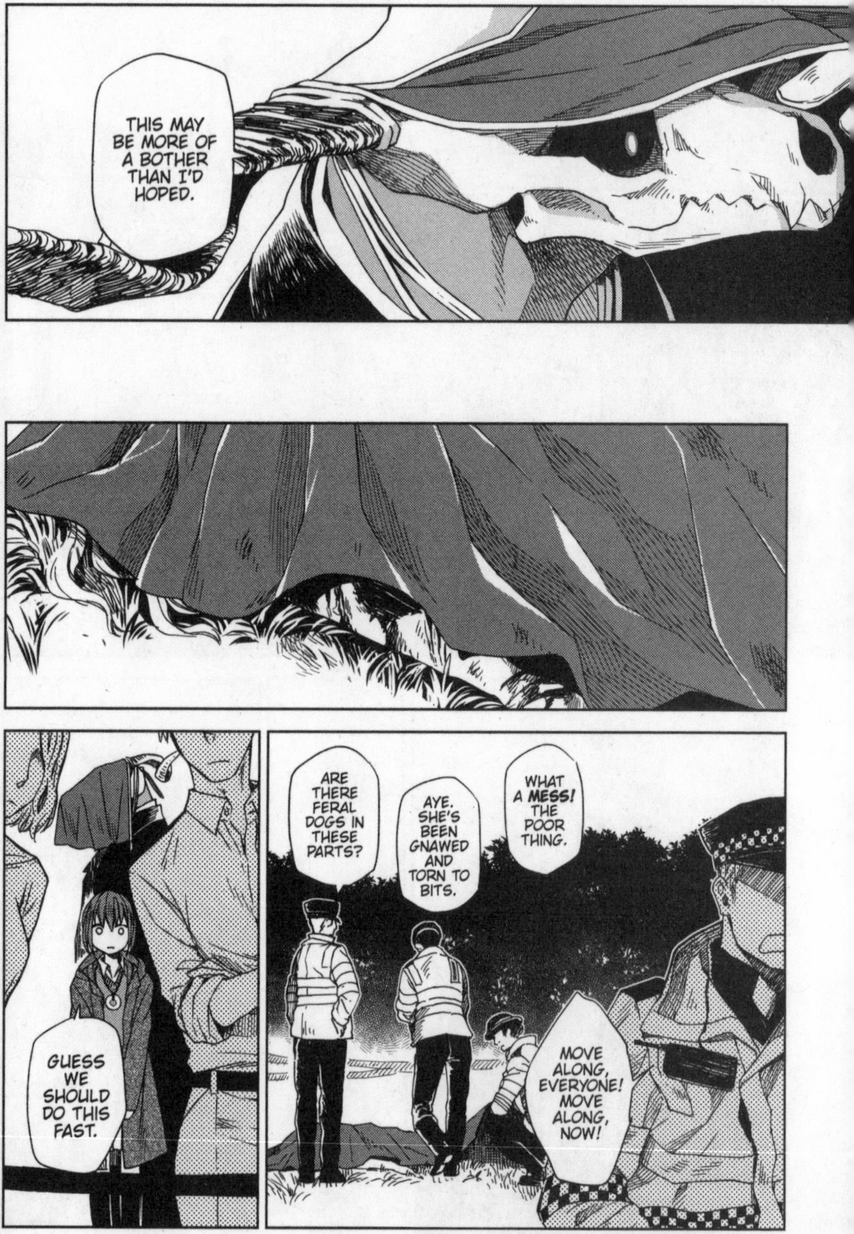
THIS MAY BE MORE OF A BOTHER THAN I'D HOPED.
WHAT A **MESS!** THE POOR THING.
AYE. SHE'S BEEN GNAWED AND TORN TO BITS.
ARE THERE FERAL DOGS IN THESE PARTS?
MOVE ALONG, EVERYONE! MOVE ALONG, NOW!
GUESS WE SHOULD DO THIS FAST.

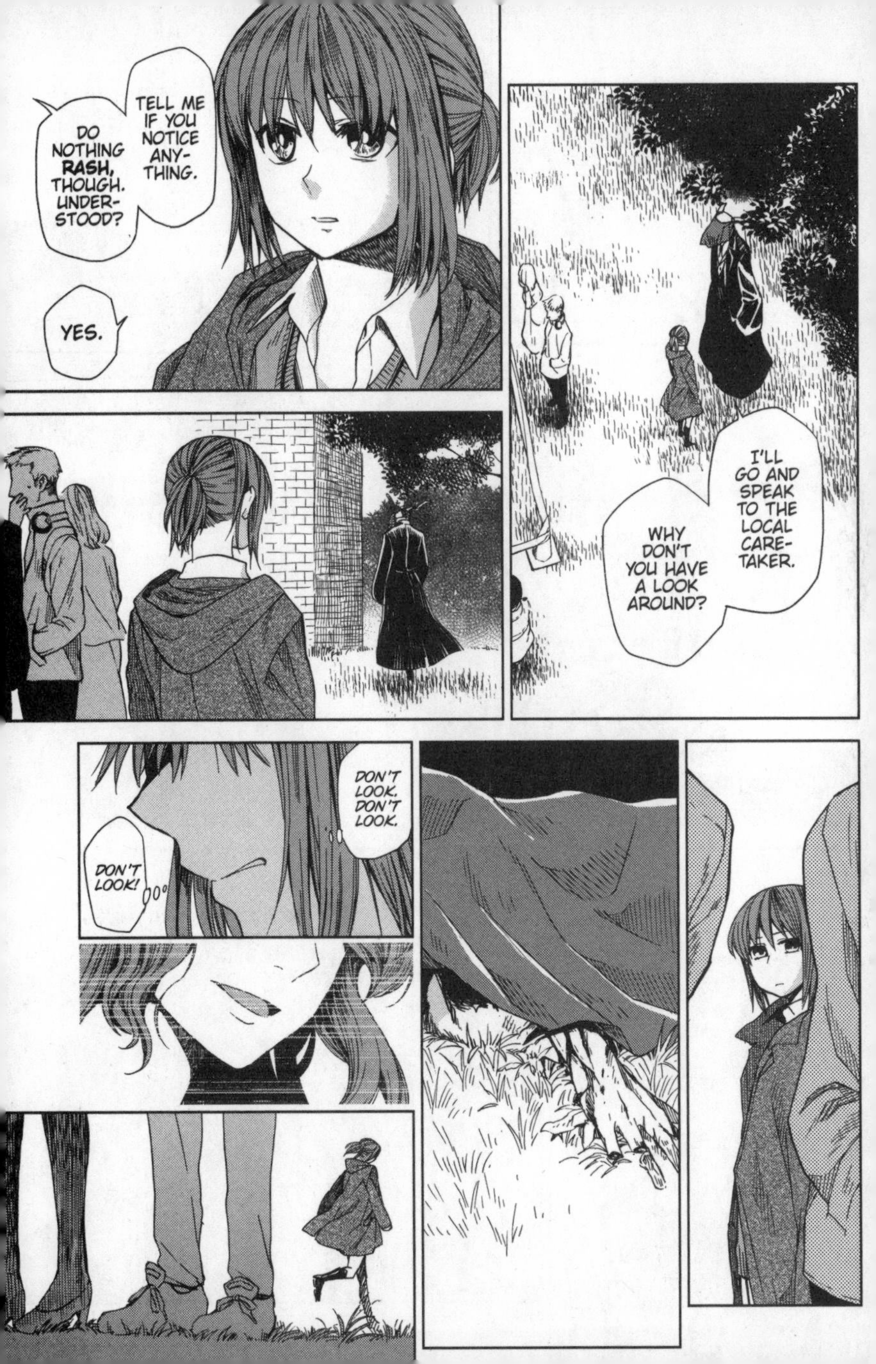
I'LL GO AND SPEAK TO THE LOCAL CARE-TAKER.
WHY DON'T YOU HAVE A LOOK AROUND?
TELL ME IF YOU NOTICE ANY-THING.
DO NOTHING RASH, THOUGH. UNDER-STOOD?
YES.
DON'T LOOK. DON'T LOOK.
DON'T LOOK!

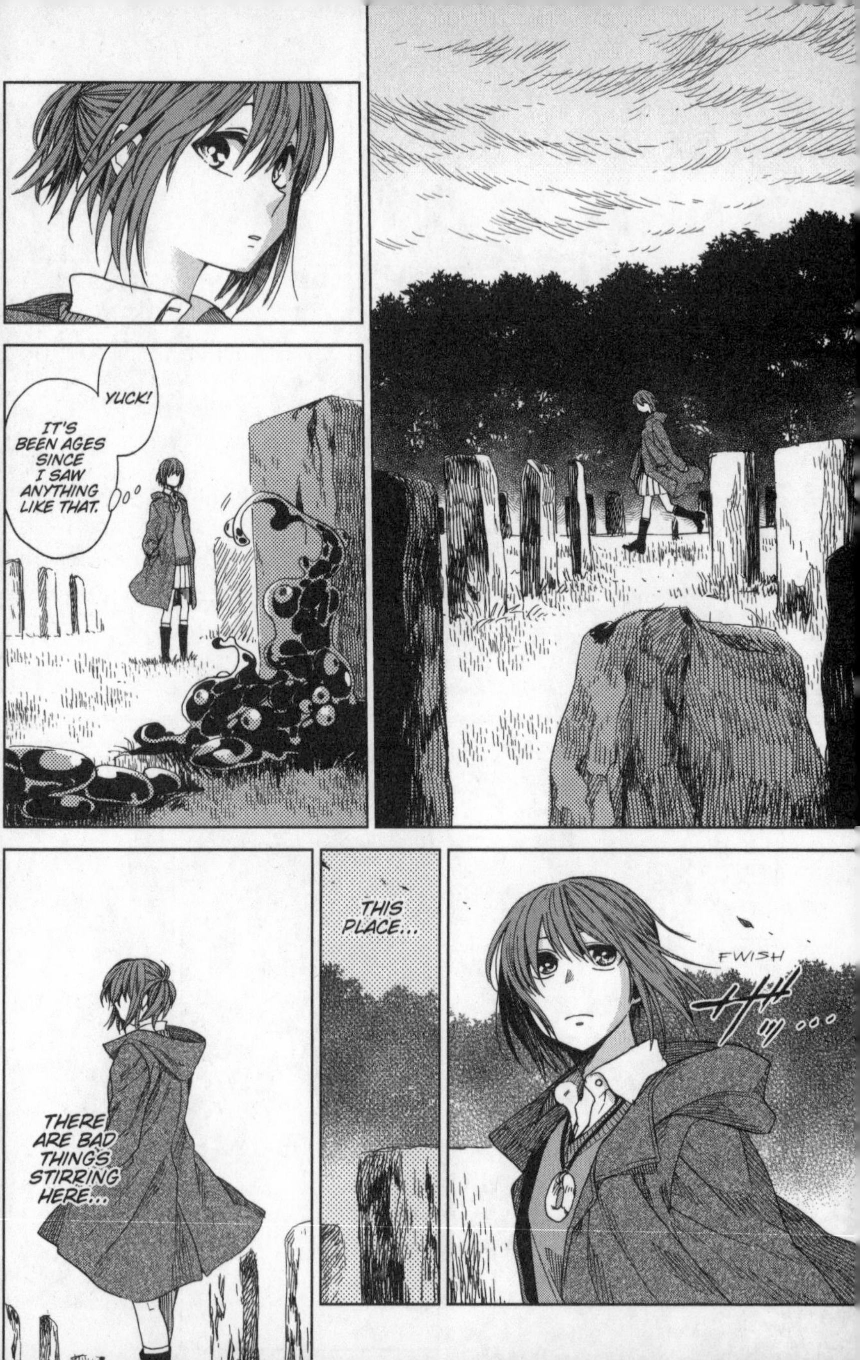
YUCK!
IT'S BEEN AGES SINCE I SAW ANYTHING LIKE THAT.
FWISH
THIS PLACE...
THERE ARE BAD THINGS STIRRING HERE...

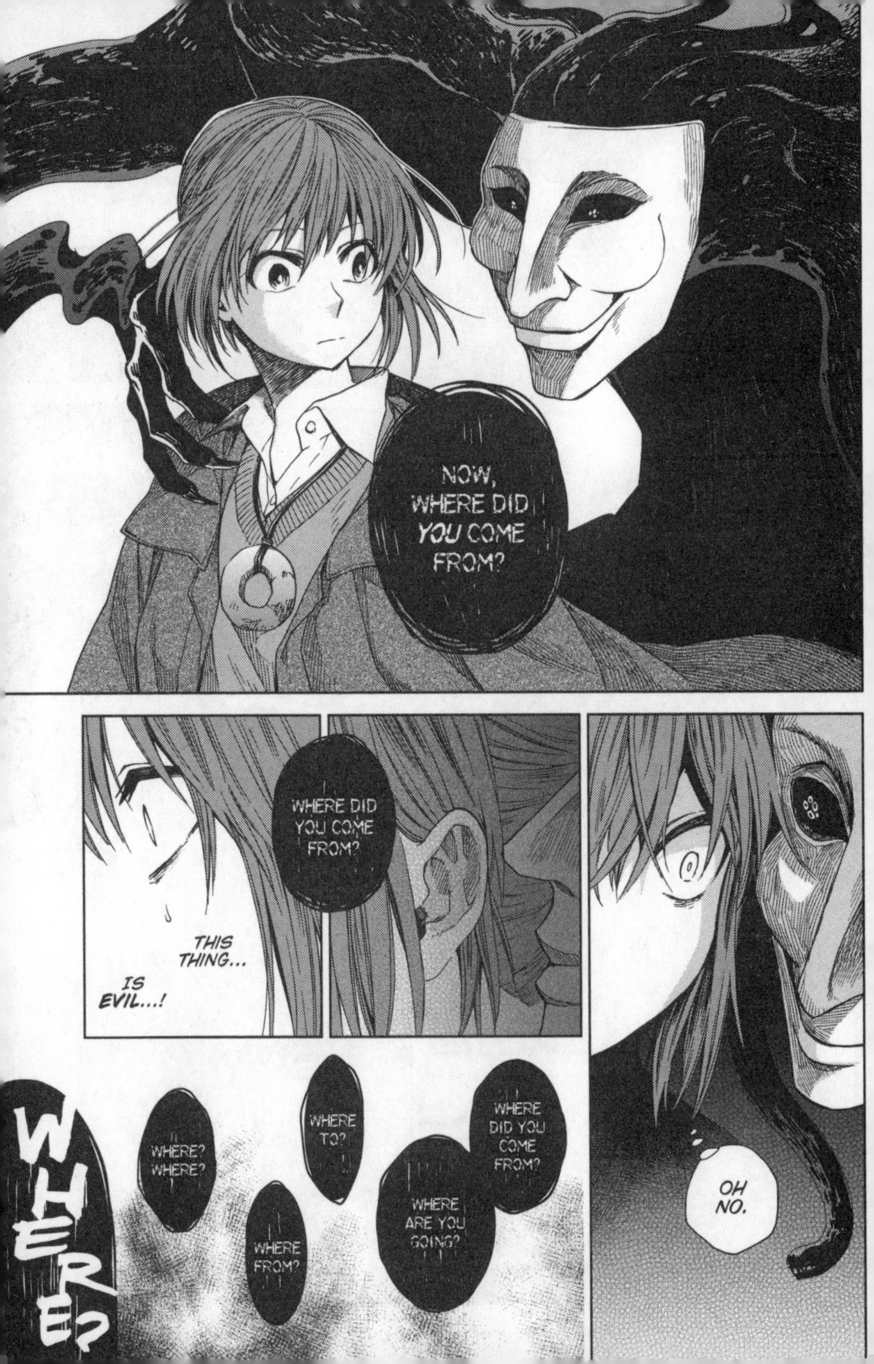
NOW, WHERE DID YOU COME FROM?
WHERE DID YOU COME FROM?
THIS THING...
IS EVIL...!
OH NO.
WHERE DID YOU COME FROM?
WHERE ARE YOU GOING?
WHERE TO?
WHERE FROM?
WHERE? WHERE?
WHERE?

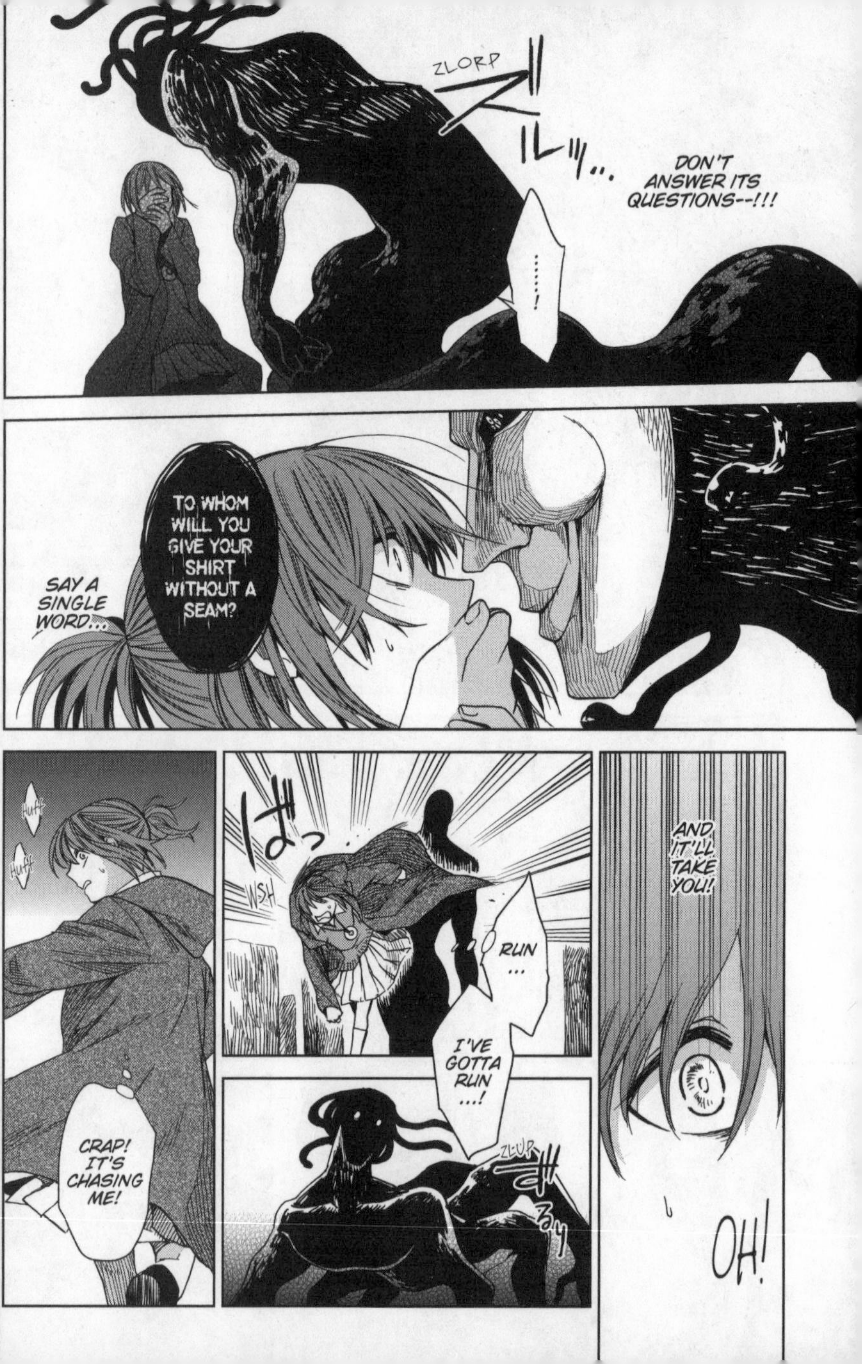
DON'T ANSWER ITS QUESTIONS--!!!
ZLORP
......!
TO WHOM WILL YOU GIVE YOUR SHIRT WITHOUT A SEAM?
SAY A SINGLE WORD...
AND IT'LL TAKE YOU!!
OH!
ばっ
WSH
RUN...
I'VE GOTTA RUN...!
ZLUP
HUFF
HUFF
CRAP! IT'S CHASING ME!

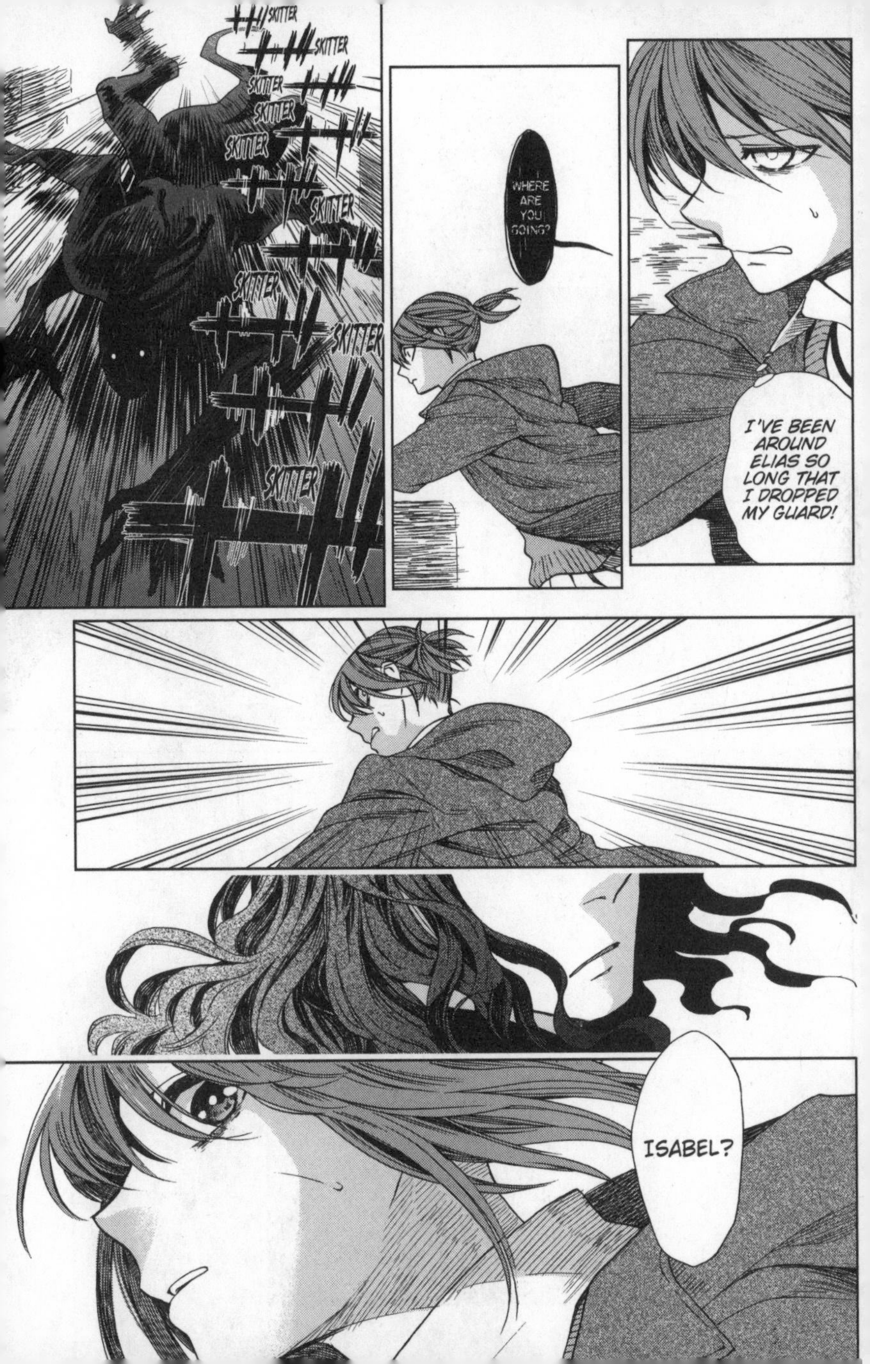
I'VE BEEN AROUND ELIAS SO LONG THAT I DROPPED MY GUARD!
WHERE ARE YOU GOING?
SKITTER
SKITTER
SKITTER
SKITTER
SKITTER
SKITTER
SKITTER
SKITTER
SKITTER
ISABEL?

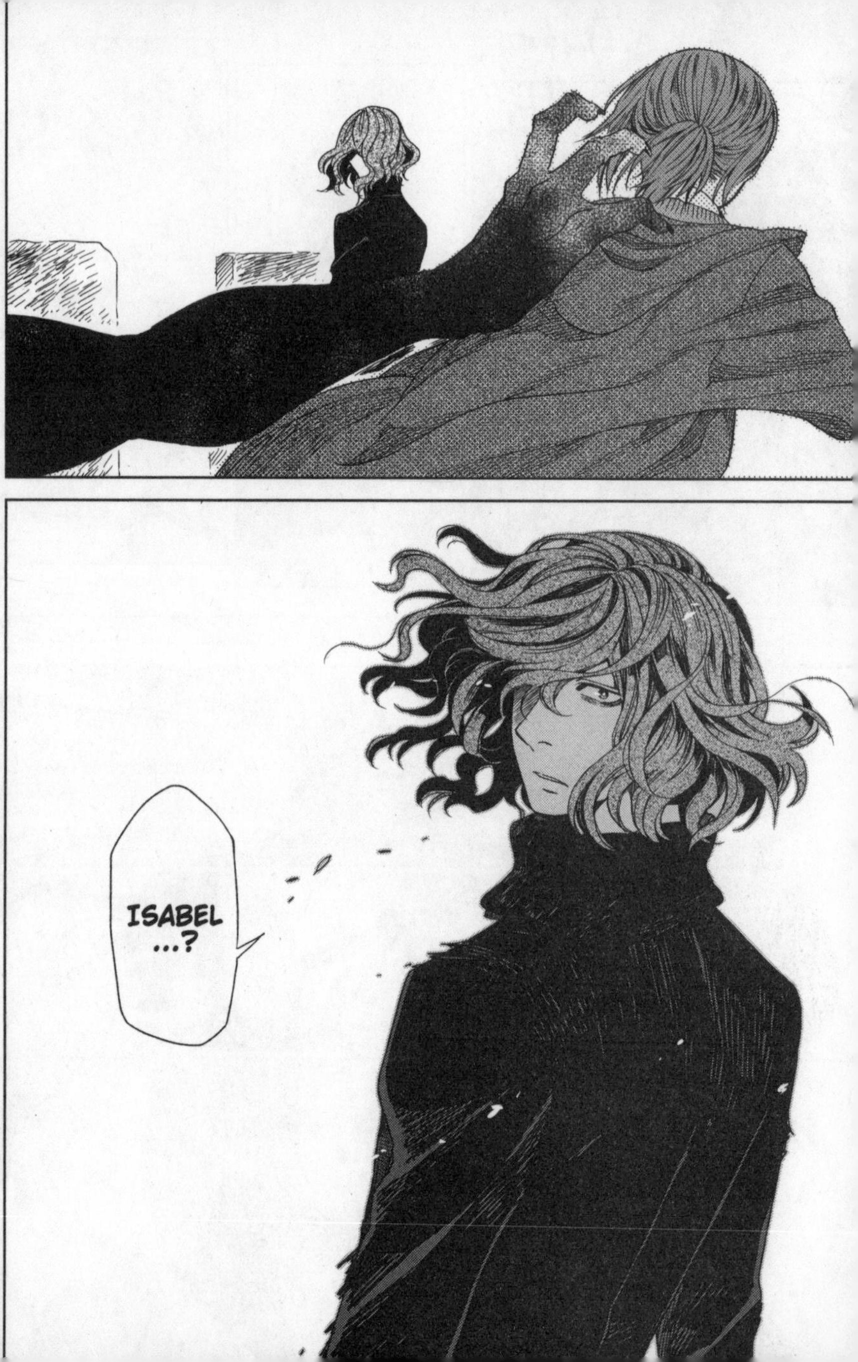
ISABEL ...?

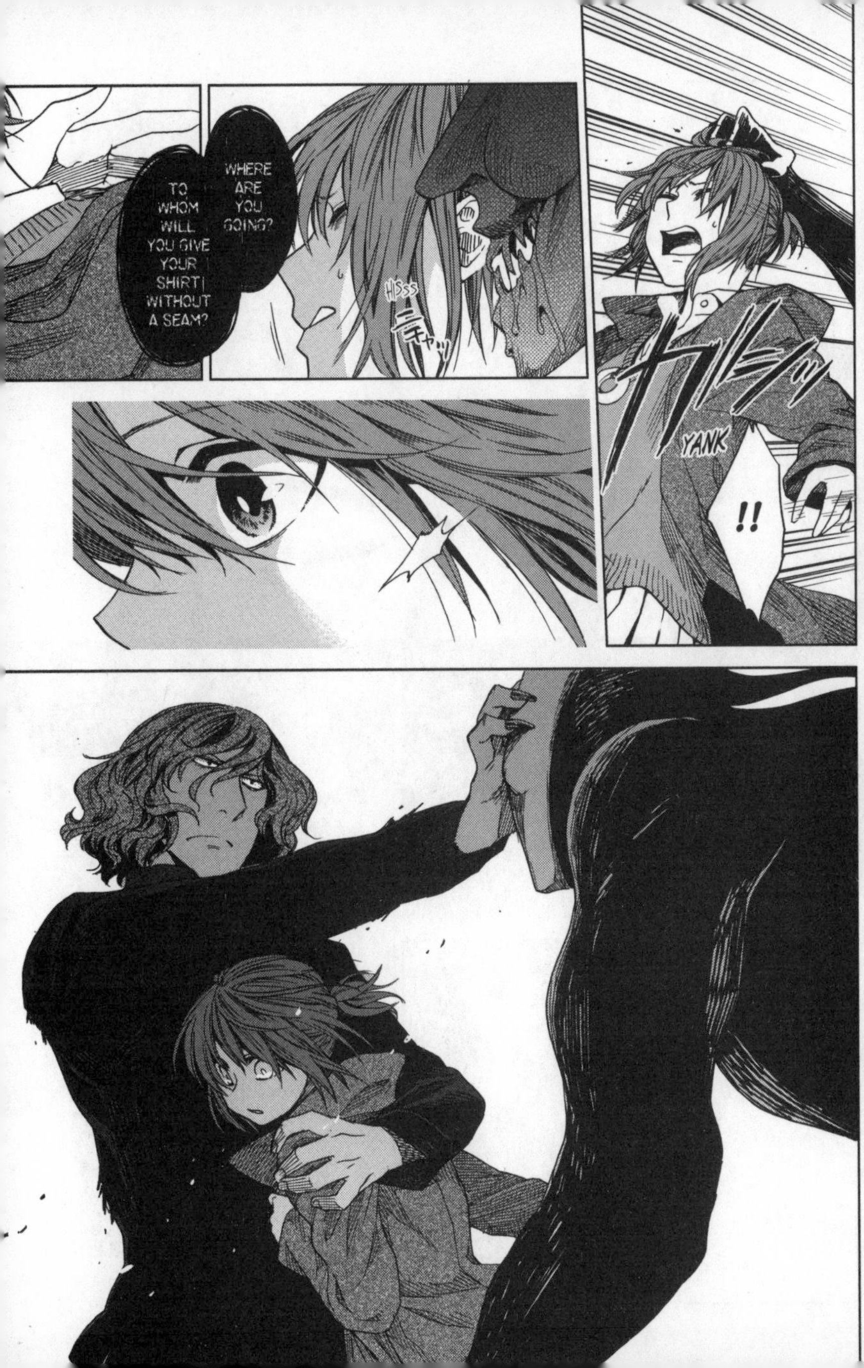
YANK
!!
WHERE ARE YOU GOING?
TO WHOM WILL YOU GIVE YOUR SHIRT WITHOUT A SEAM?
HISSS

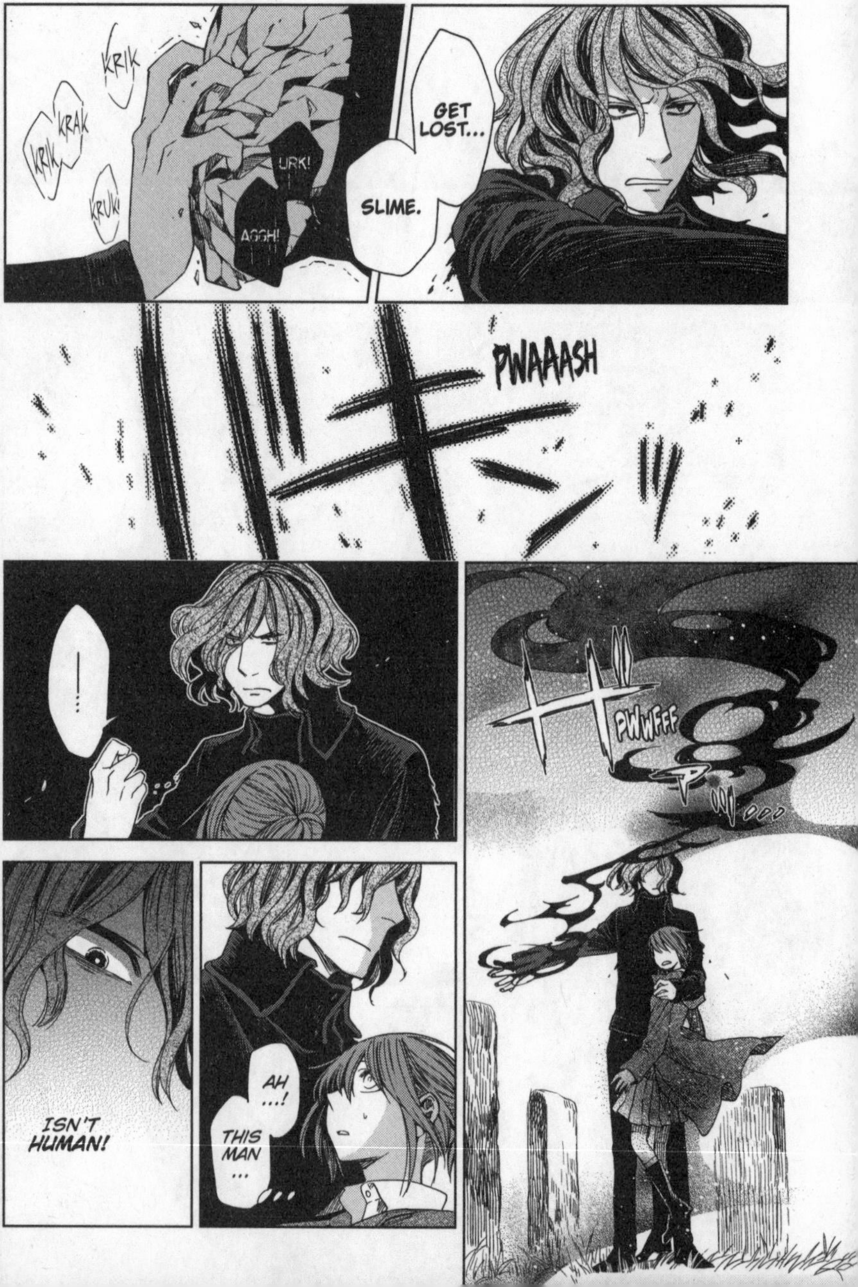
GET LOST...
SLIME.
KRIK
KRAK
KRIK
URK!
KRUK
AGGH!
PWAAASH
PWWFFF
!
AH ...!
THIS MAN ...
ISN'T HUMAN!

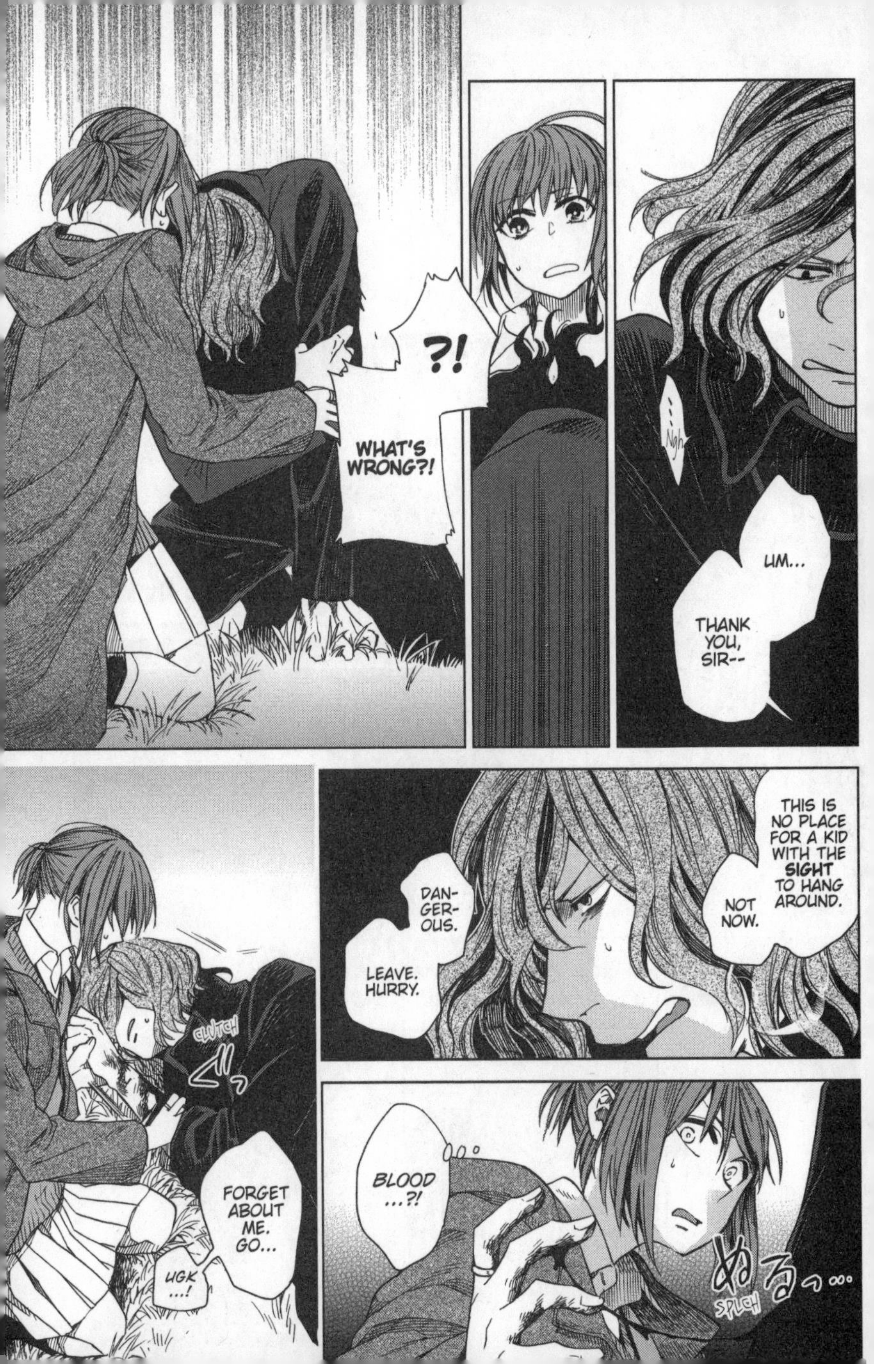
...Ngh
UM...
THANK YOU, SIR--
?!
WHAT'S WRONG?!
THIS IS NO PLACE FOR A KID WITH THE SIGHT TO HANG AROUND.
NOT NOW.
DAN-GER-OUS.
LEAVE. HURRY.
BLOOD ...?!
ぬるっ...
SPLCH
CLUTCH
FORGET ABOUT ME. GO...
UGK ...!

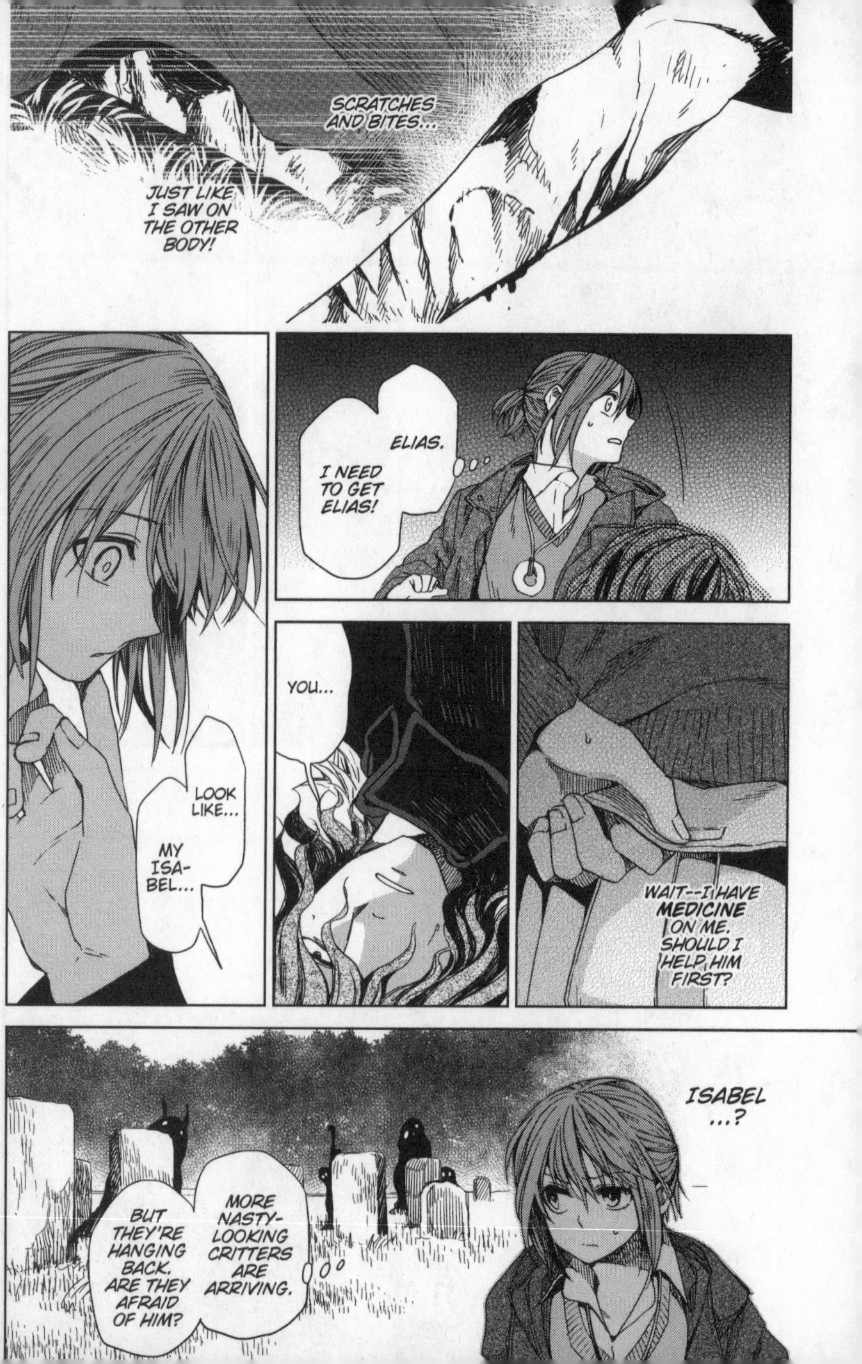
SCRATCHES AND BITES...
JUST LIKE I SAW ON THE OTHER BODY!
ELIAS.
I NEED TO GET ELIAS!
WAIT--I HAVE MEDICINE ON ME. SHOULD I HELP HIM FIRST?
YOU...
LOOK LIKE...
MY ISA-BEL...
ISABEL ...?
MORE NASTY-LOOKING CRITTERS ARE ARRIVING.
BUT THEY'RE HANGING BACK. ARE THEY AFRAID OF HIM?

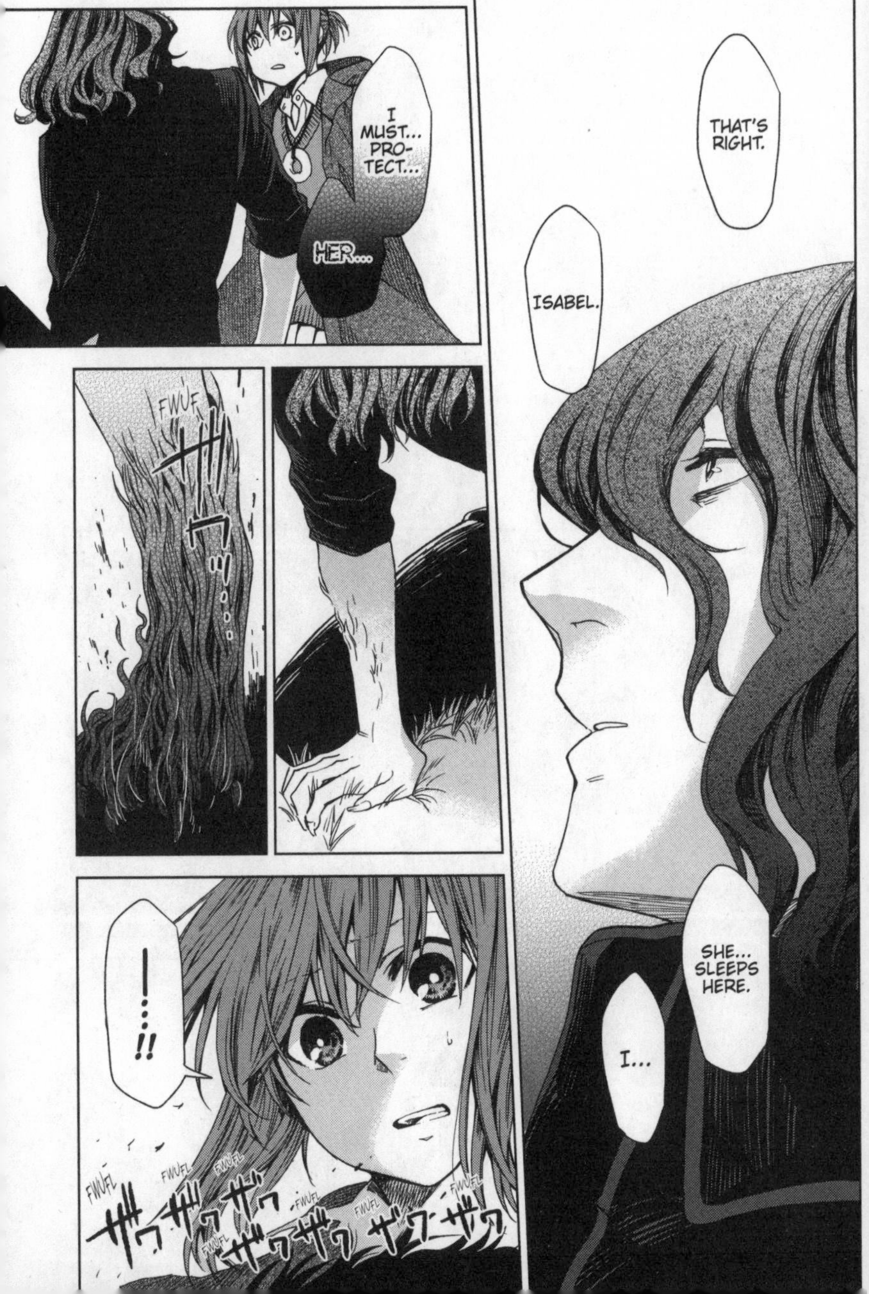
THAT'S RIGHT.
ISABEL.
SHE... SLEEPS HERE.
I...
I MUST... PROTECT...
HER...
FWUF
ザッ
...!!
FWUFL
ザワザワザワザワザワザワ

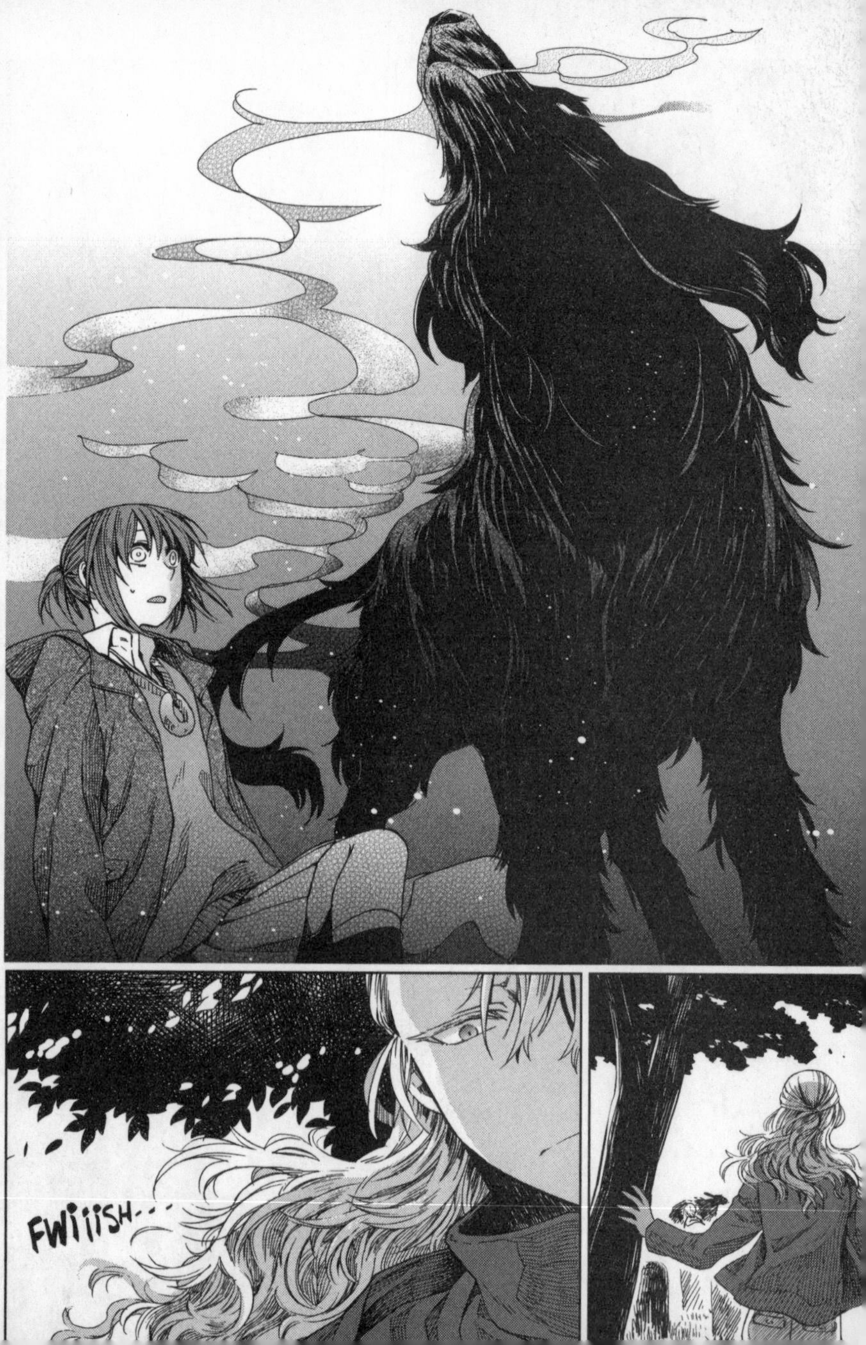
FWiiiSH...

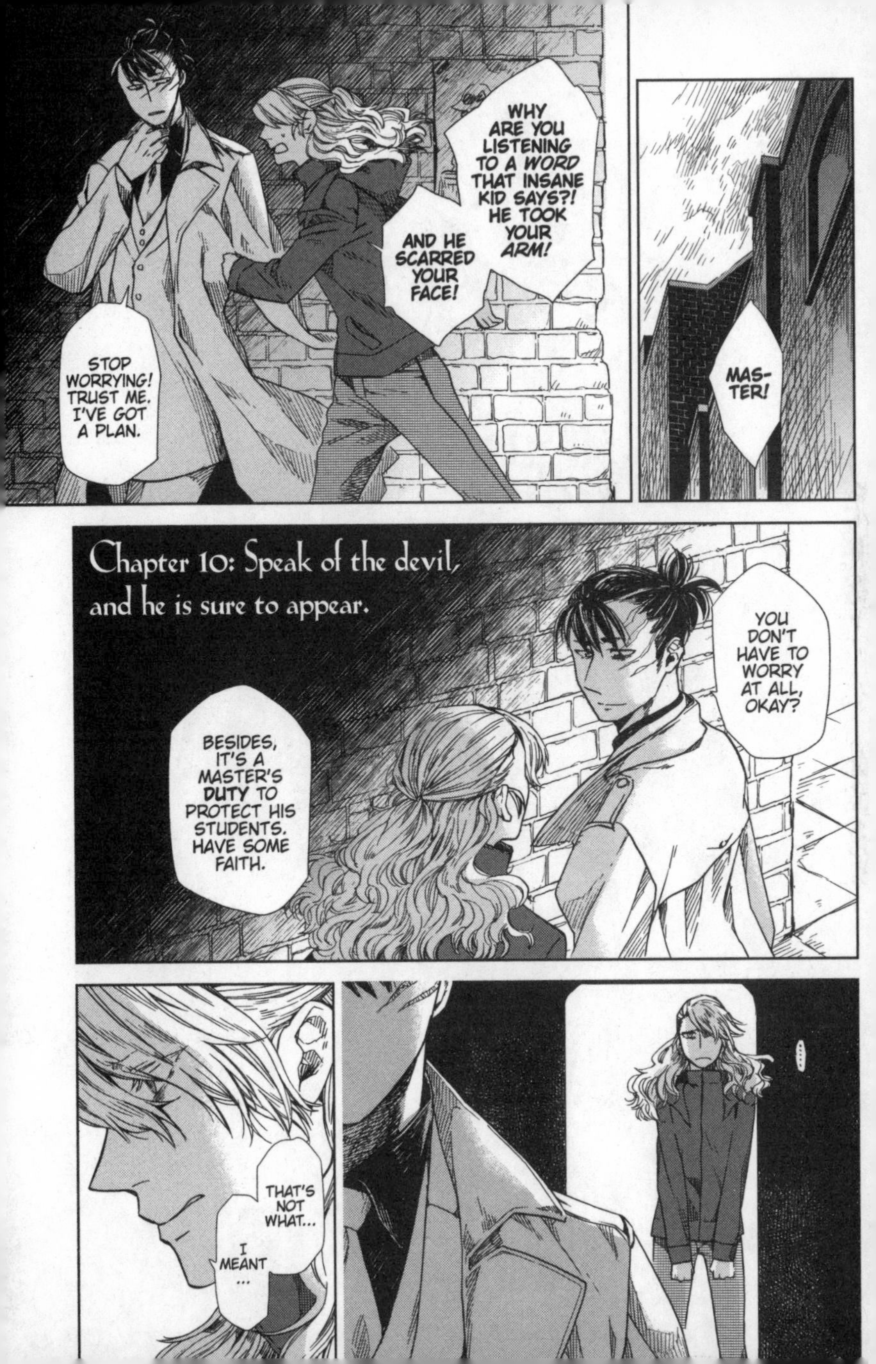
MAS-TER!
WHY ARE YOU LISTENING TO A WORD THAT INSANE KID SAYS?! HE TOOK YOUR ARM!
AND HE SCARRED YOUR FACE!
STOP WORRYING! TRUST ME. I'VE GOT A PLAN.
Chapter 10: Speak of the devil, and he is sure to appear.
YOU DON'T HAVE TO WORRY AT ALL, OKAY?
BESIDES, IT'S A MASTER'S DUTY TO PROTECT HIS STUDENTS. HAVE SOME FAITH.
...
THAT'S NOT WHAT...
I MEANT ...

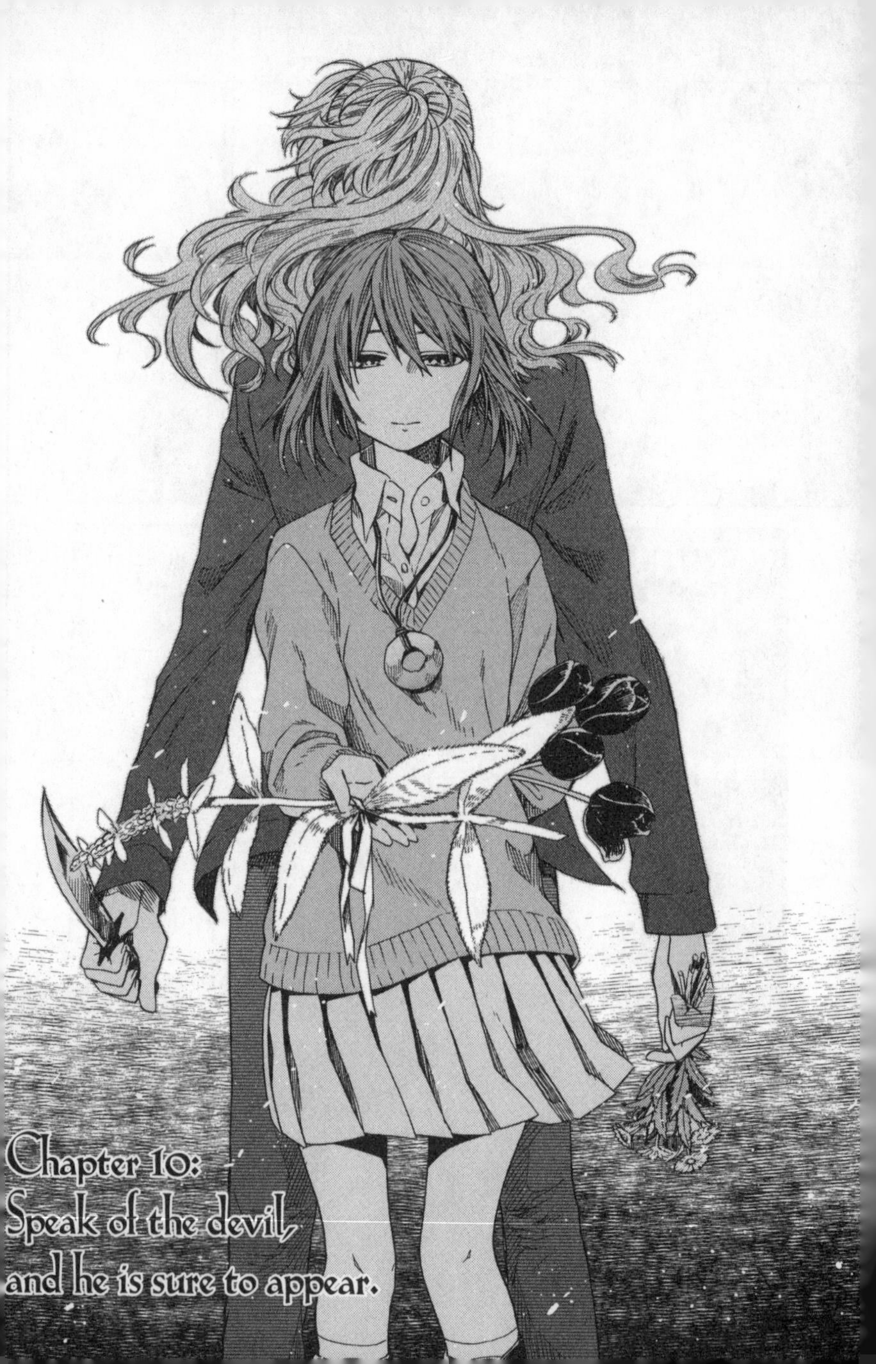
Chapter 10:
Speak of the devil,
and he is sure to appear.

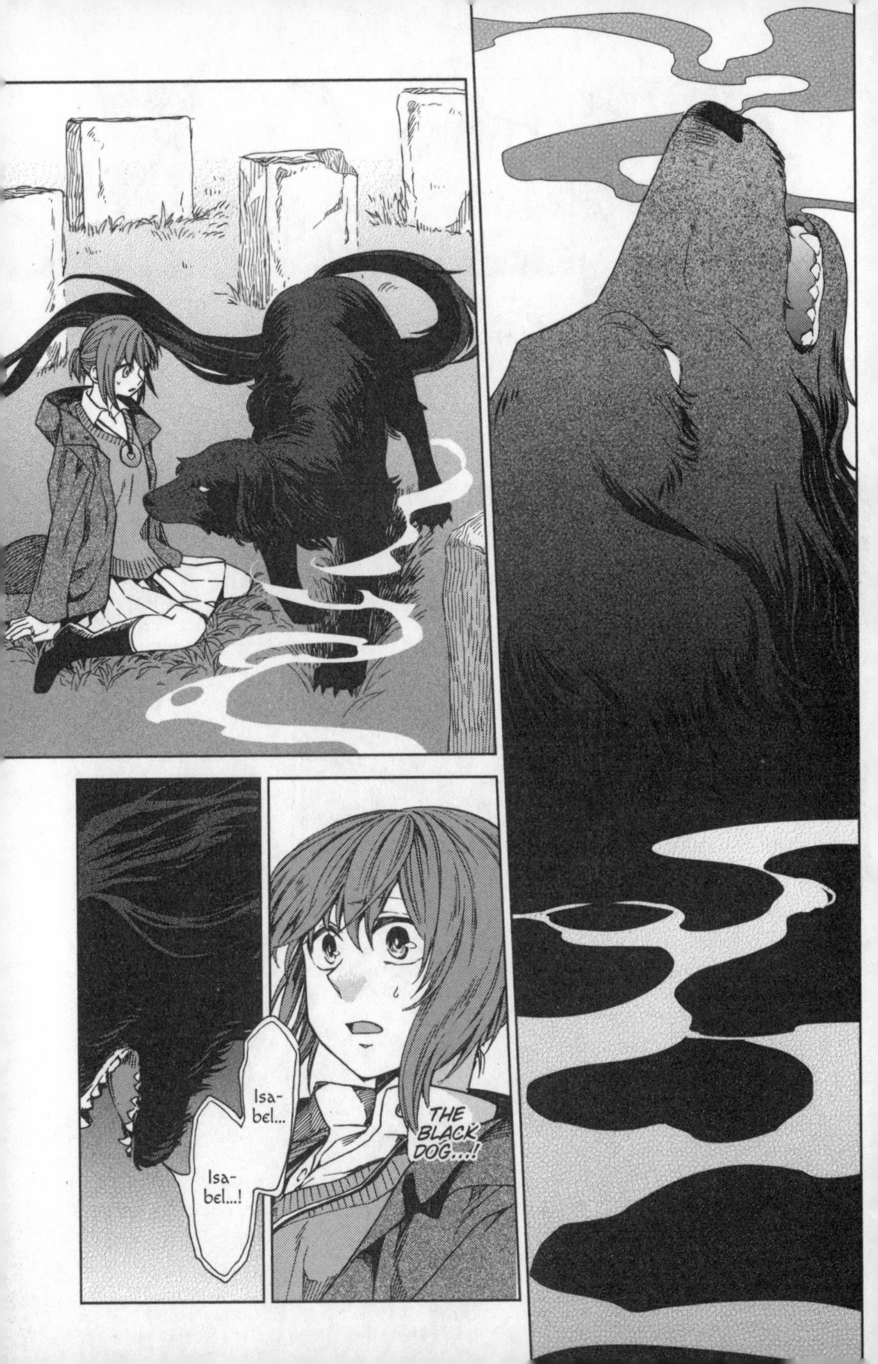
THE BLACK DOG...!
Isa-bel...
Isa-bel...!

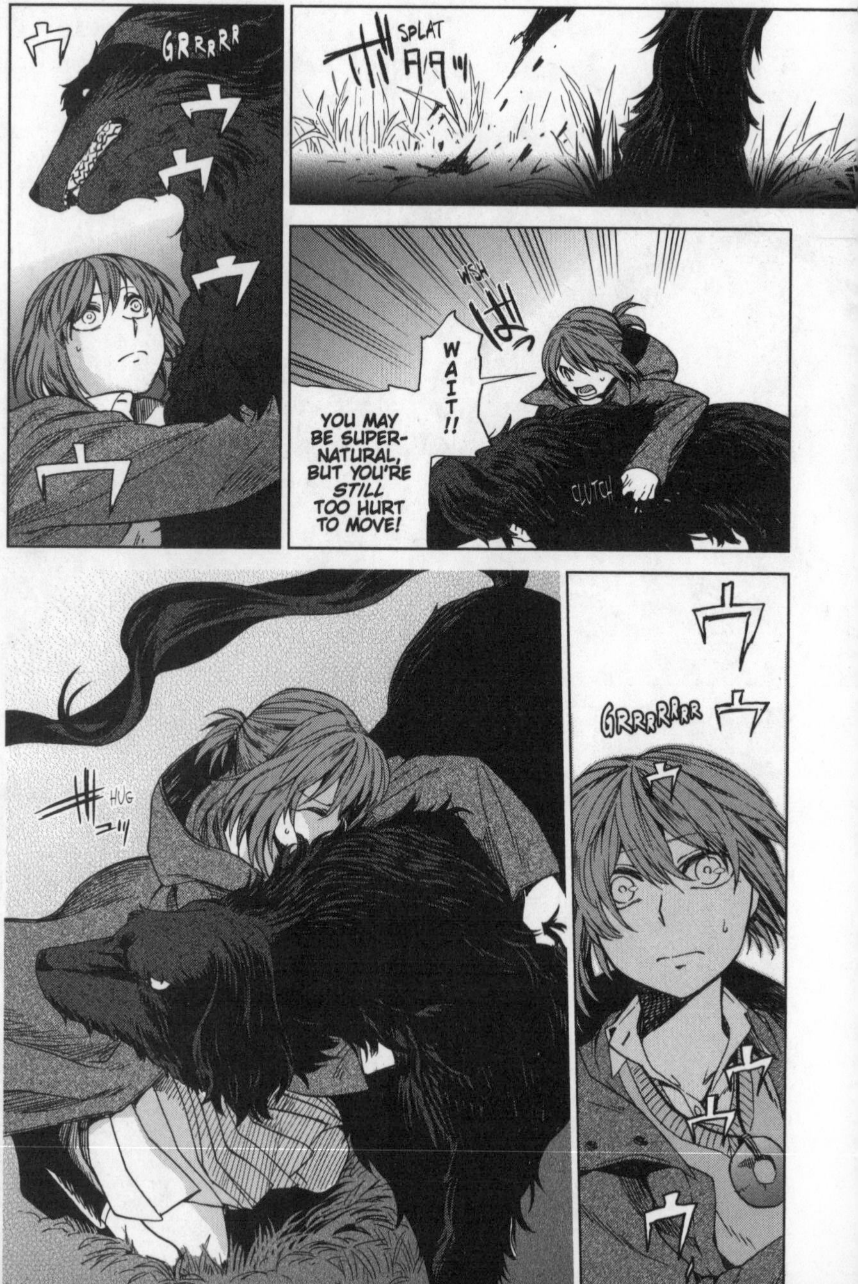
SPLAT
WSH
ばっ
WAIT!!
YOU MAY BE SUPER-NATURAL, BUT YOU'RE STILL TOO HURT TO MOVE!
CLUTCH
ウ
GRRRRRR
ウ
ウ
ウ
ウ
GRRRRRRR
ウ
ウ
ウ
ウ
ウ
ウ
HUG

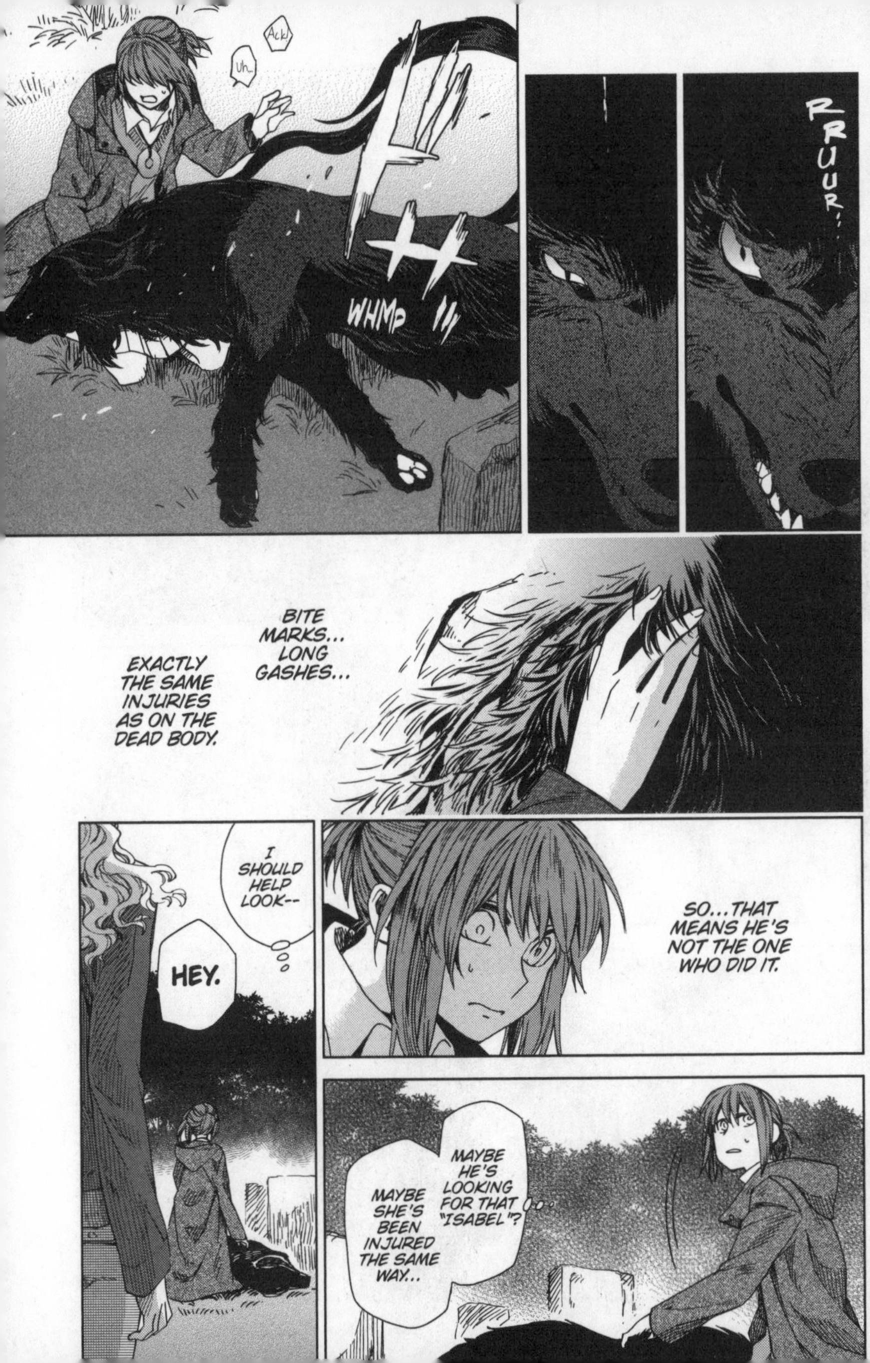
RRUUR...
Ack!
Uh...
WHMP
BITE MARKS... LONG GASHES...
EXACTLY THE SAME INJURIES AS ON THE DEAD BODY.
SO...THAT MEANS HE'S NOT THE ONE WHO DID IT.
MAYBE HE'S LOOKING FOR THAT "ISABEL"?
MAYBE SHE'S BEEN INJURED THE SAME WAY...
I SHOULD HELP LOOK--
HEY.

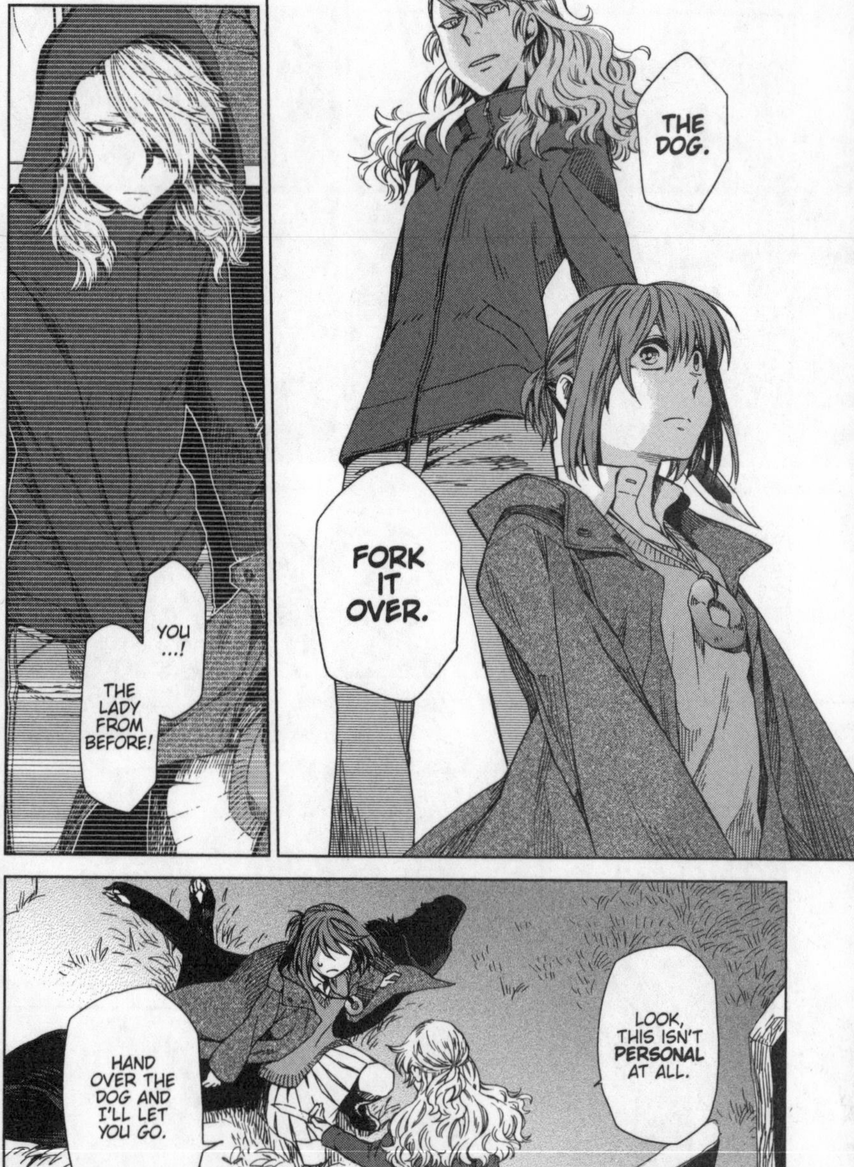
THE DOG.
FORK IT OVER.
YOU ...!
THE LADY FROM BEFORE!
LOOK, THIS ISN'T **PERSONAL** AT ALL.
HAND OVER THE DOG AND I'LL LET YOU GO.

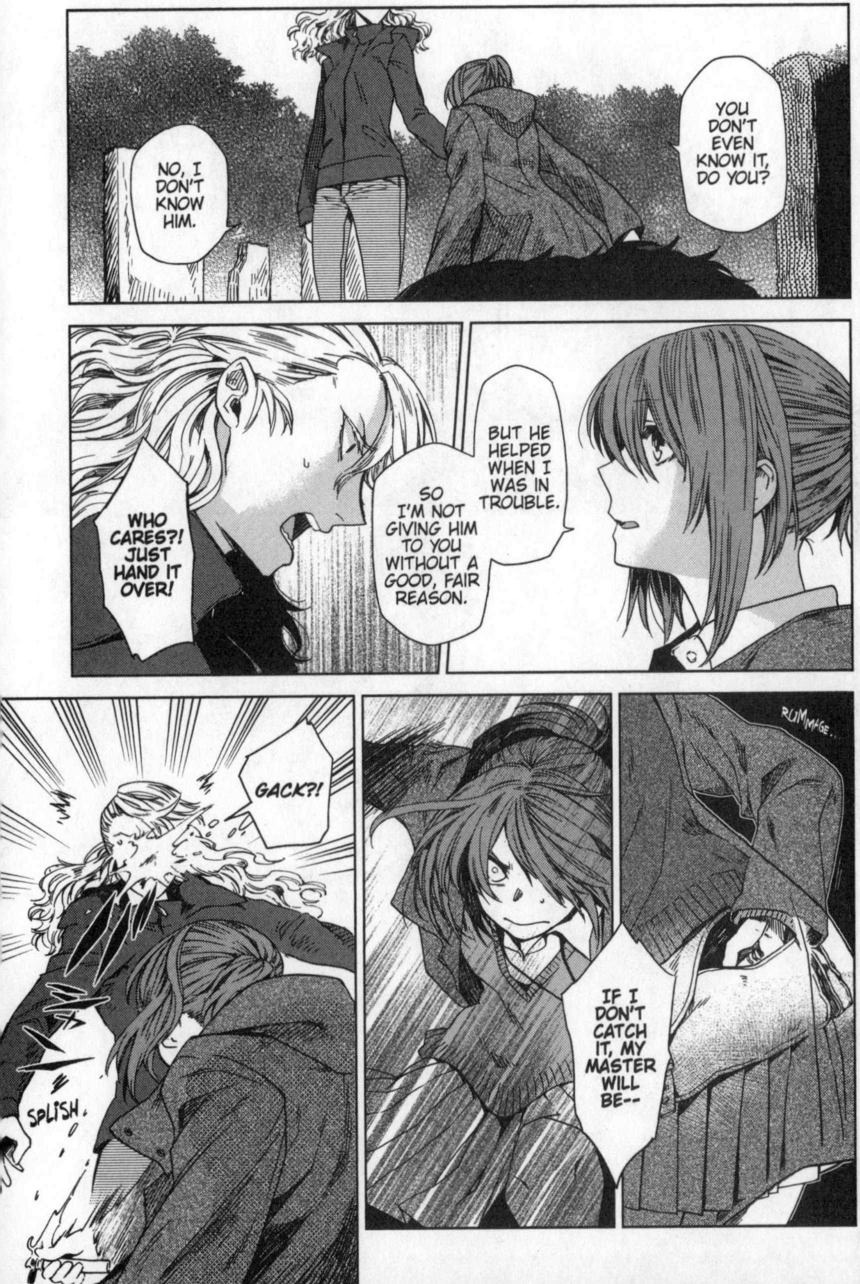
YOU DON'T EVEN KNOW IT, DO YOU?
NO, I DON'T KNOW HIM.
BUT HE HELPED WHEN I WAS IN TROUBLE.
SO I'M NOT GIVING HIM TO YOU WITHOUT A GOOD, FAIR REASON.
WHO CARES?! JUST HAND IT OVER!
RUMMAGE...
IF I DON'T CATCH IT, MY MASTER WILL BE--
GACK?!
SPLISH.

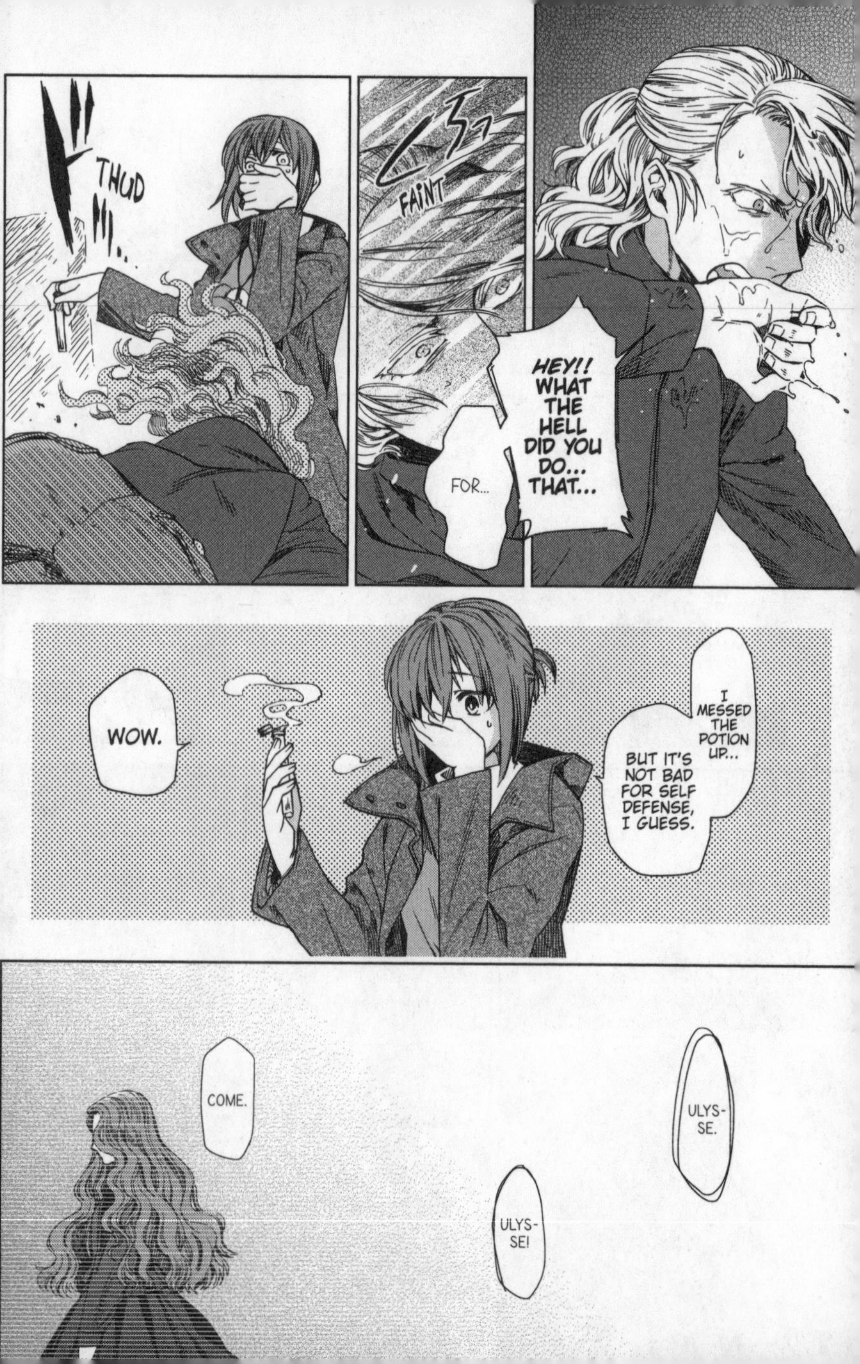
HEY!! WHAT THE HELL DID YOU DO... THAT...
FOR...
FAINT
THUD
I MESSED THE POTION UP...
BUT IT'S NOT BAD FOR SELF DEFENSE, I GUESS.
WOW.
ULYS-SE.
ULYS-SE!
COME.

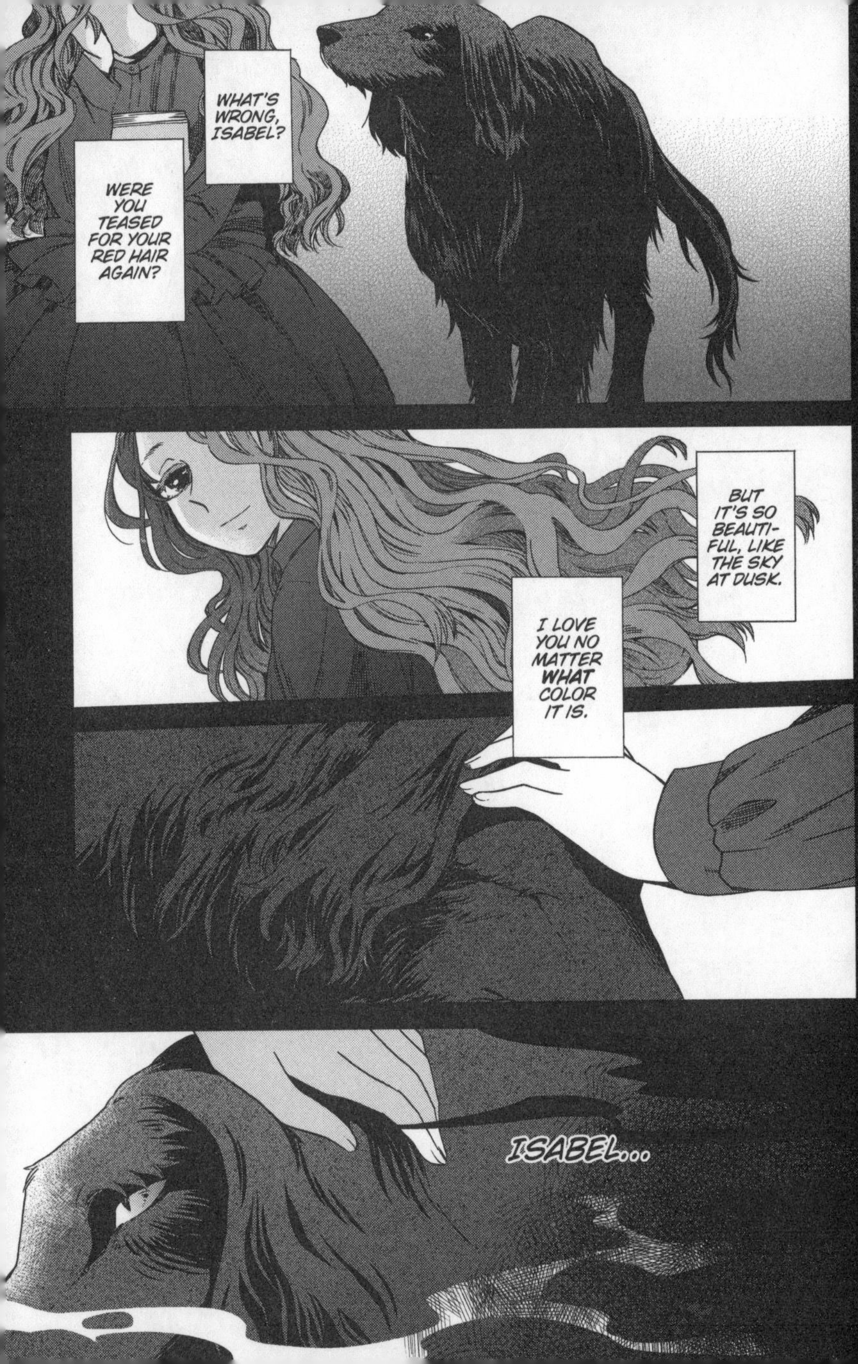
WHAT'S WRONG, ISABEL?
WERE YOU TEASED FOR YOUR RED HAIR AGAIN?
BUT IT'S SO BEAUTIFUL, LIKE THE SKY AT DUSK.
I LOVE YOU NO MATTER WHAT COLOR IT IS.
ISABEL...

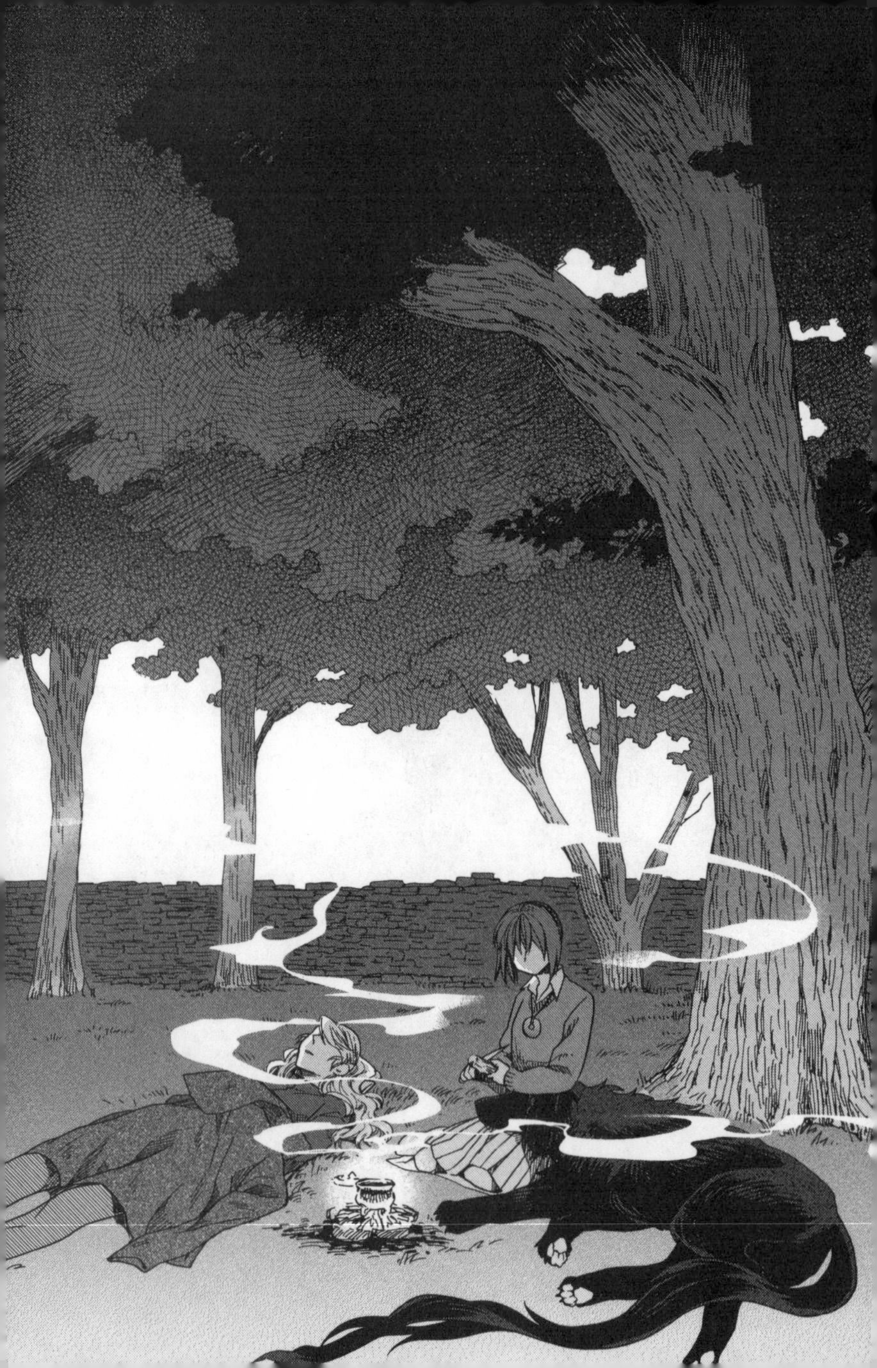

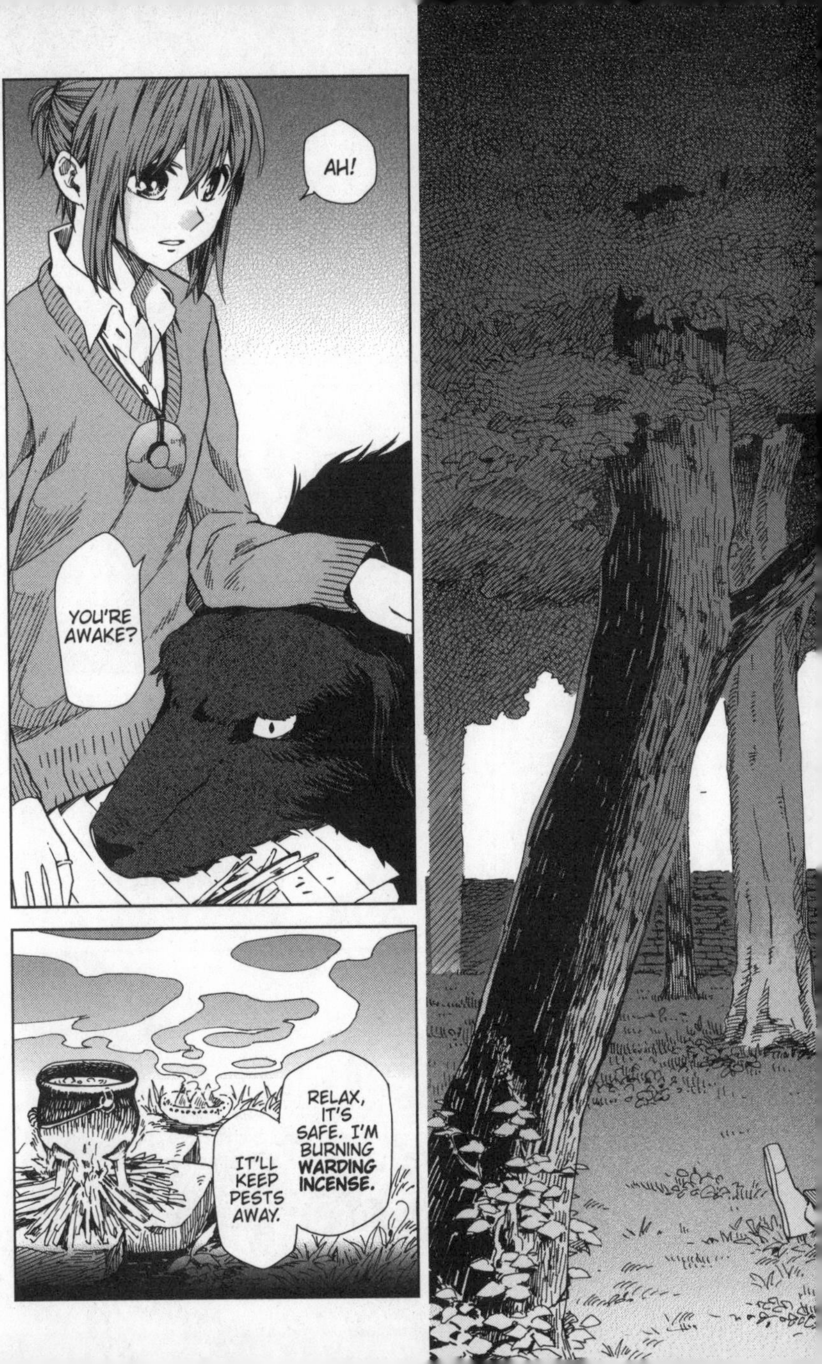
AH!
YOU'RE AWAKE?
RELAX, IT'S SAFE. I'M BURNING **WARDING INCENSE.**
IT'LL KEEP PESTS AWAY.

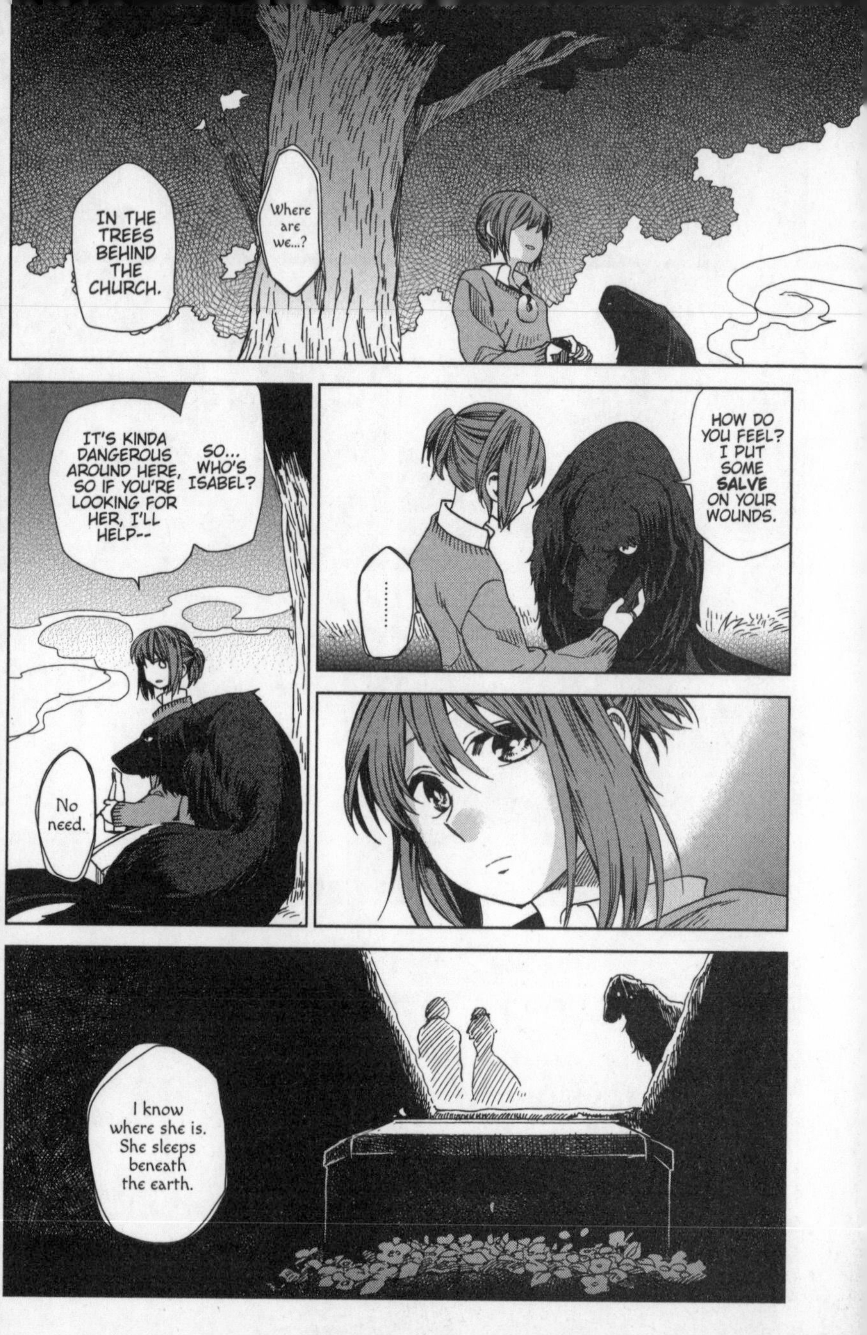
Where are we...?
IN THE TREES BEHIND THE CHURCH.
HOW DO YOU FEEL? I PUT SOME **SALVE** ON YOUR WOUNDS.
......
SO... WHO'S ISABEL?
IT'S KINDA DANGEROUS AROUND HERE, SO IF YOU'RE LOOKING FOR HER, I'LL HELP--
No need.
I know where she is. She sleeps beneath the earth.

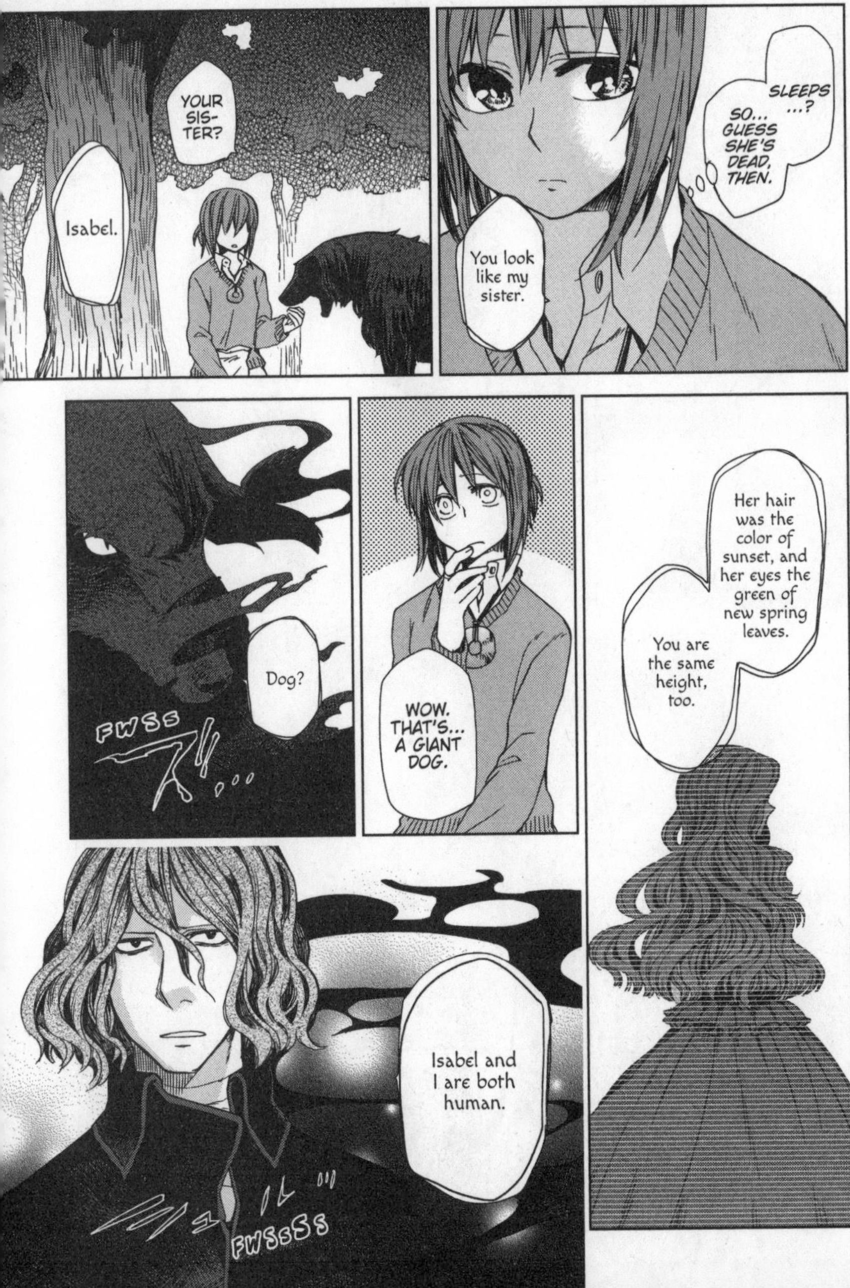
SLEEPS ...?
SO... GUESS SHE'S DEAD, THEN.
You look like my sister.
YOUR SIS-TER?
Isabel.
Her hair was the color of sunset, and her eyes the green of new spring leaves.
You are the same height, too.
WOW. THAT'S... A GIANT DOG.
Dog?
FWSS
Isabel and I are both human.
FWSsSS

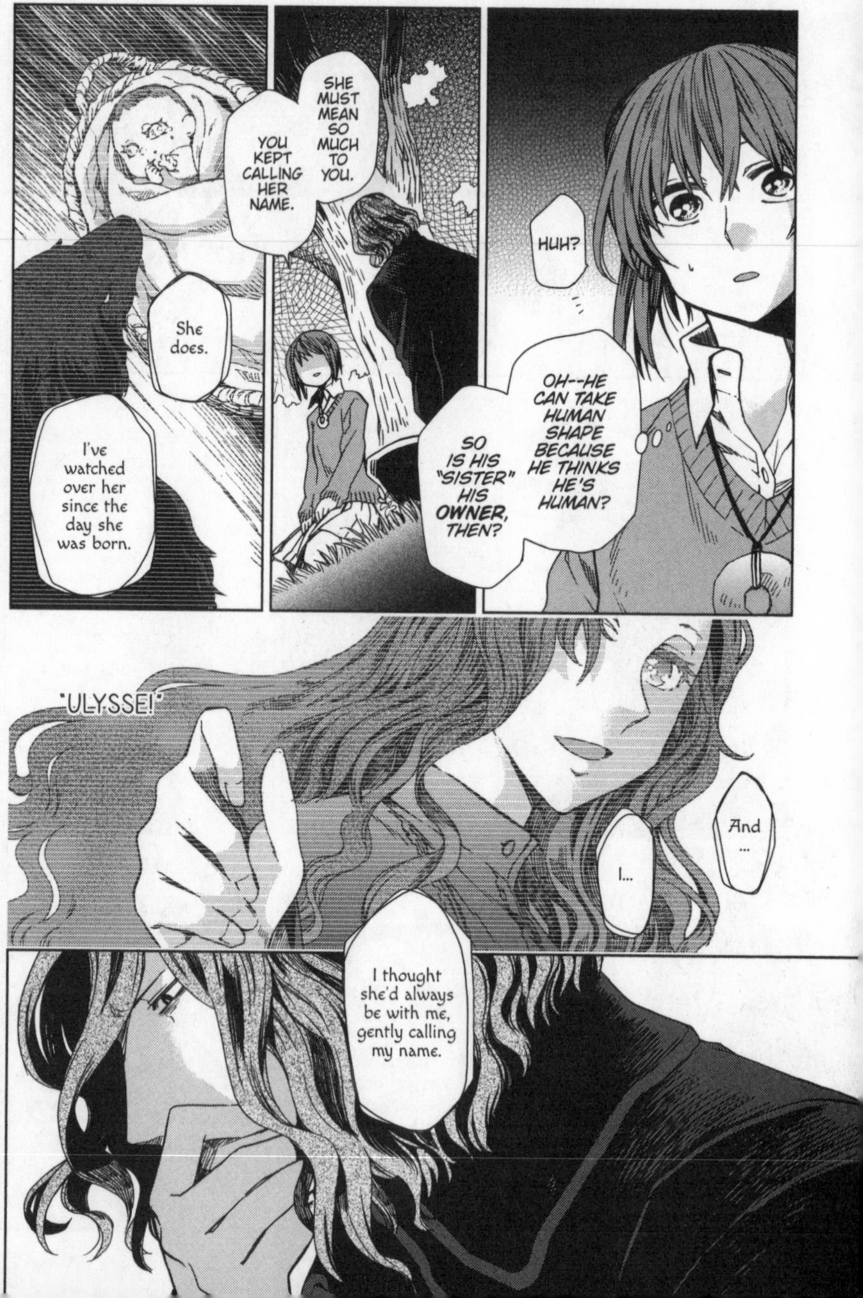
HUH?
OH--HE CAN TAKE HUMAN SHAPE BECAUSE HE THINKS HE'S HUMAN?
SO IS HIS "SISTER" HIS OWNER, THEN?
SHE MUST MEAN SO MUCH TO YOU.
YOU KEPT CALLING HER NAME.
She does.
I've watched over her since the day she was born.
"ULYSSE!"
And ...
I...
I thought she'd always be with me, gently calling my name.

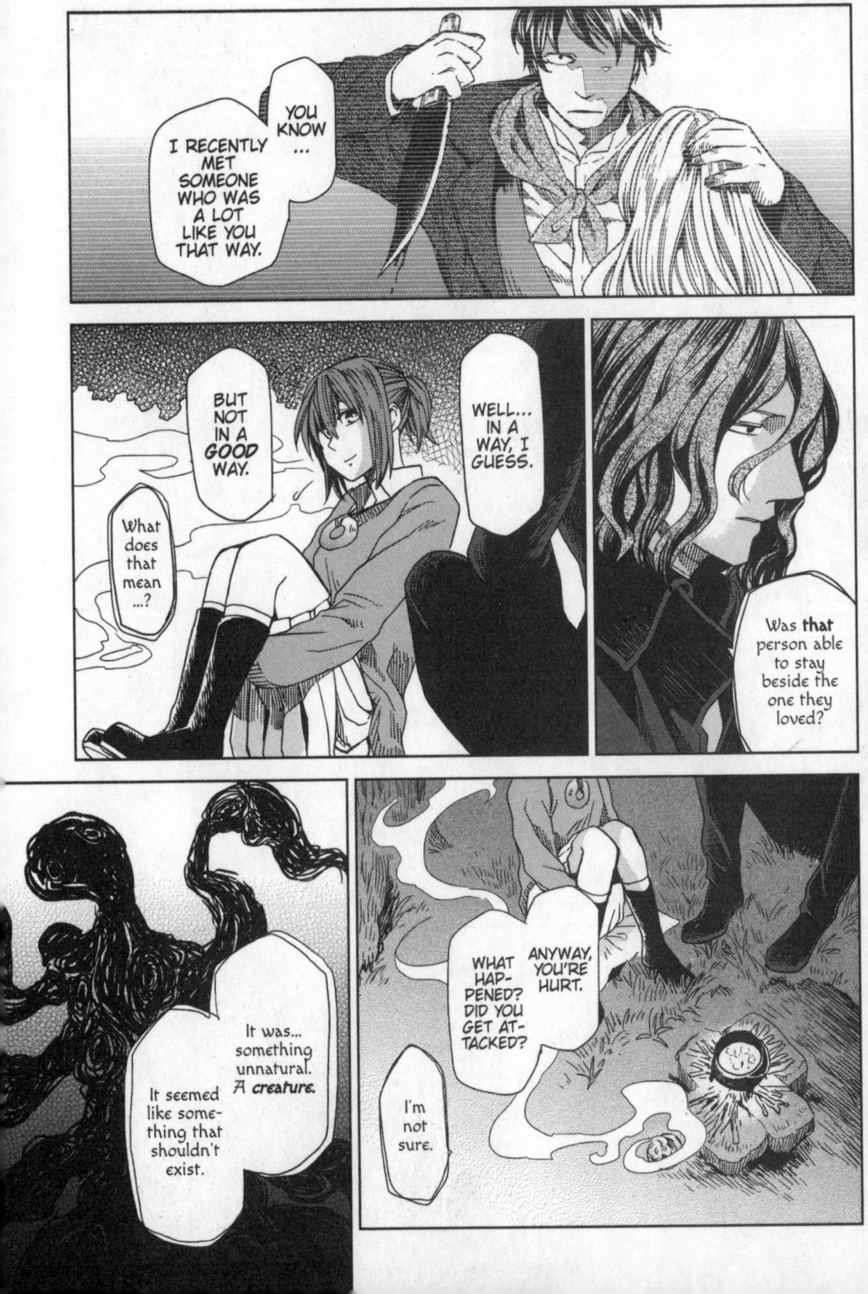
YOU KNOW ...
I RECENTLY MET SOMEONE WHO WAS A LOT LIKE YOU THAT WAY.
Was that person able to stay beside the one they loved?
WELL... IN A WAY, I GUESS.
BUT NOT IN A GOOD WAY.
What does that mean ...?
ANYWAY, YOU'RE HURT.
WHAT HAPPENED? DID YOU GET ATTACKED?
I'm not sure.
It was... something unnatural. A creature.
It seemed like something that shouldn't exist.

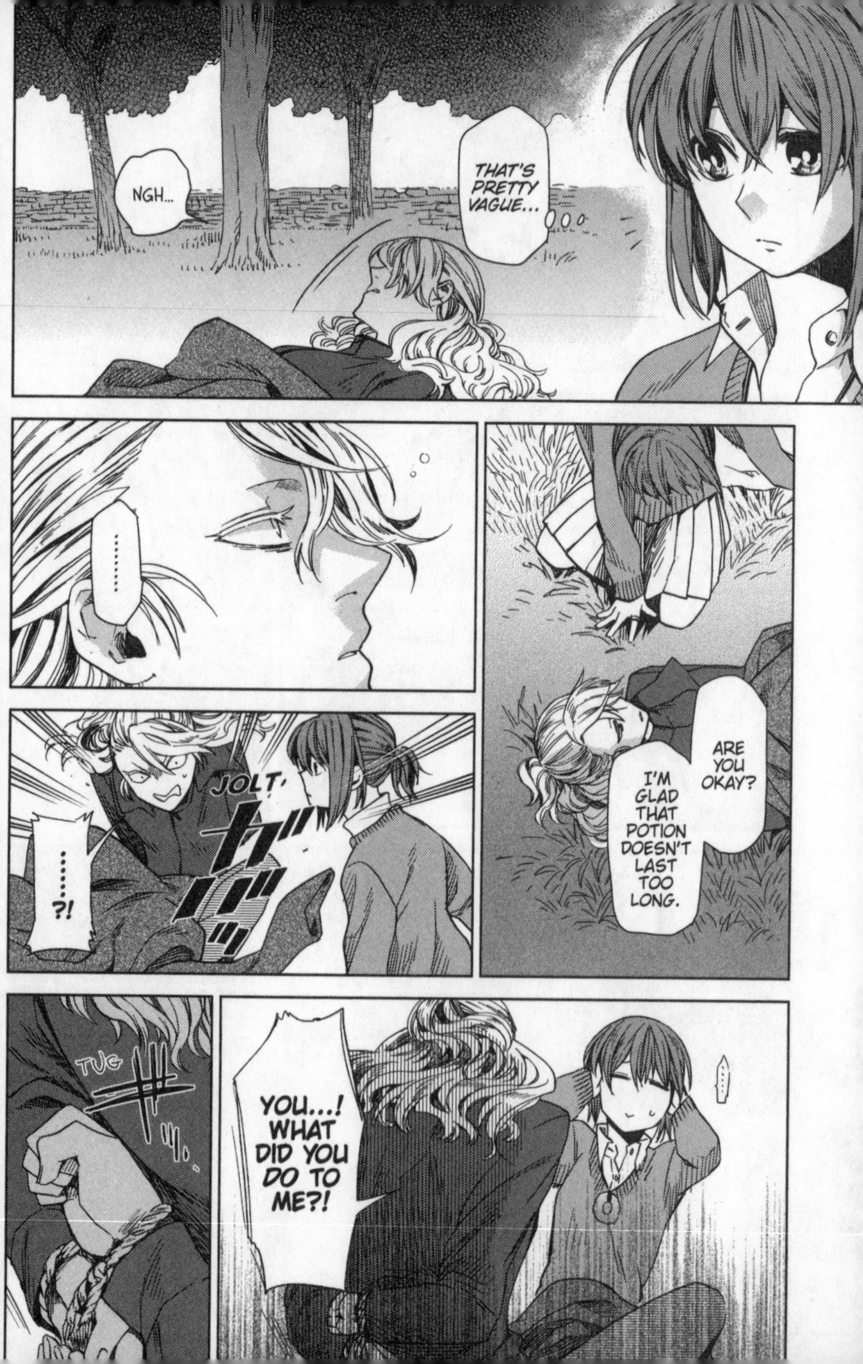
THAT'S PRETTY VAGUE...
NGH...
ARE YOU OKAY?
I'M GLAD THAT POTION DOESN'T LAST TOO LONG.
......
JOLT
......?!
......
YOU...! WHAT DID YOU DO TO ME?!
TUG

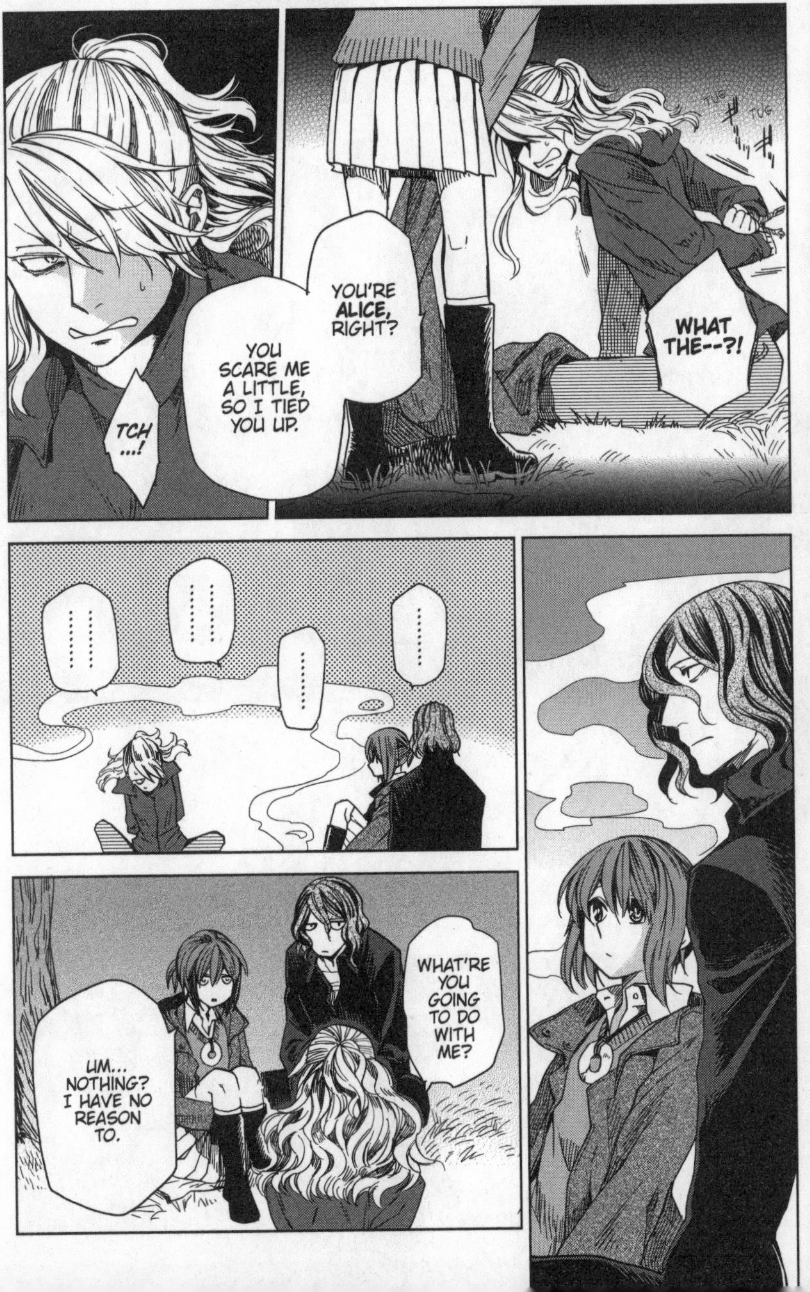
TUG
TUG
WHAT THE--?!
YOU'RE ALICE, RIGHT?
YOU SCARE ME A LITTLE, SO I TIED YOU UP.
TCH ...!
......
......
......
......
WHAT'RE YOU GOING TO DO WITH ME?
UM... NOTHING? I HAVE NO REASON TO.

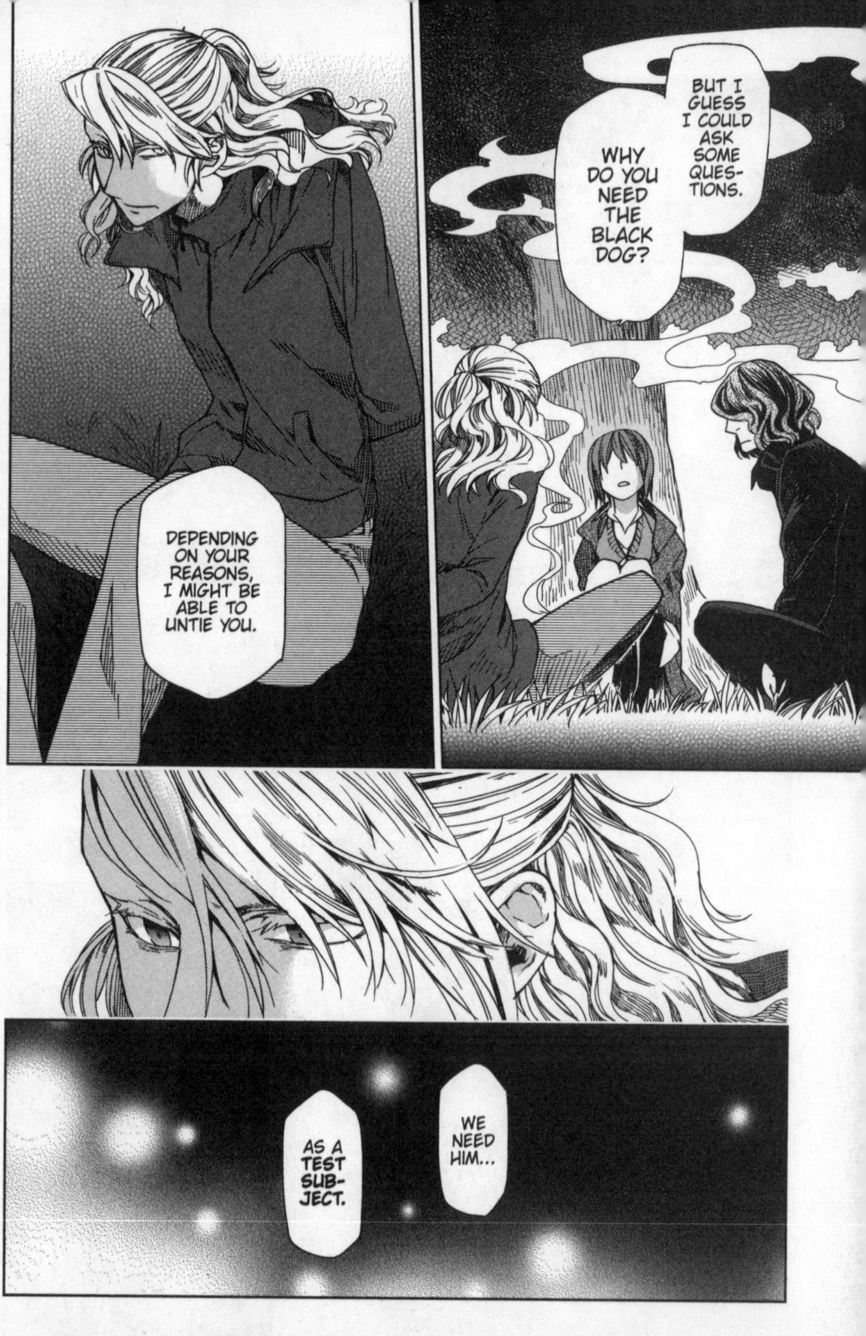
BUT I GUESS I COULD ASK SOME QUES-TIONS.
WHY DO YOU NEED THE BLACK DOG?
DEPENDING ON YOUR REASONS, I MIGHT BE ABLE TO UNTIE YOU.
WE NEED HIM...
AS A TEST SUB-JECT.

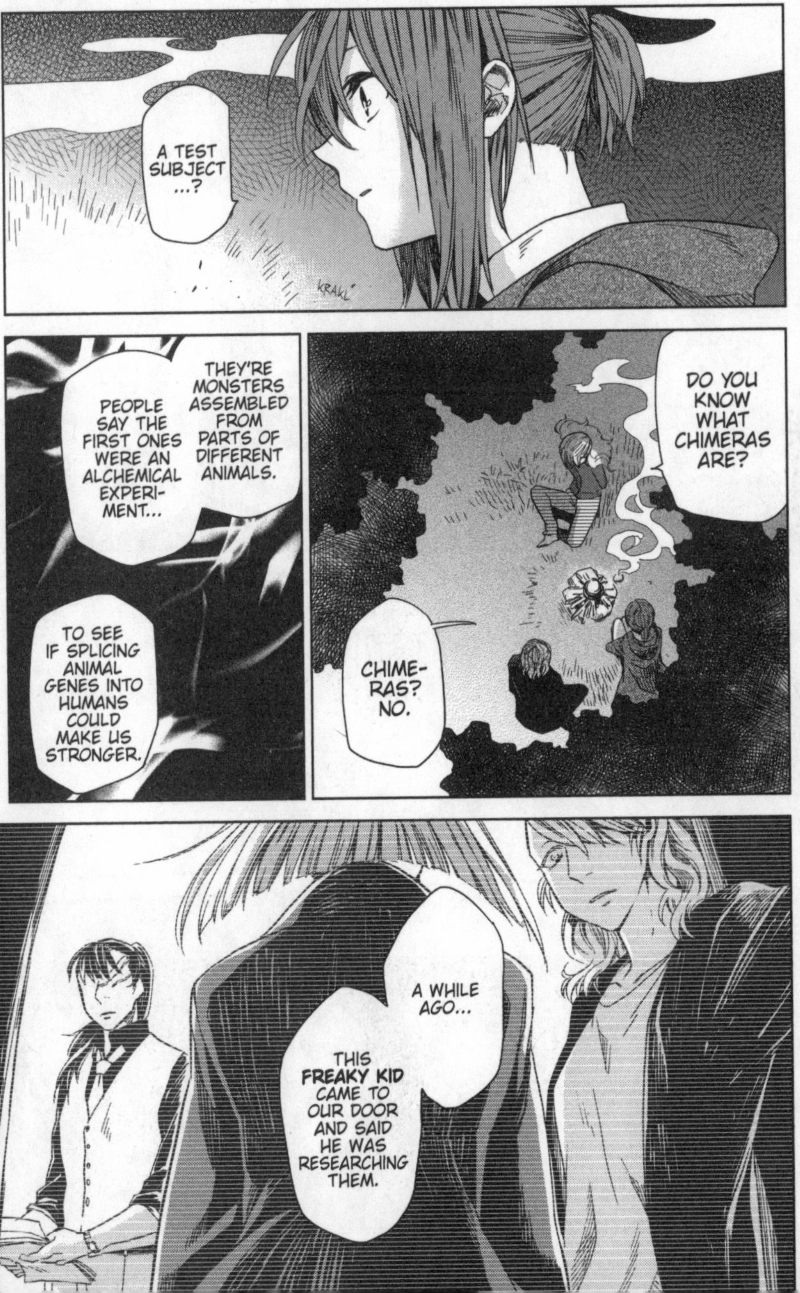
A TEST SUBJECT ...?
KRAKL
DO YOU KNOW WHAT CHIMERAS ARE?
CHIMERAS? NO.
THEY'RE MONSTERS ASSEMBLED FROM PARTS OF DIFFERENT ANIMALS.
PEOPLE SAY THE FIRST ONES WERE AN ALCHEMICAL EXPERIMENT...
TO SEE IF SPLICING ANIMAL GENES INTO HUMANS COULD MAKE US STRONGER.
A WHILE AGO...
THIS **FREAKY KID** CAME TO OUR DOOR AND SAID HE WAS RESEARCHING THEM.

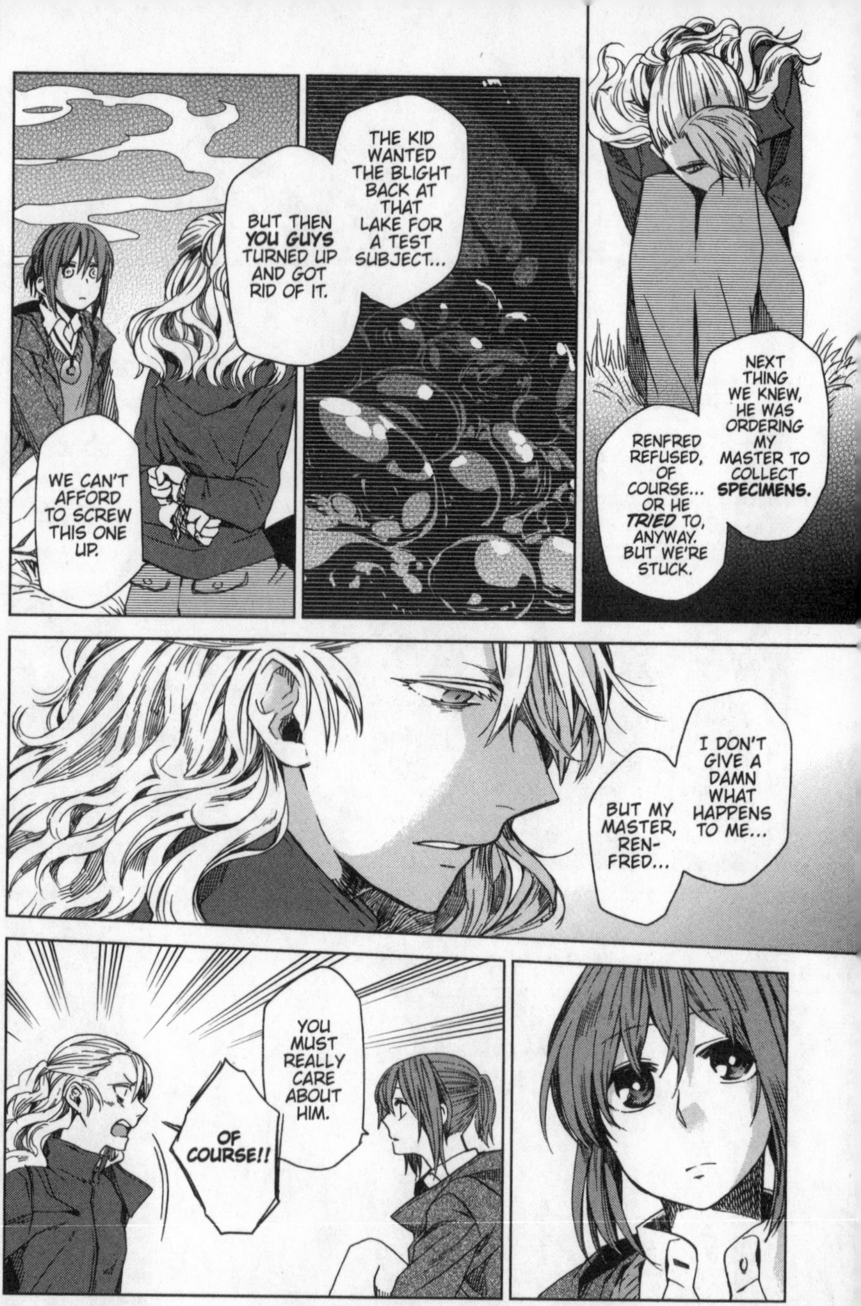
NEXT THING WE KNEW, HE WAS ORDERING MY MASTER TO COLLECT SPECIMENS.
RENFRED REFUSED, OF COURSE... OR HE TRIED TO, ANYWAY. BUT WE'RE STUCK.
THE KID WANTED THE BLIGHT BACK AT THAT LAKE FOR A TEST SUBJECT...
BUT THEN YOU GUYS TURNED UP AND GOT RID OF IT.
WE CAN'T AFFORD TO SCREW THIS ONE UP.
I DON'T GIVE A DAMN WHAT HAPPENS TO ME...
BUT MY MASTER, REN-FRED...
YOU MUST REALLY CARE ABOUT HIM.
OF COURSE!!

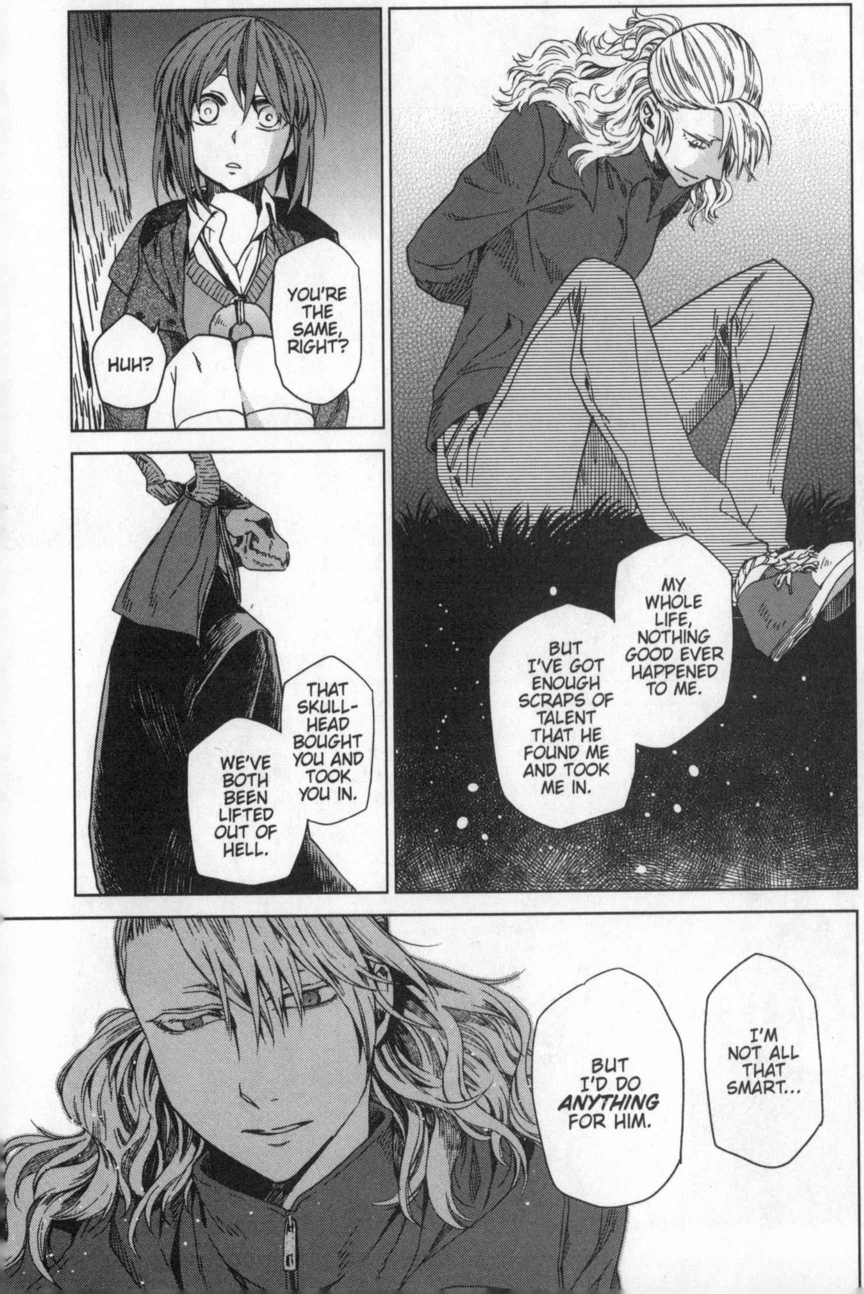
MY WHOLE LIFE, NOTHING GOOD EVER HAPPENED TO ME.
BUT I'VE GOT ENOUGH SCRAPS OF TALENT THAT HE FOUND ME AND TOOK ME IN.
YOU'RE THE SAME, RIGHT?
HUH?
THAT SKULL-HEAD BOUGHT YOU AND TOOK YOU IN.
WE'VE BOTH BEEN LIFTED OUT OF HELL.
I'M NOT ALL THAT SMART...
BUT I'D DO *ANYTHING* FOR HIM.

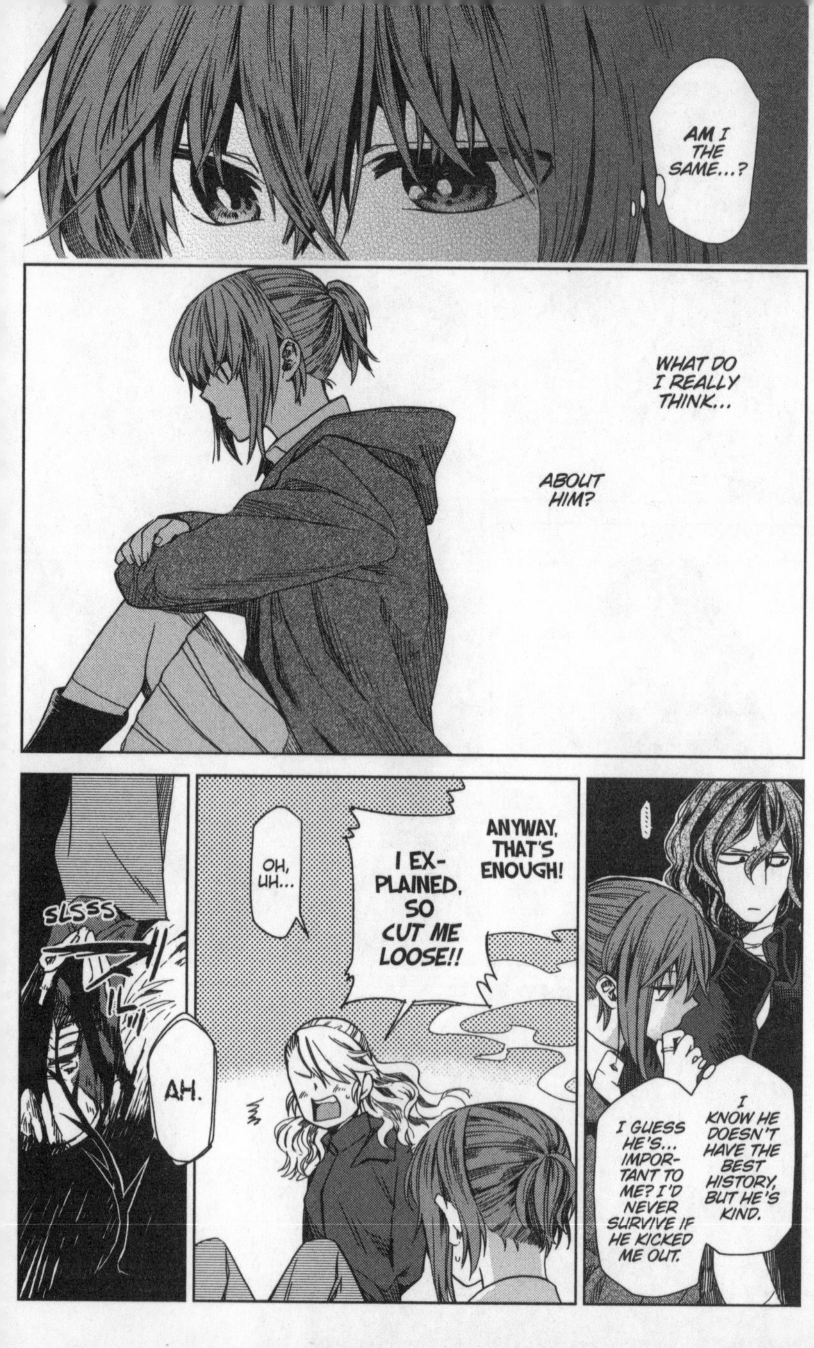
AM I THE SAME...?
WHAT DO I REALLY THINK...
ABOUT HIM?
......
I KNOW HE DOESN'T HAVE THE BEST HISTORY, BUT HE'S KIND.
I GUESS HE'S... IMPORTANT TO ME? I'D NEVER SURVIVE IF HE KICKED ME OUT.
ANYWAY, THAT'S ENOUGH!
I EX-PLAINED, SO CUT ME LOOSE!!
OH, UH...
SLSSS
AH.

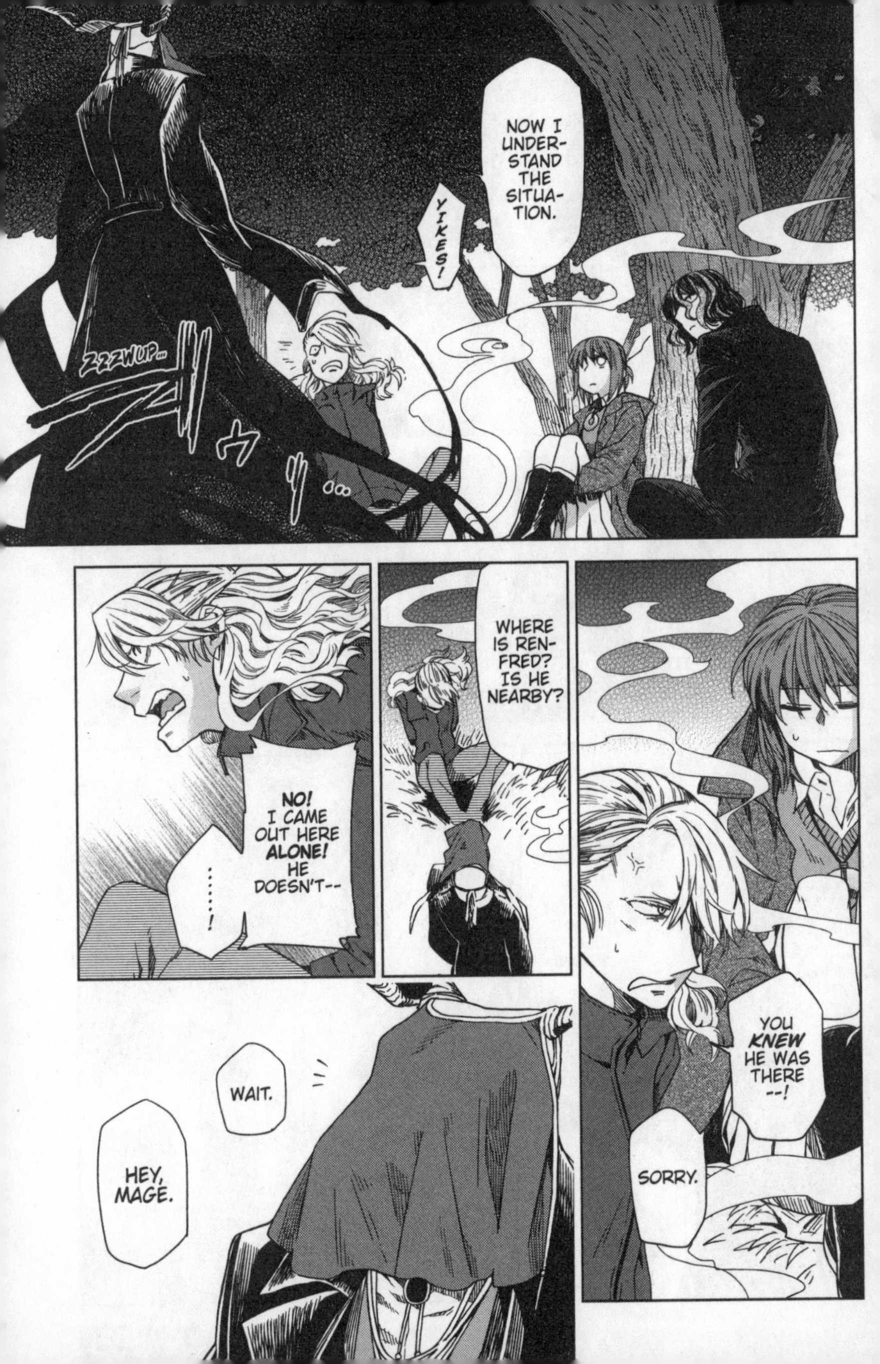
NOW I UNDERSTAND THE SITUATION.
YIKES!
ZZZWUP...
YOU KNEW HE WAS THERE--!
SORRY.
WHERE IS RENFRED? IS HE NEARBY?
NO! I CAME OUT HERE ALONE! HE DOESN'T--
......!
WAIT.
HEY, MAGE.

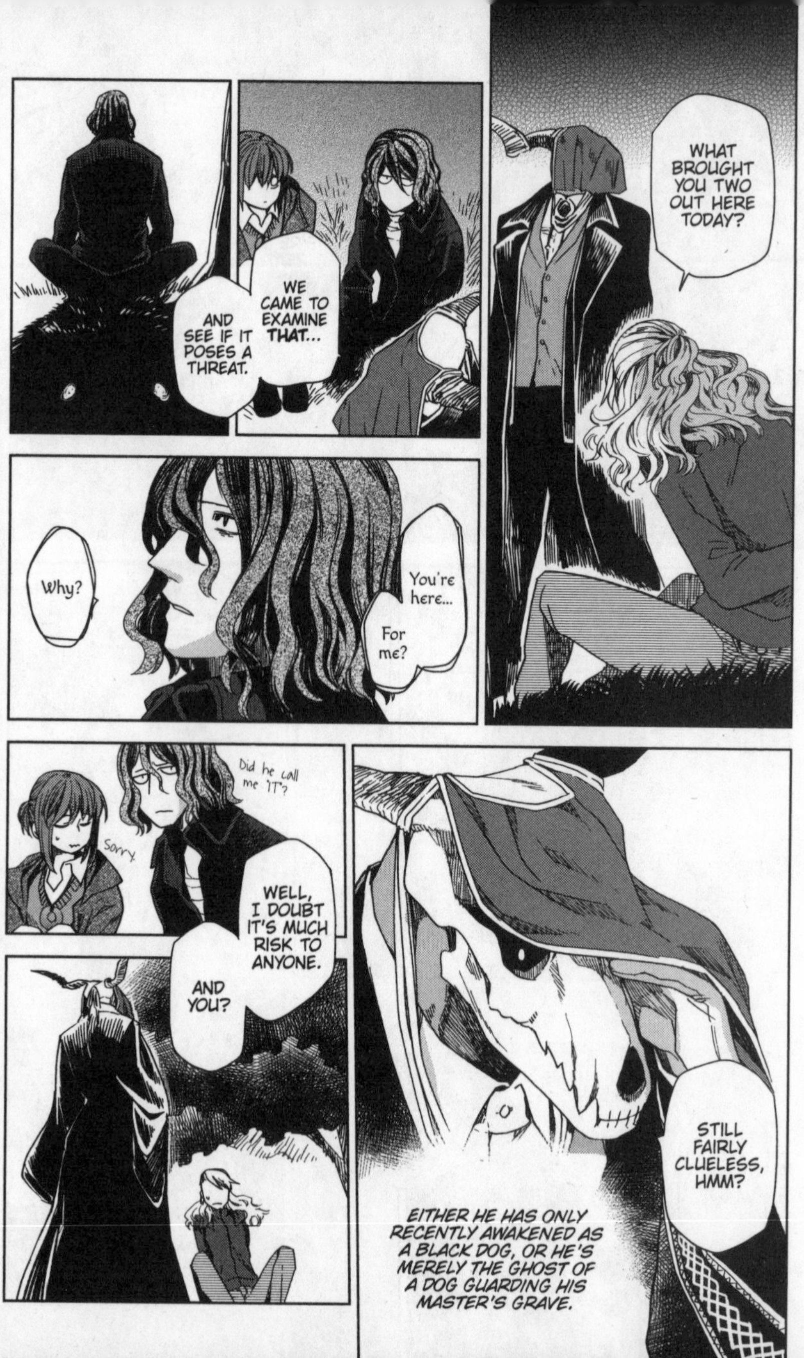
WHAT BROUGHT YOU TWO OUT HERE TODAY?
WE CAME TO EXAMINE THAT...
AND SEE IF IT POSES A THREAT.
You're here...
For me?
Why?
Did he call me 'IT'?
Sorry.
WELL, I DOUBT IT'S MUCH RISK TO ANYONE.
AND YOU?
STILL FAIRLY CLUELESS, HMM?
EITHER HE HAS ONLY RECENTLY AWAKENED AS A BLACK DOG, OR HE'S MERELY THE GHOST OF A DOG GUARDING HIS MASTER'S GRAVE.

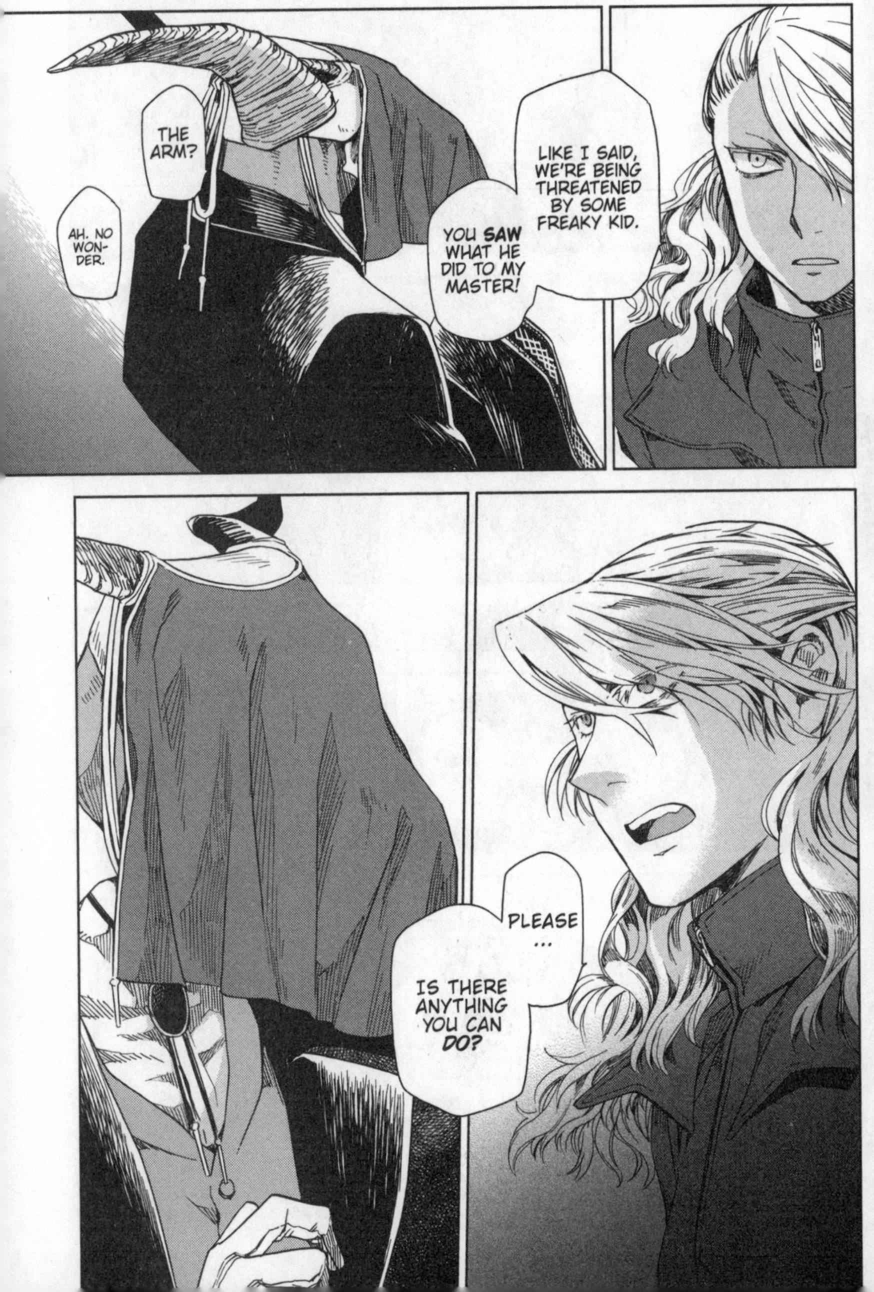
LIKE I SAID, WE'RE BEING THREATENED BY SOME FREAKY KID.
YOU **SAW** WHAT HE DID TO MY MASTER!
THE ARM?
AH. NO WON-DER.
PLEASE...
IS THERE ANYTHING YOU CAN ***DO?***

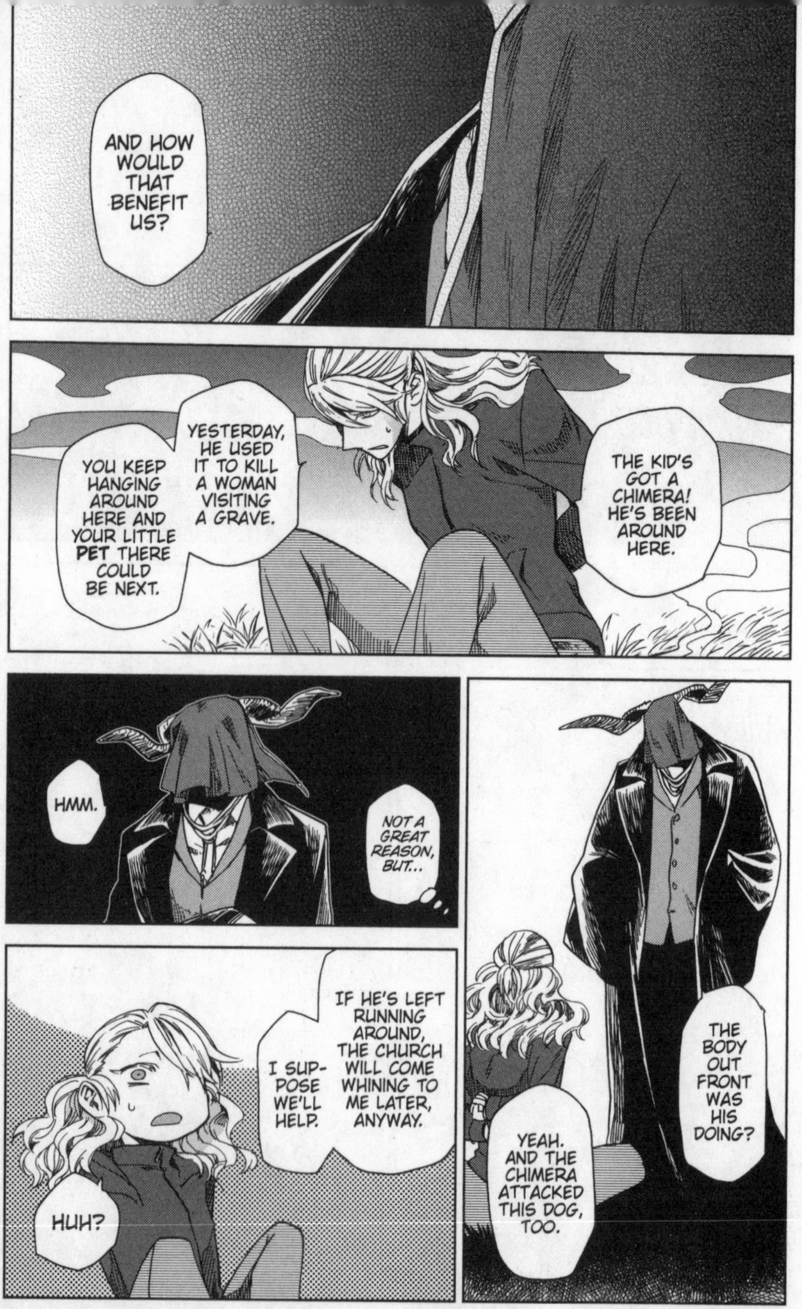
AND HOW WOULD THAT BENEFIT US?
THE KID'S GOT A CHIMERA! HE'S BEEN AROUND HERE.
YESTERDAY, HE USED IT TO KILL A WOMAN VISITING A GRAVE.
YOU KEEP HANGING AROUND HERE AND YOUR LITTLE **PET** THERE COULD BE NEXT.
THE BODY OUT FRONT WAS HIS DOING?
YEAH. AND THE CHIMERA ATTACKED THIS DOG, TOO.
HMM.
NOT A GREAT REASON, BUT...
IF HE'S LEFT RUNNING AROUND, THE CHURCH WILL COME WHINING TO ME LATER, ANYWAY.
I SUP-POSE WE'LL HELP.
HUH?

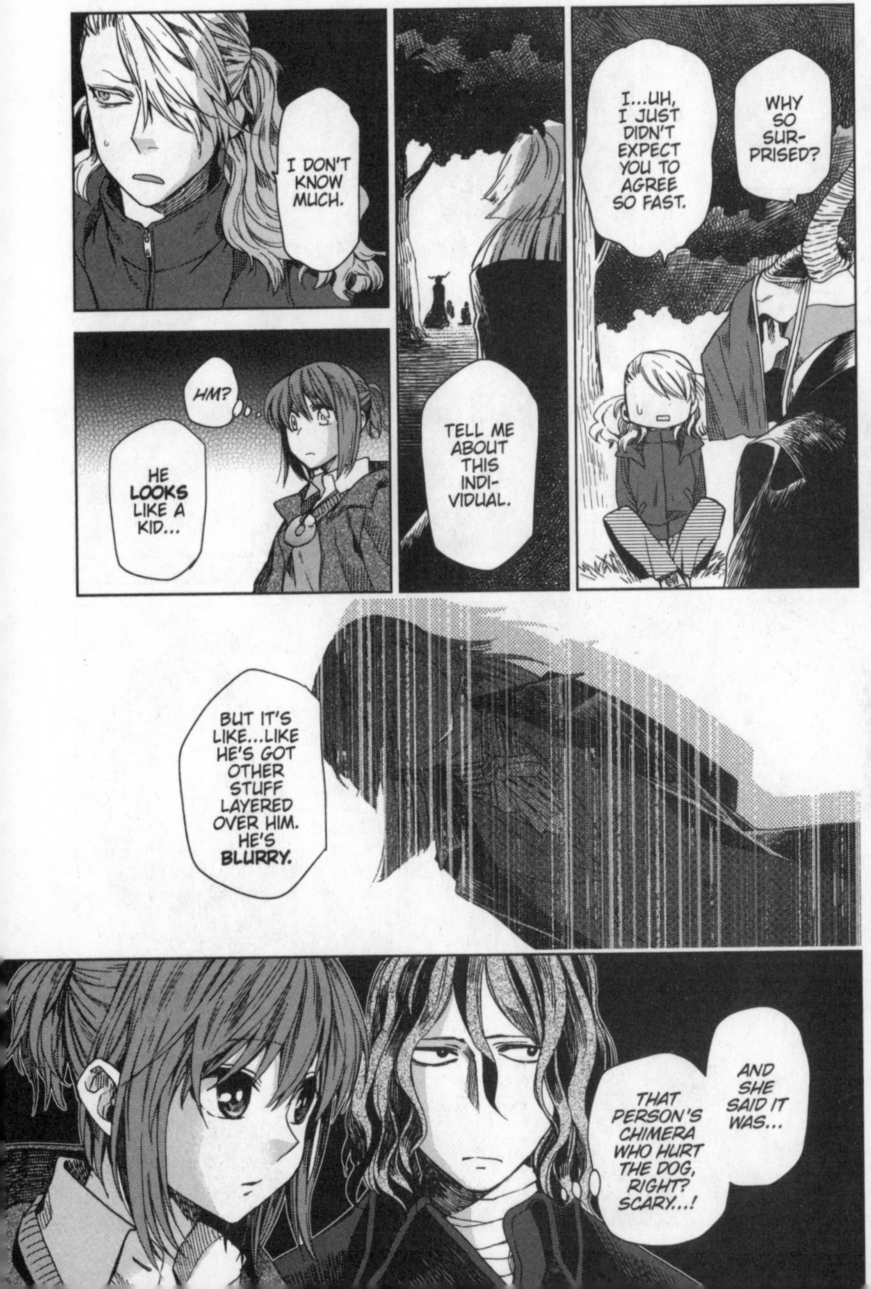
WHY SO SUR-PRISED?
I...UH, I JUST DIDN'T EXPECT YOU TO AGREE SO FAST.
TELL ME ABOUT THIS INDI-VIDUAL.
I DON'T KNOW MUCH.
HM?
HE **LOOKS** LIKE A KID...
BUT IT'S LIKE...LIKE HE'S GOT OTHER STUFF LAYERED OVER HIM. HE'S **BLURRY.**
AND SHE SAID IT WAS...
THAT PERSON'S CHIMERA WHO HURT THE DOG, RIGHT? SCARY...!

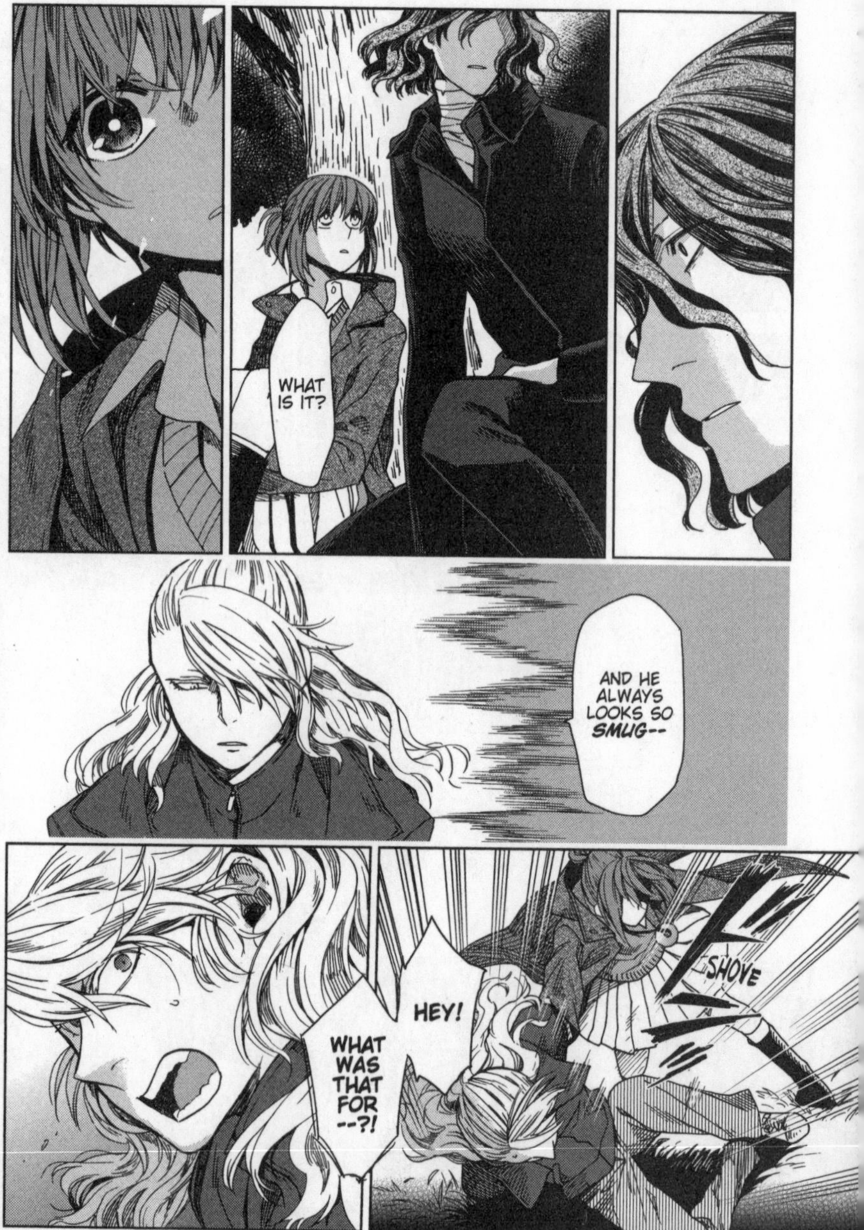
WHAT IS IT?
AND HE ALWAYS LOOKS SO SMUG--
SHOVE
HEY!
WHAT WAS THAT FOR --?!

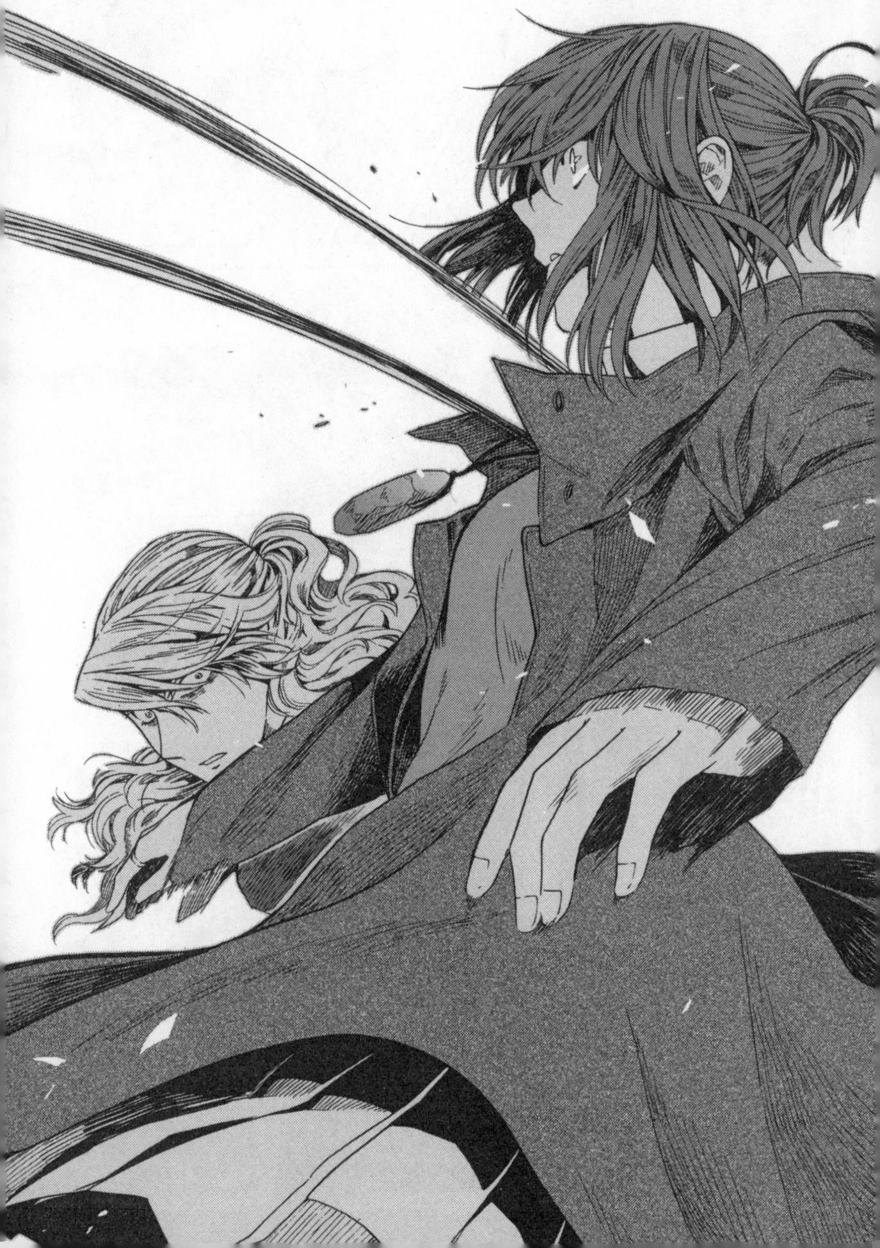

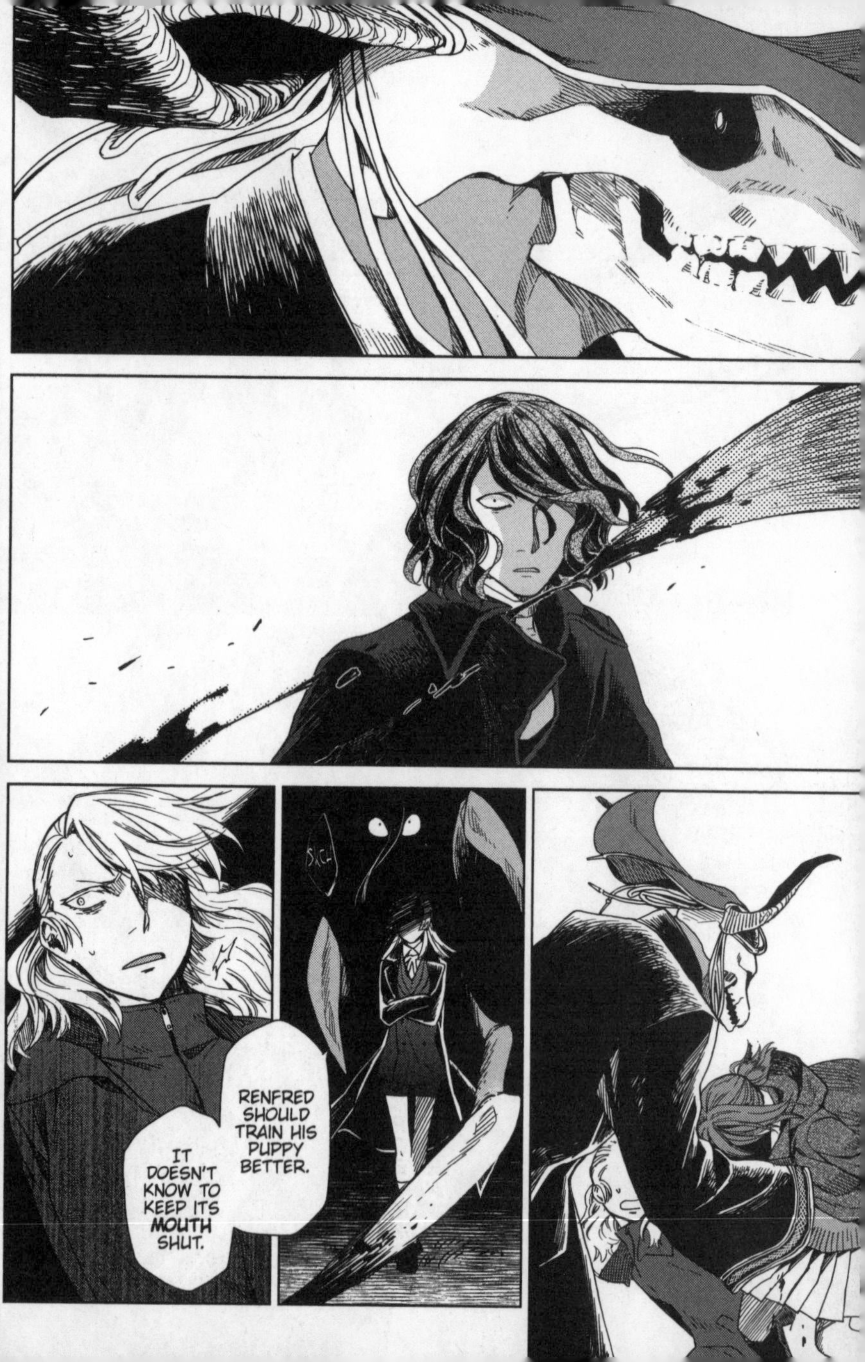
SKCH
RENFRED SHOULD TRAIN HIS PUPPY BETTER.
IT DOESN'T KNOW TO KEEP ITS MOUTH SHUT.

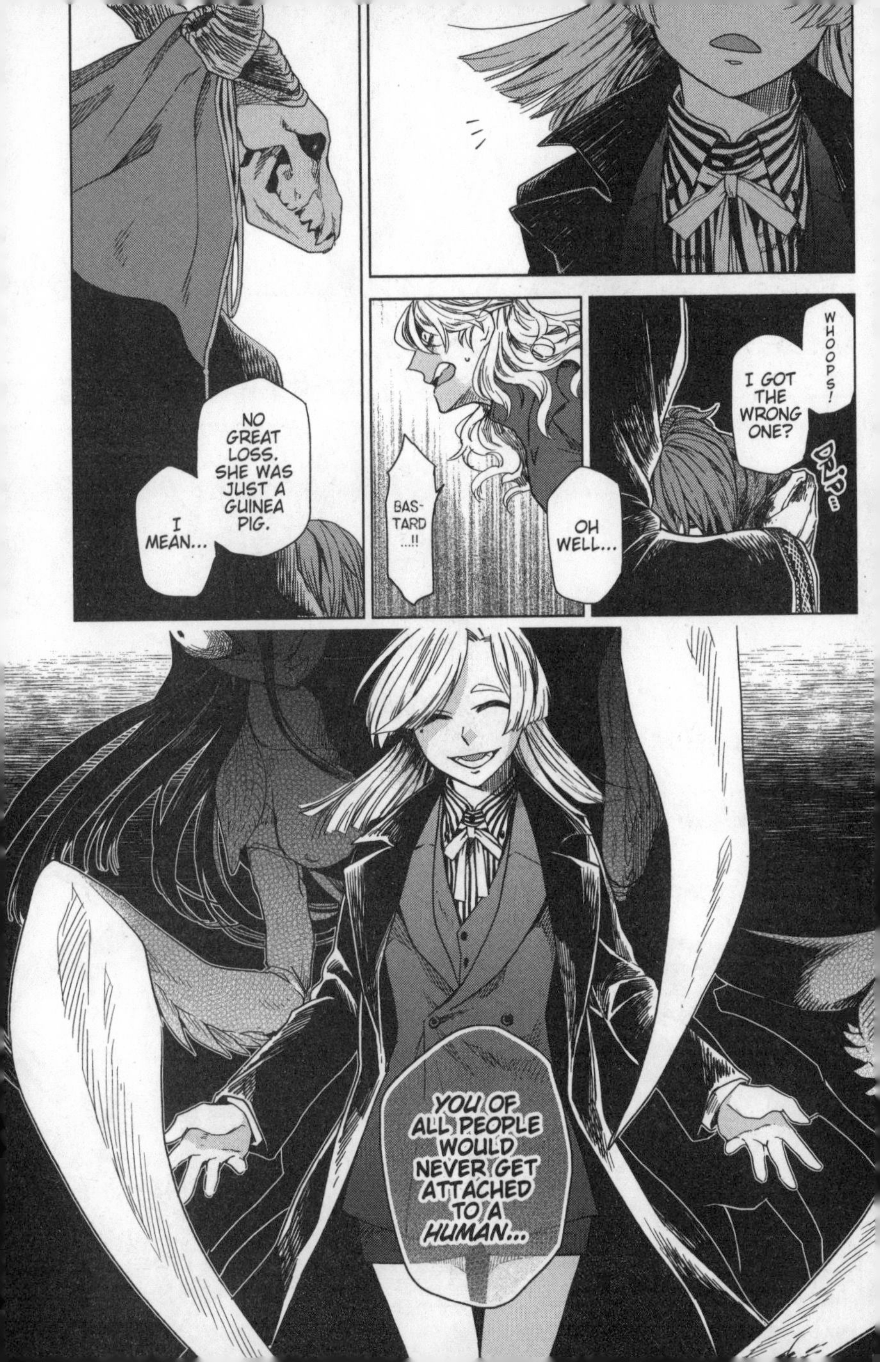
WHOOPS!
I GOT THE WRONG ONE?
DRIP...
OH WELL...
BASTARD...!!
NO GREAT LOSS. SHE WAS JUST A GUINEA PIG.
I MEAN...
YOU OF ALL PEOPLE WOULD NEVER GET ATTACHED TO A HUMAN...

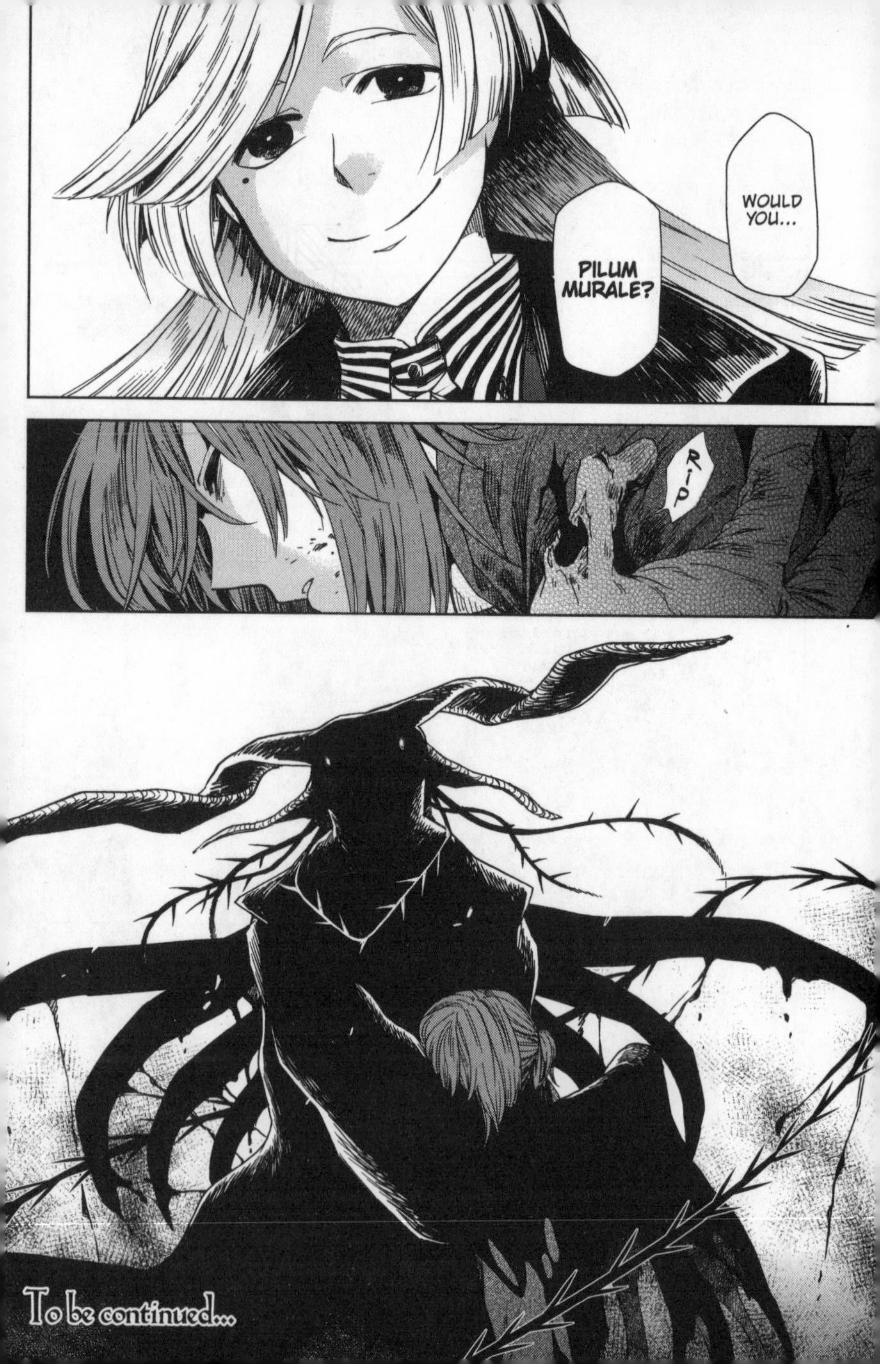
WOULD YOU...
PILUM MURALE?
RIP
To be continued...

Something That Could Be Called an AFTERWORD

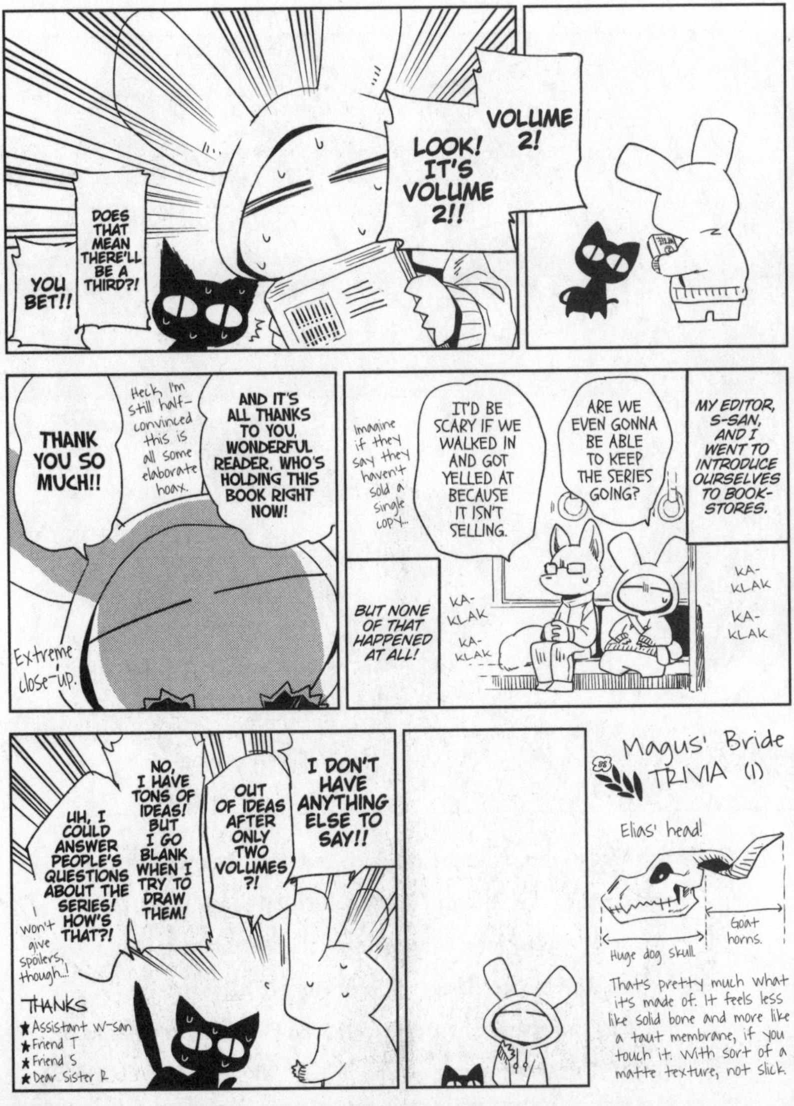
VOLUME 2!
LOOK! IT'S VOLUME 2!!
DOES THAT MEAN THERE'LL BE A THIRD?!
YOU BET!!
MY EDITOR, S-SAN, AND I WENT TO INTRODUCE OURSELVES TO BOOK-STORES.
KA-KLAK
KA-KLAK
ARE WE EVEN GONNA BE ABLE TO KEEP THE SERIES GOING?
IT'D BE SCARY IF WE WALKED IN AND GOT YELLED AT BECAUSE IT ISN'T SELLING.
Imagine if they say they haven't sold a single copy...
BUT NONE OF THAT HAPPENED AT ALL!
KA-KLAK
KA-KLAK
AND IT'S ALL THANKS TO YOU, WONDERFUL READER, WHO'S HOLDING THIS BOOK RIGHT NOW!
Heck, I'm still half-convinced this is all some elaborate hoax.
THANK YOU SO MUCH!!
Extreme close-up.
Magus' Bride TRIVIA (1)
Elias' head!
Goat horns.
Huge dog skull
That's pretty much what it's made of. It feels less like solid bone and more like a taut membrane, if you touch it. With sort of a matte texture, not slick.
I DON'T HAVE ANYTHING ELSE TO SAY!!
OUT OF IDEAS AFTER ONLY TWO VOLUMES?!
NO, I HAVE TONS OF IDEAS! BUT I GO BLANK WHEN I TRY TO DRAW THEM!
UH, I COULD ANSWER PEOPLE'S QUESTIONS ABOUT THE SERIES! HOW'S THAT?!
I won't give spoilers, though...!
THANKS
★Assistant W-san
★Friend T
★Friend S
★Dear Sister R

Your Fate.

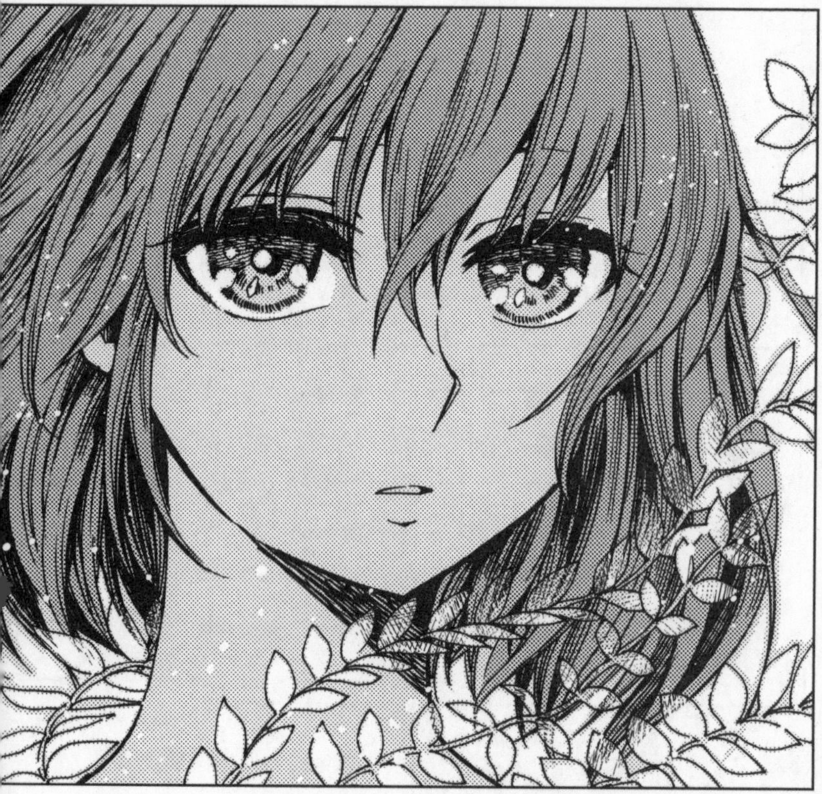

A *Sleigh Beggy* holds great power...but that power comes at a high cost, and a Sleigh Beggy's ultimate fate is cruel. The strange young man who caused the blight in Ulthar cuts Chise down mercilessly. Holding her bleeding body, Elias unleashes the power that earned him the name "Pilum Murale"--the Spear Wall!

Child, Fight

A fairy tale tinged with otherworldly romance...
Volume 3 Coming Soon!

SEVEN SEAS ENTERTAINMENT PRESENTS

The Ancient Magus' Bride
VOLUME 2

story and art by KORE YAMAZAKI

TRANSLATION
Adrienne Beck

ADAPTATION
Ysabet Reinhardt MacFarlane

LETTERING AND LAYOUT
Lys Blakeslee

COVER DESIGN
Nicky Lim

PROOFREADER
Shanti Whitesides

ASSISTANT EDITOR
Lissa Pattillo

MANAGING EDITOR
Adam Arnold

PUBLISHER
Jason DeAngelis

ISBN: 978-1-626921-92-4

Printed in Canada

First Printing: September 2015

10 9 8 7 6 5 4 3 2 1

FOLLOW US ONLINE: *www.gomanga.com*

READING DIRECTIONS

The manga prelude and epilogue sections that bookend this light novel read from right to left, Japanese style. If this is your first time reading manga, you start reading from the top right panel on each page and take it from there. If you get lost, just follow the numbered diagram here. Enjoy!!

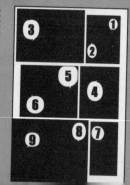